Faith and Reason

SUMMER THOMISTIC INSTITUTE 1999

sponsored by

THE JACQUES MARITAIN CENTER
UNIVERSITY OF NOTRE DAME
RALPH MCINERNY, DIRECTOR

with support from

THE MOONEY FAMILY
THE SAINT GERARD FOUNDATION
GEORGE STRAKE AND THE STRAKE FOUNDATION

Faith and Reason

The Notre Dame Symposium 1999

Edited by Timothy L. Smith

Introduction by Ralph McInerny

ST. AUGUSTINE'S PRESS

South Bend, Indiana

2001

Library of Congress Cataloging in Publication Data
Faith and reason : the Notre Dame symposium 1999 / edited by
Timothy L. Smith ; introduction by Ralph McInerny.
      p. cm.
Includes bibliographical references.
ISBN 1-890318-49-3 (pbk. : alk. paper)
1. Catholic Church. Pope (1978– : John Paul II). Fides et
ratio – Congresses. 2. Faith and reason – Congresses. I. Smith,
Timothy L. (Timothy Lee)
BT50 .F345 2000
231'.042 – dc21   00-010653

∞ *The paper used in this publication meets the minimum requirements of the
American National Standard for Information Sciences – Permanence of
Paper for Printed Materials, ANSI Z39.48-1984.*

Contents

THE THOMISTIC SEMINAR 1999
Introduction
Ralph McInerny

On behalf of the Jacques Maritain Center as well as the University of Notre Dame, I welcome you to this seminar devoted to John Paul II's 1998 encyclical *Fides et Ratio.* These seminars began some years ago with the aim of bringing together Catholic philosophers from around the world for whom their faith had philosophical significance. In inaugurating these seminars, we might have been anticipating the appearance of the encyclical that will be occupying us during the next few days.

Apart from welcoming you, as I have just done, my task this evening is to say something both innocuous and provocative. It would be presumptuous of me to take this occasion to make sweeping remarks about *Fides et Ratio,* as if there were some official reading of the encyclical that is meant to characterize out meetings. What I shall rather do much more modest but not, I think, wholly devoid of philosophical interest.–

What I intend to do is reflect on a remark to be found in paragraph 4 of *Fides et Ratio,* to the effect that there is an "implicit philosophy" held by all which provides a reference point for the rival philosophical systems. My remarks will allude to Common Sense Philosophy, with particular reference to Pere Buffier, and, even more glancingly, to Anti-foundationalism, for reasons which, if not already obvious, will emerge.

The Fundamental Questions

In the Introduction to the encyclical, the Pope adopts as a motto for his initial remarks the words carved over the door of the temple at Delphi: *Know thyself.* The opening paragraph, having noted that faith and reason are two means by which the mind rises to the contemplation of the truth, exhibiting in this an innate desire of the human heart, appears to make knowledge of God instrumental to knowledge of ourselves. "[S]o that by knowing and loving God, men and women may also come to the fullness of truth about themselves" (§1). Or is self-knowledge taken to be a bonus of knowledge of God?

An understanding of what has come to be called the Pope's Personalism surely depends on grasping the import of this liminal assertion. Man's deeper grasp of the truth over the ages "has unfolded – as it must – within the horizon of personal self-consciousness: the more human beings know reality and the world, the more they know themselves in their uniqueness" (§1). As a result, the question of the meaning of things and their existence becomes ever more pressing.

This almost Cartesian order of procedure – self - God - world – gives way to a milder claim. Only humans among earthly creatures have self-awareness. And only they are prompted to ask the big and fundamental questions:

Who am I?
Where have I come from and where am I going?
Why is there evil?
What is there after this life?

This observation is supported by appeal to the sacred writings of Israel and of other peoples, to epics and tragedies, to the philosophical writings of Plato and Aristotle. Such questions reveal the search for meaning which drives us. How we answer such questions decides the direction of our lives.

We cannot think of Delphi without thinking of Socrates and of his wry claim that he knew nothing. When in our youth we first read of Socratic ignorance, it seemed a *façon de parler*, but with age it takes on the allure of an inescapable admission. Among the things Socrates did not know was himself.[1] Was he a beast or half-divine? Self-awareness paradoxically becomes the awareness that we do not know what we are. How do we go about the quest for such knowledge? In part, perhaps, by setting the self aside as a thematic object.

Implicit Philosophy

Philosophy is introduced as a resource whereby men can have greater knowledge of the truth "so that their lives may be ever more human" (§3). Philosophy addresses the fundamental questions and is thus one of the noblest of human tasks: it is the love of wisdom. The wisdom sought is not of course deeper knowledge of what human beings are, though knowledge of the divine will provide a measure of our finitude and ontological imperfection. But philosophy has had a long and checkered history since its Greek beginnings. It might seem to have become an equivocal term. A needed clarification of the term is offered in paragraph 4. These are the steps:

1. "Driven by the desire to discover the ultimate truth of existence,

human beings seem to acquire those universal elements of knowledge which enable them to understand themselves better and to advance their own self-realization." [Again, an apparently humanist *telos.*]

2. "These fundamental elements...spring from the *wonder* awakened in them by the contemplation of creation: human beings are astonished to discover themselves as part of the world, in a relationship with others like them, all sharing a common destiny." [A recognition of the primacy of knowledge of the world segues into a suggestion that individuals – autonomous? – are about to enter into a social contract.]

3. This pursuit gives rise to different philosophical systems in different times and different cultural contexts. There arises the temptation "to identify one single stream with the whole of philosophy" (§4). To overcome such "philosophical pride" we are advised to respect each system in its wholeness, "without any instrumentalization."

4. Philosophical *enquiry* enjoys primacy over each and ever system and each of them ought loyally to serve it.

The encyclical thus seems to be embracing a radical pluralism of philosophical systems or traditions which are linked by the quest or enquiry that produces each of them, But since each must be "respected in its wholeness, without any instrumentalization," the plurality of systems appears radical, with no substantive comparisons possible.

It is precisely to prevent such a relativistic interpretation that the encyclical introduces what is the topic of my remarks. Despite the need to recognize that different times and cultures have produced different philosophies, "it is possible to discern a core of philosophical insight within the history of thought as a whole" (§4). Of what does that core consist?

> Consider, for example, the principles of non-contradiction, finality and causality, as well as the concept of the person as a free and intelligent subject, with the capacity to know God, truth and goodness. Consider as well certain fundamental moral norms which are shared by all (§4).

Transcending the philosophical systems which have their different emphases and accents, there is "a body of knowledge which may be judged a kind of spiritual heritage of humanity." It is this that the encyclical calls "an implicit philosophy." This is what everyone knows, "albeit in a general and unreflective way." Such knowledge can serve as a "reference point" for the different philosophical schools. This implicit philosophy is then spoken of in terms first of intuiting and then formulating "the first universal principles of being."

A Preliminary Characterization

If such truths are implicit in any philosophical system, and if we are willing to speak of Thomism as a system, then such an implicit philosophy should be discernible in it. And indeed it would be an easy matter to attach references to writings of Thomas for each of the truths which make up that body of knowledge. The claim is that this could be done for other philosophical systems as well. That is puzzling, needless to say, since there are philosophical systems which were fashioned precisely to exclude such claims. It would seem somewhat Pickwickian to say that the fundamental truths are negatively present in systems which reject them.

This difficulty could be circumvented by saying that these truths are implicit in any philosophy in the sense that they are antecedent to any philosophical system, but which unfortunately some philosophical systems seemingly forget or perversely deny. On that understanding, this paragraph of the introduction would be taken to embrace some form of Common Sense Philosophy. I shall return to that, as General MacArthur did to the Philippines.

How would Thomas Aquinas characterize the elements of the body of knowledge listed?

    i. the principle of contradiction
    ii. the principle of finality
    iii. the principle of causality
    iv. Human person as free and intelligent
    v. with the capacity to know God, truth and goodness
    vi. fundamental moral norms

The recurrence of "principle" suggests that these are starting points, where knowledge begins, that is, things known as such, in themselves, *per se*. (i) is of course the example *par excellence* of perseity. Could the same be said of (ii) and (iii)? A mark of a first principle is that it cannot be reasoned *to*, there is nothing prior from which it could be shown to follow. Argument on behalf of principles thus takes a peculiar form: the *reductio*. If one denies *P*, it must be shown that P leads the naysayer into incoherence and self-contradiction. But finality is defended in that way and so too is causality. The burden of disproof is on the one who denies that things act for an end or that this thing is brought about by the agency of that.

A clear instance of this can be found in the case of the defense of the notion of ultimate end in Chapter 2 of Book One of the *Nicomachean Ethics*. That there is an ultimate end is proved by showing that its denial leads to incoherence. And of course Chapter 1 of Book One begins with the assertion that all human activities are undertaken for the sake of an end, with a listing of the various kinds of human acts.

As for (iv), Thomas often remarks (e.g. *Q. D. de malo, q. 6, art. un.*) that one who denies freedom denies the very foundation of human society, that is, the very context within which he makes and is capable of making this denial. (v) might seem to offer an exception to this interpretation of the list since Thomas would of course deny that knowledge of God's existence is *per se notum*. Nonetheless, he does hold that the Supreme Good is implicitly desired in any human act, and the Supreme Truth implicitly recognized in any judgment.

The fundamental moral norms suggest the first principles of practical reasoning, that is, natural law precepts, which Thomas explicitly argues are known of themselves, *per se nota*.

The Principles as Common

To reflect in this way on the elements of the implicit philosophy to which the encyclical draws attention could have the effect of making these fundamental truths appear as deliverance of Thomism, and seem therefore to be an example of that "philosophical pride," close cousin of *odium theologicum*, against which the encyclical warns us. Yet nothing is more familiar than to hear Natural Law referred to as a Thomistic tenet, with the suggestion that the adoption or defense of Natural Law is a move into or within one philosophical system among many. This has the unfortunate effect of making the elements of the implicit philosophy tenets which divide rather than unite. But of course the claim is that knowledge of these truths is, however implicit and inchoate, prior to any formal philosophizing, so much so that it gives us a reference point by which we can measure the results of formal philosophizing, that is, particular philosophical systems. And this suggests the parallel to Common Sense philosophy about which I would now like to say a few things.

Pere Buffier and Common Sense

Pere Buffier (1661-1737) was a Jesuit who lived more or less a century after Descartes (1596-1650); their lives did not quite overlap. Descartes haunted and defined Buffier's thought, and it is perhaps significant, that so relatively soon after Descartes, Jesuits like Buffier seem utterly unaware of even the remnants of the Scholasticism that Descartes was taught at LaFleche, a college with which Buffier himself was later associated. The Jesuit is primarily interested in defending common principles from the skepticism or even solipsism that may seem to follow on Cartesian methodic doubt. The relation of Buffier to Descartes is complicated and I do not presume to comment on it here. But this can be said: If Descartes thought it reasonable to doubt that of which he was not certain, Buffier was committed to showing that what Descartes thought could be doubted cannot be.

In his *Traite des premieres verites*, Buffier first discusses what is meant by a primary truth and what it is that primary truths have in common; second, he discusses primary truths based on a general consideration of beings; third, he turns to first truths concerning spiritual matters. What does Buffier mean by the common sense?

> J'entend donc ici par le *sens commun*, la disposition que la nature a mise dans tous les hommes ou manifestment dans la plupart d'entre eux, pour leur faire porter, quand ils ont atteint l'usage de la raison, un jugement commun et uniforme sur des objets differents du senti-ment intime de leur propre perception; jugement qui n'est point con-sequence d'aucun principe anterieur.[2]

As examples of such truths, Buffier gives the following:

> *that there are other beings and other men than myself in the world
> *that there is among them something that is called truth, wisdom, prudence, and it is not arbitrary
> *that there is in me something called intelligence and something that is not, namely, body, such that the properties of the one differ from those of the other
> *that there is no conspiracy among men to deceive and mislead me

And so on. These are harder to characterize than the elements of the implicit philosophy given in the encyclical. But perhaps this is sufficient to base the claim that the implicit philosophy of the encyclical is not to be iden-tified with such a philosophy of common sense as Buffier's.[3]

It is interesting that Buffier, along with his list of truths no one could fail to know, provides an analysis of Vulgar Prejudices.[4] Presumably these are falsehoods that carry the allure of the self-evident due to familiarity. There are some surprising items on Buffier's list.

> *that two people can contradict one another on the same subject and both be right
> *that science does not consist of knowing a lot
> *that women are capable of learning all the sciences
> *that savages are as happy as the civilized
> *that all languages are equally beautiful
> *that is wrong to complain of the multitude of bad books

All in all, a strange list. But at least it serves the purpose of showing that for Buffier, the existence of truths that no one can fail to know, does not exclude a good number of falsehoods that have become commonplaces. (Of course what Buffier called vulgar prejudices may appear to us to be prejudices of Buffier.) Many would take common sense to include both of these. If so, Buffier would then doubtless maintain that common sense contains the capacity to correct itself – not in its entirety, but with respect to mere prejudices.

Buffier's procedure would seem to be the obvious one of (1) recognizing some non-gainsayable propositions; (2) asking what characterizes them; (3) asking if they or other candidates for primary truths actually deserve the appellation.

Thomism and Implicit Philosophy

The encyclical, from its opening paragraph, links the two ways in which the mind arrives at the truth, faith and reason. The believed truths which characterize Christian faith are the presuppositions of theology: the theologian accepts those truths in the same way as any other believer, but unlike most believers he reflects on them in a special way. Bringing reason to bear on the truths of faith includes a number of distinct tasks: to defend revealed truth against the charge of falsehood or nonsense; to seek an understanding of the mysteries of faith; and to draw out the implications of revealed truths.

Believed truths may be rejected on the basis that they are in conflict with what we know. Nothing is more familiar than the claim that science has shown something that has rendered belief impossible. What the critic is relying on, as deep background, is the principle of contradiction. Let *P* stand for some mystery of the faith. The attack consists in the claim that we now know that P is true. That being the case, *P* is false. The believer who responds to this, does so of course within the ambience of the same presupposition. He will seek to show that no such contradiction exists. *If* it did, the result would be as the critic claims.

Since the principle of contradiction is one of the elements of the implicit philosophy of paragraph 4, it looks as if the implicit philosophy is presupposed by both philosophical and theological reasoning. But, as the name suggests, implicit philosophy is more closely akin to explicit philosophy. How might we characterize the relation between implicit and explicit philosophy?

There are certain things that all men know prior to and independent of explicit philosophizing. This is of course a retroactive, explicit remark. What is said about implicit philosophy is perforce explicit. The claim is not that throughout the world people will be found asserting that there are things that they and others know prior to explicit philosophizing. To utter this, is to philosophize explicitly, along the lines of Aristotle's remark that to ask whether or not one ought to philosophize is already to answer the question affirmatively.

One of the merits of the philosophizing of Thomas Aquinas to which reference is made in *Fides et Ratio* is that it represents a sustained effort to root
itself in what everyone already knows, that is, in some version of what the
encyclical calls "implicit philosophy." The *principia communia* that are prior
to all *scientiae* are presupposed by the latter and are that into which arguments
are analyzed in order to show their cogency. Unless there were such common
truths, known to be such *per se*, derived knowledge would be impossible.
Thomas learned this from Aristotle, needless to say.

This whole conception of knowledge and of philosophy has been contested by labeling it Foundationalism, and then arguing that Foundationalism
makes no sense. Friends of mine – as Aristotle said of the Platonists – are pal-
adins of anti-foundationalism. It would be preposterous to seem to settle such
a quarrel in these introductory remarks. It suffices that friend and foe alike
recognize this assumption in Aristotle and Thomas Aquinas.[5] What this also
serves to show, of course, is that the assumption of the encyclical concerning
Implicit Philosophy is itself a controversial issue. Needless to say, the fact that
a truth causes controversy does not tell against it. But the constituents of the
Implicit Philosophy indicate the kind of argument that would be appropriate
to denials of it.

Away from Subjectivism

I began by calling attention to the surprising emphasis on self-knowledge
in the opening remarks of *Fides et Ratio*. Some passages seem to imply that
the whole point of knowledge is to get clear about ourselves, as if man were
the most noble and intelligible thing in reality. John Paul II's personalism presumably entails no such enormity. But there is undeniably the suggestion that
the self is some sort of lens through which others things are best seen. Or perhaps it is the other way around: the greater our knowledge of other things, the
greater will be our knowledge of ourselves, the latter being put forward as the
ultimate point of enquiry. However this might be, it is important to distinguish
that from the turn to the subject of which Cornelio Fabro wrote: *Sic incoepit
tragedia moderna*. Fabro located this turn, unsurprisingly, in the Father of
Modern Philosophy.

Descartes famously sought the beginnings of certain knowledge, its primary instances, as the result of the application of a method. The application
of this method to the contents of his mind, the inventory of cognitive claims
he and others would make, revealed them all to be dubitable. This means that
every claim to know for certain has been shown to be mistaken. More precisely, all knowledge claims dependent on sense perception and all mathematical propositions are susceptible of doubt – it is imaginable or conceivable
that they are false – and therefore they must be set aside. No one has any war-

rant simply to assert that he knows these to be true. All judgments based on sense perception and all mathematical propositions could be false since any one of them might be. Only the act of thinking all these possible false propositions could not be set aside, and thus Descartes' confidence in the fact that he, a *res cogitans*, exists, is the first successful upshot of the application of his method.

If one wanted a full-blooded alternative to Thomas Aquinas and Aristotle, surely this is it. In terms of the encyclical, Descartes can be seen as rejecting the notion of an Implicit Philosophy, that is, knowledge claims that have status prior to and independently of the activity of the philosopher. It is not sufficiently noticed that on the Cartesian alternative the first justifiable knowledge claim is the *result of*, not a *presupposition* to, formal philosophizing.

Clearly, the encyclical's claim that there is a body of truths, an implicit philosophy that provides a reference point for every philosophical system is false – unless the claim is meant to incorporate philosophical systems which deny implicit philosophy. There are some – Corrnelio Fabro is one of them – who would characterize the modern turn precisely as denying such an implicit philosophy.

Perhaps a more fruitful way of understanding the introduction of Implicit Philosophy is to see it as a primary task of any philosophical system to make explicit that implicit philosophy. That is, to link its – implicit philosophy's – characteristic claims to what, when formulated, will have the ring of the self-evident. This suggests a barefoot characterization, *ut ita dicam*, of "implicit philosophy" and its relationship to "explicit [that is formal] philosophy."

1. Anyone who begins the study of philosophy has been around for some years. He has been raised in a certain culture, learned a given language, thought and spoken for years about himself and the world. An obvious first consideration in beginning the formal study of philosophy is to ask how it relates to all that cognitive and verbal activity which preceded it.

2. One possibility would be to say to the tyro: forget all that. Everything you have previously thought or said is hopelessly muddled. It arose out of a hundred sources, some discernible, some not. Think of your tendency to say *X*. [The value of *X* could be "The world is flat", "The moon is made of green cheese," or "$2 + 2 = 4$".] How do you really know? So let's start from scratch.

3. But whence the itch? And what language are we using in Lecture One? The student is likely to suspect that not everything can be set aside that easily. He might think that unless he knows what knowing is – has some or many instantiations of it – he will be unable to assess what philosophy promises him. Unless of course there is no relationship between what the philosopher calls knowing and what everyone else does. Among the papers of Charles Sanders Peirce, often a sensible fellow, there is a piece called "The Ethics of Vocabulary." In it Peirce suggests that philosophy must devise a technical lan-

guage on the model of botany, full of neologisms, phony Greek derivatives, etc. so that there will be no question of confusing what the philosopher means and what anyone else does. It is interesting that Peirce says all this in English. In order to learn Philosophese, its terminology would have to be put into relationship with the language of the learner. This makes clear that the habitat at least of what the encyclical calls Implicit Philosophy is an inescapable reference point of any philosophical system.

Call this the minimalist understanding of Implicit Philosophy. The fact that any introduction to formal philosophy has to address novices where they are, and reflection on the fact that communication is possible, together undermine the notion that the addressee begins such study by knowing nothing. The encyclical encourages reflection on what the cognitive condition of the potential philosopher is. The suggestion is that such reflection will turn up such items as the encyclical lists as part of the cognitive repertoire of the postulant, and the recognition of that content could have a powerful effect on how we assess the plurality of philosophical systems.

So understood, implicit philosophy may remind us of other efforts to overcome the Scandal of Philosophy. It might even be said that Modern Philosophy began precisely with the effort to overcome that scandal. The encyclical suggests that the net effect has been to deepen the scandal. And as it begins, *Fides et Ratio* dares to say some blindingly obvious things about philosophical initiation. Alas, in these remarks, I have perhaps made the obvious obscure. But, as Kierkegaard asks, Why else do we have philosophers, except to make the simple difficult? Of course the obvious contains many mysteries. In token of which I will end with Richard Wilbur's little poem on Doctor Johnson's refutation of Bishop Berkeley's claim that all is thought, *esse est percipi.*

> *Kick at the rock, Sam Johnson.*
> *Break your bones.*
> *But cloudy, cloudy*
> *Is the stuff of stones.*

Notes

1. Plato, *Phaedrus* 230A.

2. *Oeuvres philosophiques de Pere Buffier de la Compagnie de Jesus, avec notes et introduction par Francisque Bouillier* (Paris: Charpentier Librairie-Editeur, 1843), p. 15. This volume contains the *Traite des Premieres verites, Elements de meaphysique* and *Examen des prejuges vulgaires.*

3. Reginald Garrigou-Lagrange, *Le sens commun* (Paris: Nouvelle Pibrairie Nationale, 3rd ed., 1926) criticizes the Scottish School and argues that its conception of common sense differs from the Thomistic sense he develops. In my essay *Notre Dame and Dame Philosophy,* written on the sesquicentennial of this university, I wrote, "Perhaps some grasp of Miltner can be had by noting that in 1937 he wrote the foreword to and caused to have published here a little work of James A. Staunton, *Scholasticism, the Philosophy of Common Sense.* In counterpoint to that cheerful verdict must be set the *Dictionary of Terms Commonly Used in Scholastic Philosophy,* published in 1930 by the university press. One flips through it and cannot escape thinking that students had to regard philosophy as on the order of learning a foreign language."

4. Buffier, *Oeuvres philosophiques,* pp. 313–470.

5. Attention should be drawn to the posthumous volume of Olaf Tollefsen, *Foundationalism Defended: Essays on Epistemology, Ethics, and Aesthetics* (Bethesda, MD: Cambridge Press, 1995), especially the titular essay.

Passchendaeles of the Mind
Opening Homily
Michael Sherwin, O.P.

In Flanders fields the poppies blow
Between the crosses, row on row,
That mark our place; and in the sky
The larks, still bravely singing, fly
Scarce heard amid the guns below.
 We are the Dead. Short days ago
We lived, felt dawn, saw sunset glow,
Loved and were loved, and now we lie
In Flanders fields.
 Take up our quarrel with the foe:
To you from failing hands we throw
The torch; be yours to hold it high.
If ye break faith with us who die
We shall not sleep, though poppies grow
In Flanders fields

— John McCrae

The battle of Passchendaele, which McCrae's poem commemorates, offers us an apt analogy for the landscape of Catholic thought during much of the past thirty years. In those rainy days of 1917, the fields of Flanders were the worst possible place for a battle, and the tactics employed there were the worst possible tactics: bombing the lowlands with heavy artillery turned them into a murderous muddy mire, a veritable "Passion dale" for the men who fought there. By the time it was over the British had lost more men in those fields than in any other battle in their history as a people.[1]

Yet, the remarkable thing was how Britain's leaders failed to recognize the peril they were in; they failed to see what any young officer in the field knew: that the battle should have been pursued elsewhere and that other tactics should have been employed.

How well this describes the battles of the Catholic mind these recent years. We have been mired in fights about law and who has authority to make it and who should obey it; about rules and exceptions to them. And too often the tactics we have employed have been enfilades of heavy bombast and acrimony. All this has bogged us down and has left many a young person mired in a viscous mental ooze of bad ideas and confusion.

What many have failed to recognize is that although these issues are important, they are not the battle we should now be fighting, nor are these the tactics we should be employing. These issues are important, but we cannot address them fruitfully until we recognize more clearly the landscape in which we now find ourselves, and until we change our tactics. *Fides et Ratio*, I would like to suggest, is a call by the Pope for us to recognize the landscape, and to employ new tactics.

The field in which we now find ourselves is the dry ground of our young people's thirst for meaning. The ground is hard and students are thirsty because many of the intellectual denizens that inhabit the post-modern landscape are telling our students that there is no meaning: that meaning is merely ideology, that truth is merely a construct of the powerful to control the weak. The dry winds of this teaching lead many into a desert of despair, a desert reminiscent of the early days of this century. I am keenly aware that we are gathered here under the auspices of the Maritain Center. In the early years of this century, Raissa Maritain was a young college student eager for truth.

> It was already an immense joy to know that others besides myself had sought truth and had not scorned to devote their lives to that search. How many treasures had revealed themselves to the activity of the human intelligence! I thought that one day among them all I would find my own treasure—absolute truth, unshakable truth! I should know the meaning of life and the truth about God.[2]

Yet, here is how she describes her teachers at the Sorbonne during those same years: "They despaired of *truth*, whose very name was unlovely to them and could be used only between the quotation marks of a disillusioned smile."[3] The result was that she and Jacques gradually descended into despair. Here's how she describes it.

> We swam aimlessly in the waters of observation and experience like a fish in the depths of the sea, without ever seeing the sun whose dim rays filtered down to us. . . . And sadness pierced me, the bitter taste of the emptiness of a soul which saw the lights go out, one by one.[4]

That was their Passchendaele, and it was as veterans of that spiritual field of battle that they dedicated their lives to understanding the relationship between the human intellect and the life of faith. Jacques and Raissa were able to undertake this vocation because they encountered the person of Christ. In the desert of their despair, Christ spoke to them and refreshed them, giving them strength for the journey. I suspect that if Jacques and Raissa could speak to us who are trying to understand the relationship between faith and reason, they would call us to remember the centrality of Christ; they would invite us to ask Christ in the Eucharist for his help and strength, for it is only in him that we will find the strength to undertake our task.

The Maritains struggled, and they have passed this struggle onto us. Although they are not buried in Flanders but in Kolbsheim, with little adjustment they could speak the words of the poem to us as well.

> Take up our quarrel with the foe:
> To you from failing hands we throw
> The torch; be yours to hold it high.
> If ye break faith with us who die
> We shall not sleep, though poppies grow
> In Kolbsheim's fields.

Notes

1. Leon Wolff, *In Flanders Fields: the 1917 Campaign* (New York: Longmans and Green, 1959).

2. Raissa Maritain, *We Have Been Friends Together* (New York: Longmans and Green, 1942), p. 35.

3. Ibid., p. 68. Italics in the original.

4. Ibid., pp. 63, 64.

John Paul II, Defender of Faith and Reason
Jude P. Dougherty

I

Although *Fides et Ratio* is the 13th encyclical written by John Paul II, and published after twenty years into his Pontificate, one can be sure that it is not the first time he has had occasion to consider the relationship between faith and reason. As a philosopher and teacher of philosophy, Karol Wojytla could not avoid it. To open the *Summa Theologiae* is to confront the subject in Question 1, article 1, wherein St. Thomas defends the necessity of revelation in spite of philosophy's ability to demonstrate the existence of God and "other like truths about God." For Thomas faith presupposes natural knowledge.

The relationship between faith and reason is a subject of interest not only to the Holy Father as teacher of the universal Church but also to contemporary minds of various intellectual persuasions. *Ratio und Fides*, for example, is the title of a work by the German, Bernard Lomse (1958). *Faith and Reason* is a collection of essays by the noted British philosopher, R. G. Collingwood (1968). The same title is used by Richard Swinburne, another English scholar who at book length discusses the nature of religious belief and its relation to reason (1981). These are only a few of the many authors who have examined the relationship, but none has done so with greater authority than John Paul II. Although it makes no reference to any contemporary author, *Fides et Ratio* was not written in an intellectual vacuum. It was produced in full awareness of the dominant trends in philosophy, which in their implication not only cut one off from faith but even render suspect the rational character of the natural sciences.

In contemporary literature the terms "faith" and "belief" are often used interchangeably, and "faith" is sometimes taken as a synonym for "hope." Given this diversity of usage, a lexicographer would have difficulty in fixing a meaning. In the history of Western philosophical thought the term "belief" has been used to designate diverse mental states and attitudes. To consider just a few, Plato distinguished between the realm of opinion and the realm of knowledge, and in the realm of opinion he further distinguished between conjecture and belief (*pistis*). Belief in this Platonic sense denotes the comparatively firm assent that the plain man gives to whatever he directly sees or hears or feels.

Aquinas also distinguished between belief and knowledge, but for Aquinas, belief (*fides*) cannot refer to something that one sees or to what can be proved; belief is the acceptance of an assertion as true on the testimony of someone else. John Locke employs this concept when he defines belief as "the assent to any proposition not . . . made out of the deductions of reason, but upon the credit of the proposer, as coming from God in some extraordinary way of communication. This way of discovering truths to men we call revelation," Locke says (*Essay IV*: 182). Hume defined belief as practical certainty about matters that cannot be justified theoretically. Kant looked upon belief as the subjectively adequate but objectively inadequate acceptance of something as true. In contemporary psychological literature, belief is often identified with emotional conviction. Pragmatic conceptions emphasize the operative character of conviction. Some authors maintain that belief is relative to what the agent has at stake.

Even with the history of Western thought before us, certain key words remain ambiguous. Words like "belief," "faith," "knowledge," and "truth" vary in meaning from context to context and from author to author. And yet all of the authors cited have produced insights into the cognitive process, or, if you will, into the dynamics of rational assent. At different periods of history, interests are specific. Medieval discussions of belief focused upon religious belief and its relationship to empirically derived knowledge. Some of the most profound contemporary discussions of belief analyze the concept within the context of the physical sciences. The relatively recent works of a number of English-speaking philosophers carry such titles as *Knowledge and Belief, Belief and Probability,* and *Belief, Existence and Meaning,* all written from a purely secular perspective, have a bearing not only on our understanding of science but also on our understanding of religious faith.

II

One wrinkle in discussions of belief is the fact that some philosophers assume that the object of belief is propositional. They argue that one's internal commitment to the truth of a given proposition depends upon the external circumstances governing one's needs for action and one's stakes in these circumstances. There is merit in this analysis, but it is not the whole story. We do know, believe, or assent to many truths that have no bearing on our practical life. Furthermore, the giving of assent to propositions cannot be primary. The proposition, verbal or written, is simply the assertion of a judgment taken to be true.

If we start with the notion that each of us has a set of beliefs that can be expressed in propositional form, we must affirm that our beliefs depend in some way upon our awareness. That which is believed are judgments which we have previously accepted and which are usually asserted by means of propositions. Assertion, it should be noted, is closely tied to language but not exclusively so. Usually we speak or write to makes an assertion. Of course, not everything spoken or written is an assertion. Certain conditions must be met. The speaker must know what it is that he asserts. Usually by his assertion he intends to reveal his conviction in the proposition asserted. Certain non-standard cases come to mind, i.e., where a man does not believe what he asserts, or where he asserts a proposition other than that intended. These non-standard cases may be a problem, but they are not important for the present discussion. It should also be noted that there are conventions which enable assertions to be made without actual speech or writing. Hilaire Belloc noted that we daily communicate much more by our grunts and groans than we do through polished speech. Even so, this does not loosen the bonds between assertion and language for what is asserted is always capable of being expressed in language.

Any analysis must eventually establish the relationship between belief and judgment. From a Thomistic point of view, judgment is very much like private assertion. One may make a judgment without asserting it and later assert what he has judged. Judgments need not be manifested in the public conduct of the judger. For one thing, opportunities for such manifestation do not always arise. For another, the agent may be reluctant for prudential reasons to let his judgments be known. From the outside, it is often difficult to establish criteria for deciding when a person has or has not made a judgment. We all know what it is like to make a judgment, but the phenomenology of judgment is itself elusive. Judgment, it seems, has only partial and inconstant connections with an agent's conduct. The operative character of a man's belief in a given situation depends on his desires and the many other beliefs that he holds.

The enduring characteristic or nature of belief may be contrasted with the relative transitory character of judgment. Judgments made here and now may remain as lifelong beliefs or as components of a belief system. A person's beliefs remain while he sleeps or is otherwise unaware of them, and, indeed, many of one's beliefs, some of which are held with great security and endurance, are rarely, perhaps never, brought to consciousness. Consequently, an individual as a moral agent may have many beliefs that are never overtly manifested or consciously recognized. If a particular occasion had not arisen, the belief may never have been apparent to the person or to others.

If belief is not necessarily manifested directly by a person's conduct, it must nevertheless be admitted that by its endurance, dispositionality, and causal relation with the person's awareness that belief does seem to be more closely related to action, and in a different way, than does judgment. A person's beliefs may be more public and objective than his judgments. And because a person can be surprised by his beliefs, he may be mistaken about them; i.e., he may judge falsely that he does or does not believe something. In short, a person may have incorrect beliefs about what he believes. Interestingly, we are much readier to contest an agent's assertions about his beliefs than we are to contest what he says about his judgments.

III

A final note regarding belief, judgments, and truth. Belief and truth may coincide, but a person may believe certain things to be true which ultimately turn out to be false. Those philosophers may be right when they acknowledge the dispositional character of belief although belief may not be identical with preparedness to act. Much of what we hold to be true is of a speculative nature, consisting of the science that we have inherited. Disposition, as a psychological state, characterizes the subjective side of the cognitive process and is not be ignored. Recognizing the dispositional character of belief, we are more likely to avoid the danger of hasty judgment. But it must be emphasized that it is in the judgment act of intellect that we achieve truth. In the judgment act of affirmation or denial we assert that reality is in fact as we have grasped it. Propositions are merely the vehicles by which acts of judgment are expressed first internally, then externally. Our statements may become objects of belief for others, but they are not primary objects of knowledge for us or even for others. In this analysis, John Paul II would concur. If I explain to a student that the electron configuration of the copper atom is such and such, I am making a statement which I hold to be true. I hold be true on faith because I have not performed the chemical analysis that revealed the element's structure nor have I made the observations that lead to the structural explanation. A disposition to assent is not the assent itself. A student is disposed to accept the word of his teacher. A teacher is careful to substantiate his assertions, though in many cases substantiation may elude him. Substantiation amounts to demonstration. Demonstrative knowledge we normally call scientific knowledge. Some, but not all of our beliefs, are based on demonstration. When certitude which depends on demonstration is not available, we get opinion. The strength of our opinion will determine action or inaction. The conviction that intervention by the Federal Reserve will create monetary stability may lead a president to take action. Where there is no certainty that a given action will have the desired result an intemperate move may nevertheless lead to action. But does action really demonstrate the strength of the opinion held?

Rashness remains possible. This analysis may help to explain the permanence of scientific knowledge, on the one hand, and the rashness or disparity between belief and action on the other.

IV

We return now to the key issue addressed by *Fides et Ratio*. Although discussions of the above sort are not explicitly invoked, John Paul II is aware of the many insights and distinctions provided by contemporary literature. Aware, too, of the distrust of reason found in much contemporary philosophy, he is at once a defender of reason *per se* and of the reasonableness of belief. To accept the Catholic Faith is not to take a leap into the dark. Reason lays the foundation for belief, insofar as philosophy can demonstrate the existence of God and disclose something of His nature. As a result of rational inquiry, it is reasonable to believe that a benevolent God, out of love for mankind, has revealed truth about himself that unaided reason could not attain. John Paul II speaks of the *intellectus fidei* and its innate unity and intelligibility, a body of knowledge, logically coherent in itself, consistent with experience, and perfective of natural understanding. Such knowledge comes to us as a logical and conceptual structure of propositions through the teaching Church. Of necessity the Church's teaching is framed in language that draws upon a host of definitions and distinctions provided by natural reason, that is to say, by philosophy. While philosophy assists in articulating and clarifying the truths of the Faith, John Paul II is convinced that philosophy is valuable only insofar as it remains true to its own methods. Philosophy is not apologetics. He is convinced that if it retains its professional integrity, it will remain open, at least implicitly, to the supernatural. "The content of Revelation can never debase the discoveries and legitimate autonomy of reason." Yet to the believer, "Revealed truth offers the fullness of light and will therefore illumine the path of philosophical enquiry." Reason must never lose its capacity to question, but is not itself above being questioned.

These reflections have implications for Catholic education at all levels, especially for the training of future priests and for the curriculum of Catholic colleges and universities. John Paul II is aware that some remedial work needs to be done where second-order disciplines have been substituted for logic, metaphysics, and philosophical anthropology. To fully master the Catholic intellectual tradition, one needs to be steeped in the history of Western philosophy, but such mastery does not cut one off from insights to be garnered from other traditions. The Holy Father specifically mentions India as a locus of a major cultural and intellectual tradition.

While his appeal to philosophers not of the Catholic faith to recover the great classical tradition flowing from ancient Athens and Rome, a tradition commented on and amplified in every generation since, is an appeal that may go unheeded, it is rightly proffered. In a previous generation it would have been endorsed by Werner Jaeger, Etienne Gilson, and Jacques Maritain among countless others. Only someone standing on the shoulders of his giant predecessors can say with assurance to his now-directed contemporaries, "Look what you are missing."

The Place of Philosophy in Moral Theology[1]
Servais Th. Pinckaers, O.P.

I will begin by sharing a confidence with you: I am very satisfied with the encyclical *Fides et Ratio* taken as a whole; I confess, however, to being somewhat troubled by section 68, which concerns moral theology, because it can easily be misinterpreted. According to this passage, moral theology has more need of philosophy than dogmatic theology does, because human life is much less regulated by prescriptions under the New Covenant than it was under the Old Covenant. Thus, while the Old Covenant contains a vast amount of moral precepts, imperatives and prohibitions, the New Covenant has far fewer, leaving much to the freedom of the Spirit. The encyclical suggests, therefore, that philosophy has an important role to play in moral theology: philosophical reflection about human nature and society can help the theologian better understand the nature of the freedom to which we are called in the Spirit. So far so good. The temptation, however, is to read section 68 from within the perspective of a morality of obligations, which is the legacy of the post-Tridentine manuals of theology, or from within the perspective of a morality of duty and of imperatives such as the one proposed by Kant. From this perspective section 68 is telling us that the New Covenant merely provides general principles and a new inspiration to a morality that essentially remains a natural morality. As such, according to this view, the role of philosophy is to help the theologian apply general moral principles to concrete cases.

I can understand this perspective. It is logical from within a framework that makes morality the domain of obligatory precepts, imperatives and prohibitions. Does not St. Thomas himself say that the New Law does not add any new precepts concerning external acts, and thus does not impose any additional obligations?[2] One could conclude from this that the New Testament merely reasserts the moral teaching of the Decalogue, which is itself identified with the natural law, and that theology merely adds to moral teaching a few new sources of inspiration. As a result, morality principally becomes the concern of philosophy, and consequently the preferred name of the discipline becomes "ethics." Furthermore, the New Testament, especially such texts as the Sermon on the Mount in St. Matthew's Gospel and the apostolic catechesis in the St. Paul's letters, is displaced from moral theology properly so called, and is relegated instead to the domain of spirituality.

One's perspective and conclusions change, however, once one adopts the point of view of St. Thomas: in other words, the perspective changes completely once one adopts a morality of happiness and virtue that seeks excellence in action and in the moral agent himself, giving priority to interior acts, which form the virtues at the very root of one's personal actions. Once one views Christian morality from the perspective of the primary virtues, one immediately perceives the role played by theology with its virtues of faith, hope and charity. Theology plays a direct role in moral analysis, but it is a role that in no way diminishes the part played by philosophy with regard to the cardinal virtues, studied with the aid of Aristotle and other philosophers. Moreover, if we turn our attention to Scripture, we find that the Decalogue is vivified and enkindled by being drawn into charity's love of God and neighbor. This aspect of Gospel morality is especially evident in the moral teaching brought together by St. Matthew in the Lord's Sermon on the Mount and ably presented in the apostolic catechesis.[3] It is a morality that aims above all at the perfection of the heart and mind through a wisdom and a love that enliven the other virtues. The doctrines in the Sermon on the Mount and in the apostolic catechesis form the principal sources of the moral teaching of the Fathers and of St. Thomas in particular.

From this perspective, theology recovers its place and its active role in the study of the moral life. From within this perspective we are in a better position to address our question concerning the respective roles of theology and philosophy in moral science.

Before confronting St. Thomas with this question, it will be helpful to remember that philosophy has been a vitally important issue to Christianity since apostolic times. St. Paul poses the question dramatically in the *First Letter to the Corinthians* where he confronts human wisdom with the wisdom of the cross (1.18-25). But, Paul offers a guideline for responding to the question of philosophy in the *Letter to the Philippians*, where he states: "whatever is true, whatever is noble, whatever is just, whatever is pure, . . . if there is any virtue, if there is anything worthy of praise, consider these things" (4.8). Debate concerning the value of philosophy was continued by the Fathers of the Church. The greatest among them knew how to take up what was best and most useful in pagan philosophy, especially in the teachings of the Platonists and of the Stoics, while at the same time firmly respecting the priority of the Gospel received in faith. St. Thomas is firmly within this positive stream of thought. Following the example of Albert the Great, he had the audacity to introduce into Christian theology Aristotelian doctrine, which had not received at that point a favorable reception. We should add that since the Renaissance, modern philosophy has complicated the issue by placing its center of gravity in the human person and no longer in God, and by claiming for itself complete autonomy in the name of sovereign reason, which claims for itself the ability to understand and explain everything, including the Scriptures and Christian revelation.

In this debate, morality continues to be a sore point, revealing the limits of modern philosophy and the sciences to those who have eyes to see it. This is so, because even the most ordinary voluntary actions, as Maurice Blondel has demonstrated, engage the human person in his concrete totality and leave him open, through his deepest inclinations, to the fullness of reality, to a reality that is beyond what we know or can know from reason alone. Moral action is, so to speak, the existential stage of philosophy and the sciences, and it puts them decisively to the test.

This is what makes studying the theology of St. Thomas so interesting. Thomas succeeded in constructing a theology that was in harmony with Greco-Roman philosophy and did so precisely in the area of morality. Our interest is deepened when we realize that Thomas offers us the completed version of a virtue morality inherited both from the Fathers of the Church and from ancient philosophy, while most modern philosophies and the sciences remain tied to a morality reduced to the level of imperatives and prohibitions.

Does theology need philosophy? What place should philosophy have in theology and what role should it play there? In a word, what interaction should philosophy have with theology in Christian moral reasoning? These are the questions we shall pose to St. Thomas. To answer them, we have chosen four structural elements of his moral theology, elements that are evident in the very plan of the *Prima Secundae*; we have, however, shifted the question of free choice to the end; since this question arises at the end of the process of moral reflection, it leads us to the consideration of concrete cases.

We can reduce the essential components of Thomistic moral theology to four structural elements:

> 1. The moral life is essentially a response to the question of happiness and the ultimate end of human action, a conception of the moral life that was the general view held by the philosophers of antiquity and the Fathers of the Church. This corresponds to the *Treatise on Happiness and the Ultimate end.*
>
> 2. Humans progress toward beatitude by their actions. These actions flow from two types of principles corresponding to the two parts of the human act: the interior act and the exterior act. First, there are the interior principles or personal sources of action. These are the *virtues* and their contrary *vices and sins.*
>
> 3. There are then the exterior or superior principles of action: *law and grace.*
>
> 4. This construction presupposes an analysis of the human person as God created him: God created him in his image with the faculties that together constitute the proper act of the human person, namely, *free*

choice, the voluntary act. The entire goal of moral theology is to form, from universal principles, the choice that generates the concrete act.

We note here that the thought of St. Thomas, from its study of principles all the way to its analysis of choice, is "unitive" in the sense that it emphasizes the collaboration of all human faculties under the guiding interaction of reason and will. In this way, the decision to act is constituted by a practical judgment and a free choice that are indissolubly united. The unitive character of action is also evident in the structure of the treatises concerning particular virtues. Each treatise first studies a virtue, as the interior principle of action, and then considers an associated gift caused by grace and a precept of the Decalogue, as the exterior principles of action, concluding with an analysis of the sins opposed to the virtue. We shall consider under these four points the place and role of philosophy in the moral theology of the Angelic Doctor.

The Treatise on Beatitude

In the five questions that comprise the treatise on beatitude, the role of philosophy, especially of Aristotle and Boethius, seems so vast that some interpreters have regarded these questions as being purely philosophical in nature. They have not noticed, however, that the study of the ultimate end and of the different goods that present themselves to us forms a threefold way – comparable to the "five ways" that lead us to God's existence – a threefold way that leads to the Christian response to the question of happiness. The vision of God in the next life is our ultimate end, because "God alone" can fully satisfy the human longing for happiness. To explain this conclusion, Thomas no longer bases himself upon the Philosopher, but upon a theologian, St. Augustine. Augustine also begins his exposition of Catholic moral theology with the question of happiness, which according to Augustine all people ask themselves even before they consciously express it. The one who can fulfill this deep desire is the Trinity, revealed and made accessible in Jesus Christ.

We also often fail to notice that Thomas's analysis of the beatitudes in his Commentary on the Gospel of St. Matthew is an underlying source of his treatise in the *Summa*. In the Commentary on St. Matthew, Thomas already follows the itinerary of a progressive search for the true good – something that he will later employ in question two of the *Prima Secundae* – showing that Christ alone reveals perfect happiness, a happiness that none of the philosophers, not even Aristotle, were able to discover. Moreover, the treatise on beatitude is itself structurally linked to the analysis of the evangelical beatitudes in question 69. Indeed, question 69 brings the treatise on beatitude to its completion. It is there that Thomas presents the beatitude attainable to the Christian in this life by living the virtues and the gifts.

Philosophy and theology, therefore, both play large roles in the treatise on beatitude, but in doing so they are not merely juxtaposed. They are connected to each other in a relationship that we could call "natural." They, in fact, respond together to a question that flows from the spiritual nature of the human person: what is the true good, what is real happiness? Enlightened by revelation, the theologian perceives that, because of the openness of the human intellect and will toward the infinite, this spontaneous desire can only be fulfilled by the vision of God. Hence, the famous argument affirming the natural desire to see God, which forms the principal wellspring underlying St. Thomas's reasoning on this point. In the face of this vocation, philosophy is both necessary and insufficient. It cannot attain, nor even imagine, such a beatitude, a beatitude that is a complete gift and properly supernatural. Yet, the theologian for his part, although by faith he knows about our call to beatitude in God, he cannot trace the ways that lead to it without the labor of reason, without engaging in philosophical reflection concerning human acts and the virtues.

Laid out in this way, the treatise on beatitude controls the entire moral part of theology. The relationship between philosophy and theology sketched above is maintained by Aquinas throughout the *Secunda Pars*. In each treatise, whether it be the treatise on the virtues, on law or on sin, the guiding principle of analysis is each thing's relationship to beatitude as the ultimate end.

We note as well that the treatise on beatitude will disappear in the post-Tridentine manuals of moral theology, as well as in modern ethics of the Kantian variety, following the critique of eudaemonism. It has not been replaced by anything except the search for a material and sensate happiness that is prone to utilitarianism and rightly suspected of being a form of egoism. Happily, the *Catechism of the Catholic Church* has reintroduced the question of happiness, placing it at the beginning of its presentation of Christian morality, which it describes as a vocation to the beatitude revealed in the evangelical beatitudes.[4]

The Virtues and the Gifts

The vast treatise on the *habitus* and the virtues is a masterpiece of Thomistic moral theology. It contains the heritage of ancient philosophy and the thought of the Fathers, both of which regard virtue as the essence of human and Christian perfection. Here again, the role of philosophy is so extensive that one might even view it as primary. Indeed, St. Thomas's teaching concerning the virtues is the result of the patient research of medieval theologians who were guided not only by St. Augustine but also by the works of

Aristotle, which were progressively being rediscovered. Especially significant is Thomas's extended study of the *habitus*, which serves as the foundation of his treatise on the virtues. In some places, such as his treatise on prudence, Aquinas even follows the precise structure of Aristotle's analysis in close detail. Moreover, to establish the definition and division of the virtues annexed to the cardinal virtues, he draws upon the lists of virtues compiled by Cicero and Macrobius, a choice that makes it difficult for Aquinas to know where to place such Christian virtues as humility, obedience or vigilance. The impression that the treatise on the virtues is above all a philosophical treatise is accentuated by our practice of conceiving the virtues as essentially the product of human effort and as being entities acquired through repeated action.

Yet, when one reads the treatise on the virtues in its entirety, one perceives that it is principally a work of theology. Indeed, the virtues form a living organism comparable to the human body with its organs. They do not exist or function separately, even though a structural analysis of the *Summa* might lead a superficial reader to conclude that they do. Instead, united in a dynamic bond established by charity and prudence, the virtues work together, like the members of our own body.

We see this dynamic especially present in the relationship between the theological virtues and the moral virtues. Faith, hope and charity constitute the head of the Christian organism of virtues. Like a vital energy, the theological virtues animate the human virtues from within, ordering them toward divine beatitude and even transforming them to a certain extent. St. Thomas perceived this transforming influence so strongly that he judged it necessary to add to the acquired moral virtues certain infused moral virtues in order to perfect them. Moreover, in each treatise on the moral virtues, one can detect that Thomas has made changes to the Aristotelian conception of moral virtue. Thus, instead of courage in battle, martyrdom becomes the supreme act of fortitude, while virginity consecrated to Christ becomes the perfection of chastity. Thomas even maintains that true patience does not exist without charity, and thus not without grace.[5]

Furthermore, and this is fundamentally important, Thomas links the virtues to the gifts of the Holy Spirit. In this way, the gifts enter into the organic life of the virtues and they perfect it. The gifts are an integral part of the Thomistic view of the moral life, in accordance with the definition of the New Law as the grace of the Holy Spirit. For Aquinas, the gifts are a necessary part of every Christian's life. They add to the virtues a receptive dimension, which is a docility to the promptings of the Holy Spirit. In this way, the action of the Holy Spirit can, like the virtues, permeate all the actions of a Christian. The moral life truly becomes a "life in the Spirit," as the Catechism calls it.[6] We do not see here a separation between the moral life and the mystical life.

Subsequent theology will regard the gifts as belonging to the mystical life and will view the mystical life as something that is reserved to a chosen few. For Aquinas, however, the gifts, like the virtues, belong to all believers.

In fact, under the guidance of revelation and Christian experience, the conception of virtue itself is transformed: to the acquired virtues are added the infused virtues, which are caused by the grace of Christ and no longer by mere human effort. These virtues, beginning with the theological virtues, are vitally associated with the human virtues. They animate them from within to such an extent that the acts of the virtues become the work both of God and of the human person united together in charity.

We note too that apostolic catechesis, notably the teachings of St. Paul about the virtues and the vices in the *Letter to the Romans*, was virtually forgotten by modern moralists.[7] For St. Thomas, however, whose commentary on the *Letter to the Romans* was preparatory for his work in the *Summa Theologiae*, the apostolic catechesis was the principal source and "authority" of his teaching, in conjunction with the interpretations of this catechesis offered by the Fathers, especially by St. Augustine and St. Gregory the Great, among others. The Thomistic analysis of the virtues in this way draws together the principal streams of Scriptural, theological and philosophical reflection.

We find once again, therefore, that philosophy is closely associated with revelation at the very heart of theology, following the prescription of St. Paul: "if there is any virtue, if there is anything worthy of praise, consider these things" (Phil. 4.8); but, at the same time we also find Aquinas asserting that the Word of God deepens philosophical knowledge and develops it beyond human hopes and expectations.

Laws and Precepts

In Christian teaching, the Decalogue has always been regarded as fundamentally important. Scholastic theology linked it to the natural law inscribed in the hearts of all people. Post-Tridentine theology made the Decalogue the cornerstone and threshold of the very structure of moral theology. Theology during this period no longer organized its material according to the virtues, as St. Thomas had done – although it still regarded Thomas as a principal authority – but instead organized it according to the ten commandments, which it interpreted as expressing obligations and prohibitions imposed upon the human person by the divine will.

St. Thomas also regarded the Decalogue and the natural law as fundamentally important. But he places them in a larger legislative context that makes them dependent upon Christian revelation. In his view, the laws form an organic whole that have their origin in God in the eternal law. The eternal law is made manifest to the human person first in the natural law inscribed in the heart; it serves as the foundation of human law. Divine Revelation, especially necessary because of sin, is revealed in order to bear witness to, perfect and make more precise this natural legislation. Revelation comes from God in two forms. It comes as the Old Law, concentrated in the Decalogue, and as the New or Evangelical Law, principally expounded in the Lord's Sermon on the Mount. The New Law is the summit of the moral law and brings the divine law to perfection on earth. The Decalogue and the natural law are thus drawn into a legislative dynamic that has its source in God and that returns to him by means of the Gospel. It causes a reinterpretation of the Decalogue whereby the Decalogue becomes interiorized and is given a higher perfection through the gift of charity. For St. Thomas, the Decalogue presents the rules for exterior acts that the New Law perfects by regulating the interior acts that inspire them. The New Law does this with the aid of the virtues, especially the virtues of faith, hope and charity. In this way the Decalogue becomes the servant of the virtues. It particularly plays a role in the first stage of the divine pedagogy, in the formation of beginners who must struggle against sin and refrain from vice.

The philosophical part of Christian moral teaching principally concerns its foundation, the natural law and the Decalogue that places the natural law in the context of the Covenant. The task of the philosophical part of Christian moral teaching is to develop human and civil law through a process of deduction or addition, which is properly the work of reason. It adds to this, reflection on the nature of the virtues, something that requires experience and maturity.

We should note that the natural law is not a hindrance to freedom. For St. Thomas, it has a profoundly dynamic character: it flows from natural inclinations and aspirations for the good and for happiness, for the preservation of one's being, for the gift of life, for truth and for life in society, inclinations that one already finds listed in the *De Officiis* of Cicero.[8] These inclinations are developed by the virtues. With regard to the negative precepts, they prohibit acts that are incompatible with the formation of the virtues and by doing so the negative precepts prepare the way for the birth of the virtues. In this way, the natural law and the Decalogue can be ordered to the Evangelical law as to a superior perfection, a complete fulfillment. In this way also theology takes up and brings to completion the investigations of philosophy.

Let us note also the sapiential nature of law in St. Thomas's works: Law is a work of reason; it is the product of the ordering reason of the divine or human legislator, and not of the solitary will of one in authority, as generally is the case in the modern conception of law. Thomas's view of the obedience that law requires is equally sapiential, associating the intellect with the will. The task of this wisdom is to coordinate the different levels of moral legislation, the philosophical level with the theological level.

We should add that, for St. Thomas, philosophy also has something to say concerning the Evangelical Law. Aquinas takes up the Aristotelian division between the pleasurable life, the active life and the contemplative life, in order to explain the beatitudes and to present Christ as the true philosopher. Even more interesting, he will use the analysis of friendship in the *Nicomachean Ethics* in order to define charity.

Prudential Judgment

The principal task of practical reason in the moral domain consists in the application of precepts to personal action in concrete circumstances. We can present this operation as a deduction from the first principles of the moral order, provided that we link these principles with the natural aspirations that are the foundation of law and the first source of human acts. These principles, therefore, are not abstract and theoretical, even if their formulation is universal and seemingly impersonal. They correspond to the sense of truth and goodness, of love of self and of neighbor, that are natural to the human person and that proceed from that spiritual spark that Thomas calls *synderesis*.

The work of applying the principles of practical reason is the work of prudence integrating the input of moral science and of conscience, which is the law's interior witness. It does not limit itself to establishing what is permitted or forbidden, but tends toward quality, toward a certain perfection of action in the present situation, like an artisan who seeks to make a good work in the exercise of his craft. A work like this requires intelligence, experience, effort and vigilance. This is why moral action requires the participation of all the faculties of the subject, as well as the use of exterior contributions received from such sources as one's education.

Prudential judgment is distinct from other forms of judgment because it goes beyond ideas, as beautiful as they may be, and beyond intentions, counsels and commandments, as judicious as they may be. Prudential judgment goes beyond these to reach the decision to act, which engenders the act, and to its execution, which transforms the acting subject himself: it makes the subject better and enables him to grow. This is why true prudence needs the other virtues, which regulate one's affectivity and one's relations with others. We can say that prudential judgment or choice is holistic; it engages the human person in his entirety, including the past that he has inherited, and even his subconscious. It is from these acts that one judges the character of a person, as one judges a tree from its fruit.

The holistic character of concrete action requires the joint intervention of philosophy and theology, of reason and of faith in Christian moral judgment. The study of "cases," especially cannot be limited to a rational examination, nor to a material application of revealed principles. It requires that one put faith into action; by doing so, one receives the light of the Spirit, as well as the light of reason, and one seeks to discover concretely the best good that one should do. The Christian moral theologian should, therefore, assimilate the message of the Gospel, often quite concrete in its formulation, such as the golden rule, and employ the philosophical and scientific resources available to him as he engages in reflection. In doing so, the moral theologian recognizes that his labors will be incomplete and even in vain if he does not attempt to put his personal prudence into action, which is the only way for him to attain the experience of, and a taste for, good fruits.

In the *First letter to the Corinthians*, St. Paul offers us an excellent example of what we could call apostolic casuistry. In examining the different cases that are brought to him, his method is consistent. It is characterized by the interpenetration of two levels: first, there is the level of rational criteria as found among the philosophers and the rabbis. For example, in the case of fornication, he writes that "every other sin a person commits is outside the body, but the immoral person sins against his own body" (6.18). At the same time, St. Paul offers criteria that are taken from the level of faith: "Do you not know that your bodies are members of Christ? . . . Do you not know that your body is a temple of the holy Spirit within you?" (6.15, 19). Thus, we see that there exists in St. Paul's discernment a close link between human meaning and the meaning of Christ, the one takes up and reinforces the other. But the Christian criteria become predominant, especially through the work of charity, which unites all believers as brothers and sisters, as members of one body under the impulse of the Spirit.

Conclusion

The interaction, therefore, between philosophy and theology is quite close in the moral works of St. Thomas. Far from being separated from each other, or in competition with each other, these sciences work together, because philosophy, in the practice of moral theology, has been integrated into the work of theology, an integration that is nothing less than vital. Influenced by the work of the theologian, the philosopher begins to consider the fundamental questions concerning the goal and meaning of life, concerning good and evil, happiness and suffering, death and the afterlife, even though the philosopher recognizes that on his own he cannot offer a complete answer to these questions. The theologian, for his part, needs the philosopher. The philosopher teaches the theologian how to reason with rigger and discernment in investigating the human dimensions of action. He also provides the theologian with the categories and the language he needs to make a solid presentation of the richness of the Gospel and of Christian experience.

This type of relationship between philosophy and theology rests upon the adage of St. Thomas: *"Gratia non tollit, sed perficit naturam,"* which could be transcribed as: theology does not destroy philosophy, but perfects it. This adage can be understood in two complimentary ways. The most frequent interpretation consists in thinking that one can construct philosophy as a work of reason, with the assurance that if it is true it will be confirmed by grace and the content of the faith. This is the perspective of the philosophers. Yet, one can also understand this adage from the opposite angle: one must have the audacity to believe in the word of God as the source of a superior light, with the certain conviction that, far from destroying what is true, good and reasonable in philosophy, faith teaches us to make these things our own, to value them and to bring them to perfection. Faith reveals to us a wisdom that is deeper and vaster than any human wisdom. It reveals a wisdom given to us by the Holy Spirit who unites us to the person of Christ and to his cross, teaching us to "live in Christ." This perspective is the perspective of the theologian. Both the philosopher and the theologian are called to encounter each other in the light of the truth that shines upon them.

Notes

1. Translated from the French by Michael Sherwin, O.P.
2. Aquinas, *Summa Theologiae* I-II, q. 108, a. 2.
3. Cf. *Catechism of the Catholic Church* (1994), n. 1971.
4. *Catechism*, nn. 1716–29.
5. *Summa Theologiae* II-II, q. 136, a. 3.
6. *Catechism*, n. 1699.
7. Cf. *Catechism*, n. 1971.
8. Cicero, *De Officiis*, bk. 1, c. 4.

The Immutability of the Sense of Dogmas and Philosophical Theories
Rev. Leo Elders, S.V.D.

Numerous sections of the encyclical *Fides et Ratio* are devoted to a description of the nature and mission of philosophical studies as well as to an appraisal of some main currents in contemporary thought. The question of the collaboration between theology and philosophy occupies several chapters of the text: chapter II deals with the way in which in the Bible reason and faith are associated; chapter IV examines the relationship between faith and reason in the course of history; this part of the encyclical culminates in §43 and 44 which affirm that in the works of St. Thomas Aquinas a most harmonious synthesis between faith and reason was reached. The chapter concludes deploring the drama of the separation between faith and reason in modern time. After some pages on the position of the Magisterium of the Church with regard to philosophical systems and theories (chapter V), Chapter VI of the text deals with the interaction and collaboration of philosophy and theology.

In this connection, following in the footsteps of *Fides et Ratio,* I propose some reflections on the bearing of philosophical views on how one conceives the nature and value of the dogmas of the faith and the role of philosophy in defense of their immutability. Let me first briefly recall what is meant by a dogma, even if to many of you this reminder may be totally redundant.

Dogmas as the Church Sees Them

In the Hellenistic world the term "dogma" had the sense of opinion, decision and ordinance. In Stoic philosophy it acquired the connotation of the doctrine to which one must conform one's moral life.[1] St. Paul uses the word to signify religious doctrine.[2] In the early Christian centuries "dogmas of Christ" came to be used indiscriminately with "doctrine" or "teachings". In later centuries the term got the meaning of revealed truth as proposed by the Church and distinguished from what is not revealed. The First Vatican Council used it in its definition of papal infallibility.[3] So a dogma is that truth which is revealed and as such formally ascertained and defined by the Church: "All those things are to be believed by divine and catholic faith which are con-

tained in the written or transmitted Word of God and which are proposed by
the Church, either by a solemn judgment or by the ordinary and universal
magisterium, to be believed as having been divinely revealed."[4] The content
of dogmas depends on divine revelation, but dogmatic propositions as such
have been made by the Church. They are the answer of the Church to God's
self-communication and show that the Church understood the message of salvation. Dogmas bind the faithful together into a community of believers in the
same creed.[5] They signify the immutable truth of God's being and his perfect
faithfulness. In this way they become the starting-point for jubilant thanks-
giving and praise of God's marvelous love.[6]

Revelation itself took place in history and stretches from Abraham until
the end of the apostolic period. The understanding of what was revealed also
shows a historical dimension The constitution *Dei Verbum* of Vatican II
speaks of a growth in the understanding of what has been handed down to us.
"This happens through the contemplation and study made by believers, who
treasure these things in their hearts (cf. *Luke* 2, 19. 51), through the intimate
understanding of spiritual things they experience, and through the preaching
of those who have received through episcopal succession the sure charism of
truth."[7]

Speaking of the historical dimension of dogmas one may first point to the
language used in their formulation. The expressive power of words may
sometimes change in the course of time. However, as the encyclical
Mysterium fidei of Paul VI says, it is not without the help of Holy Spirit that
the Church has established a rule of language and confirmed it with the
authority of the councils.

> This rule must be religiously observed and let no one presume to
> change it at his own pleasure or under the pretext of new science.
> Who would ever tolerate that the dogmatic formulas used by the ecu-
> menical councils for the mysteries of the Holy Trinity and the
> Incarnation be judged as no longer appropriate for men of our
> times...? These formulas, like the others which the Church uses to
> propose the dogmas of faith, express concepts which are not tied to a
> certain form of human culture, nor to a specific phase of history, nor
> to one or other theological school. No, these concepts present that
> part of reality which necessary and universal experience permits the
> human mind to grasp and to manifest with apt and exact terms, taken
> from either common or polished language. For this reason, these for-
> mulas are adapted to men of all times and all places.[8]

What the Church defines is the sense of the proposition as she understands
it, that is the objective intellectual contents signified by the sentence. This
sense will often imply an analogous use of the terms, as when a dogma defines

a supernatural mystery. The sense defined by the Church, always remains the same and remains true for ever, as Vatican I teaches.[9] This Council condemned the opinion that dogmas once proposed must with the progress of time be given a meaning other than that which was understood by the Church or which she understands."[10] The terms in which the dogmas are stated, have been chosen with great care and not without the guidance of the Holy Spirit. This does not exclude that the dogmas may not always be readily understandable to modern man or to people living in a different culture. They may need to be explained. "It may also happen that in the habitual usage of the Church certain of these formulas gave way to new expressions which, proposed and approved by the Sacred Magisterium, presented more clearly the same meaning."[11] It must also be noted that in the Eastern and Western Church different formulae have been proposed which, without mutual contradiction, express each an aspect of a particular mystery, as, for instance, the mode of procession of the Holy Spirit.[12]

The above lines present very briefly the position of the Church with regard to the dogmas of the faith and their use of terms and propositions consecrated by Councils, the Magisterium, Tradition and Christian piety. The Church upholds the immutability of the contents of these propositions. The dogmas unfold the riches of Gods love, preserve the mind from subjectivity and aberrations; they bring us closer to the eschatological fulfillment of our present life, when faith will be turned into vision. Vatican II expresses the wish that the treasure of revelation entrusted to the Church may increasingly fill the hearts of men.[13]

However, in recent years this doctrine has been criticized by some theologians. Several difficulties have been raised against it. In order to solve them one has to make use of philosophical considerations.

The Desire Not to be Tied to Anything

A first objection appears to be based on the desire of freedom. Certain Christians do not want to be bothered by a set of complicated propositions they cannot understand. Instead of being a group of people who profess the same faith, they want to be a community of people seeking truth, each in his own way. Only what we feel or experience ourselves is authentic. Their battle cry is: "Away with dogmatism."

This objection proceeds from a fundamental misunderstanding of the Christian faith, which is not an undertaking like a cultural club where each member can pursue his own way of thinking. The faith is an invitation to something beyond nature and the visible world. When one does not understand this aspect of our Christian vocation,, it is obvious that the dogmas – which summarize what the faith is about – do not make much sense. Quite typical of modern man is the desire not to be tied to anything. In his encyclical *Veritatis splendor* John Paul II writes that the desire of freedom of modern man is that of a freedom which has lost its connection with truth, i.e., with the ontological order. The desire of autonomy and of disengagement from rules and institutions leads to serious consequences: a certain disorder in organizing one's life and a lack of consistency in one's actions. Instead of reason, instincts become the commanding factor. One's personal life has no longer an overall purpose but obeys the urge to be uninhibited in what one does. Institutions become something threatening. Virtues and traditional moral rules are no longer considered positive values, for they impose constraints. This position leads to the collapse of faithfulness. Instead of being attached to stability, people crave for constant change. Philosophy shows that the roots of this attitude lie in existentialism, and beyond it in a view which reduces the faculty of free choice to a power cut loose from the intellect.[14] To counter and overcome this powerful trend we should develop ethics along the lines of Aquinas's insight that the good of man is to live according to reason.[15]

Are True Sentences Possible?

A second criticism concerns dogmas as propositions. It is very problematic whether there are true sentences as such. The terms of a proposition come to be understood differently in the course of time, as reality itself is constantly changing. According to this view there is a disjunction between reality and our knowledge. Knowledge is at best a process parallel to reality; our concepts may show some similarity with things, but do not really grasp their intelligible contents. In other words, our mind considers its own concepts but not things, and the outside world is not really attained.[16] For all practical purposes one could say that propositions are simultaneously true and false.[17] If propositions which are thought to contain and to express the same truth for ever do not exist, dogmatic definitions cannot be absolute statements and will have to be replaced by ever new formulas.

That dogmatic formulas do not express the fullness of the mystery of faith has been known ever since the beginning of Christianity.[18] St. Augustine drew attention to the poverty of our language which hardly succeeds in expressing what we inwardly think.[19] However, this does not mean that absolutely true propositions are not possible. As the philosophy of Aristotle and Aquinas shows, things have an essence. In the process of knowledge they give their intelligibility and truth to our intellect which, with the help of the senses and in particular the *cogitativa*, can form judgments about reality which are absolutely true.[20] Our knowledge is not about likenesses but about things. In the field of scientific studies also certain propositions are believed to remain always true. Propositions about the message God sent us are necessary: we would not even be able to think about it and give account of it, if we could not seize and express it in judgments. To this effect the dogmas are necessary.

Dogmas are anything but a sort of straight jacket of thought. We are invited to enter by faith into a new realm; a window opens on God's being, but in the still obscure twilight of the faith we would lose our bearings if we did not have the dogmas to guide us and to teach us. They invite us to penetrate ever deeper into the treasures of revelation and to grow in love of God.

The changing circumstances of our lives and our own individual needs may cause us to consider the revealed message from an angle which differs somewhat from that of earlier generations. Yet this does not lead to a reformulation of dogmas because these convey God's immutable truth and are so intimately connected with man's deepest being, needs and longings and formulated in such a profound and general way, that they always retain their validity.

Nowadays a special difficulty is that the set of values prevailing in modern society is very different from the world of faith. Instead of there being a harmonious unity between the doctrine of the faith and prevalent ways of thinking, there is often a rupture and faith is juxtaposed to other convictions. It is the duty of Christians to adapt their thinking to that of the Church, and not to that of the society in which they live, and, if necessary, to take even a heroic stand in defense of the faith.

The Critique of Analytical Philosophy

A further difficulty against reliance on dogmas is raised by some analytical philosophers: propositions which are supposed to express a truth beyond our experience are meaningless. They may perhaps be emotionally significant to some people, but in reality they are non-sensical, because they cannot be related to valuable experiences.[21] If the propositions of the creed are to have a meaning, they must be understood as referring to certain aspects of our life.[22]

In answering this objection we first make a concession: human knowledge is in fact derived from sense experience; our mind cannot think without uninterrupted reference to the contents of sense knowledge. Yet the intellect forms general concepts and formulates laws of being and even infers the existence of causes which as such do not fall under sense experience.

In the act of faith there is real contact with God, but this takes place in the darkness of our defective and analogical way of knowing: we use concepts which God has chosen among the words of our language and our experiences (or which at least reflect these experiences in those dogmas in which are expressed in a more philosophical language). These concepts obtain an analogous sense in order to express the mystery of God's being and will, who decided to save us because of Jesus, his only begotten Son. By faith we touch God himself through the intermediary of revealed doctrine. Our language and our concepts become instruments to express a truth which is far beyond the immediate significance of the words. In this way they are an anticipation of a coming experience. In the last analysis, all propositions of the faith go back to the original message of the apostles, that is to human experiences of those who witnessed the events through which God revealed himself and who received a message in order to hand it on to others.

It is not surprising that each individual Christian does not have an immediate experience of the events of salvation nor receives a personal revelation. We may see here an analogy with what happens in human society: we are born in a certain society and receive a language as a house we did not build ourselves. In a similar way we also receive the language of the faith. Because of its particular nature, dogmatic language combines several seemingly opposed characteristics: it states facts, but it is also tied to an attitude of the will; it expresses convictions but is also adorative. To those who do not have the faith, it is only mythical, because it proposes things of which we have no evidence.

The Immutability of Dogmas and The Historicity of Man

Another difficulty with regard to dogmas is believed to be caused by the historicity of human thought. The assumption of ever true statements does not seem to do justice to this historicity. If man himself constantly evolves, there is no place for a body of unchangeable dogmas. The Church too lives in history and cannot produce ready made formulas applying to all situations. Faith is not present in its purest form when one hands on a set of dogmas which have no connection with the historical situation of contemporary Christians.[23]

The answer to this difficulty comprises a philosophical and a theological consideration. There are undoubtedly people in the Western world who experience the historicity of their being and feel that they are constructing their own truth which is valid only now. However, relativism as the denial of any absolutely true statements is simply impossible. If we think that there are no absolutely true statements, we already assume that there is at least one. A real skeptic would have to seek refuge, like Pyrrho, in *aphasía.*[24] The theory of the relativity of our knowledge goes against the grain of thought itself which tends to become certitude. The case of Hans Küng illustrates this point: in his *Unfehlbar? Eine Anfrage* he doubts about the possibility of affirming wholly certain propositions, yet he seems entirely sure of the correctness of his own theories. To be of value thought must possess certitude. No one cares for mere opinions, if they do not help to reach certitude.

It is a fact that we can grasp the truth of doctrines proposed in other periods of history. We can indeed, accompany in thought Socrates, as he is arguing in Plato's dialogues, and evaluate his arguments. Our present instant becomes enlarged and is extended so as to comprise the intelligible contents of a discussion said to be held 2400 years ago. Our immaterial mind is able to reach beyond the moment of time in which it now exists: it makes scientific statements which are true for ever as are statements about historical facts. Things have their truth which can be grasped by the mind. Were there nothing but a Heraclitean flux, there would not be such a permanent intelligibility. Because things have their essences and their meaning, a truly certain knowledge is possible, a knowledge which is not subject to the fleeting moment of time.

It follows that on the level of supernatural faith propositions are possible which always retain their truth. The dogmatic formulas are supra-temporal. Ever since the beginning of the Church this permanence of the Christian message has been stressed.[25] It was solemnly defined by the First Vatican Council.[26] In the *Constitution on Divine Revelation*, §8, the Fathers of the Second Vatican Council, while dwelling on the fact that further understanding of the revealed message is possible, refer nevertheless to the text of Vatican I, thereby indicating that the permanence of the same sense of the dogmas is presupposed. The identity of revealed doctrine to be preserved and to be handed down to the next generation of men does not exclude, rather demands that this doctrine is proposed to the faithful in a language which they can more easily understand.

Obviously dogmas are historical in so far as they are also, accidentally, the reflection of the thought of the Church at a particular moment of time and of the circumstances which surrounded their definition. History is the soil in which dogma grows and develops. This is a logical consequence of the Incarnation. There is dogmatic development, but there is no change in the meaning of what the Church believed and defined at a particular moment of time.

Does Historico-critical Exegesis Undermine Dogmatic Formulas?

Dogmatic formulas are based on Holy Scripture either as restating what is explicitly written in the Bible, or as a systematic representation of its contents or as inferences from what is implicitly contained in it. Opponents of the Catholic view of dogmas argue with Bultmann that the world of the Bible is a mythical world: a divine man, the logos, angels and devils, descent into hell, resurrection and ascension into heaven are typical myths.[27] Since dogmatic formulas use and define material explicitly or implicitly contained in Holy

Scripture, it would seem that they must be interpreted on the basis of our understanding of the Bible and be divested of their mythological presentation.

Vatican II has answered this difficulty: through Tradition the full canon of the sacred books is known and are these books more profoundly understood. The faith of the Church is subordinated to Holy Scripture, but it is also decisive for the determination of the sense of the text. This is obvious in such questions as the primacy of Peter and his successors, the sacred ministry and the special place of Mary. The mere scientific study of the text of Holy Scripture provides no guarantee for understanding the revealed truth contained in it. If some biblical scholars would hold that the New Testament references to the resurrection of Jesus do not imply the physical reality of the event, they understand the texts differently from the Church and thus fail to see the real meaning of inspired Scripture.

With regard to Bultmann's theory of the so-called mythological view of the world which, as he thinks, pervades the writings of the New Testament, we argue that there is no question of such a total opposition between the view of the New Testament and that of modern man. Because of the supra-temporal aspect of man's thought there cannot be such a discontinuity between two mentalities. In the second place, certain events such as the virgin birth of Jesus and his resurrection were no less difficult to believe in for the people of those days than for our contemporaries. That certain expressions of Holy Scripture are figurative was known to the early Church and there is no need to demythologize these propositions. Furthermore, what Bultmann calls the mythological mentality is far from being as primitive as he assumes it to be. It is rather a permanent aspect of the way in which man grasps reality. A consistent demythologization along the lines stipulated by Bultmann would lead to a sort of anti-profession of the faith: "I believe in Jesus Christ who is not born from all eternity from the Father; who is not born in time from a virgin; who suffered under Pontius Pilate and died but not in expiation of our sins; who was buried but did not rise from among the dead; who did not ascend to heaven and does not sit at the right hand of the Father."[28]

The Distinction Between Truth and Formulation

Some refer to Pope John XXIII to express their doubts about permanently valid dogmas. In his opening address to the Bishops gathered for the Second Vatican Council John XXIII spoke about the need to express the Christian message in a way which agrees with our time, making a distinction between the truth contained in the dogmas on the one hand and the manner in which they are formulated on the other.[29] Some authors drew the conclusion that apparently the formulas are not the essence of the dogmas and can be changed They saw a basis for their view in a philosophical theory which distinguishes between the gist of a proposition and the terms in which it is expressed. This theory was proposed by some theologians of the Jesuit scholasticate of Lyon-Fourvières, such as H. Bouillard[30] and partly by H. de Lubac: the concepts used in the dogmas are not very relevant and are subject to changing cultural conditions. Behind this theory lies a view which sees divine revelation not as the communication of conceptual knowledge but as the manifestation of a Person. Some went far beyond the initial intention of these authors and suggested that the dogma about the transsubstantiation might not mean more than that the religious truth of bread and wine are changed in a eucharistic celebration[31] or that the definition of papal infallibility of Vatican I should be understood in this sense that the Magisterium of the Church proposes in each period of history the message of Christ in a way which is convenient to people.[32]

In his encyclical *Humani generis* of 1950 Pius XII rejected the theory which assigns no more than a relative value to the terms in a dogmatic proposition. Who embraces this theory risks espousing certain tenets of modernism.[33] As is obvious the debate also evokes a philosophical question, i.e., the relation of the terms of a proposition to the proposition itself. A statement is nothing else but the acknowledgment that a term belongs to, is present in or characterized by another term. The statement itself is nothing but this connection of two terms: that of the subject and the predicate. St. Thomas speaks of *componere* and *dividere*. The judgment sees and pronounces the reality of this composition.[34] Those who underestimate the importance of the terms in the propositions of the faith are likely to have been influenced by the intuitionism of Bergson.[35]

If the enunciation of a dogma would not have its own particular signification, all the articles of faith would flow together in confusion. Faith would no longer be distinguished from a mystic feeling or a surrendering to the unknown. This would be against man's dignity and responsibility. God will only propose the message of salvation in a form adapted to man's intellectual life.[36] The terms of the dogmatic formulas signify the realities of man's salvation. Some of these terms have been taken from Holy Scripture, others have been consecrated by their use and acceptance by Tradition. In fact, the dogmatic formulas are often the result of ages of prayerful meditation on the contents of revelation and were defined under the guidance of the Holy Spirit.[37]

It is understood that the Church does not define any particular philosophy but, in her definitions, she may use philosophical terms, when she judges that these terms aptly express an objective fact of the revealed reality she wants to state. Those who reduce the significance of the concepts used in dogmatic for-

mulas sometimes appeal to St. Thomas Aquinas who writes that the act of
faith is directed to the reality which is signified and not to the terms of the articles of faith.[38] However, Thomas does not say that the terms of a dogma are
irrelevant, but that the object of the faith, God in his simplicity, is expressed
by means of a composition of terms in the human mind. God himself transcends our enunciations. To signify even better that the reality to be attained
in the act of faith is God himself, we use the form "I believe IN."[39]

Dogmas and Archetypes

Over the past hundred years several authors have argued that dogmas are
no more than an expression of religious feeling.[40] In its most modern form this
explanation is proposed by C. Jung. Dogmas such as that of the Trinity, the
Divinity of Christ, the Assumption of Mary, must be explained with the help
of archetypes. In all these dogmas the spontaneous activity of the psyche is at
work.[41] Almost the entire life of the collective unconscious has been chan-
neled into the dogmatical archetypical ideas and flows along like a well-con-
trolled stream in the symbolism of creed and ritual.[42] In this view the objec-
tivization of psychic contents into dogmas is not quite harmless. Although
dogmas do in fact protect the mind against the unknown forces of religious
experience, they may be instrumental in the drying up of this experience.
Hence, Christians should not pay too much attention to these formulas, something which seems to be happening today.

Our answer is that this difficulty rests on subjectivism and the prejudice
that revelation cannot come to man from God. As the modernists said, "revelation cannot be put into us from outside; it can be occasioned but it cannot be
caused by instruction."[43] If this line of thinking would be true, one might as
well resort to Jung's explanations which would allow us to discover some
sense and beauty in the numerous dogmas. But over and against this sort of
attempts at a re-interpretation, Christians cannot but stress the objectivity of
revelation, without which the Christian message is no better than a dream or
an illusion. When God reveals, something takes place in the prophet's mind,
due to which the prophet or apostle understands the sense of the events he sees
or of the words he hears and of ideas he receives, in relation to God's love for
mankind. It is in this way that the apostles were given the understanding of
the meaning of Jesus' death and resurrection.[44] The modernists appear to
exclude this specific intervention of God. But the so-called "religious sense"
to which they resort in order to explain the genesis of Christian dogmas, is a
category of reality which subtracts itself from scientific research.

The doctrine of revelation does not say that revelation is necessarily an
abrupt or violent invasion of man's mind. The ordinary perception of events

and the mechanism of man's sensitive and intellectual life are in most cases an integral part of it. With regard to Jung's theory one could say that a psychologist may discover that certain dogmas show an analogy with the contents and basic structures of the conscious or unconscious life of the mind. It could be that what Jung calls the archetypes did facilitate awareness and the formulation of certain dogmas. However, when Jung does not want to consider (and perhaps does not want to admit) the objective meaning of dogmas and their basis in revelation, he locks himself up in the subjectivity of psychic facts.[45]

Dogmas Have No Relation to Modern Life

There are also those who argue that dogmas serve little if any purpose. Dogmatic formulas are frequently the result of a theological dispute and are a reaction of the Church against certain dangerous developments. They have a "Sitz im Leben." In recent years Christians have become very sensitive on the question of the teaching authority of the Pope and the Bishops. They also feel that the faith has become far too complicated. Jesus himself did not speak in dogmas and taught only two commandments. Therefore, dogmatism should be transcended and the function of dogmas should be reduced to that of signposts for Christians underway.[46] W. Kasper argues that a reduction of dogmas to simpler affirmations is possible.[47]

Many of us have noticed that there is a gap between Christian doctrine and the pattern of life and thought of a good number of our contemporaries. But does this mean that Christian doctrine has to go into the melting pot? At first sight it may seem that the vast mass of dogmas is too much of a challenge and too much of Greek intellectualism to modern man. Moreover, there has been a shift of interest. Nowadays people are more concerned with questions of social justice and personal freedom than with that of their own salvation.[48] However, there is no obligation to know and to study all dogmas in order to be saved. As J. H. Newman has pointed out, a Christian may approach the dogmas in a more intellectual or in a more "real" way, meaning that he uses them as an inspiration in daily life.[49] In this second way, Christians of good will, who have no theological training, can certainly discern the sense of the dogmas. If the sometimes abstract formulas seem far removed from daily life, it is the task of catechists to make Christians see the meaning and value of the treasures of the doctrine of the faith.

It is doubtlessly true that heresies, theological controversy and other external factors have led to the formulation of many dogmas. Yet if the Holy Spirit guides the Church, those factors had a special function in bringing about more clearly the true doctrine. The accidental origin of certain dogmas does not detract from the lasting value of their substance. This becomes even clearer if one reads the acts of the councils, such as Trent. The only thing the Fathers were concerned about was to render account of the Catholic faith, as this faith lived in the tradition of the Church. If the expression of this faith as to certain points of doctrine has become especially difficult for modern man, could it not be that modern man has adopted certain ways of thought and attitudes which do not favor acceptance of the faith.[50] What is called for is a conversion of man rather than a change in the doctrine of the Church.

In certain ecumenical endeavors a number of Christians seem to be willing to bypass doctrinal differences in order to bring about a practical union with our separated brethren in Protestant churches. They pay special attention to some central dogmas and neglect what according to them lies at the periphery of the faith. However, Vatican I reminds us that all dogmas must be believed with the same faith with which we believe the Incarnation and Redemption.[51] When God reveals his being and his plan of salvation, this divine truth is not known by us in one single intuition but by means of a variety of concepts and propositions. Some of these are more fundamental than others which are derived from them or related to them.[52] There is a certain order in which the faith must be presented, but a reduction of the doctrine of the faith to a few simple propositions is illegitimate and contrary to the faith.

Epilogue

An examination of the attempts to attenuate, to change or even to reject a number of the dogmas of our Catholic faith reveals some underlying common facts and tendencies: a lack of interest in the supernatural and a this-worldly attitude. Supreme value is given to one's own experience and to sense perception over and against objective statements. People seem to seek what is of immediate usefulness to them. There is furthermore the conviction that nothing is definite: laws and rules ought to be changed in the course of time. Many are reluctant to accept as binding a doctrine proposed by others, worse, by bishops of past ages who had no inkling of modern life. Finally, pluralism in doctrine appears to have become the normal situation in our modern societies. In addition there are underlying philosophical theories, such as conceptualism, idealism and its derivatives, historicism and neo-positivism. The debate about the lasting value of dogmatic formulas illustrates the need of adherence to sound philosophical views about the mind and human knowledge which one will find in the works of Aquinas.

One may hope that when people become aware of the spiritual impoverishment brought about by the above mentioned factors, they will acquire again a greater esteem for objective order, tradition and doctrinal authority.

Yet the conversion necessary for believing the doctrine of the faith can only be the work of the Holy Spirit who renews the face of the earth.

Notes

1. See M. Else, "Der Begriff des Dogmas in der alten Kirche," *Zeitschrift für Theologie und Kirche* 61 (1964), pp. 421–38.

2. Ephesians 2. 15; Colossians 2. 14.

3. H. Denzinger, *Enchiridion symbolorum* (hereafter DS) (Barcinone: Herder, 1963) n. 3073.

4. DS 3011.

5. Cf. Karl Rahner, "Was ist ein Dogma?" *Schriften zur Theologie*, 15 vols. (Einsiedeln, 1960), vol. 5, pp. 54–81.

6. L. Scheffczyk, "Satzwahrheit und Bleiben in der Wahrheit," in *Zum Problem der Unfehlbarkeit. Antworten auf die Anfrage van Hans Küng*, ed. K. Rahner (Freiburg, 1971), pp. 148–73, esp. 166 ff.

7. *Dei Verbum*, §8.

8. Paul VI, *Mysterium fidei*, §14 and 15. See also idem, *Credo*, §5.

9. DS 3020.

10. DS 3043.

11. *Mysterium Ecclesiæ*, in *Acta Apostolicæ Sedis* 65 (Vatican, 1973), §5.

12. Cf. Vatican II, *Unitatis redintegratio*, §14.

13. *Dei Verbum*, §26.

14. See L. Elders, "Contemporary Theories of Freedom and Christian Ethics", in *Freedom in Contemporary Culture. Acts of the 5th World Congress of Christian Philosophy (20–25 August, 1996)*, 2 vols. (Lublin, 1999), vol. II, pp. 7–21.

15. Aquinas, *Q. d. de veritate*, q. 13, a. 1: "Bonum hominis est secundum rationem vivere." See L. Elders, "Bonum humanæ animæ est secundum rationem esse," *Revue théologique de Lugano* IV (1999), pp. 75–90.

16. The type of conceptualism was upheld by Avicenna, Suarez (*In de anima*, lib. III, c. 2, n. 5ff) and is found in the philosophies of Kant and many other modern authors.

17. H. Küng, *Unfehlbar? Eine Anfrage* (Zürich: Benziger, 1970), pp. 95–121.

18. Cf. 2 Cor. 3. 16; Justinus, *Dialogus cum Tryphone* 127. 2; Clement of Alexandria, *Stromateia* II. 2; Irenœus, *Adv. hœreses*, IV. 20. 5.

19. De *Trinitate* IX. 7. 12. Cf. also Vatican I, *De fide catholica*, chapters 2 and 4.

20. See our *The Philosophy of Nature of St. Thomas Aquinas* (Frankfurt am Main: Peter Lang, 1997), p. 182.

21. A. J. Ayer, *Language, Truth and Logic* (New York: Dover, 1952), ch. 1.

22. Cf. R. B. Braithwaite, *An Empiricist's View of the Nature of Religious Belief* (Philadelphia: R. West, 1955).

23. W. Kasper, "Geschichtlichkeit der Dogmen," *Stimmen der Zeit* 181 (1967), pp. 401–16.

24. Sextus Empiricus, *Pyrroneion Hypotyposeis* I (Frankfurt: Suhrkamp, 1968), p. 192.

25. Cf. Matthew 28. 20; Galatians 1. 8; Hebrews 1. 2; 12. 2; 2 Timothy 1. 13; 3. 10.

26. DS 3020: "Hinc sacrorum dogmatum is sensus perpetuo est retinendus, quam semel declaravit sancta mater Ecclesia nec umquam ab eo sensu altioris intelligentiœ specie et nomine recedendum." Cf. also the *Decretum Lamentabili* of 1907.

27. R. Bultmann, *Das Evangelium des Johannes* (Göttingen, 1941); *Die Theologie des Neuen Testamentes* (Mohr, 1961), pp. 162 ff.; *Offenbarung und Heilsgeschehen* (München, 1941).

28. H. Sasse, *Flucht vor dem Dogma. Bemerkungen zu Bultmann's Entmythologisierung des Neuen Testaments* (Bleckmar, 1965).

29. *Acta Synodalia Sacrosancti Concilii Vaticani* II, 6 vols. (Vatican, 1970–78), vol. I, p. 172.

30. H. Bouillard, *Conversion et grâce chez S. Thomas d'Aquin* (Paris, 1944).

31. Cf. C. Vanneste, "Bedenkingen Bij de Scholastieke Transsubstantiatie-Leer," *Collationes Brugenses et Gandavenses* 2 (1956), pp. 322–35.

32. This is the thesis of A. Houtepen in his *Onfeilbaarheid en hermeneutiek* (Brugge, 1973).

33. A refutation can be found in the collective work, *Dialogue théologique*, ed. M. Labourdette (Saint-Maximin: Les Arcades, 1947).

34. Cf. *In I Peri hermeneias*, lectio 5, n. 73; R. McInerny, "Some Notes on Being and Predication," *The Thomist* 22 (1959), pp. 315–35.

35. See M. Labourdette and M.-J. Nicolas, "Analogie de la vérité et l'unité de la science théologique," *Revue thomiste* 47 (1947), pp. 417–66.

36. Cf. L. Malevez, "L'invariant et le divers dans le langage de la foi," *Nouvelle revue théologique* 95 (1973), pp. 353–66.

37. *Mysterium Fidei*, in *Acta Apostolicae Sedis* 57 (1965), p. 758.

38. Aquinas, *Summa theologiæ* IIa–IIœ, q. 1, a.2 ad 2: "Actus autem credentis non terminatur ad enuntiabile, sed ad rem."

39. Aquinas, *Q.d. de malo*, q. 6, a. 1, ad 14.

40. In particular, F. Schleiermacher.

41. Cf. Jung, "Psychologie und Religion," *Gesammelte Werke*, 20 vols. (Zurich, 1958-), vol. 11, pp. 46 ff; also, "Versuch einer psychologischen Deutung des Trinitätsdogmas," Ibid., pp. 119–218.

42. C. Jung, *Psychological Reflections* (Princeton, 1970), pp. 46 ff.

43. G. Tyrrel, *Through Scylla and Charybdis* (New York: Longmans and Green, 1907), p. 306.

44. Aquinas, *Q.d. de veritate,* q. 12, a. 3, ad 11.

45. On the epistemological difficulties which beset Jung's theory of archetypes, see L. Gilen, "Das Unbewusste und die Religion nach C. G. Jung," *Theologie und Philosophie* 42 (1967), esp. pp. 494–500.

46. Cf. B. Sesboué, "Autorité du Magistère et vie de foi ecclésiale," *Nouvelle revue théologique* 93 (1971), pp. 327–59; Y. congar, "Du bon usage de Denzinger," in *Situations et tâches présentes de la théologie* (Paris, 1967), pp. 11–133; J. Nolte, *Dogma in Geschichte* (Frieburg, 1970), speaks of an "Exodus aus unhaltbaren Positionen."

47. W. Kasper, *Einführung in den Glauben* (Mainz, 1975) pp. 96–98.

48. Cf. G. Widmer, "Sens et non-sens des énoncés théologiques," *Revue des sciences philosophiques et théologiques* 51 (1967), pp. 644–65.

49. J. H. Newman, Grammar of Assent (London, 1895), ch. 4, §3; and his "Letter to the Duke of Norfolk," Certain Difficulties Felt by the Anglicans in Catholic Teaching Considered (London: Basil Montagu Pickering, 1876), vol. 2, pp. 171–347.

50. See R. Guardini, *Die Sinne und die religiöse Erkenntnis* (Mainz, 1950), p. 36: "Wir nehmen unsere heutige Erkenntnissituation als ob sie die natürliche und wesentliche wäre. Wir müssen unsere Erkenntnissituation als Ergebnis einer Geschichte sehen, die voll Schuld ist und Bekehrung fordert."

51. DS 3011. See also Pius XI, *Mortalium animos*, in *Acta Apostolica Sedis* 20 (1928), pp. 10–15.

52. *Mysterium Ecclesiæ* (see note 11 above)

Truth and Truths: A Crucial Distinction in the Encyclical Letter *Fides et Ratio*
William J. Hoye

Needless to say, in the encyclical on faith and reason "truth" is obviously a fundamental notion, from the point of view of both faith and reason. In its opening sentence the encyclical compares faith and reason to "two wings on which the human spirit rises to the contemplation of truth." There is no over-looking the fact, furthermore, that the term is used with different meanings. As an analogous term it is not always free from the danger of equivocation and for this reason requires careful attention. What I would like to concentrate on in the present paper is the distinction between "truth" used in abstract and *quasi*-abstract senses, although certainly not always as an abstract *notion*, on the one hand, and "truth" used in concrete senses, on the other hand. If Latin were strictly consistent, then it would be appropriate to distinguish neatly between *veritas* and *verum*, but unfortunately the word *veritas* is in fact used in both senses, i.e., for truth itself and for *a* truth, or truths. The distinction becomes palpable with respect to the use of the singular and plural forms of the word. For sometimes the term lends itself to the plural form and some-times putting it in the plural is out of the question – and occasionally one is unsure. Now, although the difference between the two uses would seem to be ingrained in common language, in reflective thought it is often ignored, occa-sionally giving rise to misunderstandings. Since in the encyclical itself there is no explicit elucidation of the various uses, I have been prompted to try to reflect more closely upon this relationship and its import.

The Two Dimensions of Truth

First, let me exemplify the different uses of the term "truth" in the encycli-cal. The Pope can speak, for example, – concretely – of "certain truths, whether philosophical or theological" (§54) as well as of the truth of philoso-phy or "philosophical truth"(§30) – in the singular – and (in the same para-graph) of "the truths of philosophy." There is the divine truth of faith[1] and "the truth of Christian faith" (§40), or "Christian truth" (§38), along with the "truths of faith" (cf. §43; 44; 45; 97) (also rendered as "the contents of faith"

§43). Sometimes the ambivalence can be observed in a comparison of translations. In §105, for example the English translation has the plural ("the truths of the faith") where the Latin text has the singular (*fidei veritatem*). There exist, of course, "numerous truths" (§30; 31: "many more truths"), "philosophical truths" (§30), "religious truths" (§30), and "philosophical-religious truths" (§30). And naturally one raises "the question of the link between, on the one hand, the truths of philosophy and religion and, on the other, the truth [singular!] revealed in Jesus Christ" (§30). But here too we are to distinguish between "revealed truth," (e. g., §15) or "the truth of Christian Revelation" (§14), on the one hand, and "revealed truths," or "the truths of Revelation" (§92; 100; 76), on the other.

When the Pope speaks of "the Truth which is the living God" (§92) and in the same paragraph of "the Truth, which is Christ,"[2] then this is certainly not to imply that we are dealing here with *two* truths. But what about the sentence "philosophy seeks truth"? Is that the same meaning of "truth" (regardless of the fact that the English translation, in conformity with the Italian version, capitalizes "truth" in the one instance and lower cases it in the other)? Or is it in turn different from "the total and ultimate truth, that is, the essence itself of the objects of knowledge" (§82), to which philosophy is addressed. And when I enquire, as I am presently doing, about the meaning of the term "truth," I am of course using the word in still another way, namely, as an abstract, general notion. Similarly, when the Pope cites the scholastic definition of truth as *adaequatio rei et intellectus* (§82), presumably he is not offering us a definition of God, nor, of course, is God to be understood as an abstract notion. What, then, is the difference between these two *quasi*-abstract uses? Perhaps the most difficult distinction in the entire encyclical is the one between "revealed truth" and "truth pure and simple," which seems to extend beyond revealed truth. In §73 we read: "It is as if, moving between the twin poles of God's word and a better understanding of it, reason is offered guidance and is warned against paths which would lead it to stray from revealed Truth and to stray in the end from the truth pure and simple [which the Latin refers to as "truth itself" (*ipsam veritatem*)]."

For the purpose of analyzing the essential relationship between theology and philosophy, the Pope proceeds by taking the point of view of abstract truth – a decisive choice of a basis for comparison and a good example for the importance of distinct thinking in regard to the notion of truth. "Since God's word is Truth (*cf.* Jn 17. 17)," so he argues, "the human search for truth – philosophy, pursued in keeping with its own rules – can only help to understand God's word better." The clear distinction made at the beginning of Chapter VI (§65) between hearing God's Word [*auditus fidei*] and understanding it [*intellectus fidei*], as the twofold principle of theological method,[3] makes it possible to speak of a circular relationship – of interdependence, of mutual influence – between theology and philosophy. Although theology receives the whole truth through Revelation, it does not stop there. As the Pope approaches the question, it is mandatory to *understand* what has been revealed, and this necessitates the "philosophizing mind" (§73). For according to the radical teaching of Augustine's that the Pope cites, "If faith does not think, it is nothing."[4] At this point philosophy becomes unavoidable. However, it does not replace Revelation nor does it really go beyond it; it remains within the horizon of revealed truth, while searching for truth, its truth. In this way, theology and philosophy meet. Taken in the abstract singular: "Truth can only be one" (§79). Hence, Revelation does not imply that the search for truth has found its goal; to the contrary, the search receives renewed motivation.[5] Revelation is not simply the solution to the questions posed by philosophy. While, of course, maintaining their own "different aspects of truth" (§6), they both are striving after the same goal, and this goal that the two have in common the Pope surprisingly defines as the supernatural beatitude of Christian Revelation: "The ultimate purpose of personal existence, then, is the theme of philosophy and theology alike. For all their difference of method and content, both disciplines point to that "path of life" (Ps 16. 11) which, as faith [!] tells us, leads in the end to the full and lasting joy of the contemplation of the Triune God" (§15). We are thus urged to place ourselves freely "in the truth," for we "can find fulfilment only in choosing to enter the truth" (§107) – and it is noteworthy that here, i.e., in a Christian context, there is no further specification of truth.

But Pope John Paul II goes even further. He explains that philosophy is required not only for *understanding* what one has heard through Revelation but even for the very *hearing* of the Word of Revelation from the first.[6]

The reason why "the relationship between revealed truth and philosophy" has a circular form (§73), is that both revolve, spirally, within the compass of one and the same abstract "horizon of truth"(§107).[7] Viewed "in the context of this highest horizon," as the Latin puts it, the encyclical states: "This relationship imposes a twofold consideration, since the truth conferred by Revelation is a [!] truth to be understood in the light of reason. It is this duality alone which allows us to specify correctly the relationship between revealed truth and philosophical learning" (§35).

The key to the principal thesis of the encyclical, which asserts not just the convergence of philosophy and theology, but their unity, is, once again, the notion of truth. Philosophy and theology are linked together by "necessity" and the Pope goes so far as to claim even "the impossibility of their separation" (§77). The unity of truth, considered from the perspective of truth viewed as a horizon, or, to use another metaphor, in the light of truth, as opposed to truths, encompasses philosophical and theological truth. In §34 this is explained as follows (without employing the orthographical device of capitalizing "truth," which would hardly be feasible here):

> This truth, which God reveals to us in Jesus Christ, is not opposed to the truths which philosophy perceives. On the contrary, the two modes of knowledge lead to truth in all its fullness. [Note that we have here one and the same truth.] The unity of truth is a fundamental premise of human reasoning. . . . It is the one and the same God who establishes and guarantees the intelligibility and reasonableness of the natural order of things upon which scientists confidently depend, and who reveals himself as the Father of our Lord Jesus Christ. This unity of truth, natural and revealed, is embodied in a living and personal way in Christ, as the Apostle reminds us: "Truth is in Jesus" (cf. Eph 4. 21; Col 1. 15–20). . . . What human reason seeks "without knowing it" (cf. Acts 17. 23) can be found only through Christ: what is revealed in him is "the full truth."

Thus, we have, in short, a two-dimensional picture of truth: a vertical dimension, which is singular, and a horizontal dimension, where a plurality of truths occur. Both dimensions come together in the idea of searching for truth.

Searching for Truth

The Revelation of "universal and ultimate truth" does not mean that the believer has reached his or her intellectual goal and can now be content to come to a standstill, so that independent philosophy becomes dispensable. – For Aquinas, incidentally, the question takes on just the opposite form: For him the question is not whether philosophy is necessary but why Revelation is necessary? – Rather than bringing the person to rest, revealed truth "stirs the human mind to ceaseless effort; indeed, it impels reason continually to extend the range of its knowledge until it senses that it has done all in its power, leaving no stone unturned" (§14). The human situation is thus one of existing among truths, not statically, but, so to speak, suspended in motion between truths and truth: Seeking truth while finding truths. Life in truth has the form of a journey on "truth's way" (§48).

Our basic state in the light of truth is one of searching, as the encyclical does not tire to repeat.

> It is by the nature of the human being to seek the truth. This search looks not only to the attainment of truths which are partial, empirical or scientific. . . . Their search looks towards an [!] ulterior truth which would explain the meaning of life. And it is therefore a search which can reach its end only in reaching the absolute (§33).

Precisely in "the human being's unceasing search for truth and meaning" lies "the grandeur of the human being, who can find fulfillment only in choosing to enter the truth" (§107). It is not just that the human being possesses a capacity for truth, in the sense of being capable of finding individual truths, its very definition consists in the searching: "One may define the human being, therefore, as the one who seeks the [!] truth" (§28). "By its very nature reason is orientated to truth" (§49). This holds true even in regard to revealed truth (cf. §105). Life in truth takes place in the manner of a "journey towards the one full truth" (§92). We have a "vocation to full truth" (§71). Put in other terms, our essential relationship to truth occurs more in the will than in the intellect. It is more important, at least in our present state, to love truth than to find what we can of it, in other words, to be truthful rather than actually knowing. Loving truth is more important, and is capital in the argumentation of the encyclical.

The search is called in the encyclical "humanly unstoppable" (§33). Revelation presupposes this natural state. "In Jesus Christ, who is the Truth, faith recognizes the ultimate appeal to humanity, an appeal made in order that what we experience as desire and nostalgia may come to its fulfilment" (§33). With or without faith, "the human being's ceaselessly self-transcendent orientation towards the truth" (§23), the human's "progression toward full truth" (§22), determines life. For the whole of human life is encompassed by truth. As Thomas Aquinas says: "Truth itself, which is the object of faith, is the goal of all of our desires and actions."[8] In fact, Thomas even teaches that truth is the goal of the entire universe.[9]

I would now like to draw out some of the implicationis arising from the distinction between the two different dimensions of truth by turning directly to Thomas Aquinas and noting briefly some of his developments of this principle. By appealing to Thomas as "an authentic model for all who seek the truth" (§78), I am interpreting the encyclical in a way which it itself clearly recommends.

The Truth of Faith and the Truths of Faith[10]

Does supernatural Revelation not serve to clarify the ambivalence of the truth situation? Is it not the Revelation of the truth that we are ultimately seeking? No doubt, in the Thomistic view Revelation contributes knowledge that philosophy is unable to attain. But does Revelation contribute answers to the questions that philosophy poses but is itself *a priori* incapable of answering on its own strength? To the best of my knowledge, nowhere does Thomas Aquinas make such a claim. It is a frequent misunderstanding of philosophical researchers of Thomism that they often all too readily presume that theology can compensate for the deficiencies of philosophy. In regard to the question treated here, at least, the case is in fact just the opposite. Far from resolving the predicament of the *conditio humana*, faith accentuates the irony of a temporal life in truth. The fulfillment of all longings, that is to say, happiness, or, as one might say, standing in truth, is not achieved by faith itself. Thomas poses the surprising question whether happiness, the goal of all human striving, consists in faith, and answers negatively. To the contrary, he explains, faith intensifies the longing for fulfillment.[11] It makes the disillusionment only worse by proposing truths like the Trinity, which are utterly incomprehensible.

The Thomistic conception of faith has, to a large extent, been adopted by the Magisterium. The *Cathecism of the Catholic Church* (§155) quotes Thomas's conception of faith, whereby "Believing is an act of the intellect assenting to the divine truth by command of the will moved by God through grace."[12] Thomas himself clarifies what he means by "divine truth." He refers to it as "first truth" (*veritas prima*), or perhaps one could say: "primordial truth." (When, in contrast, the encyclical uses this term, it occurs only one time, has a quite different meaning and is obviously to be taken in a concrete sense.[13]) The object of faith is defined by Aquinas in a twofold manner: on the one hand, its object is truth itself (*veritas prima*), and on the other hand, truth is attained precisely as unknown: *Veritas prima est obiectum fidei secundum quod ipsa est non visa.*[14] Accordingly faith brings about a twofold effect: it renders truth as well as certain truths present to our consciousness, while guaranteeing the unknowableness of truth itself. Believers are explicitly aware that they are not in possession of truth itself. Human thought is capable of grasping individual truths, but truth itself in the sense in which it is predicated of God remains beyond the grasp of human knowledge, with or without faith and Revelation. Expressed in another way, what is believed by supernatural faith is truth itself, taken in the most "abstract" sense, attained, however, not primarily as an act of the intellect, but of the will, which believes without knowing, without experiencing. Faith is a relationship of the will by way of reason to truth itself.[15] What, then, is its relationship to truths, taken in a concrete sense, that is, what our encyclical refers to as "fundamental truths of Catholic doctrine" (§6)? On this question Thomas arrives at the necessary conclusions.

He refers to truth as the formal object of faith (*obiectum formale*), the formal object being understood as "that which is known."[16] Individual truths he accordingly interprets then as the materiality of the proper object of faith. The particular truths of faith, the *credenda*, the dogmas, are for Aquinas merely the matter of faith,[17] they are not what is really known. Hence, truth itself is present to the mind through concrete truths, remaining, nonetheless, in itself unknown. Thomas compares it to light, which is perceived in concrete colors, without however being apprehended in itself.[18] He also draws a comparison to the object of medicine, the formal object of which is health,[19] whereas everything that a physician concretely does is just the materiality of that with which he is really concerned.

The relationship between truth and truths in the content of faith can be viewed under another aspect. Thomas distinguishes between "implicit" and "explicit faith." He maintains that the only articles of faith that must be explicitly believed are the existence of God and divine providence. Everything else may in principle remain implicit.[20] This implies that Revelation is, as Thomas calls it, "secondary" and "accidental" with regard to the object of faith.[21] What Revelation does is simply to explicate.[22] Thomas even goes so far as to refer to revealed truths as mere examples which serve as an occasion for the occurrence of faith itself:

> And thus it is clear that faith comes from God in both parts, namely both in regard to the interior light that induces to assent and in regard to things which are proposed exteriorly, that is, which have their source in divine Revelation. And such things are related to faith-knowledge as that which is taken from sensual knowledge is related to principles, for by each there comes about a certain determination of knowledge. Hence, just as the knowledge of principles is taken from the senses and nevertheless the light by which the principles are known is innate, so does faith come from hearing, and nevertheless the habit of faith [i.e., that faith which offers salvation] is infused.[23]

It thus becomes understandable why Thomas denies that theology is defined by the event of Revelation. The *divinitus revelata* does not define the object of theology that would be a restriction, a concretization of truth. What defines it is the *divinitus revelabilia*, that is, whatever *can* be revealed, or, in other words, every possible truth.[24] Accordingly, Aquinas defines theology as a perspective, a *modus considerandi*, which he interprets in the *Summa theologiae* not as Revelation, but with the famous phrase *sub ratione Dei*.[25]

To be sure, Thomas consistently teaches that Revelation adds truths to our knowledge, but what he does not claim is that the ultimate truth of reason is superseded by Revelation. The ultimate insight of reason pertains to the divine mystery; in other words, it consists of the knowledge of God's unknowabilty. By no means does revealed truth extinguish mystery. In the words of the Pope:

> It should nonetheless be kept in mind that Revelation remains charged with mystery. It is true that Jesus, with his entire life, revealed the countenance of the Father, for he came to teach the secret things of God. But our vision of the face of God is always fragmentary and impaired by the limits of our understanding. . . . In

short, the knowledge proper to faith does not destroy the mystery; it only reveals it the more, showing how necessary it is for people's lives (§13).

Thomas himself teaches clearly: "That is the ultimate of human knowledge about God: knowing that one does not know God."[26] This situation, which is of course determined not by the free will of God but by the essential structure of the human intellect, cannot be changed even by supernatural Revelation: "Although we are elevated by Revelation to the knowledge of truths that we would otherwise not know," Thomas maintains,

> nevertheless, not with the effect that we know in some other way than through the senses. . . . And thus it remains that immaterial forms are not known to us in respect to *what* they are [*quid est*], but only in respect to the fact *that* they are [*an est*], regardless of whether this comes about by way of natural reason based on the effects of creatures or by way of Revelation.

"The nature of God in itself knows neither the Catholic nor the pagan."[27] Over against this background Thomas can explain revelations that are by their very nature not understandable. Through the Revelation of truths that are incomprehensible, we attain more truth in regard to God's incomprehensibility.[28] Even God is unable to reveal to human beings what their natural reason is in principle unable to grasp. Even God in His Revelation must adapt Himself to the human capacity.[29] *Gratia supponit naturam.* Faith knowledge serves to ignite desire for truth.[30]

If it were not the case that our truths are tainted with inadequacy, like broken reflections in fragments of shattered mirror-glass, in other words, if a really adequate representation of objective reality, a perfect unity of consciousness with its object, not just an assimilation (*adaequatio*) were to occur, then we would have not absolute truth, but indeed no truth at all. For something of the knowing subject (*aliquid proprium*) is a mandatory component of human truth – otherwise it would not be possible to speak of an *adaequatio*.[31] Our truths must be qualified by both similarity and dissimilarity with their object. Consequently, there exist no truths for us that do not include a certain element of distortion. In an important chapter of the *Summa contra gentiles* (III, c. 47), Thomas quotes a gloss on the passage from Psalm 12. 2: "Truths are decayed from among the children of men," and explains: "as from one man's face many likenesses are reflected in a mirror, so many truths (*multae veritates*) are reflected from the one divine truth [*ab una prima veritate*]." Concrete truths for Thomas always have the quality of "enveiled obscurations"[32] of truth. The error of the world, the ineluctable distortion inherent in all of our truths, resembles the colors filtered through the stained-glass windows of a gothic cathedral caused by the sunlight and suspended in midair, floating, as it were, in the twilight space. We can seek truth in no other place but in this twilight-world – where we never find it to our full satisfaction. We find truth merely in a human manner. Whoever has found truth, has found God's creation; whether God Himself has been found as well, i.e., something divine, depends not upon reason but upon the person's will. If one holds too tightly to this truth, refusing to continue on "walking in truth," "so that one progresses little by little in the knowledge of truth,"[33] then one remains imprisoned within the twilight world. In contrast to the tradition preceding him, Thomas is able to view curiosity (*studiositas*) as a virtue.[34] Loving truth, seeking truth is essential to the human situation, but never possessing truth absolutely. What we *can* succeed in possessing are individual truths. But these are nothing but the rungs of a ladder that points up to absolute truth. Human beings are not endowed with the eyes of Platonic eagles, enjoying the legendary capability of gazing directly into the sun; for Thomas Aquinas we are more like Aristotelian owls, moving about in a shadowy reality. For Thomas the awareness of this gives rise to wonder about this ambivalent existence, which he looks upon as the foundation of religion.

Faith assures that truth itself retains its characteristic of unknowableness, without which there can be no moral life. The threat to this ironical life situation is not only sensual concupiscence but also a common form of moral idealism. Concretizing truth itself – as opposed to truths – is inevitably immoral. The moral idealism of a fanatic involves the deception of believing one has found absolute truth, while one has in fact only discovered *a* truth. (Self-righteousness is usually the tell-tale sign.) Fanatic idealists know neither ambivalence nor doubt. They are, to be sure, in motion, but only within the context of practical activity. In respect to truth they have come to a standstill. They have put truth itself out of their minds, eclipsing it with *a* truth. For this would imply reducing God to a creature within our temporal world.

The Truth, the Truths and the Untruths of Conscience[35]

Seeing, as the Pope puts it, that "the good of the person is not only 'to be in the Truth,' but also 'to do the Truth;'"[36] considerations on truth lead naturally to ethics. In the Thomistic teaching on conscience, which exposes the inner nerve of the whole Thomistic ethics, the distinction between the two dimensions of "truth" becomes absolutely cardinal. In his encyclical letter *The Splendor of Truth*, Pope John Paul II reaffirms the fundamental principle when he states: "In any event, it is always from the truth that the dignity of conscience derives" (§63). The inner structure of morality becomes clearer when one considers the idea of the erroneous conscience. The text just quoted continues with the observation: "In the case of the correct conscience, it is a question of the objective truth received by man; in the case of the erroneous conscience, it is a question of what man, mistakenly, subjectively considers to be true."[37]

Viewed in the "truth perspective" the notion of the erroneous conscience, regardless of the fact that this may not be the usual case, can prove to be extremely helpful in understanding the structure of truth such as it exists in the ambivalent state of dynamic suspension between truth and truths in which humans find themselves. The thorough and exact treatment that Thomas Aquinas devotes to his innovative teaching on the erroneous conscience represents not just an exception within his appreciation of truth in general; thanks to the radicalness of his analysis, the notion of truth as well as the human relationship to truth acquire thereby unmistakable clarity. In my opinion, furthermore, nothing brings the religious roots of morality more clearly to light than this insight. Expressed in other terms, the acknowledgment of the meaning of the erroneous conscience is only understandable with the help of the distinction between truth taken in an "abstract" sense and truth taken in a concrete sense, or, in Thomistic terms: the difference between *veritas,* or, more precisely, *veritas prima,* and *vera,* or *veritas,* understood in a sense which is susceptible to being pluralized. Both the intrinsic difference and the relationship between the two meanings, i.e., the meaningfulness of making use of one and the same word to create an analogous term, becomes evident in Aquinas's extraordinary teaching on the truth of the erroneous conscience, for it presupposes a positive relationship to truth in spite of the fact that truth in concrete reality has actually been lost sight of. (Without such an insight, moreover, there would appear to be no way of justifying the idea of freedom of conscience.)

For what reason is it morally good to do objective evil and immoral to do what is in truth objectively good when my conscience is the reason behind my act – and this with utter disregard for the degree of incompetence of conscience (stupidity makes no difference)? If conscience is the immediate voice of God, how can it be explained that it errs at all? Thinking along these lines, Joseph Ratzinger has been moved to call Aquinas's teaching simply "incomprehensible."[38] Ratzinger objects that Thomas is guilty of contradicting himself by neglecting to distinguish sufficiently between will and reason. Ratzinger grants that the will is bound to obey reason, but reason itself, that is, conscience, he asserts, is under obligation not only to seek but also to find objective truth. This means for Ratzinger that an erroneous conscious is always itself guilty, since "reason must know of God's law."[39]

When I now treat Thomas's convictions concerning the erroneous conscience, then it goes without saying that I am presupposing a truly erroneous conscience, one, that is, which is unaware of its error; ignorance that is in any sense willed is excluded from the present reflections.[40] The fact that ignorance itself can be freely and culpably willed does not invalidate my question.

But Thomas's approach is in reality quite different from Ratzinger's; it is deeply *subjective.* He bases his conviction upon the fact that conscience attains reality precisely *qua* true (*ut verum*), not, in other words, as a really objective truth, but as what subjectively appears to be an objective truth. What is decisive for the person is how the will reacts to what conscience has found. This ironical constellation, which is absolutely crucial, arises from the distinction between truth in reality (*verum*) and truth as a "formality" (*ut verum*) in thought, i.e., as a (subjective) point of view. Even when conscience is deceived and arrives involuntarily at a false judgment, which comes down to a judgment contrary to God's eternal law, nonetheless, what it dictates is dictated *ut verum* and, precisely for this reason, "as derived from God, from Whom all truth comes."[41] Pope John Paul II quotes Thomas: "Whatever its source, truth is of the Holy Spirit."[42] And this is far from being a subjective deception. Concretely regarded, the truth reached is purely subjective, but the relationship to God, as truth itself in the abstract sense, is objective. Although conscience has not succeeding in finding concrete truth, the will, in affirming conscience, chooses truth.

Accordingly, Thomas explicitly rejects the argument that God's law deserves more obedience than conscience,[43] implying that conscience is to be relativized. In the world of concrete particulars, i.e., in the realm of moral decisions and actions, what God really wills that it happen remains, Aquinas even goes so far as to assert, unknown to us: *In particulari nescimus quid Deus velit.*[44] It is simply impossible for us to separate God's will from the norm prescribed by our individual conscience. "The voice of conscience," he explains, "is nothing other than the presence, the arrival [*perventio*] of eternal law in the person having a conscience."[45] Even when conscience errs it grasps whatever it finds *as* God's will.[46] In this sense, subjectively, to be sure, divine law infallibly "comes through" in conscience. What can be demanded of a human being is not that the individual person will what God wills, but, as Thomas put its, that he will what God wills that he will: *vult hoc quod Deus vult eum velle.*[47] And this is nothing other than that he will what his conscience prescribes.

When Thomas describes conscience as being infallible, he means this only in respect to the first principles of morality. What he intends is that whoever follows his conscience can be sure to be seeking truth. And the seeking for truth, not the actual finding of truth, is the essence of morality: the will's establishing of reason in human conduct. The moral order that Thomas has in mind is not a collection of general norms, or truths; it is simply the (abstract) relationship to truth itself. Expressed differently: It is religion. There is no infallible guarantee here that the objectively right thing will be done. Virtue and vice are a matter of character, not of practice. Should a hunter accidentally kill his father, believing that he is aiming at a deer, then there is no moral guilt involved in the act, although, considered under all of its aspects, the act is obviously not good.[48] Medieval Latin can speak here of a *peccatum*, but that is a general term and must be distinguished from *peccatum morale*.[49]

"Truth" is an analogous term. The truth of moral norms is not identical with the truth of morality itself. Abstract thought relativizes the objectification of morality. The distinction implied here is essential to Christian ethics. One result of this insight is that it sheds some light on the relationship of morality to faith. The pivotal point is the idea of truth. Precisely in its abstract sense, truth opens morality to its inherent religious dimension. Believing is necessary, declares Thomas, precisely because humans have abstract ideas.[50] According to Thomas, religion is made possible by the fact that humans think abstractly within concrete existence. Otherwise, morality would remain on the horizontal level of history. Thomistic ethics is an ethics primarily of virtues and vices, not of concrete actions or practical norms. Morality does not consist essentially in practice, but in interior character. And character is a quality of the will, not of the intellect. (But that does not mean what one calls a strong will, that is, a will that is self-assertive. It is a will that conforms to the intellect, that is, which wills nothing but truth insofar as it is attainable by human consciousness.) In fact, speaking biblically, we are to "walk in truth" (2 Jn 4), not stand in truth. In other words, it is impossible that truth itself become concrete for us in our historical situation. God's will is not identical with my will.

One can justifiably speak of the *irony of truth*. The truth of untruths and the deception inherent in truths articulate the twofold dimension of truth, namely, the horizontal and the vertical. The ambivalence of truth is emphasized by Thomas himself with the help of the distinction between truth in a material sense and truth in a formal sense. Human reason knows of the reality of absolute truth, but it is unable to apprehend it in itself, whereas it is the will, in its own way, that does attain abstract truth directly. In this sense, the will transcends the intellect. Although we are unable to know God directly, we are capable of loving him directly. Moral good and evil develop out of this ambivalent structure. Morality, the state of the will, arises "out of the apprehension of reason [*ex apprehensione rationis*]." "The cause and root of human goodness is reason."[51] We are dealing here with something individual and subjective. What the will then has as its concrete object is what is presented to it by reason. For its part, reason remains something subjective, although its whole thrust is directed towards objectivity. Is something proposed by reason as bad, then the will itself becomes bad if it chooses this – regardless of the objective situation. This effect is distinct from the objective quality of the choice under consideration. Something that is in itself good can thus become evil in that it takes on a *ratio mali* without necessarily being really evil and, *vice versa*, what is in itself objectively evil can assume the *ratio boni* in the individual's mind.

Now, an ethical position like this makes sense – I think it can be said – only within a religious perspective. The meaning of life in the world depends ultimately on our relationship to God, not on our relationship to the world, nor to our external practice within society. Our relationship to concrete reality in itself is not decisive, but our relationship to abstract truth (*veritas prima*, i. e., God) is. "In order to have a right will in willing a particular good, it is necessary that the particular good be willed *materialiter*, while the universal divine good be willed *formaliter*."[52] This means that the extent to which "the human will is required to conform to the divine will is restricted to the general formal aspect: *formaliter, sed non materialiter*."[53] In regard to the question whether a human will is in conformity with God's will, everything depends upon the *ratio*, the subjective aspect, of what is willed (*quantum ad rationem voliti*). Hence, Thomas can lay down the principle, "Whoever wills something *sub quacumque ratione boni*, conforms [*ipso facto*] to the divine will."[54]

Eternal Beatitude as the Apprehension of Truth Itself

Man's relationship to truth arrives at its final stadium in eternal life after death in fulfilling happiness. As the Pope has expressed it, "Only in the truth can he find salvation."[55] Here, too, it is the truth perspective which provides the hub of Thomas's thought. Ultimate fulfillment, he teaches, consists in the contemplation of truth itself; "Man's ultimate happiness consists in the contemplation of truth [*in contemplatione veritatis*]."[56]

Thomas enunciates this in chapter 51 of the *Summa contra gentiles* – a high point of Thomistic thought and a good example for the relevance of the distinction between truth in the twofold sense as well as of the interplay between philosophy and Revelation:

> Since truth [*verum*] is the perfection of the intellect, that intelligible which is truth itself [*veritas ipsa*] will be a pure form in the genus of intelligible things. This applies solely to God, for, since truth [*verum*] is consequent upon being [*esse*], that alone is its own truth [*sua veritas*], which is its own being [*suum esse*]; and this belongs to God alone. . . . Consequently, other subsistent intelligibles are not forms in the genus of intelligible things, but have a form in a subject; for each of them is something true but not the truth [*verum, non veritas*], even as it is a being, but not being itself [*ens, non autem ipsum esse*]. It is therefore clear that the divine essence can be compared to the created intellect as an intelligible species by which it understands; which cannot be said of the essence of any separate substance.[57]

But note that such a union with God is not ontological:

> And yet it cannot be the form of another thing through its natural being. For it would follow that, once united to another being, it would constitute one nature; which is impossible, since the divine essence is in itself perfect in its own nature. But an intelligible species, in its union with the intellect, does not constitute a nature, but perfects the intellect for understanding; and this is not inconsistent with the perfection of the divine essence.[58]

This structure can also be expressed in terms of the distinction between essence and *esse*. The uniqueness of God's nature consists in the fact that His essence *is* His being. Precisely because of this, God is able to be united to human consciousness in a strictly immediate sense, that is, as truth itself.[59]

> The divine essence is being itself [*ipsum esse*]. Hence, as other intelligible forms which are not their own being are united to the intellect by means of some entity whereby the intellect itself is informed and made in act; so the divine essence is united to the created intellect, as the object actually grasped, making the intellect in act by and of itself.[60]

In the case of any other being, the union with human consciousness without any intermediary would result not just in its assimilation, but in its complete subsumption into consciousness, so that it would be an accident of the human knower. As truth itself, God can be united to a human intellect without impeding the independent being of either Himself or of the human subject, analogous to the way light can be united to the eyes.

The intrinsic knowability of God arises from the fact that He is the cause of the knowability of beings.

> The divine essence is not something universal in being, since God is distinct from everything, but only in causing, for that which is through itself is the cause of what does not exist through itself. Hence, being subsisting through itself [*esse per se subsistens*] is the cause of all being received in another. And in this way the divine essence is an intelligible, which can determine the intellect.[61]

Thomas analyzes this even more deeply. Divine causality in this sense, he warns, is not to be understood as formal causality taken in a literal sense; God does not become the content of knowledge, a *verum*. Thomas speaks of God's being the form of the intellect only in the sense of a comparison to the ontological relationship between form and matter, "because," as he explicitly explains, "the relationship of the divine essence to our intellect is like the relationship of form to matter." The difference is subtle.

> But this should not be understood as though the divine essence were
> a *true* form of our intellect or because out of it and our intellect there
> were brought about a single entity, as in natural things something in
> constituted out of form and matter; but because the relationship of the
> divine essence to our intellect is like the relationship of form to mat-
> ter.[62]

In the *De veritate* Thomas notes: "It is not necessary that the divine essence itself become the form of the intellect [i.e., a truth], but that it have a relationship to it *like* a form,"[63] that is, like the form that is ontologically con-joined with matter. In the eschatological vision human consciousness is like matter, and God functions like the ontological form of consciousness, but not as a real cognitive form, determining the content of consciousness.

Truth and God

How far is Thomas willing to go with his exaltation of truth? His radical position seems to have provoked a question posed during a late quodlibetal discussion. There someone confronted him with the question whether truth is stronger than wine, than the king or even than a woman. In spite of all, in his response he holds fast to his conviction – although first noting that these things cannot really be compared to one another – and argues that "truth is greater in dignity, and more excellent and stronger."[64]

A deeper dilemma was posed by Dostoyevsky, who asked himself what he would do if forced to choose between truth and Jesus Christ. Dostoyevsky opted for Christ.[65] Thomas Aquinas, however, uncompromisingly chooses truth. He presents the question in the extreme case that one's conscience, undoubtedly an erroneous conscience, tells one that it is evil to believe in Christ. Under such conditions, he declares, rejecting truth and believing in Christ would be sinful.[66]

But Aquinas, not stopping at this point, even confronts himself with a final dilemma: What must be said if God were not in fact truth itself and one were then forced to choose between God and truth. This is, of course, a fictional question, but Thomas hypothetically accepts it, nonetheless, thus adding addi-tional clarity to his own position. As a conclusion of my paper, it can be remarked that it is only logical when he responds to the objection raised against the biblical figure Job that in daring to carry on a dispute on truth with God Himself he disregards the superiority of the divine person, Thomas unhesitatingly and candidly replies: "It must be answered that truth does not vary with the diversity of persons, so that when someone is speaking the truth he cannot be defeated by whomsover he might be disputing."[67]

Notes

1. Cf., e.g., §44: "Faith accepts divine truth as it is."

2. Cf. also §73: "God's word is Truth."

3. Cf. §65: "Theology is structured as an understanding of faith in the light of a twofold methodological principle: the *auditus fidei* and the *intellectus fidei*."

4. Augustine, *De Praedestinatione Sanctorum* 2. 5 (PL 44, 963).

5. "In the light of these considerations, the relationship between theology and philosophy is best construed as a circle. Theology's source and starting-point must always be the word of God revealed in history, while its final goal will be an understanding of that word which increases with each passing generation. Yet, since God's word is Truth (cf. Jn 17:17), the human search for truth – philosophy, pursued in keeping with its own rules – can only help to understand God's word better. It is not just a question of theological discourse using this or that concept or element of a philosophical construct; what matters most is that the believer's reason use its powers of reflection in the search for truth which moves from the word of God towards a better understanding of it. It is as if, moving between the twin poles of God's word and a better understanding of it, reason is offered guidance and is warned against paths which would lead it to stray from revealed Truth and to stray in the end from the truth pure and simple. Instead, reason is stirred to explore paths which of itself it would not even have suspected it could take. This circular relationship with the word of God leaves philosophy enriched, because reason discovers new and unsuspected horizons." *Fides et Ratio*, §73.

6. "Philosophy contributes specifically to theology in preparing for a correct *auditus fidei* with its study of the structure of knowledge and personal communication, especially the various forms and functions of language." *Fides et Ratio*, §65.

7. Cf. §44: "the horizon of universal, objective and transcendent truth;" §92: "The Truth, which is Christ, imposes itself as an all-embracing authority which holds out to theology and philosophy alike the prospect of support, stimulation and increase."

8. "Veritas prima, quae est fidei obiectum, est finis omnium desideriorum et actionum nostrarum." *Summa theologiae* I, q. 4, a. 2, ad 3. Cf. *Summa contra gentiles* III, c. 25, n. 10.

9. "Truth is necessarily the final goal of the whole universe [Oportet igitur veritatem esse ultimum finem totius universi]." *Contra Gentiles* I, c. 1, n. 4.

10. For a more extensive treatment see W. J. Hoye, "The Thought of Being as the Necessary Reason for Supernatural Faith in the Theology of Thomas Aquinas," Doctor Communis 41 (1988), pp. 173–83; idem, "Der

Wirklichkeitsbegriff als Grund der Notwendigkeit des Glaubens nach Thomas
von Aquin," *Knowledge and the Sciences in Medieval Philosophy*
(Proceedings of the Eighth International Congress of Medieval Philosophy
[S.I. E.P.M.], 3 vols. (Annals of the Finnish Society for Missiology and
Ecumenics, vol. 55), eds. R. Tyorinoja, A. I. Lehtinen, D. (Helsinki: Follesdal,
1990), vol. 3, pp. 409–16.

11. "Per felicitatem, cum sit ultimus finis, naturale desiderium quietatur.
Cognitio autem fidei non quietat desiderium, sed magis ipsum accendit: quia
unusquisque desiderat videre quod credit. Non est igitur in cognitione fidei
ultima hominis felicitas." *Summa contra gentiles* III, c. 40, n. 5.

12. *Summa theologiae* II-II, q. 2, a. 9; cf. Dei Filius 3; DS 3010.

13. In §26 we read: "The first absolutely certain truth [*prima veritas absolute
certa nostrae exsistentiae*] of our life, beyond the fact that we exist, is the
inevitability of our death."

14. *Summa theologiae* II-II, q. 4, a. 1. Cf. Ibid., q. 1, a. 6, ad 2: ut sit non
visum.

15. Cf. *Summa Theologiae*, q. 1, a. 1.

16. "Id per quod cognoscitur, quod est formalis ratio obiecti." *Summa
Theologiae*, II-II, q. 1, a. 1.

17. "In obiectum fidei est aliquid quasi formale, scilicet veritas prima super
omnem naturalem cognitionem creaturae existens: et aliquid materiale, sicut
id cui assentimus inhaerendo primae veritati." *Summa Theologiae*, II-II, q. 5,
a. 1, corpus. "Obiectum fidei primum et formale est bonum quod est veritas
prima. Sed materialiter fidei proponuntur credenda." Ibid., q. 7, a. 1, ad 3. Cf.
ibid., q. 1, a. 1c; *In III Sententiarum*, d. 24, q. 1, a. 1, sol. 1, ad 1.

18. Cf. *Summa theologiae* II-II, q. 1, a. 3.

19. *Summa Theologiae* II-II, q. 1, a. 1.

20. Cf. *Summa Theologiae* II-II, q. 1, a. 7; q. 2, a. 5; q. 5, a. 4c; q. 16, a. 1c;
De veritate, q. 14, a. 11.

21. "Per accidens autem vel secundario se habent ad obiectum fidei omnia
quae in Scriptura divinitus tradita continentur." *Summa theologiae* II-II, q. 2,
a. 5, corpus.

22. *Summa Theologiae* II-II, q. 2, a. 6 corpus: "explicatio credendorum fit per
revelationem divinam."

23. "Et sic patet quod fides ex duabus partibus est a Deo, scilicet et ex parte
interioris luminis quod inducit ad assensum et ex parte rerum quae exterius
proponuntur, quae ex divina revelatione initium sumpserunt. Et haec se
habent ad cognitionem fidei sicut accepta per sensum ad cognitionem princi-

piorum, quia utrisque fit aliqua cognitionis determinatio. Unde sicut cognitio principiorum accipitur a sensu et tamen lumen quo principia cognoscuntur est innatum, ita fides est ex auditu, et tamen habitus fidei est infusus." *In Boethii De trinitate*, q. 3, a. 1, ad 4.

24. *Summa Theologiae* I, q. 1, a. 3, corpus.

25. *Summa Theologiae* I, q. 1, a. 7, corpus.

26. "Illud est ultimum cognitionis humanae de Deo quod sciat se Deum nescire." *De potentia*, q. 7, a. 5, ad 14. "Dicimur in fine nostrae cognitionis Deum tamquam ignotum cognoscere." *In Boethii De trinitate*, q. 1, a. 2, ad 1. See W. J. Hoye, "Die Unerkennbarkeit Gottes als die letzte Erkenntnis nach Thomas von Aquin," in *Thomas von Aquin*, ed. A. Zimmermann, Miscellanea Mediaevalia, vol. XIX (Berlin: Walter de Gruyter, 1988), pp. 117–39.

27. "Ipsam naturam Dei prout in se est, neque catholicus neque paganus cognoscit: sed uterque cognoscit eam secundum aliquam rationem causalitatis vel excellentiae vel remotionis." *Summa theologiae* I, q. 13, a. 10, ad 5. Cf. *Summa contra gentiles* I, c. 3; *Summa theologiae* I-II, q. 3, a. 6c; *Super epist. ad Romanos*, c. 1, lect. 6.

28. "Est etiam necessarium huiusmodi veritatem ad credendum hominibus proponi ad Dei cognitionem veriorem habendam. Tunc enim solum Deum vere cognoscimus quando ipsum esse credimus supra omne id quod de Deo cogitari ab homine possibile est: eo quod naturalem hominis cognitionem divina substantia excedit, ut supra ostensum est. Per hoc ergo quod homini de Deo aliqua proponuntur quae rationem excedunt, firmatur in homine opinio quod Deus sit aliquid supra id quod cogitare potest." *Summa contra gentiles* I, c. 5, n. 3.

29. "Divina non sunt revelanda hominibus nisi secundum eorum capacitatem." *Summa theologiae* I-II, q. 101, a. 2, ad 1.

30. "Est etiam necessarium huiusmodi veritatem ad credendum hominibus proponi ad Dei cognitionem veriorem habendam. Tunc enim solum Deum vere cognoscimus quando ipsum esse credimus supra omne id quod de Deo cogitari ab homine possibile est: eo quod naturalem hominis cognitionem divina substantia excedit . . . . Per hoc ergo quod homini de Deo aliqua proponuntur quae rationem excedunt, firmatur in homine opinio quod Deus sit aliquid supra id quod cogitare potest." *Summa contra gentiles* IV, c. 7, n. 3. *Summa theologiae* I, q. 1, a. 1 argues in the same vein. In regard to truth, cf. *In III Sententiarum*, d. 24, q. 1, a. 1, sol. 2.

31. "Veri enim ratio consistit in adaequatione rei et intellectus; idem autem non adaequatur sibi ipsi, sed aequalitas diversorum est. Unde ibi primo invenitur ratio veritatis in intellectu ubi primo intellectus incipit aliquid proprium habere quod res extra animam non habet, sed aliquid ei correspondens, inter

quae adaequatio attendi potest." De veritate, q. 1, a. 3, corpus.

32. Thomas quotes the observation of Pseudo-Dionysius: "Impossibile est nobis aliter lucere divinum radium, nisi varietate sacrorum velaminum circumvelatum." *Summa theologiae* I, q. 1, a. 9, corpus.

33. "Et ideo ad hominem pertinet ut paulatim in cognitione veritatis proficiat." *In I Ethicorum*, lect. 11, n. 2.

34. Cf. W. J. Hoye, *Demokratie und Christentum. Die christliche Verantwortung für demokratische Prinzipien* (Münster: Aschendorff, 1999), pp. 253–65.

35. For a more extensive treatment see W. J. Hoye, "Die Wahrheit des Irrtums. Das Gewissen als Individualitätsprinzip in der Ethik des Thomas von Aquin," in *Individuum und Individualität im Mittelalter*, ed. Andreas Speer, Miscellanea Mediaevalia, vol. XXIV (Berlin: Walter de Gruyter, 1996), pp. 419–35; idem, "The Erroneous Conscience and Truth According to Thomas Aquinas," in *Moral and Political Philosophies in the Middle Ages. Proceedings of the Ninth International Congress of Medieval Philosophy*, eds. E. Andújar, C. B. Bazán, L. Sbrocchi (Ottawa, 1994); idem., *Demokratie und Christentum*, pp. 297–328.

36. Pope John Paul II, "Address to the participants of the International Congress for Moral Theology," (April 10, 1986), §1 (= *Insegnamenti* IX, 1 [1986], p. 970).

37. *Veritatis splendor*, §63.

38. Cf. J. Ratzinger, "Commentary on the 'Pastoral Constitution on the Church in the Modern World,'" *Lexikon für Theologie und Kirche*, 2nd ed., *vol. 14: Das Zweite Vatikanische Konzil: Konstitutionen, Dekrete und Erklärungen* (Freiburg: Herder, 1968), p. 329.

39. Ibid., p. 331. For a similar standpoint see Robert Spaemann's introduction to: *Thomas von Aquin, Über die Sittlichkeit der Handlung: Summa theol.* I-II, q. 18–21, trans. with comm. R. Schönberger, Collegia. Philosophische Texte, eds. R. Schönberger, J. Jantzen, P. R. Blum (Weinheim: VCH Verlagsgesellschaft, 1990), p. xv.

40. Cf. *Summa theologiae* I-II, q. 19, a. 6, corpus.

41. "Ratio errans iudicium suum proponit ut verum, et per consequens ut a Deo derivatum, a quo est omnis veritas." *Summa theologiae* I-II, q. 19, a. 5, ad 1.

42. *Fides et Ratio* §44, quoting Thomas Aquinas, *Summa theologiae* I-II, q. 109, a. 1 ad 1: "Omne verum a quocumque dicatur a Spiritu Sancto est."

43. Cf. *De veritate*, q. 17, a. 4.

44. *Summa theologiae* I-II, q. 19, a. 10, ad 1.

45. *De veritate*, q. 17, a. 4, ad 2.

46. Cf. *De veritate*, q. 17, a. 4, ad 1.

47. *Summa theologiae* I-II, q. 19, a. 10, corpus.

48. Cf. *Quaestiones quodlibetales* III, q. 12, a. 2.

49. Cf. *De malo*, q. 3, a. 1c; a. 6c; *Summa contra gentiles* III, c. 10.

50. What Thomas means in particular are the abstract notions of being and of the good [*universalem boni et entis rationem*]. Cf. *Summa theologiae* II-II, q. 2, a. 3.

51. *Summa Theologiae*, I-II, q. 66, a. 1, corpus. Cf. *Summa contra gentiles* III, c. 10: "In actu igitur voluntatis quaerenda est radix et origo peccati moralis."

52. "Ex fine autem sumitur quasi formalis ratio volundi illud quod ad finem ordinatur. Unde ad hoc quod aliquis recta voluntate velit aliquod particulare bonum, oportet quod illud particulare bonum sit volitum materialiter, bonum autem commune divinum sit volitum formaliter." *Summa theologiae* I-II, q. 19, a. 10, corpus.

53. "Voluntas igitur humana tenetur conformari divinae voluntati in volito formaliter, tenetur enim velle bonum divinum et commune, sed non materialiter." *Summa theologiae* I-II, q. 19, a. 10, corpus.

54. "Quicumque vult aliquid sub quacumque ratione boni, habet voluntatem conformem voluntati divinae, quantum ad rationem voliti." *Summa theologiae* I-II, q. 19, a. 10, ad 1.

55. *Veritatis splendor*, §8.

56. *Summa contra gentiles* III, c. 37, n. 1.

57. *Summa contra gentiles* III, c. 51, n. 4.

58. Ibid.

59. "Est autem hoc singulare divinae essentiae, ut ei possit intellectus uniri absque omni similitudine, quia et ipsa divina essentia est ejus esse, quod nulli alii formae competit." *Compendium theologiae* I, c. 9.

60. "Divina essentia est ipsum esse. Unde, sicut aliae formae intelligibiles quae non sunt suum esse, uniuntur intellectui secundum aliquod esse quo informant ipsum intellectum et faciunt ipsum in actu; ita divina essentia unitur intellectui creato ut intellectum in actu, per seipsam faciens intellectum in actu." *Summa theologiae* I, q. 12, a. 2, ad 3.

61. "Essentia divina non est quid generale in essendo, cum sit ab omnibus aliis distincta, sed solum in causando; quia id quod est per se, est causa eorum quae per se non sunt. Unde esse per se subsistens est causa omnis esse in alio recep-

ti. Et ita essentia divina est intelligibile quod potest determinare intellectum."
Quaestiones quodlibetales VII, q. 1, a. 1, ad 1.

62. "Quod quidem non debet intelligi quasi divina essentia sit vera forma intellectus nostri; vel quia ex ea et intellectu nostro efficiatur unum simpliciter, sicut in naturalibus ex forma et materia naturali: sed quia proportio essentiae divinae ad intellectum nostrum est sicut proportio formae ad materiam." *In IV Sententiarum*, d. 49, q. 2, a. 1, sol. From this it is clear that Karl Rahner's interpretation of Thomas's reference to formal causality in the beatific vision as implying "transcendental causality" stands in contradiction to Thomas himself. For Rahner God is not a verum, but He is nonetheless "the content" and "the object of our vision." Rahner, "Über den Begriff des Geheimnisses in der katholischen Theologie," in *Schriften zur Theologie*, 16 vols. (Einsiedeln: Benziger, 1962), vol. 4, pp. 58, 76, 79. Cf. W. J. Hoye, *Die Verfinsterung des absoluten Geheimnisses. Eine Kritik der Gotteslehre Karl Rahners* (Düsseldorf: Patmos, 1979), pp. 60–61.

63. "Non autem oportet quod ipsa divina essentia fiat forma intellectus ipsius, sed quod se habeat ad ipsum ut forma; ut sicut ex forma, quae est pars rei, et materia efficitur unum ens actu, ita licet dissimili modo, ex essentia divina et intellectu creato fiat unum in intelligendo, dum intellectus intelligit, et essentia divina per seipsam intelligitur . . . Quandocumque in aliquo receptibili recipiuntur duo quorum unum est altero perfectius, proportio perfectioris ad minus perfectum est sicut proportio formae ad suum perfectibile. . . . Et ideo, cum intellectus creatus, qui inest substantiae creatae, sit imperfectior divina essentia in eo existente, comparabitur divina essentia ad illum intellectum quodammodo ut forma." *De veritate*, q. 8, a. 1, corpus.

64. *Quaestiones quodlibetales* XII, n. 12, q. 14, a. 1.

65. F. Dostoyevsky, Letter of February 20, 1854 to Natal'ja D. Fonvizin, *Complete Works*, ed. by the Academy of Science of the Soviet Union, vol. 12 (Leningrad, 1975), p. 297. A few years later the same question is brought up in *The Demons*, pt. II, ch. 1, p. 7.

66. *Summa theologiae* I-II, q. 19, a. 5, corpus.

67. "Et supra dixerat disputare cum deo cupio, ex nunc loquitur quasi Deum habens praesentem et cum eo disputans. Videbatur autem disputatio hominis ad Deum esse indebita propter excellentiam qua Deus hominem excellit; sed considerandum est quod veritas ex diversitate personarum non variatur, unde cum aliquis veritatem loquitur vinci non potest cum quocumque disputet." *In Job*, c. 13.

The Exaltation of Metaphysics in John Paul II's
Fides et Ratio
Mario Enrique Sacchi

The encyclical *Fides et ratio* of Pope John Paul II contains an unusual exaltation of metaphysics on the part of the Church's teaching. This exaltation arises in the midst of a vast spiritual crisis which depends to a great extent on the modern aggressive and persistent rejection of the science of being as such. Two paragraphs of *Fides et ratio* are devoted to the exaltation of metaphysics (§83–84), but all the context of this document exudes the explicit aim of emphasizing the outstanding role of our science in man's intellectual life.

In *Fides et ratio* we find a significant testimony of the reassessment of metaphysics through the constant affirmation of the natural desire for knowledge as an impulse that lies in the same nature of the human soul. Moreover, several paragraphs of the encyclical dwells on man's natural motion to the knowledge of truth and to the search for wisdom. John Paul II points out that our mind has an unrestrained impetus of a very perfect intelligence to be crowned in the intellective union with an infinite object which transcends everything of this world. From that it follows that the natural desire for knowledge implies the natural desire for God because man has received the magnificent perceptive power of his reason, for he knows the first principle of everything and also of his own act of being.

John Paul II's insistence on the natural desire for knowledge has an exceptional importance because the Pope echoed here a major thesis of metaphysics. In fact, we are fully aware that the affirmation of such a natural desire for knowledge heads the famous initial statement of the *Metaphysics* of Aristotle: "All men by nature desire to know."[1] This affirmation is the key to understand the essence of metaphysics and the most decisive direction towards man's union with God. That is why St. Thomas Aquinas had recourse to this metaphysical doctrine of Aristotle. Aquinas gave a broad philosophical and theological justification of this Aristotelian doctrine where lies the Thomistic speculation on the order of the acts of rational creature to his ultimate end. Therefore, the foundation of human acts in man's natural order to the intellective knowledge of God is the first and most powerful evidence of our aspiration to eternal happiness and also the context in which the moral life of human beings is based properly.

The exaltation of metaphysics expounded in *Fides et ratio* indicates the Church's firm opposition to the modern rejection of man's association to God through philosophical knowledge. The new encyclical of John Paul II involves a further Catholic allegation against the long history of agnosticism advanced by the nominalist schools of the Middle Ages and extended by the main currents in modern thought. The plain truth is that metaphysics and agnosticism are irreconcilable enemies. The agnostic spirit discards the rational knowledge of God; on the contrary, metaphysics is an authentic philosophical theology, for the science of the first principle and of the first cause is the same science of that which all men call *God*; not as known in the intimacy of his own divine life, but as the first principle and the first cause of every being, i.e., *sub ratione entis*. That is why, above all, agnosticism is a denial of first philosophy because this science would have no *raison d'être* if the human intellect cannot attain a certain knowledge of the divine being. Due to the fact that science is the knowledge of the causes of things under our consideration, according to Aristotle's definition of epistemic knowledge,[2] the impossibility of a knowledge of the first principle and of the first cause of everything would deprive us of an understanding of the first cause and of the first principle of the subject of metaphysics, and so the science of being as such would be rendered nonsensical.

Now, if we obtain a scientific knowledge of everything by means of causes, and yet man's metaphysical discourse could not get a certain knowledge of the first uncaused cause (according to the agnostic position) then the human soul must face up to a grave dilemma: either nothing could be known or human knowledge would be limited to a mere phenomenological examination of mundane objects. But *Fides et ratio* does not accept this dilemma. John Paul II says that man is capable of obtaining a metaphysical knowledge of God because He created the human being as a compound of body and intellective soul. Now, man's intellect is potentially infinite, so that through this power we can know the infinite divine principle of our own entity. As Aristotle has proved in his *De anima*, the human soul is in a way all existing things for all them can be known by our mind. Nothing escapes the possibility of being reflected in our immaterial soul as in a mirror where all intelligible objects can be represented.[3] On the other hand, the potentially infinite extension of human intellect has an objective correlate in external things because its formal object is precisely being as such. However, bearing in mind that being is also predicated by analogy of the first being, the infinity of its essence is not excluded from the common object of man's intellect.

Philosophers must be persuaded that the denial of the order of rational knowledge to the intellective union with God finishes in the denial of metaphysics itself. The science of being as such could not be an immanent knowledge of man's soul if our intellective power does not order its proper act to the understanding of the first principle and the first cause of the universe. In that case, the science of being would not be the scientific knowledge of the causes of its subject.

Understandably, after the long agnostic evolution of modern thought, the capacity of human reason for knowing God according to the metaphysical method is still impugned nowadays. In this sense, some philosophers who agree with Martin Heidegger's criticism of metaphysics admit his identification of first philosophy with a certain *ontotheology*, as it was described in Kant's *Critique of Pure Reason*, but those philosophers add to Heidegger's opinion a complement that they think compatible with the Thomistic theory of human knowledge of God, i.e the ontotheological failure of metaphysics as a science concerned with God could be overlooked by means of an apophatic experience of divine mysteries.

Heidegger propounded an overcoming of metaphysics once he was convinced of the breakdown of its so-called "ontotheological constitution." He thought that metaphysics would be a discipline founded on speculation about being *qua* being and about God as an *ens causa sui*.[4] This strange ontotheology had arisen and grown because the *Sein* would stay hidden in the entities of all the existing things and fallen into oblivion. Not even the philosophical concept of God could avoid this oblivion for, according to Heidegger, the *Sein* would not be the essence of the divinity. So, if not divine, the *Sein* cannot be an infinite act, for Heidegger's *Sein* does not exceed the limits of the things existing in this finite world, a world full of beings that keep an "ontological difference" with regard to that *Sein*. Then Heidegger's thought about the *Sein* lies on the assumption that it would be something absolutely foreign to the being itself.

However, human thinking about the *Sein* would need to discover its truth by means of surmounting its hidden situation in the being. Also since God cannot be the finite *Sein* essentially participated in by the things of this world, such a thinking would not be a speculation about God either. If so, the authentic thought about the *Sein* would not be an ontotheology; it would be a non-metaphysical thought which overcomes the disappointment arisen from its historical oblivion in Western philosophy, especially since Plato and Aristotle, "the pioneers of ontotheology," according to Heidegger, have established a new style of philosophizing which cannot allow one to think of the *Sein* as a pure *Sein*, i.e., independently of its commitments with the being with which metaphysics deals.

After Heidegger's death, the core of his criticism of the science of being as such has been adopted by some authors who compared it with St. Thomas's metaphysics. In general, these philosophers are persuaded that Heidegger's challenge of our science would affect completely and fairly the history of metaphysics, with the exception of Aquinas's own metaphysical conception. St. Thomas's metaphysics would be exempt from Heidegger's criticism of first philosophy because it would not be impregnated with the ontotheological compounds that would corrupt the remaining contributions to the science of being as such put together throughout its turbulent historical evolution.

It is said that ontotheology deals with a concept of being that is predicated univocally both of the creatures and of God, but not a concept which would favour the fact of the knowledge of being (the formal object of the intellect) as a perception of the *Sein* founded in the intelligibility of its common predication both of God and of his effects. This would confirm Heidegger's favourite opinion: the *Sein* would be hidden in the darkness of being, so that metaphysics, the science of being as such, would cease to think of the *Sein* as a pure *Sein* because of its obstinate concealment into being. Nevertheless, St. Thomas's metaphysics would be free from this typical ontotheological deceit.

It is certainly unquestionable that Aquinas put the act of being at the vertex of his metaphysical speculation. He demonstrated that the *esse*, or the *actus essendi*, is the first act of the being by participation and also the nature of God, the uncaused cause of all those things which are not by virtue of their own essences. The being composed of essence and act of being is an effect of the *ipsum esse subsistens* that can be known metaphysically starting from the intellection of created things, but being as such is not predicated of these things and of the divine being in an univocal sense. The finite being receives the act of being within the limits of its essence, whereas God is the *esse irreceptum* whose nature exceeds entirely the entity commonly predicated of the creatures whose essences are not their act of being. This is a brief synthesis of the famous Thomistic theory of the real distinction of the essence and the act of being of every finite and composed thing and, at the same time, of the very perfect identity of the *esse* and the divine substance.[5]

Philosophers who follow Heidegger's rejection of ontotheology raise the question of whether the concept of being would be also predicated of the uncaused cause of everything understood under the universal reason of the *ens inquantum ens*. As God transcends the *ens commune* predicated of all his effects, the divine being would be excluded from the notion of being as such. Therefore, if metaphysics is the science of the common being, and if its notion is not predicated of the divine being, then first philosophy would not be a knowledge of God. Moreover, we cannot attain an understanding of the deity through metaphysical speculation because God's entity is not predicated of the subject of the science of being *qua* being. But if metaphysics speculates about all its matters in the light of the concept of being, and as God exceeds the common being, then his truth would remain beyond the ontotheological intellection of the metaphysician's reach.

Now St. Thomas taught that we cannot perceive naturally God's essence in itself because the enormous disproportion existing between his dazzling intelligibility *quoad se* and the weak powers of our natural reason in view of the knowledge of an object infinitely distant from the diminished entity of God's effects. According to this Thomistic doctrine, some authors think that, if all our intellective perceptions are reduced to the concept of being, and if God transcends the common being, metaphysics "the science of being as such" must keep silent with regard to the mystery of a deity, because God cannot be predicated of the concept of being. Now, if so, how can we avoid the relapse into agnosticism? Is the human reason compelled to limp when the *horizon* of the act of being impedes the knowledge of the uncaused cause placed beyond the objective borders of the common being?

Philosophers who admit Heidegger's criticism of metaphysics think that St. Thomas had eluded these queries through an explicit overcoming of ontotheology. Whereas Plato and Aristotle reduced the pure act to the common conception of being, Aquinas's theological theory would include another way of knowing the divine essence. The Thomistic approach to God would not be an ontotheological speculation of the uncaused cause of all caused beings. Traditional metaphysics has tried unsuccessfully to speak about the divine being throughout the history of Western philosophy, but a process with an apophatic character would be able to do just this. Thus God can be known by man's intellection, but not as a being. So, we can know God as something unknown and ineffable. He would be seen in a penumbra beyond beings. His mystery would surpass every entity and yet we attribute *esse* to his essence because we lack a name uncontaminated with the imperfections of the act of being participated by creatures. As a consequence of that, St. Thomas's apophatic thought would be free from the ontotheological vice which reduces God to the concept of being.

The apophatic way would allow our mind to know God as something unknown, but provided that man's intellect gains access to the "gloominess of ignorance" and meditates plunged into the "dark night" of intelligence. It would be in the midst of these shadows that the excellence of the divinity would show the brilliance of its infinite remoteness with respect to the act of being conceived by onto-theologist metaphysicians. It would be so because the act of being, conceived in metaphysics as the act of common being, would gather all the intelligible things in the brightness of a presumed univocal conception. Therefore, man cannot obtain a knowledge of God if he has unfounded hopes of the doubtful goodness of the onto-theological structure of metaphysics. On the contrary, we can know the divine being by means of an apophatic thinking, which would be the only sort of thinking suitable for grasping the mystery of the *Deus ignotus* (cf. *Act.* 17:23), a divinity that refuses to remain itself locked in the schemes of the science of being *qua* being.

Nevertheless, knowledge is an essentially affirmative act. I know the horse in affirming that it is such as it is. Instead if I say "the horse is not a lion," this statement is not false, but for the fact that I deny that the horse be a lion, I do not know what is a horse. As Aquinas pointed out, the nature of negation demands that it always follows affirmation: *Affirmatio naturaliter est prior negatione.*[6] Even more, St. Thomas wrote that affirmative knowledge is more worthy than the knowledge which depends on negative demonstrations. The foundation of this Thomistic theory lies in the relationship of our affirmations with by its because its participation in the *actus essendi*. Negations, on the contrary, are related both to being and non-being. However, although non-being, absolutely considered, is unknowable negations, as related to being do participate in a certain way in affirmative propositions.[7]

As in all the human knowledge, metaphysical intelligence also responds to these epistemological rules. The knowledge of the first philosopher is an affirmative one of being as such because his intellection starts and sustains itself with the supreme affirmation of every intellect: being *is*. It is not in vain that the fundamental knowledge had by our intellect is that things *are*. Thereby, as metaphysical intelligence progresses through its scientific discourse, all its judgments, now affirmative, now negative, find their basis in the aforementioned affirmation with an absolute necessity. But when the science of common being must face up the main aporia of its investigation into the causes of caused being, the theory of causes contained in the theorems of metaphysics concludes affirmatively that all the caused things depend necessarily on a first uncaused cause.

In his demonstration of the uncaused cause, the metaphysician answers the question *an est* by means of an apodictical reasoning whose conclusions are reached through consecutive affirmations. It is true that this reasoning also includes several negations, as it happens in every intellective process ruled by the first principles of intelligence, especially by the principle of non-contradiction, but the presence of these negations in the demonstrative argumentation does not hinder the conclusion of theological discourse from being an affirmative knowledge of God: *quod Deus sit*. And yet human reason does not satisfy its own natural desire of knowing only by affirming the uncaused cause. St. Thomas asserted that once the cause of things investigated by the human intellect is known, our intellectual power does not content itself with the mere determination of the existence of such a cause. The natural desire for knowledge drives one to search for an explicit knowledge of the very essence of that uncaused cause.[8] Now, does it mean that the science of being as such, once deduced affirmatively that God is, can likewise advance towards obtaining an affirmative knowledge of his essence, a knowledge about *quid est Deus*?

This is the knotty point of our problem. Philosophers who admit Heidegger's criticism of metaphysics raise the question within the following antithetical terms: on the one hand, philosophy proves that God is and subsequently demonstrates the attributes of divine nature; on the other hand, these philosophers exploit some statements of St. Thomas which would deny the aptitude of man's reason for knowing God's essence. So the struggle would be unavoidable for God's pure act, which is his own essence, being the highest mystery *quoad nos*, cannot be known through the perceptive potency of our natural reason. But in spite of the impenetrability of this mystery, metaphysicians seek to know the secrets of the divine nature because they want to reach an affirmative knowledge of the subsistent pure act of God's substance.

The problem lies on the disillusion of some philosophers with regard to the human possibility of an affirmative knowledge of the divine nature. They think that such an affirmative knowledge would be impossible because the infinite distance which separates the creatures from God would not allow one to perceive his substance. So, an affirmative metaphysical knowledge of God would imply an arrogant offense against his mysterious essence. That is why the unknowability *quoad nos* of his nature drives us to this alternative: either the theological suitability of metaphysics must be rejected as a result of its irreverent aspirations to show itself as an affirmative knowledge of God's essence, or our knowledge of God must be restricted to a negative approach to his mysterious unknowability. In a word, it would be absolutely necessary that God be reached by means of a mode of knowing really distinct from metaphysics, the science of being such as it was exalted in the Western philosophical tradition.

Now then, the simple fact that some philosophers deal with this question as philosophers, makes clear that they are overrunning the matter of sacred theology, a matter they cannot pursue as mere philosophers or *inquantum huiusmodi*. Even more, metaphysics cannot solve that question. After the solution of the question *an est* through the affirmative demonstration of the first uncaused cause, *quod omnes Deum nominant*, the science of being as such advances in view of the deduction of the divine essence's attributes starting from the same conclusions –of those arguments through which the first philosopher inferred that God is. In this sense, all the theoretical argumentation of philosophical theology about the uncaused cause is ruled by the three ways originally outlined in the *Corpus areopagiticum* and later promoted by St. Thomas to their highest scientific expression: the *viae causalitatis, negationis et eminentiae*. But why is metaphysics unable to solve the problem of the scope of man's knowledge of the divine essence? It would be wrong to think that its solution would not be possible through metaphysical analysis because its supposed powerlessness with regard to the evaluation of its own cognitive virtues.

In fact, our problem has been affected by further complications by reason of the opinions of Christian authors who deal with it on the assumption that they may act as metaphysicians, but in this case, against what they think, it is plain that these philosophers, not *inquantum huiusmodi*, but *inquantum Christiani*, are carrying out an apologetical task which belongs to sacred theology exclusively. They act as experts in *sacra doctrina* because they theologize about the several ways man can know God, now through the own power of our natural reason, now through this same reason elevated by the divine grace of faith, now through a permanent comparison between these two modes – natural and supernatural – of knowing the uncaused cause of metaphysics, which is the same God who revealed himself his mysterious truth to all men for their eternal salvation.

The metaphysician is conscious of the scope of his science. In fact, metaphysics deals with its own principles because it is not only an epistemic habit, but also a true wisdom. But first philosophy deals with itself, with its principles and with its analytic process without exceeding the knowledge that human reason can obtain about its perceptive act by means of the efficacy of its natural capacity for knowing. So, in the measure that our intellect is in potency with regard to a supernatural object which cannot be known naturally by man's mind, in this same measure the science of being *qua* being cannot demonstrate if and how such an object is knowable by human reason. Much less metaphysics can demonstrate the attributes of the essence of something supernatural whose transcendence makes its understanding impossible for the first philosopher who treats being commonly predicated by analogy of everything.

Nevertheless, the natural limits of metaphysical knowledge do not hinder entirely the possibility of a certain knowledge of the essence of the uncaused cause. It is not necessary to have recourse to sacred theology to know it, for metaphysics itself manifests this aptitude for its scientific function. So, once having demonstrated that there is a God, metaphysics deals immediately with the question *quid est Deus*. In this new phase the science of being as such concludes that the affirmation of the first unmoved mover, of the first uncaused caused, of the being absolutely necessary, of the first principle of being of all the creatures and of their perfections, and of the governor of the universe allows us to predicate of his nature several attributes knowable with certainty by our natural reason. So, man's intellect speculates about God's essence making use of the ductility of the three ways described by the Pseudo-Dionysius and Aquinas, every one of them empower human reason to obtain naturally a certain knowledge of God's substance.

The metaphysical knowledge of God is fundamentally affirmative since the key to its philosophical intellection lies in this statement: God *is*. Starting from this affirmation, metaphysics rises to the understanding of the attributes of his essence. So, it infers that God is one, simple, immutable, eternal, wise, true, good, provident, and absolutely separated from all the mundane things He created, etc. Still, the primacy of the metaphysical affirmation of God is diminished by the weakness of human reason for knowing appropriately a being whose nature is absolutely simple; hence, the *via negationis* is an indispensable resort to complement concomitantly the weakness of our affirmative knowledge of the divine essence. This is a testimony of the frailty of our philosophical reasoning in its order to the accomplishment of the science of being as such by means of the intellective union of man's mind to the first and supreme truth.

The absolute primacy of affirmative metaphysical knowledge includes the necessity of negative judgments that complements the rational process ordered to the demonstration of the attributes of the divine essence. St. Thomas stated fittingly this primacy of affirmative knowledge when he interpreted the scope of Pseudo-Dionysius' apophatic theology. Aquinas said that nothing can be denied of God, if we do not have a certain affirmative knowledge of his nature. That is why the author of the *Corpus dionysianum* wrote that the divine names mean positively God's essence, although they cannot hide the deficiencies and the imperfections of the words of our human language when we use them to signify those things predicated of the Creator's nature.[9] Man's language does not signify God's essence through names taken from an understanding of his nature such as the saints *in patria* have in seeing him face to face, but starting from the knowledge of created beings we perceive during our life in this world.[10]

The recent attacks against metaphysics, wrongfully confused with the ontotheology rejected in Heidegger's works, would leave open only one way to obtain a certain knowledge of God, that is to say an apophatic approach to his mystery, but this way is not of a philosophical nature. This apophatic way is closer to a mystical experience which presupposes the supernatural revelation of God's truth. But if it is not founded on such a revelation, then it dissolves in to an esoteric gnosticism or in to an outlandish theosophy. However, the fact is that metaphysics is not a science of mysteries. It is a philosophical science whose principles are taken from natural evidence; not from the divine revelation. The apophatic way appears as reason's surrender, for reason has resigned from knowing things and their first uncaused cause according to the only way to this end, namely metaphysics.

In *Fides et ratio* John Paul II exalted metaphysics just at that moment when the science of being as such is being confuted once more by reason of its supposed ontotheological vices. The clash between this pontifical exaltation of metaphysics and the apophatic way to a non-metaphysical knowledge of God is beyond all doubt. In short, this apophatic way is a restoration of the old agnostic trend grafted onto modern thought in which the foundations of first philosophy were undermined by nominalist tendencies. But Pope John Paul II has just confirmed that the Church thinks that metaphysics, in spite of its innumerable detractors, is still alive in the heart of philosophical speculation.

Notes

1. Aristotle, *Metaphysics* I. 1: 980a21.

2. Cf. Aristotle, *Analyt. post.* I. 2: 71b9–12.

3. Cf. Aristotle, *De anima* III. 8: 431 b 21.

4. Cf. M. Heidegger, "Die onto-theo-logische Verfassung der Metaphysik," in Idem., *Identität und Differenz* (Pfullingen: Günther Neske, 1957), pp. 35–73.

5. A masterly explanation of this thesis can be read in the book of N. del Prado O.P., *De veritate fundamentali philosophiae christianae* (Fribourg, Switzerland: Ex Typis Consociationis Sancti Pauli, 1911).

6. Aquinas, *In I Peri hermen.*, lect. 1, n. 10. Cf. lect. 8, n. 3; and lect. 39, n. 8.

7. Cf. Aquinas, *In I Post. analyt.*, lect. 39, n. 5. Cf. n. 8.

8. Cf. Aquinas, *Comp. theol.* I. 104.

9. "Intellectus negationis semper fundatur in aliqua affirmatione: quod ex hoc patet quia omnis negativa per affirmativam probatur; unde nisi intellectus humanus aliquid de Deo affirmative cognosceret, nisi de Deo posset negare, non autem cognosceret, si nihil quod de Deo dicit, de eo verificaretur affirmative. Et ideo, secundum sententiam Dionysii, dicendum est, quod huiusmodi nomina significant divinam substantiam, quamvis deficienter et imperfecte." Aquinas, *De potentia*, q. 7 a. 5 resp.

10. "Considerandum est quod nomina, cum sint a nobis imposita, sic significant secundum quod res in cognitionem nostram cadunt. Cum igitur hoc ipsum quod Deus est, sit supra cognitionem nostram, ut ostensum est, cognitio autem nostra commensuretur rebus creatis, nomina a nobis imposita non sic significant secundum quod congruit divinae excellentiae, sed secundum quod convenit existentiae rerum creatarum." Aquinas, *In I De div. nomin.*, lect. 1, n. 29.

The Validity of Metaphysics:
The Need for a Solidly Grounded Metaphysics
Benedict M. Ashley, O.P.

In his great encyclical *Fides et Ratio,* Pope John Paul II opposes the anti-rational tendencies of our postmodern times and urges the importance for faith and theology of a sound metaphysics. By the need for a sound "metaphysics" he means "the need for a philosophy of *genuinely metaphysical range,* capable, that is, of transcending empirical data in order to attain something absolute, ultimate and foundational in its search for truth. He adds,

> I do not mean to speak of metaphysics in the sense of a specific school or particular historical current of thought. I want only to state that reality and truth do transcend the factual and empirical, and to vindicate the human being's capacity to know this transcendent and metaphysical dimension in a way that is true and certain, albeit imperfect and analogical (§83).

But where is such metaphysics to be found? Perhaps the most influential philosopher of this closing century was Martin Heidegger. In his book *An Introduction to Metaphysics,*[1] he also insistently raised the "question of Being." Yet he concluded, if I understand him rightly, that what has been thought of as metaphysical inquiry in the West since Aristotle wrote the first work given that title has now come decisively to an end. It must be replaced, thinks Heidegger, by a type of thinking more akin to that of the East. He argues that this is the case because what Plato and Aquinas initiated was an attempt to get a mental control over Being that has inevitably led to our technological age of physical control over things. In this technological culture the questioning of Being is inevitably stifled. Hence, to use that kind of meta-physics in theology will inevitable lead, Heidegger thought, to an "onto-theology" that will certainly end in atheism. Yet one searches in vain in his writings for any answer to the question of Being except that it is the flowing truth of historical events unveiling themselves to human beings and then conceal-ing themselves. It attains expression in some form of language such as poet-ry or philosophy that conceals as it reveals. This plea of Heidegger's for an anti-metaphysical metaphysics opening the way to an anti-theological theology drew only ridicule from the logical positivist Rudolf Carnap.[2] Carnap mocked Heidegger's discourse, along with any metaphysics or theology, as pretentious nonsense.

It is evident from John Paul II's commendation of Thomism (§43–45) that although he insists that the Church has no philosophy of its own, he also believes that it provides at least one version of a valid metaphysics needed by theology, particularly if it incorporates the data of a personalist phenomenology. That means that as students of the thought of Aquinas it is incumbent on us to show that, in fact, a Thomistic metaphysics can validate itself in the face of the attack on any kind of metaphysics launched by Heidegger, Carnap, and so many of our contemporary thinkers. In this paper I want to show how I think this can be done on the basis of Aquinas's Aristotelian epistemology which I assume to be preferable to Platonist, Empiricist, or Kantian theories of knowledge.[3]

Last year in this conference I argued, not to everybody's satisfaction, that Aquinas holds that no science proves the existence of its own subject. Hence, for metaphysics to be a valid science, we must first establish that its proper subject, namely, "being as such" actually exists. In the twentieth century most Thomists have either assumed this without proving it, or have given unconvincing arguments. At least this is the case if we also accept the view of Aquinas, attacked by Duns Scotus, that the "being" in question is analogous and extends to immaterial as well as material being.[4] Too many Thomists have assumed that the proof of the existence of God or of any kind of immaterial being is the exclusive task of metaphysics itself, thus producing a circular argument in which metaphysics proves the existence of its own subject. Aquinas provides the way out of this vicious circle. He explicitly maintains that the required proof of the existence of immaterial being is provided not by metaphysics but by physics, that is, natural science whose proper subject is not "being as such" but changeable being, *ens mobile.*[5]

For natural science itself no such proof of the existence of its subject is required, since it alone among the sciences has a proper subject whose existence is immediately and directly evident to human knowledge. This is so because its formal subject is the essence of material things that is also the proper object of human intelligence.[6] Although metaphysics does not depend formally on natural science (otherwise it would not be distinct from it), it does depend on it as its necessary condition, just as does mathematics, ethics and all the other special sciences. If natural science did not establish the existence of quantity, mathematics, according to Aquinas, would not be a science.[7] Ethics also presupposes the account of human nature supplied by natural science while the other practical sciences also presuppose its account of the natural materials and forces with which they have to work.

Why Thomists Have Avoided Aquinas's
Own Approach to Metaphysics

Why have not Thomists generally accepted this establishment and defense of metaphysics through natural science? I would suggest two reasons. One that has influenced John Paul II's own thought and left its mark on *Fides et Ratio* is his special concern always to maintain the dignity of the human person in the face of our "culture of death."[8] He says, "In a special way, the person constitutes a privileged locus for the encounter with being, and hence with metaphysical inquiry" (§83).

I believe we must acknowledge that classical Thomism in its search for scientific objectivity and universality sometimes paid too little attention to the subjective, individual, and historical aspects of knowledge. Modern philosophy with its Cartesian "turn to the subject" has made its most important contributions in its exploration of precisely these topics. Karl Wojtyla in *The Acting Person*[9] and the Lublin School of Thomism, with their use of a phenomenological method, have shown how this aspect of Aquinas's thought can be profitably developed.[10] Since however, a phenomenological study of the person can attain metaphysical depth only by passing through psychology and the proof of the spirituality of the human person, this personalist Thomism ought to encourage rather than inhibit the approach to metaphysics through natural philosophy.

Hence, I believe that a second reason for the neglect of an approach to metaphysics through natural science has been far more significant. This is the fear that a close relation between metaphysics and natural science would imperil the certitude of metaphysics, since, it is claimed, science can only lead to probabilities.[11] This fear has especially troubled theologians who point out the attempt to base apologetics on scientific theories has frequently led to the ridicule of the Faith. Thus, in a brilliant historical study Michael J. Buckley, S.J. *The Origins of Modern Atheism,*[12] has tried to show that nineteenth century apologists such as Samuel Butler exposed the Christian Faith to mockery by their attempts to use science as an argument through design for the existence of God. Similarly, Ernan McMullin in many publications and lectures has urged that Catholics take a positive and realistic view of modern science.[13] Yet he is always concerned to urge that we keep ever in mind that what theology needs from philosophy is a sound metaphysical grounding rather than put our trust in an apologetics built on the sands of current scientific hypotheses. Stanley Jaki advises a similar reliance on metaphysics rather than natural science and takes a very negative view of the Aristotelian tradition for its failure to keep science and metaphysics clearly distinguished.[14]

This reluctance to bring metaphysics into any sort of dependence on natural science was especially fostered in the United States by the predominating influence of the eminent Thomists Etienne Gilson and Jacques Maritain. Gilson wanted, for this and other reasons, to disconnect the thought of Aquinas from that of Aristotle, by reconstructing Aquinas's metaphysics from the *Summa Theologiae* without regard to his commentaries on Aristotle's works, especially his natural science treatises.[15] Maritain, on the contrary, was concerned to do justice to Aquinas's obvious interest in the study of sensible nature.[16] Yet he retained the Wolffian distinction between natural philosophy and empirical science. He argued that modern empirical science was a new species of science formally distinct from the natural philosophy of Aquinas, because the latter was a "dianoetic" science of "being" (*ens mobile*) while modern science was only "perinoetic." By "perinoetic" Maritain meant that modern science deals only with the phenomena of sensible beings and does not attain to their essences.

Maritain's defense of a natural philosophy is logically compatible with a natural science approach to metaphysics since that approach depends only on the arguments for the existence of immaterial beings contained in Aristotle's *Physics* and *De Anima.* It does not depend on the more detailed and now utterly out-dated parts of his natural science. Nevertheless, Maritain remained so cautious about any entanglement with modern science that his own defense of metaphysics rests not on the physical arguments for the existence of immaterial causes just mentioned, but on a supposed metaphysical intuition of "being as such."[17] Gilson vigorously criticized this stance as a mere conceptualism, and Maritain had in the end to agree that what he had really intended was Gilson's grounding of metaphysics in the judgment of the act of being, the "to be" or *esse*.

In my opinion these valiant attempts to shield metaphysics from the threat of modern science are in vain. They rest on the claim that since the proper subject of metaphysics is "being as being," this subject can be known to be real independently of natural science. Aquinas maintained, against the whole Platonic tradition and in contradiction to Scotus, Suarez, Descartes, Leibnitz, and Kant, that the proper object of the human intellect is indeed being, but only *changeable* being.[18] Furthermore, he held that metaphysical being is known only by analogy to this changeable, physical being.[19] It follows necessarily that a valid metaphysics cannot be independent of natural science by which these analogates are critically known. It even supposes the other special sciences that also presuppose natural science. As Aquinas says, "This science [metaphysics] that is called "wisdom," although it is first in dignity is nevertheless last to be learned."[20]

Joseph Owens, vigorously defended by John F. X. Knasas,[21] grants that metaphysics begins with *ens mobile* known by our senses to exist, but then proceeds to separate the *ens* as the subject of metaphysics from the *mobile* as the subject of natural philosophy. This, however, ignores that without a proof that non-mobile being exists such a merely verbal or conceptual separation has no critical value. The common error of all these positions is to suppose that one can make a real judgment that the subject of a supposed science of metaphysics exists before one has proved *a posteriori* from their sensible effects that immaterial beings *really* exist. If, as Aquinas repeatedly says, no immaterial beings exist, then natural science would be First Philosophy. For example,

> [I]f there is no substance other than those which exist in the way that natural substances do, with which the philosophy of nature deals, the philosophy of nature will be the first science. But if there is some immobile substance, this will be prior to natural substance; and therefore the philosophy of nature, which considers this kind of substance, will be first philosophy. And since it is first, it will be universal; and it will be its function to study being as being, both what being is and what the attributes are which belong to being as being. For the science of the primary kind of being and that of being general are the same.[22]

Nor can I agree with my good friend Lawrence Dewan, O.P. that in such texts as the one just quoted

> Aristotle there in fact says nothing about discoveries made by natural science. There he says that if there were no natural entity, natural science would be first philosophy. . . . Thus, he says that physics would be metaphysics if there were no separate entity. It is not said that physics discovers the existence of a separate entity. What certainly could be said is that, until they discover the existence of separate entity, the thinkers who do it, though they are metaphysicians, might not be able to distinguish themselves from physicists.[23]

While I do not deny that there can be a common sense intuition of *ens in commune* prior to the study of natural science, the issue is not common sense intuition, but the order of critical, scientific thinking. I would ask what kind of metaphysicians are unable to distinguish themselves from physicists except persons who are thinking in a merely common sense mode and not a scientific one?

I would also ask Dewan, Owens, and Knasas how it is possible to have a metaphysics about being as such if we are not critically certain that there are any beings but material beings and how can we sure of this prior to metaphysics without a proof from natural science. They seem simply to assume that in the phrase *ens mobile*, the *ens* can be abstracted from the *mobile*. But if the only being we know exists is being that is liable to change, then the study of "being as being" is the study of that kind of being and no other. Nor would I concede without qualification that the advances made by modern science in the study of the material world add nothing to metaphysical first principles. It is true, of course, that Aquinas proves the existence of immaterial being in the foundational part of natural science the certitude of which is independent of the rest of the science that deals with the details of nature with which modern science is chiefly concerned. Indeed, in any science the truth of its own first principles is independent of the conclusions in whose demonstration they are premises. Yet as conclusions are drawn from them the sense of these same principles becomes clearer and is enriched. This must be true in a special way in metaphysics where the principles are so broad and analogous as to be quite empty until we see how they apply to the analogates from which they are drawn. No wonder beginning students of metaphysics find a discussion of "being as being" so vacuous! That is why Aquinas warns against the young studying metaphysics. For those who have not acquired a fund of knowledge about reality, metaphysics can only be empty words.[24]

What Is Thomistic Metaphysics?

What then is metaphysics as Aristotle and Aquinas understood it? In the *Metaphysics* Book I (Alpha Major), Aristotle describes what true wisdom would be and calls it "first philosophy." It is not "first" in the sense that it is the first science knowable to us as Scotus thought,[25] but in the sense of a "supreme wisdom." Hence, Aristotle also calls it "theology" since it is a participation in divine knowledge. In Book Two (Alpha Minor) he adds an argument to show that even if a First Philosophy may be difficult to attain and its results relatively minimal, the effort is eminently worthwhile. In the *Nicomachean Ethics* VIII[26] he had already shown that the life of contemplation, especially in its highest form humanly possible, is the very goal of human living.

Aristotle then proceeds in the course of the subsequent books, at least as I read them, to ask whether any of the recognized sciences is First Philosophy. He enumerates the theoretical sciences, namely, natural science and mathematical science with its two species arithmetic and geometry, the practical sciences of ethics, with its three species, individual, family, and political ethics, and the indefinite number of productive arts. Finally, he recognizes logic, that he again divides into poetics, rhetoric, sophistics, topics or dialectics, and analytics or demonstrative logic, as well as grammar or linguistics.[27]

In the course of his treatise, he then eliminates each of these special sciences as a candidate for First Philosophy. Logic and linguistics are eliminated because they do not deal with mind-independent reality but only mental constructs. One should note that for Aristotle each real science has its own appropriate methodology and type of demonstrative logic, since he says that while every science deserving the name arrives at certitude, one should not expect the same type of certitude in all.[28] Hence, the questions today grouped under "epistemology" (a name only as old as 1854[29]) do not pertain to a distinct science, nor even a distinct part of metaphysics. For Aquinas each science applies the principles of analytic logic to determine the proper criteria for judging the critical value of its own hypotheses and conclusions as part of its own foundations. In metaphysics these various criteria are compared under the analogical concept of "truth," as it is a transcendental property of being as such. The psychology of knowing, on the other hand, pertains to psychology, mainly a part of natural science, although insofar as it presupposes the existence of a spiritual soul it pertains to metaphysics.

Aristotle also quickly eliminates the various kinds of practical knowledge as candidates to be "First Philosophy" because all practical knowledge presupposes some theoretical knowledge, every "ought" presupposes an "is." He devotes special attention, in particular in the last two books of the *Metaphysics* (Mu and Nu), to eliminating mathematics as First Philosophy because for Plato mathematics was superior to and independent of natural science. Thus, Aristotle and Aquinas come to the crucial question, whether natural science is First Philosophy and, hence, whether it is the ultimate wisdom possible to unaided human reason.

By temperament and background, his insistence that all human knowledge begins empirically, his extensive writings on natural science, and his reaction to the intuitive idealism of his teacher Plato, Aristotle was inclined to hold that natural science is the highest kind of objective, critical human knowledge. In this he was as much an empiricist as are today's scientists. Yet in his critical development of the principles of natural science in the *Physics* and in his analysis of human nature in the light of these principles in the *De Anima*,[30] he was forced to admit that natural science itself proves that changing material things have immaterial first causes. Hence, natural science cannot be ultimate wisdom, First Philosophy.

Thus, it became evident to Aristotle and Aquinas that First Philosophy is formally a science in its own right. Its subject is "being as such" in the sense that each of the recognized sciences is about a particular type of being while First Philosophy can be none of these since it studies "being" universally as including the non-material.[31] It must be distinct even from the science of nature that is presupposed by all these other sciences and which is presupposed even by First Philosophy itself. First Philosophy, therefore, does not have any data of its own but derives all its data from the special sciences and ultimately from natural science. It cannot reduce these sciences to a single science, however, since the various kinds of being with which these sciences deal are only analogously one. Its task is to distinguish and relate the various sciences and to inquire in what way they have common principles. Thus, metaphysics is an interdisciplinary science which seeks to unite all human knowledge, not by reduction to a single science, as Plato attempted by his dialectic that supposedly leads to a vision of the One,[32] but by preserving their autonomy and empirical grounding. That is, it coordinates them in view of their ultimate, spiritual causes.

Aristotle's own *Metaphysics* is a puzzling and disjointed work. Its essential unity has been well defended by Giovanni Reale in his excellent *The Concept of First Philosophy and the Unity of The Metaphysics of Aquinas*.[33] This is not the place to try to explain the order of the *Metaphysics* or to defend its general agreement with the account of the science that I am here proposing. In my view First Philosophy treats of being in its widest analogical scope as established by the demonstration of the existence of immaterial beings. Therefore, the first part of metaphysics is concerned with answering the question not of the existence of the subject but of its real definition, i.e., an analysis of what the subject is.[34] In the case of metaphysics this foundational part is an analysis of the analogical unity of being in its many senses. Because the subject of this science is only analogically one, being as such cannot be strictly defined but can be described by analysis.

The second part of metaphysics, the science proper, is the causal demonstration of the properties of the subject in terms of the quasi-definition established in the first part. These properties are designated by terms that transcend the categories established in natural science and are, therefore, called "transcendentals." They are not properties in the same way as the properties of material things that are included in the nine categories of accidents established in natural science, since they are distinguished from the analogical notion of being as such only by relations of reason. They are usually listed as *unity, truth,* and *goodness,* and some wish to add *beauty*. In fact, there may be an indefinite number of such transcendental terms, a question open for metaphysical exploration. Aristotle confined himself to the discussion of transcendental unity, along with some remarks on truth and goodness.[35] "Unity" adds to the notion of being as such only a negative note, an absence of division. It would seem then that this second part of First Philosophy deals with three principal topics, being as such and its relation to knowing minds (truth) and to free wills (goodness).

Aquinas insists, against Avicenna, that God and, it would seem, finite created intelligences as well are not properly part of the subject of First Philosophy but pertain to it only as the principles of being as such.[36] This might seem contradictory. If the subject of metaphysics extends to immaterial things, why do they not fall under its subject? I suggest that what Aquinas means is that since the immaterial principles of being are known only as the causes of material things, they must be studied under that formality, i.e. as principles of the subject, not part of the subject. Yet such knowledge as we can have of immaterial existents by reason must be achieved in a science of being as such, not in a theology properly speaking, that is, in a science for which they are the subject. Such a science whose subject is God is possible only through principles that are revealed by God. Thus, Aristotle's use of the term "theology" for First Philosophy, while defensible, is in a sense improper. Yet it should be noted that Aristotle never denied the possibility of a superhuman revelation. Abraham Bos in his fascinating *Teologia cosmica e metacosmica,*[37] shows that the surviving fragments of Aristotle's dialogues suggest that he pondered such questions but did not find an appropriate way to treat of them in his scientific writings.

Metaphysics is principally about being as substance.[38] Since, however, God is not part of the subject of metaphysics, it is not contradictory for Aquinas to deny that God is a "substance."[39] Hence, Heidegger's strictures against "onto-theology" cannot possibly apply to Aquinas's thought. In view of these distinctions, the treatment of immaterial substances in Book IX (Lambda) of the *Metaphysics* should be considered the third principle part of metaphysics, since it answers the fourth question of any science, namely why the subject has its properties, that is, their causes. Relative to material things their causes are immaterial things, not indeed, their material causes, but their efficient, formal, and final causes. Immaterial things, however, are only exemplary and not intrinsic formal causes with respect to material things.

Thus, First Philosophy has three parts corresponding to the last three of the four scientific questions. The first defines being as such analogously. The second describes how its transcendental properties are realized in the special sciences. The third shows that God and created spirits are the ultimate causes of these properties of things as they are demonstrated in the special sciences.

The fact that Aristotle chiefly considers God as the final cause of the world in the *Metaphysics* led some ancient commentators and many modern ones to assert that he did not consider God to be the efficient cause of the world. Others have held that Aristotle only makes God the efficient cause of motion, not of the existence of the world. Surely, Aquinas's opinion that these assertions fail to take into account the relation of the *Metaphysics*, probably an *opus imperfectum,*[40] to Aristotle's other works is defensible. Having proven God's existence in *Physics* VIII as the First Efficient Cause of all beings and recapitulated much of what he had written there in *Metaphysics* X (Kappa), Aristotle had no need to again discuss God's efficient causality in *Metaphysics* X.[41] What remained to be shown there is that while God is the efficient cause of all beings, he must also be their final cause, because these two causes are correlative.[42] Aquinas explicitly rejects the often-repeated assertion that for Aristotle God is the cause of the motion of material things but not their being, their *esse.*[43] Material things exist only because their matter has been given form by their efficient causes. Hence, even if, as Aristotle hypothesized, the world is eternal, it remains true that the First Cause of its motions must also cause its total being. The First Efficient Cause of being as such, therefore, is also its Final Cause.

Aristotle also shows that God is the Formal Cause of all things, since he is says that God is "Thought Thinking Itself" and thus the exemplar by which it produces all things in its own likeness. In saying that the proper object of God's knowledge is Himself Aristotle is not asserting, as has also often been claimed, that God does not know the world that he causes.[44] If God is Thought Thinking Itself, he must know his own acts and in doing so the things he makes and causes to act.

Perhaps the reason that God's knowledge and providence over the world is not very explicit in Aristotle's works is the incompleteness of his discussion in the *Metaphysics* of the created spiritual intelligences. It has often been noted that Aristotle omits a discussion of the human soul, although in *De Anima* he concluded that the human intellect by which humanity is specified is a spiritual being. Suarez was led by this fact to omit discussion of the human soul in his *Disputationes Metaphysicae* and leave it to psychology in natural science.[45] I believe this omission by Aristotle was due to the well-known problem of the eternity of the world implying the existence of an infinite multitude of human souls separated from their bodies. Aquinas solved this problem when he showed that the Neo-Platonized version of Aristotle presented by the Arabian philosophers who held that there is a single intelligence for all humanity is inconsistent with Aristotle's own principles.[46] Generally, treatises in metaphysics have not only omitted the discussion of the human soul but even more often of the created intelligences. I believe both of these omissions are serious errors, but I will not here say more on this difficult topic.[47]

Suarez, in the second volume of his treatise, has an elaborate discussion of the categories.[48] These properly belong to natural science, but of course metaphysics can reflect on them in its exploration of immaterial reality. For example, Aquinas shows that while quantity, time, place, etc. cannot be applied to immaterial things, yet substance, quality, relation, action and passion can be analogically applied to them.[49] Moreover, one can discuss how with respect to time and place the categories of material things can have some analogical meaning, since angels are virtually limited by place and have angelic time, while when we speak of God as loving we apply the category of quality to Him analogically.

It is also customary to treat in metaphysics of the ultimate principles of reasoning, such as the principle of contradiction and causality and to devote much attention to epistemology. It is best, I think, to deal with these topics under the consideration of transcendental truth and the distinction between mind-dependent or logical truth and mind-independent or ontological truth. Again the problem of act and potency, to which a major part in many treatises in metaphysics is given, is best treated along with the quasi-definition of being principally as substance in its unity. The division of being into uncreated and created and in into its various kinds, often called "special metaphysics," should be treated first at this point and then again in respect to truth and goodness, under those transcendentals. Hence, the discussion of the principles and causes of being belongs, as we have seen, to the third part of metaphysics.

Thus, a valid metaphysics for today that could perform the service to faith and theology that John Paul II calls for would look rather different from the standard treatises that followed on Suarez' seminal work. It would even seem quite different than the somewhat fragmentary *Metaphysics* that has survived in the Aristotelian corpus and on which the medievals commented as best they could. It would be an inter-disciplinary effort to compare the various now existing disciplines without any pretense to reduce them to a single science; instead, it would protect their autonomy. It would, however, explore the foundations of each of these sciences, natural science, mathematical physics, mathematics in its branches, ethics in its branches, the arts liberal, fine, and mechanical, logic, and linguistics or semantics to see if they meet critical standards. Under the transcendental of truth it would critically separate the dialectical and probable from the certain and demonstrative in each field.

Moreover, by comparing the foundational levels of these sciences it would expose the fallacies that have arisen from the improper intrusion of one discipline in another and yet show how they could be related in the interests of the unification of knowledge. It would serve the apologetic function of Sacred Theology by showing the credibility of revelation. Under the heading of the transcendentals of goodness and of beauty, it would show the harmony of the "ought" and the "is" studied respectively by ethics and natural science. It would also compare and relate morality and esthetics, and provide the instrument of that "theology of glory" that Hans Urs Van Balthasar so perceptively restored.[50] In all these clarifications it would not be content with the efforts of current analytic philosophy to clarify language but would go deeper into ontological questions.

Finally, it its study of God the Eternal Spirit and the created persons whose end is union with him, it would restore to us a sense of the spiritual universe that is far vaster than its material portion and supply that emphasis on personalism that John Paul II supports. I believe that metaphysics so understood would also show how much there is in common between the two great theologians of the Middle Ages, St. Thomas Aquinas and St. Bonaventure. Bonaventure brought out the many ways in which the metaphysical structure of created things reflects the Triune personalism, if I may use that expression, of God as the exemplary cause of all things. This will become clear also in Thomistic terms if our metaphysics centers on unity (reflecting the Father), truth (reflecting the Son), and goodness (reflecting the Holy Spirit).

Furthermore, this type of metaphysics will seize the opportunity in our postmodern times to bridge the great gap between our Catholic tradition and the modernity of modern culture, resting as that does on the objectivity of natural science and the creative subjectivity of the fine arts. Once we have become thoroughly faithful to the Aristotelian empiricism of Aquinas, we can show that a valid metaphysics can be grounded in natural science, provided that the foundations of that science are critically rethought to remedy the confusions of modernism that postmodernism is exposing but cannot remedy. Both the well established conclusions and the working hypotheses of such a rethought natural science, as well as of the other rethought special sciences, will enrich our understanding of general metaphysical truths without imperiling a *philosophia perennis.*

Finally, this will make possible a reform of our universities and reunification of knowledge without loss to the autonomy of the individual disciplines. For Catholic universities it will make possible the restoration of Sacred Theology as the president, but not an autocratic queen, of the sciences. As Miguel de Beistegui has shown in his *Heidegger and the Political Dystopias,*[51] Heidegger, the herald of the end of metaphysics, in his notorious rectoral address proposed such a unification of the university, as had Kant in his essay, *The Conflict of the Faculties* and as had also Fichte. Their views, however, where narrowly nationalistic and vaguely idealistic. In a far nobler and realistic Christian way John Henry Newman proposed such a view in his *Idea of a University* that has had, I believe, an influence on *Fides et Ratio.*

Notes

1. *An Introduction to Metaphysics,* trans. Ralph Manheim (Garden City, NY: Doubleday/Anchor, 1961).

2. "The Elimination of Metaphysics Through Logical Analysis of Language," trans. Arthur Pap, in *Logical Positivism,* ed. A. J. Ayer (New York: Free Press, 1966), pp. 60–81.

3. Since I believe that Aquinas is generally in harmony with Aristotle, in this paper I always intend to refer to both together when I speak of Aquinas's views, unless I wish explicitly to distinguish them.

4. On this see C. L. Schircel, OFM, *The Univocity of the Concept of Being in the Philosophy of Duns Scotus* (Washington, DC: Catholic University of America, 1942); Robert P. Prentice, *The Basic Quiditative Metaphysics of*

Duns Scotus in his "De Primo Principio" (Rome: Ed. Antonianum, 1970), pp. 124–29. The view originated with Avicenna and was held by many medievals; cf. Etienne Gilson, *History of Christian Philosophy in the Middle Ages* (New York: Random House, 1955), p. 764, n. 59.

5. My arguments for this with documentation were given in this workshop in the Summer of 1998 and will be published in *The Thomist*. See also my article, "The River Forest School of Natural Philosophy," in *Philosophy and the God of Abraham, Essays in Memory of James A. Weisheipl*, ed. R. James Long (Toronto: Pontifical Institute of Medieval Philosophy, 1991), pp. 1–16.

6. The terms "subject" and "object" often lead to confusion. In Thomistic terminology human faculties are specified by their proper *objects*. Sciences, however, are specified by their proper or formal *subjects* because it is the task of a science to prove the properties of their generic and specific subjects which are also the logical subjects of the various propositions whose properties are proved in that science as predicates of these subjects.

7. Aristotle, XI. 1. 2162, "Now the truth of the matter is that the objects of mathematics are not separate from sensible things in being but only in their intelligible structure, as has been shown above in Book VI (n. 1162) and will be considered below (n. 2185)." This and other translations of texts from this work are from *St. Thomas Aquinas: Commentary on Aristotle's Metaphysics*, trans. with Introduction by John P. Rowan, Preface by Ralph McInerny (Notre Dame, IN: Dumb Ox, 1995).

8. *Evangelium Vitae*, §12.

9. *The Acting Person*, trans. Andrezej Potocki, in *Analecta Husserliana,* vol. 10 (Dordrecht/ Boston, 1979). See also Rocco Buttiglione, *Karol Wojtyla: The Thought of the Man who Became Pope John Paul II* (Grand Rapids: W. B. Eerdmans, 1997), pp. 117–76.

10. See Andrew N. Woznicki, "Lublinism – A New Version of Thomism," *Proceedings of the American Catholic Philosophical Association* 58 (1986), pp. 23–27. Also see the "Translators' Afterword," in *Karol Wojtyla*, pp. 307–51.

11. I developed this theme in an article, "The Loss of Theological Unity: Pluralism, Thomism, and Catholic Morality," in *Being Right: Conservative Catholics in America*, eds. Mary Jo Weaver and R. Scott Appleby (Bloomington/Indianapolis: Indiana University Press, 1995), pp. 63–87.

12. New Haven: Yale University Press, 1990.

13. On these various views including McMullin's, see Ian G. Barbour, ed., *Religion and Science: Historical and Contemporary Issues*, (San Francisco, CA: Harper San Francisco, 1997), pp. 77–105. Barbour classifies opinions as

Conflict, Independence, Dialogue, and Integration and says, Three Roman Catholic authors Ernan McMullin, Karl Rahner, and David Tracy seem to me to be advocates of Dialogue, though with varying emphases. McMullin starts with a sharp distinction between religious and scientific statements that resembles the Independence position" (p. 91). I would hold for Integration, but with the qualifications and distinctions that I have put forth.

14. On Jaki's great contribution, see Paul Haffner, *Creation and Scientific Creativity: A Study in the Thought of S.L. Jaki* (Front Royal, VA: Christendom Press, 1991). I agree with Jaki's emphasis in his *Cosmos and Creator* (Chicago: Gateway Editions, 1981) and *Uneasy Genius: The Life and Work of Pierre Duhem* (Dordrecht: Martinus Nijhoff, 1984) on how the Christian doctrine of creation freed science from Greek errors. Yet as Haffner makes clear Jaki has been much influenced in his philosophical views by Gilson and Maritain and in his view of the history of science by Duhem. His view of Aristotle is, in my opinion, flawed.

15. "There is no philosophical writing of Thomas Aquinas to which we could apply for an exposition of the truths concerning God and man which he considered knowable in the natural light of human reason. His commentaries on Aristotle are so many expositions of the doctrine of Aristotle, not of what might be called his own philosophy," Gilson, *History of Christian Philosophy*, p. 367. For a very different view see James A. Weisheipl, O.P., *Friar Thomas D'Aquino: His Life Thought, and Work* (Garden City, NY: Doubleday, 1974), pp. 281–85.

16. For a comparison of Maritain and Gilson's views, see John F. X. Knasas, *The Preface to Thomistic Metaphysics: A Contribution to the Neo-Thomist Debate on the Start of Metaphysics* (New York: Peter Lang, 1990). Maritain develops his view on natural philosophy and the natural sciences in his Philosophy of Nature (New York: Philosophical Library, 1951), as well as in *The Degrees of Knowledge*, trans. Gerald B. Phelan (New York: Charles Scriber's Sons, 1959). Matthew S. Pugh, "Maritain and Postmodern Science", in *Postmodernism and Christian Philosophy*, ed. Roman T. Ciapolo, American Maritain Association (Washington, DC, The Catholic University of America Press, 1979), pp. 168–82, in an otherwise helpful article attempts to answer criticism by me and others. Yet he does not answer the objection that a perinoetic discipline as Maritain describes it would, by Aquinas's criteria, not be related to a dianoetic discipline as a formally distinct *scientia* but as a dialectic that would be a purely ancillary part of the dianoetic discipline.

17. *A Preface to Metaphysics* (New York: Mentor, 1962); cf. Raymond Dennelly, "Maritain's 'Intellectual existentialism:' An Introduction to His Metaphysics and Epistemology," in *Understanding Maritain: Philosopher*

and Friend, eds. Deal W. Hudson and M. J. Mancini (Macon, GA: Mercer University Press, 1987), pp. 201–33.

18. "Intellectus autem humani, qui est conjunctus corpori, proprium objectum est quidditas sive natura in materia corporali existens; et per huiusmodi naturas visibilium rerum etiam in invisibilium rerum etiam aliqualem cognitionem ascendit." Aquinas, *Summa Theologiae* (ST) I, q. 84, a. 7. "The proper object of the human intellect as it is joined to the body is the essence or nature existing in bodily matter and through this it ascends to some knowledge of the nature of invisible things."

19. See *ST I*, q. 4, aa. 1–3 in which Aquinas makes clear that we cannot define God but can know him only as the analogical cause of the creatures that are his effects. Note that this requires us first to prove that God exists as the cause of these effects before we can infer anything positive about him. Thus, an analogy of attribution (effect to cause establishing existence) must precede an analogy of proportionality by which various positive things are said of God.

20. "Ista scientia, quae sapientia dicitur, quamvis prima in dignitate, est tamen ultima in addiscendo." Aquinas, *In Metaphysics* I. 2. 46.

21. Owens writes, "If metaphysical inquiry is to proceed in the light of the being that is found in sensible things, it will try first to isolate that being and examine it as far as possible just in itself. In that manner it may well make evident a viewpoint from which all things whatsoever can be investigated, including the supersensible," *An Elementary Christian Metaphysics* (Houston, TX: Center for Thomistic Studies, University of St. Thomas, reprint, 1963), p. 29. He fails, however, to explain how, if only material *ens mobile* is known really to exist, that one can meaningfully speak of that "being" in isolation from the only way in which it is actually known to exist. For other works of Owens in which he elaborates this view see the references in Kansas, *Preface to Metaphysics* (pp. 72ff). Knasas himself in great detail expounds and defends Owens view as preferable to that of Maritain and others.

22. "Si non est aliqua substantia praeter eas quae consistunt secundum naturam, de quibus est physica, physica erit prima scientia. Sed si aliquis sustantia immobilis, ista erit prior substantia naturali; et per consequences philosophia considerans huiusmodi substantiam, erit philosophia prima. Et quia est prima, ideo erit universalis, et erit eius eo speculari de ente inquantum es ens, et de eo quod quid est, et de his quae sunt entis inquantum est ens: eadem enm est scientia primi entis et enti communis, ut principio quarti habitum est." Aquinas, *In Metaphysics* VI. 1. 1170 on Aristotle, *Metaphysics* VI. 1. 1026a 31, Aquinas notes this earlier, "Sicut si non essent aliae substantiae priores substantiae mobilibus corporalibus, scientia naturalis esset

philosophia prima, ut dicitur infra in sexto." Ibid. III. 6. 398. "Thus if there were no other substances prior to changeable corporal substances, natural science would be First Philosophy, as is said below in Book VI."

23. For my replies to Rev. Dewan's argument see *Addendum* to this paper.

24. Aristotle, *Nicomachean Ethics* VI. 9. 1142a17; Aquinas, VI. l. 7. n.1210

25. See references in Note 6 above.

26. Aristotle, *Nicomachean Ethics* X. 7. 1177a11.

27. Aquinas, *Expositio super librum Boethii De Trinitate*, ed. Bruno Decker, (Leiden: E.J. Brill, 1959), trans. Armand Mauer, *The Division and Methods of the Sciences* (Toronto: Pontifical Institute of Medieval Studies, 1963), qq. 5 and 6.

28. Aristotle, *Nicomachaen Ethics* I. 1. 1052b18–22; Aquinas, *ST* II-II, q. 96, a. 1, ad 3; II-II, q. 47, a. 9, ad 2, etc.

29. According to the article "Epistemology," *Encyclopaedia Britannica*, 14th ed., vol. 8., p. 660. On the inventor, the Scottish philosopher, James Frederick Ferrier, see the article by George E. Davie, *The Encyclopedia of Philosophy*, ed. Paul Edwards (New York: Macmillan), vol. 3, pp. 188–89 (The terminological invention is not mentioned there).

30. Aristotle, *Physics* VIII. 10.

31. Aristotle, *Metaphysics* IV. 1. 1003a; Aquinas, IV. 1. 530

32. In the allegory of the cave (*Republic*, Note II. 514a–18d1), Plato reduces all knowledge to the vision of the One symbolized by the Sun.

33. Trans. John R. Catan (Albany, NY: State University of New York Press, 1980).

34. Aristotle, *Metaphysics* I. 1. 71a11. See also Aquinas, *In Metaphysics*, "It is not possible for everything to be demonstrated since the subject [of a science] is not demonstrated but only the properties of the subject. For it is necessary to know of the subject both that it exists and what it is, as is said in the Posterior Analytics, Book I. This is because a demonstration must be from principles which are axioms (*dignitates*) and must be about something that is a subject and others thing that are [its] properties. Thus it is immediately evident that one of these three, namely, the axioms, are not demonstrated, since otherwise that they would have to have others axioms prior to them, which is impossible." (My translation) III. lect. 5. n. 390.

35. In medieval thought the transcendental terms are *res, aliquid, unum, verum, bonum* (thing, something, one, true, good). Aristotle in the *Metaphysics* speaks mainly of "unity" X. 1–4 and the other transcendentals only in scattered texts. Aquinas says, "Among these four [being, one, true,

good] much the first is being. Therefore it is necessary that it be positively predicated, since negation or privation can not be what is first conceived by the intellect, since always that which is negated or privated is a negation or privation of understanding. The other three, however, add something that does not limit "being," or it would not be first. This cannot be the case, however, unless what is added is something of reason only and this is either a negation which, as was said, is added by "one," or a relation that is able to be referred to ens universally. This last either pertain to the intellect to which "true" implies a relation, or to the appetite to which "good" implies a relation." *De Potentia* 9. 7 ad 6 (My translation).

36. Aquinas says in the Prologue to his on the *Metaphysics* says. "From this it is evident that, although this science studies the three classes of things mentioned above, it does not investigate any one of them as its subject, but only being in general. For the subject of a science is the genus whose causes and properties we seek, and not the causes themselves of the particular genus studied, because a knowledge of the causes of genus is the goal to which the investigation of a science attains. Now although the subject of this science is being in general, the whole of it is predicated of those things which are separate from matter both in intelligible constitution and in being. For it is not only those things which can never in exist in matter which are said to be separate from matter in their intelligible constitution and in being, such as God and the intellectual substances, but also those things which can exist without matter, such as being in general. This could not be the case, however, if their being depended on matter."

37. Milan: Vita e Pensiero, 1990.

38. Aristotle, *Metaphysics*, IV. 2. 1003a33; Aquinas, IV. 1. 534–46.

39. Aquinas, *ST* I, q. 3, a.5, ad 1.

40. For the current state of research on the history of the Aristotelian Corpus and the development of Aristotle's thought see William Wians, ed., *Aristotle's Philosophical Development: Problems and Prospects* (Lanham, MA: Rowman & Littlefield, 1996). In one sense the Metaphysics is complete since all the questions posed in Book III (Beta) are answered in it; see William H. Kane, O.P., "An Introduction to Metaphysics," in his *Approach to Philosophy: Elements of Thomism: A Collection of Essays* (Washington, DC: The Thomist press, 1962), pp. 121–42. See also Giovanni Reale, *The Concept of First Philosophy*, note 33 above. Nevertheless, it is clear that it is a work put together from various originally distinct writings without final revision, that is, a work in progress.

41. Aquinas says at the very beginning of the *Metaphysics* I. 11. 180 that *Maxime haec scientia considerat causam formalem et finalem and aliquo*

modo etiam moventem. "This science chiefly gives consideration to the formal and final cause and somewhat (*aliquo modo*) to the efficient cause." This *aliquo modo* as regards the efficient cause, indicates that the conclusions of metaphysics hold both for changeable and unchangeable beings it is less concerned with efficient causality. One cannot, therefore, conclude from the fact that Aristotle hear speaks chiefly of God as formal exemplary cause and as final cause that he denies that he is the first efficient cause of the material world.

42. Aristotle, *Metaphysics* V. 2. 1013a 18; Aquinas, V. 2. 775. Final causality is a predetermination of efficient causality and cannot exist unless there is something predetermined to seek that end. Created things could not desire God as their end unless he had created first them and so created them to desire him.

43. Aquinas says, "Since, as it is said in II *Metaphysics* [1. 280] that the disposition of things is the same in being and in truth, therefore just as some things are always true and nevertheless have a cause of their truth, so Aristotle understood that some beings, namely the celestial bodies and separated [immaterial] substances exist always, yet have a cause of their being. From which it is clear that although Aristotle assumed the world was eternal, nevertheless he did not believe that God was only the cause of the world's motion and not the cause of its being as some have asserted." Aquinas, *In Physics* VIII. 3. 996. See the similar statement in I*n Metaphysics* VI. 1. 1164.

44. On this see Leo Elders, S.V.D., *Aristotle's Theology: A Commentary on Book Lambda of the Metaphysics* (Assen: Van Gorcum and Co., 1972), pp. 251–68. Elders, who is often less benign in his reading of Aristotle than I would be, says "I do not think that it is necessary to assume that Lambda 9 excludes from the First Being all knowledge of the world. According to the metaphysics of Lambda 7 and 9 the world is dependent on the First Being, if not in its being, at least in its activity. As I have pointed out in the commentary on chapter seven, the first or highest being contains the fullness of being. In so far, its self-knowledge is also a knowledge of the world. It comprises, in a sense, the changes occurring in the world, for all change is in view of a terminus, which is a formal perfection. Now the first being is the best of all things. Hence it is the *telos* of all process. It would follow that by knowing itself it knows whatever is really the object of *episteme*. This knowledge never is a knowledge turned toward the world, but remains entirely concerned with the being of the First Mover; it does not even regard its causality in as far as this produces certain effects. – Aristotle did not work out this point, yet it is his merit to have made plain the first being cannot have things outside itself

as an object of its knowledge. That this supreme Mind thinks the essences of all being is also intimated by the comparison of its activity with of the productive sciences" (p. 257 f).

45. Copleston says that this greatly influenced later writers. Cf. Frederick Copleston, S.J., *A History of Philosophy*, 3 vols. (New York: Doubleday/Image Books, 1955), vol. III, p. 355.

46. *De unitate intellectus contra Averroistas*, dated by Weisheipl somewhat before 1270. English translation: *The Trinity and the Unicity of the Intellect*, trans. Re. Breenan (St. Louis:St. Louis University, 1946); unfortunately not from the critical text.

47. In my opinion the existence of superhuman created intelligences can be demonstrated in natural science with the sort of certitude proper to that science. This was the opinion of the noted Thomist, Charles de Koninck, Dean of theology of Laval University, and I have defended it in my *Theologies of the Body: Humanist and Christian*, 2nd ed. (Boston: National Catholic Bioethics Center, 1998), pp. 650–60. I am puzzled therefore why Aristotle discusses this only in *Metaphysics* Lambda, where his argument clearly depends on astronomical facts that pertain to natural science but omits any discussion in his natural science works. I can only attribute this to the imperfect character of that text.

48. Francisco Suarez, *Disputationes Metaphysicae* (Hildesheim: George Olms, 1965 reprint of Paris 1866 ed., original 1597).

49. For example, see *ST* I, q. 52–53 on in what way spiritual beings are in place q. 54–58; and in time q. 61. 2 ad 2 and q. 63. 6 ad 4; and have the faculties (active qualities) of intelligence, qq. 54–58, and will, qq. 59–69; and have action, qq. 106–7, etc.

50. Hans Urs von Balthasar. *The Glory of the Lord: A Theological Aesthetics*, 7 vols. (San Francisco: Ignatius Press; New York: Crossroad, 1993).

51. London: Routledge, 1998.

ADDENDUM

Lawrence Dewan, O.P., "St. Thomas, Physics, and the Principle of Metaphysics," *The Thomist* 61 (1997), pp. 549–66 has courteously criticized the thesis I am defending and my interpretation of Thomistic texts. In lieu of a more detailed reply the following indicates his main points and my replies.

1) Dewan says that as he pondered my thesis, "I think of such facts as that Thomas nowhere presents us with such a view of the formation of metaphysical concepts: he everywhere treats the metaphysicals as a domain unto themselves, even though they are objects first encountered by us in sensible reality." True, but Aquinas makes clear in IV. 15. 594 on Aristotle IV. 3. 10005a13 that *Non enim omne ens est hujusmodi: cum probatum sit in octavo Physicorum, esse aliquod ens immobile.* "Not all being is of this kind [*ens mobile*], because in *Physics* VIII it was proved that some kind of unchangeable being exists."

2) Dewan also says that "For Aquinas it is not only the concepts of physics that are encountered in sensible things." Yes, in fact all valid concepts originate in our knowledge of physical things, including mathematical, ethical, and metaphysical concepts, but in each case Aristotle and Aquinas are careful to show that these other types of concepts are derived from those of natural science in a valid manner. Thus, abstract mathematical concepts are grounded in the natural science proof that physical quantity is a necessary property of existing bodies. Ethical concepts are grounded in the natural science demonstration of the ends of human behavior fixed in human nature. Similarly there must be a demonstration that metaphysical concepts are grounded in natural science.

3) Dewan in footnote p. 552, n. 7 quotes *ST* I, q. 85, a.1 ad 2 and says that such terms as "potency and act" and "a being" "can be abstracted from universal matter" and "can be found existent without any matter, as is clear in the case of immaterial substance." Again true enough, but why can they be so abstracted?

4) In some of these texts, Dewan says, "The Aristotelian metaphysician is presented as already on the scene, and yet not knowing if there is any separate entity" (p. 552–53). This backed by note 9 on p. 553 referring to VII *Meta.* I. 1268–69. On this Aquinas says, as does Aristotle (*Meta* 7. 2 .1028b30–31) that the question of whether there are other than sensibles will be discussed until later. I grant that it would have been be more consistent if (*salve reverentia*) Aristotle and Aquinas had here referred back to the proof in *Physics* VIII rather than forward to that in *Metaphysics* Lambda but the essential point is that the proof in Lambda, as many commentators emphasize, is through final causality and thus presupposes the one in *Physics* VIII from efficient causality that, as Aquinas says in *ST* I, q. 2, c. is "more evident" than the others four of the *Quinque Viae* . See also Aquinas, *SCG* I. 13, nn. 109–10: *Quorum primum est quod procedunt ex suppositione aeternitatis motus quod apud Catholicos supponitur esse falsum. Et ad hoc dicendum quod via efficacissima ad probandum Deum esse est ex suppositione aeternitatis mundi, quo posita, minus videtur esse manifestum quod Deus sit. Nam si mundus et motus de novo incoepit, planum est quod oportet poni aliquam causam quae*

de novo producat mundum et motum: quia omne quod de novo fit, ab aliquo innovatore oportet sumere originem; cum nihil educat se de potentia in actum vel de non esse in esse.

5) Dewan (pp. 554–55) quotes Aquinas on IV *Meta* lect 1 (533), concerning Aristotle at *Meta* 4, 1 (1003a28–32) that early philosophers were seeking the highest causes. Yes, but it is also true that Aristotle complains they went no further than sensible causes. Even Parmenides is often quoted as a metaphysician for his talking about "Being" as though Being was a sphere. Aristotle commends the exception of Anaxagoras who introduced "Mind" as a principle. Anaxagoras never showed that Mind is immaterial and may well have agreed with the Stoic opinion that the Logos was a kind of fire.

6) Dewan quotes III *Phys.* lect 2 (285)," [This] text makes clear that the very definition of motion, used in science has as its subject mobile being, uses notions intelligibly prior to that of motion. These are presented as differences of being. Obviously, being *as* being is meant. The notion of being that is being employed can hardly be conceived as limited to the mobile, since mobility is a posterior intelligible. We are witnesses to the role of metaphysical consideration at the very origins of physical thought." Yes, potency and act are concepts that are indeed prior to that of motion. Aristotle begins not with the concept of motion but with that of "changeable being" (*ens mobile*) and then proves that motion is the proper act of changeable being. At this point the study of "Being as being" is the study of changeable being and there is no critical certainty that "being' has any other valid sense. When Dewan says "being *as* being is meant" he equivocates on what "being" means at this point in the order of sciences. If we only know that material things exist, then to study them as being, i.e., as existent is to study "being as being," which, in fact, is what Aristotle does in the *Physics*. There he studies changeable being according to the mode proper of being to it. To study it as *ens commune* would be to claim knowledge one does not scientifically possess.

7) Dewan says, "If we find, in the treatments pertaining to physical science, some approach from the viewpoint of being, this will be, not properly physical science . . . but a case of the physicists taking on the role of the metaphysician. Along these lines, Thomas tells us that the geometer proves his own principles by taking on the role of the metaphysician." (p. 557). In note 18 he refers to I *Post. Anal.* 21. 177 concerning Aristotle at 77b3–5, that reads. *Nulla enim scientia probat sua principia, secundum quod ostensum est supra. Dicit autem, secundum quod geometra est, quia contigit in aliqqua scientia probari principia illius scientiae, in quantum illa scientia assumit propria alterius scientiae; sicut geometra probat sua principa secundum quod assumit formam philosophiae primi, idest metaphysici.* I would grant that there is a sense, and an important one, in which metaphysics (once its subject has been established by natural philosophy) is said by Aristotle and Aquinas to demon-

strate the principles of the particular science, namely, that it shows whether they are or are not absolutely necessary, i.e., if to deny them would entail a contradiction. Some are necessary in this way, some are not, but for natural science are largely only hypothetically necessary, e.g., given our actual world, so and so must be true. Since, however, Aristotle and Aquinas assert that metaphysics is last in knowledge *quoad nos*, if these principles were not known with certitude before metaphysics natural science mathematics, and ethics would not be sciences, which is contrary to everything Aristotle and Aquinas do to show that these are true sciences. Is Dewan agreeing with Scotus that metaphysics must be known prior to the other sciences? He says that "Thomas sees the principles, precisely as known first of all and to all, as having a properly metaphysical character. This does not make the beginner a finished metaphysician, but it does mean that the principles of metaphysics are precisely those very first-known principles, not some newly constructed conception of being resulting from the study of physics. If we did not start with metaphysical principles, no particular science would ever provide them" (p. 558).

8) Dewan denies that Aquinas thought the proper object of the intellect is the essence of material beings (p. 558, note 20). Dewan says, "Thomas never says to my knowledge, and never would say, in my judgment, that the proper object of the human intellect is *ens mobile*. When he needs to underline the humble beginnings of human intellection, he uses such a formula as 'ens vel verum, consideratum in rebus materialibus,' that is 'a being' or 'the true,' considered in material things (*ST* I, q. 87, a. 3 ad 1). This is a formula that, while indicating the mode of being that is the connatural object of the human intellect, preserves the metaphysical starting point from confusion with the notions proper to physical science." This ignores *ST* I, q. 84, a. 7 *Intellectus autem humani, qui est conjunctus corpori, proprium objectum est quidditas sive natura in materia corporali existens; et per huiusmodi naturas visibilium rerum etiam in invisibilium rerum etiam aliqualem cognitionem ascendit (ST* I, q. 84, a. 7). "The proper object of the human intellect as it is joined to the body is the essence or nature existing in bodily matter and through this it ascends to some knowledge of the nature of invisible things."

9) On another text he says that Aristotle says in *I Post. Analyt*. 5. n. 50, of propositions known to all that "belong precisely to being," for "a being is the first conception of the intellect involved in such principles as that of contradiction and the whole is greater than the parts." Hence, they "are received from metaphysics, to which it belongs to consider being, just in itself [*ens simpliciter*] and those things which belong to being. But there are other principles such as that right angles are equal that belong to particular sciences." Yet Dewan in note 22, p. 559 refers to VI *Meta* lect 1. 1146. "Those Principles either are more certain for us, as in natural [objects] which are closer to sen-

sible [objects], or else they are simpler, and prior as regards their nature, as is [the case with] mathematical [objects]. Thus, Dewan does not observe that *ens mobile* is being and hence natural science is also about being. Therefore, the principles of non-contradiction and the whole is greater than the part can be established in natural science within the scope of its proper subject and can ground the principles of mathematics and the practical sciences. However, once it is established that there are immaterial beings, it can be shown that these principles also apply to immaterial being and more profoundly. This, however, cannot be assumed but must be demonstrated.

10) In the final section of his article Dewan uses his excellent article regarding the development of the intellectual virtues, "St. Thomas and the Ground of Metaphysics" (*Proceedings of the ACPH* 54 [Washington, DC: ACPA, 1980], pp. 444–54), to show that metaphysics is the highest of the sciences and properly deserves the name of "wisdom." I heartily agree, but I do not think that this doctrine can be used to imply that it is known prior to the other sciences (the Scotistic view) but to the contrary that it comes last and defends the other sciences and their principles from contradictions.

In conclusion it seems to me that in trying to show that metaphysics can be constructed independently of the natural science proof of the existence of immaterial beings Dewan (a) relies on a merely common sense intuition that material things cannot be all that exists; (b) assumes that prior to this proof the term "being as being" has any other real referent than to "changeable being as its exists in it proper mode" and can be the subject of a real science. The metaphysical mode of being has to be critically shown to have a real referent or it will not be a real science.

The Social Foundation of Realist Metaphysics[1]
Grace Goodell

Lamenting that many contemporary scholars shrink from the Big Questions of life, the Pope exhorts us in *Fides et Ratio* to respond to these questions' call with fresh energy and imagination. Few Big Questions have fallen into greater neglect and yet await our exploration with greater promise than that of the social bond at the core of reality. The social bond bears upon virtually every question we have considered in this meeting. It lies at the center of the nature of God, the nature of man, and their connection to one another.

A failure to embrace the profoundly *social* nature of God and man is a main cause of the crisis in philosophy that the encyclical addresses. The eclecticism, historicism, modernism, scientism, pragmatism, nihilism and postmodernism against which John Paul II warns us, all spring from a denial of community across cultures and through time. Even if the fundamental principle of sociation is not yet central to Western Christian philosophy and theology, all the more, then, it invites our creative exploration. The encyclical urges us not just to reinvigorate what we have inherited, but with a passion for ultimate truth to take the search into new realms (§56).

Theology, philosophy and social science all stand to contribute richly to our knowledge of the social bond, though just as the Pope would have it, theology takes the lead. Its sublime truths – the Trinity, the Incarnation, our Redemption, the Resurrection, we as the Body of Christ, the timeless communal solidarity of the Holy Mass – these stir us to contemplate sociation at the heart of our knowledge of God. Nor can we enter into such key philosophical concerns as the nature of the moral order, individuality, personal identity and responsibility, freedom, conscience and the will if we focus on the isolated individual. The isolated individual does not exist. How can we penetrate the nature of faith, hope and love – all, exercised in union with others – without a thorough understanding of corporate solidarity and the individual's part-whole relationship to it? What is the meaning of suffering without community? What is teleology? Ecclesiology? Law? St. Thomas insists that it is first and foremost for "the multitude," not the individual. Thus, through the "telic arc" many virtues and sins are seen primarily in terms of their effects upon "the common good."[2]

The Church, with her birth in the upper room, her early roots in little communities of faith that gave the martyrs courage, with her great flowering in medieval Europe and whose genius was the corporation, can only be understood in light of sociation. Consider the sacraments: baptism, confirmation, reconciliation, the banquet of friends in the Eucharist, matrimony, Holy Orders and even the last rites – all, *quintessentially* social. Let us then turn to the social bond at the foundation of experiential truth and goodness.

Social Metaphysics

Addressing itself to *Fides et Ratio*'s exhortation that philosophers restore metaphysics to our overall culture[3] – even what one might call popular culture – our discussion here focuses on phenomena generally pervasive throughout a society. While it addresses questions about the vitality of professional philosophy and theology, the paper primarily deals with laymen's "metaphysics" and what underpins it. In no way, however, should this be taken to refer only to *educated* laymen.

But the paper focuses on the social dimension of realist metaphysics for two reasons that are more important: 1) it considers realism as essentially affirming relational wholes, relational truths, rather than primarily breaking up unities; and 2) the support as well as the threats to realist metaphysics are to be found in a thinker's and a culture's social foundations, not just in philosophical argumentation.

Notwithstanding John Paul II's acknowledgment of our social nature, his discussion of metaphysics takes the individual to be the unit of thought, action and hence of scholarly analysis, a perspective characteristic of virtually all Western philosophy. A perspective that, one may argue, leads to nihilism. To complement that emphasis, this paper explores the enterprise of metaphysical thought as usually if not always taking place within the context of a social group or influenced by social experience. We consider the processes of metaphysical reflection as ultimately comprising complex *combinative* rather than reductionist dynamics, processes that mirror the unity inside social bonds. It seems then that all important objects of metaphysical speculation have in this sense an irreducibly social nature. These objects may elude the analyst who sees the world only through the lens of individualism. In response to one of the final challenges the Pope presents to philosophers, we ask what a culture friendly to and indeed positively oriented to realist metaphysics looks like, and what the social conditions that foster it are. Perhaps our exploration will help Catholic philosophers and theologians recognize how starkly individualistic – hence nominalist – much of their discourse seems, despite their occasional nod to social ties.

In this light, then, how do we define realist metaphysics? Here we see realist metaphysics to be constructed upon three interdependent foundations.
These foundations partly overlap with those that John Paul emphasizes as the
most salient aspects of metaphysics, aspects that our culture most desperately
needs restored. These foundations are:

- First, a general affirmation of reason: the *belief that nature is
intelligible,* and hence that nature, life and society have meaning,
which we can partly discover.
- Second, *the society-wide acceptance of the reality of universal,
abstract forms.* These forms or categories are apart from particular
existence, knowledge given us by the senses, linguistic conventions,
thought processes of the individual mind, or peculiarities of a single
culture. While these forms do not simply comprise generalities
derived from the particulars through induction, their reality is confirmed by properties that laymen perceive as they generalize from
direct experience of nature – properties such as actual, objective vis-
ibility, regularity of occurrence, hierarchical arrangement, constancy
over time, interdependence, internal complexity, and boundedness.
When we refer to a society-wide belief in the reality of universal
forms, we limit this to key *social* forms or categories. For example,
such abstractions as the family, fatherhood and the Church. Whether
a culture that believes in these realities is also inclined to affirm such
concepts as "chair" or "dog" comprises an important question, but
one beyond our speculation here. To an anthropologist, and arguably
to a Thomist as well, it is more significant that people consider the
family as real than that they are realists about "chair" or "dog."
- Third, springing from the first two fundamentals, there is a *concern for the Great Questions* that give meaning to life. We trace a
connection between the nihilism of contemporary culture, its nominalism, its disinterest in the Big Questions, and the loss of social reality in modern Western society. This third dimension of realist metaphysics rejects the notion that we as a species and as concrete human
groups are mere accidents overwhelmed by the universe, a position
directly related to overemphasis on individuality at the expense of
our social nature. To the contrary, we are confident that life has meaning when and because we are members of transcendent social bonds.
The metaphysician is impelled by a desire for not solitary but collective answers to these questions because they affect us all and every
generation. The Big Questions derive their bigness from their social
weight.

Our discussion proposes a close connection between each of these three key dimensions of realist metaphysics, on the one hand, and a particular type of social organization on the other, the same type underpinning all three metaphysical preoccupations. In elaborating how these components of realist metaphysics are contingent upon social organization, we will begin with the *second* dimension, epistemological *realism*. After that we will turn to realist metaphysics' *third* dimension, showing the link between a concern for life's Big Questions and particular social configurations. Only then, after exploring the social ground beneath these two pillars of realist metaphysics, can we return at the end of the essay to why the *first* one, the affirmation of reason itself, is also in large part contingent upon social organization.

Secular Anthropology May be of Assistance

In considering the reality of the social bond as the foundation for realist metaphysics, theology and philosophy can count on assistance from secular anthropology. It is as a social and cultural anthropologist that I offer these contributions to our Thomistic Institute. Having no training in philosophy, I request you to correct my misuse of concepts in your disciplines that you understand in fullness and with technical precision. In this same vein, I invite you into the nuances of selected terms and concepts which, though familiar to you as lay-persons, may have special meanings in my discipline.

The first of these is the term "social." It may be worthwhile to consider seeing the central truths of our faith and their various philosophical and moral ramifications in light of this anthropological concept as distinct from the concept of "love," which is more familiar to your disciplines. Both "social" and "love" connote affective inclination, but by pointing to society the former opens us onto less subjective ground. In its broadest sense "social" entails less exercise of the will, if any at all. A person *is* born into society and can never get away from it, not having to choose to develop and maintain it as with love. Then too, "love" suggests the subject-object dualism which "social" does not.

While it is understandable that most philosophical writing defines culture mainly as ideas, in this analysis we will emphasize concrete social structures, observable patterns of behavior, as an essential aspect of culture. Here "social" refers to a group bond larger than a dyad (larger than, for instance, a friendship between two people – or, as in the psalms, the humble petitioner and his Lord). Within the broad genre of the social union, we are concerned with the social *group,* and within that class with *corporate groups* as exemplified by the corporate family. The term "corporate" refers to incorporation through social and moral bonds, not legal incorporation: that is, with internally generated cohesion, not externally governed. Rev. Pinckaers's exposition of this distinction in his monumental history of ethics has no equal.[4]

Now let us elucidate how each of the three dimensions of realist metaphysics requires that the corporate group is the pervasive building block of society, especially the corporate family.

The Social Foundation of Realist Metaphysics: An Hypothesis

We open our exposition with this hypothesis: that realist metaphysics is not likely to be restored to a position of prominence within Western culture – perhaps not even within Christian philosophy – without a restoration of the transgenerational and translocal corporate family, fundamentally because a belief in the reality of metaphysical forms is directly connected to the social experience and objective, society-wide "truth" of transcendent, morally-bound groups, whose paradigm is such a family.

The traditional concept of nature which Rev. Ashley so powerfully elaborates in his work, uniting man with God metaphysically, depends on the irreducibility of the transgenerational, no-exit corporate family. Unless the family as an unseen, timeless reality is as immutable, as *given*, as the sun or the Alps – neither constructed nor possible to de-construct – it is improbable that a society will put forth and be open to serious metaphysical affirmation in any of its three dimensions outlined above. Ordinary people believe in the objective reality of essential forms and of invisible things like nature and God when they live in a non-contrived social order – when the primary units in their social landscape have an existence and authority not dependent upon a reference point in the political order, not requiring fundamental concessions from enacted law. When such primary building blocks have social substance, then God, abstract forms and the great metaphysical questions can be real, and metaphysics' confidence in reason seems reasonable.

Rev. Pinckaers comes close to my proposal when he indicates the connection between nominalism in the realm of philosophy and in society the transformation of the "natural" social bond into *humanly constructed* aggregations, created and maintained instrumentally out of individual self interest and validated in terms of convention or contract.[5] While it is true that most societies in which we find a basic set of *pervasive and immutable* social forms, beginning with the family and others modeled on it, have not produced professional metaphysicians, the people in these societies are solid realists, they take with high seriousness the encyclical's Big Questions of human life, and they have no doubt about the efficacy of logic, reasoning and common sense. The corporate family as a social reality seems to be a necessary but not sufficient social condition for realist metaphysical thought.[6]

This hypothesis is likely to have unpalatable ramifications for philosophers, ramifications which make it akin to some of the errors discussed in the encyclical. I hope that these difficulties will open us to fruitful exchange, because I intend to assert an argument of general import, and to employ a method of analysis that has broad, not idiosyncratic application. While it does not endorse social or cultural determinism, it does urge theologians and philosophers to turn their attention in a more systematic way to the social aspects of God's nature, our nature, and our relationship to Him, as being central to Roman Catholic Christianity. Further, there are substantive parallels between what we might call the structure of philosophy's truths and approaches, on the one hand, and social organization on the other. More particularly, it suggests correlations between realist metaphysics and observable patterns of sociation in a society whose predominant organizational principle is the morally bound Great Vertical Order. Let us turn, then, to the social foundation that underpins each of the three key dimensions of realist metaphysics, beginning with epistemological realism.

Metaphysics' Epistemological Realism: The Corporate Family as its Precondition

Asking how the corporate family's pervasiveness in a culture plays an indispensable role in fostering epistemological realism throughout that society, we find much of our answer in the definition and description of the corporate family. What is it? I doubt that the corporate family any longer exists in Western society, and in some places has not for many generations. Rev. Ashley cites the ancient Jewish idea that a living community has a "corporate personality" from which its members derive their life, and to which they contribute in such a way that its very existence depends on them. St. Paul reminded the Christian community, which he called "the body of Christ," that "if one member suffers, all the members suffer with it; if one . . . is honored, all the members share its joy."[7] Since its birth the Church has served as a paradigm of the timeless, morally-bound family – and, we may add, a model and protector of corporate social groups in general. In one way or another she herself manifests virtually all the properties that concern us in them.[8]

In what sense is the corporate family's form "real" in those societies that take it to be so? In the following elaboration of its essential properties, it may help us to take the terms "natural" and "real" as interchangeable: Within these societies, the thing I am about to describe is natural and *real*. First, the corporate family is *primordial*, foundational. No one can imagine its ever having been created; it has always existed. Certainly it pre-dates the state with its formal legal apparatus. Ongoing presumably forever[9] – and, like nature herself, ever emerging – it transcends the life of individual members, of generational cohorts and even of political regimes. No multi-generational memory, no human faculty or archive can contain it. As one traces back, back, back through the generations of forebears that have kept the family continuity, new branches come into view and spread out; with each generation the family expands, becoming more populous, variegated, abstract and morally compelling. Its beginning is lost in the misty past where as one recedes farther and farther even in any specific instance the family approaches a metaphysical "form" – that is, a group which is abstract, comprehensive, universal, and certain. Each family in its particularity realizes the form by extending itself back to its misty origins.

A society composed of such families requires that every human being belong in one. Absolutely everyone, even still-born babies. Family identity is personhood. It is inconceivable that one could be human apart from his family of birth. That a person might try to change his name in order to disguise his identity in a new place, or could do so legally, is preposterous. There is no escaping membership in one's natal family – not even by death. When a member pioneers in a new land the family does not lose him but realizes its translocal potential as he establishes its beachhead on new soil. Consider, for instance, the gigantic but solidary overseas Chinese families that have their flags on five continents. Some of them count into the hundreds of thousands of members.

The reason I call these corporate groups "no-exit" is that by its very nature the moral bond is irreversible, whereas contract stipulates a temporal beginning and end. Thus, the corporate family is trans-temporal as well as transgeographical. Both factors make it invisible. Though an integral, corporate whole, it is unseen. The ancestors are alive and present as constituent parts of the family. But it is absurd to refer to them as a "line." Not only does the huge assemblage possess depth in time, but in social variation and semantic texture also: two more properties that it shares with the natural order. Every corporate family manifests the eccentricity, complexity and ever-changing internal movement that characterize the reality of the world as we know it: babies growing up, some dying in a day or two; tottering senility; colorful characters, deviants, bitter internal struggles, traitors – plus heroes, scholars, poets, high officials, saints and millions of ordinary souls. Deaths and replacements here on earth, i.e, continual emergence.

The corporate family's social density is matched by its semantic complexity: multi-layered references and connotations, collective memories, stories, symbols, lies and secrets that only insiders can interpret. Lessons from the unfathomable particulars of history and that change internally over time without losing their coherence. Shame that pierces an insider's being, but only an insider's. In its internal economic, social and semantic exchanges and interdependencies, the whole exceeds the sum of its parts. Rev. Ashley writes that "as we go up the scale of more and more complex natural units, the number and interrelations of the parts increases . . . [and] there is an increase in the interiority of its activities."[10] Such cumulative personal and social texture gives the family substance, weight, and puts its densely compressed matter beyond the possibility of human tampering. The bulk is just too great, too unruly, to be deconstructed. Any efforts to do so must eventually bow to its truth.

Another hallmark of the type of group that underpins realist metaphysical thought is that despite its internal variation – or rather, because of it – this social mass is unitary. Boundary holds all this profusion together, defines it off against "others" outside, and provides the cognitive as well as behavioral enclosure for each family's unique internal organization. Virtually all important, risk-bearing exchanges take place inside the family's boundaries or those of groups consciously seen as functioning like the family.

To transmit such thick interior cross-referencing bounded off against the outside, the preferred metier of expression in such groups comprises analogy, symbol and ritual, not language "associated by law."[11] This rich particularity insures its impenetrability by non-members. The West's beloved civil society with its obsession for public transparency has no place for these social orders' private-world reality, resistant to public scrutiny. E. O. Wilson has laid bare the most intricate organizational relations of ants and bees, but the corporate human family is too deeply textured for external penetration. To those in such a culture, this opacity testifies to its reality.

Embodying two further properties of social reality, these solidary families are primary actors in society, publicly recognized and objectively observable agents of autonomous action. Each makes its mark on the here and now as a patently visible, known entity. Self-governing through its own multiple authorities, it orders its affairs independently. It assumes responsibility as one body and disciplines its members on its own. Every person in society is tagged according to kinship and held accountable for group as well as individual deeds, also credited with group and other individuals' merits, even of the ancestors long gone.

The group has its members' happiness and its own well being and continuity as its sole ends. All of society recognizes this principle's reality and pre-eminence, what St. Thomas called the common good. The group's integrity cannot be reduced to social digits like roles, to explicit language, or to single-purpose utility. These irreducibilities to part-selves and partial, "flat" meanings comprise additional evidence of its social reality. No part can impose itself on the others or use the others for its purposes. Nor can insiders ever blatantly use the group for their own designs, lest the primordial rule be violated, that the group, good in itself, has only ultimate not immediate ends. Naked instrumentality constitutes a mortal offense.

These comprise the key attributes of a corporate group: foundational, given (though arbitrarily), invisible, unitary and integral, no-exit, not amenable to individual tinkering, socially and semantically dense, bounded, publicly observable and active, its existence needing no external justification. In bolstering the social union against reason's human engineering, these properties embody and hence attest to a reality beyond our making. When everyone takes this social form for granted as a rock-solid experience authorizing all similarly constructed abstract social forms, then the corporate group gives form to nature and is the seal of reality. Specks, clumpings and even material exchanges that are not housed in or sponsored by one of these mini-sovereignties do not exist ontologically. Part and parcel of realist metaphysics is recognition of the moral and semantic void beyond the corporate family's borders.

The Corporate Family is Good

Though abstract, the corporate family is not only real, true, but it is also good. Just as all life begins in the family, so does all virtue. A corporate family is objective in the sense of being outside and larger than self, but it is never indifferent. All family members are by definition good, even if they are bad; and most non-family are neutral or suspect, even if they are good. One has to behave helpfully to family members and serve as their succor of last resort, not lie to them or cheat them. This is not due to love, duty, or concrete or emotional benefits of membership. The family is good because it is oneself. Truth governs inside. Outside, falsity is only constrained by formal Law.

Unity within such a no-exit social bond comes from all the members having an internally-embraced identity – usually to a group one has *not* deliberately joined but rather has been assigned to by society (for example, by infant baptism).[12] Contrary to Lockean theory of contract, members inside traditional morally-bound social unions, including outcast groups, take these groups to be good simply because, finding themselves assigned to them, they embrace their socially imposed identity. Each insider perceives himself to be an interchangeable exemplar of the more inclusive and abstract levels of the social whole. This intense identification can take place even when it brings avoidable opprobrium or death.[13]

Utilitarian or psychological factors to which contemporary social science attributes the self's identification with a group, such as depending on others for need satisfaction, recognizing a common fate with other members, sharing the same attitudes and values with them, enjoying proximity or frequent social contact with them, do *not* constitute the most fundamental conditions for pride in a group, mutual acceptance, intense moral cohesion and sacrifice. Rather, profound social attachment can be naturally elicited by mere *external designation*.[14] The will does not have the first move. Nature does. It arbitrarily creates social bonds, and people accept its fiat not only as being real, but also as being good.

Realist Metaphysics' Concern for the Big Questions of Life

Realist metaphysics comprises more than the affirmation and study of the abstract forms of reality. As *Fides et Ratio* asserts, it also lifts up our vision to the ultimate truths and values of life. The two tasks are connected, because the comprehensive social forms above our quotidian experience give to the world innate universal significance, which we love and want to enter into. Like epistemological realism, this second dimension of realist metaphysics – a society-wide concern, even among ordinary laymen, for the Big Questions of life – also depends upon the corporate family. To grasp how this social form influences whether or not a culture is concerned about transcendent goodness and the Big Questions, we return to an aspect of the corporate family that we mentioned above, its layered internal organization.

Recall that as one traces farther and farther back through the generations, the small, concrete and vulnerable living family takes on the qualities of an increasingly more comprehensive, permanent and immovable overall form whose certainty is anchored in the distant past. The here-and-now corporate family is part of a vast, multi-leveled Great Vertical Order whose form is shared by many other groups in society, all modeled (often consciously) on it. Thus, just as the corporate family comprises nuclear or extended families nested in lineages, which are then nested in clans – and on up – so too, the Church comprises unitary parishes nested in dioceses within archdioceses. Kinship is not the only principle out of which Great Vertical Orders evolve. Other frequently found ones include Great Vertical Orders based on religious or temple membership, mother language, ancestral place of origin, and even sonship within an ancient, hoary educational order which through its intensely moral labors has made fully human persons of the generations of the young entrusted to it, brothers one and all. These Great Orders, too, unite the living and the dead.

Each person belongs to several Great Vertical Orders, or more. A proliferation of such internested orders fills out society, giving it plural systems of authority. Though resembling each other in form, the Great Vertical orders are autonomous, each having its own hierarchical governance and semantic codes. People in societies organized on this basis can easily articulate and map out the Great Vertical Orders' regularities. Organization in gradients is essential to the character of all transcendent, no-exit, morally-bound corporate groups. Social scale is built up gradually, each level expressing an increase in membership size, hence of substantive social variety and social abstraction. The greater the internal variation, the greater the potential for interdependencies exclusively within the Great Vertical Order.[15]

Within each Great Vertical Order the levels do not overlap in content, but rather the lower groups are contained in those above them. Each individual part and each group at every level embody the essential qualities of the overarching universal form, because step by step the lowest level is in touch with and can reach the highest – indeed, is contained within it. Through such structured ascendancy, each Great Vertical Order carries its members, personally, up to the highest, most comprehensive good. The small and the great are connected, giving the particular and the individual entry into the transcendent, his Unity and Good.

Depending on circumstances and personal inclination, a member of a Great Vertical Order can and will identify with any level of social abstraction, all the way up or down. Each part carries a complete set of the entire group's cultural DNA and a positive orientation toward the whole, enabling the members to act in concert on basic matters with but minimum explicit communication. These qualities give the whole an accordion-like flexibility and adaptability without depending on external coordination – again, manifesting in visible joint action, reality's telltale sign of unitary complexity. This multileveled unity resists reductionism and dualism: every level is simultaneously true and good.

The Great Vertical Order's boundaries have profound epistemological ramifications. Truth is socially situated without contradicting its abstract universality. It flows freely up, down and laterally within the overall boundaries, but only information of little value crosses into general public circulation outside. Thinking is always readjusting itself to adapt to or bring itself in line with social reality, being. Complex truth is confined within the bounded domain because so are intention and complex meaning. Meaning requires contrast, the contrast provided by boundary off against the external void. No potential can be actualized outside the self-referential family, because there are no meaningful things out there. This internal truth-domain and its complement, the external void of mistrust and suspicion, are not founded on sentiment; rather, they are empirically upheld in everyday experience.

Thus, echoing one of the encyclical's main themes, reason is autonomous, but can only reach significant truth when operating within the domain of faith. Authority, like truth, is only active within the Great Vertical Order. The truth-seeker wants authority's collaboration, its guidance and intervention. Authority does not only pass truth downward as from teacher to pupil or master craftsman to apprentice. Particularly in the thrust of action, but by no means exclusively then, subordinates may possess greater authority than their superiors. When this happens the principle of hierarchy still governs. As the basis of order it has not been replaced by function, neither equality nor utility being compatible with truth.

The Great Vertical Order's building blocks are not static. To the contrary, such society is constantly aware of movement. On a case-by-case, situational basis individuals have to affirm one of their particular memberships, which is where the virtue of prudence comes in. Then too, families in time father new ones, becoming lineages, then later on becoming clans, and so forth, eventually taking on the qualities of a prototypical form. Thus, the lower levels are continually in motion. Fresh challenges that arise call forth new units at the particular level, nudging older forms into increased stability as they recede "upward" to where all collectivities eventually converge in unity.[16] Crucial to the order's emergent nature, if a person is to understand a thing he must understand what has gone before – the ancestors are an active part of the present.

Freed by their time-transcendent reality, the lower orders comprise living, intensely interacting fields ever changing and, in the overall, expanding. Since the Great Vertical Order's truth domain always refers back to its interior resources, and since it authorizes meaning and truth internally, it constitutes an on-going order of potentiality – but only as long as a contrast is maintained between it and the outside. If boundedness is denied, there can be no autonomous reason that the Pope so ardently defends.

The Great Vertical Orders' layered structure of morally-bound corporate groups fosters concern about the Great Questions of life and yearning for completion, because the Order as a whole constantly exerts an upward pull towards the highest, the universal, the most perfect and most stable reality. For example, a nuclear family cannot separate its core identity and actualization – not to mention its resources in time of need – from its lineage, clan and higher levels of kinship. Given two immediately contiguous levels, the higher one, the more transcendent form, specifies the meaning of the lower one while the latter gives social content to the former. Such an arrangement – and remember, we are discussing actual social organization in which people live out their lives – imbues society with that ultimate meaning indicated by the most comprehensive unity at the top. One might go so far as to say that built into the social system is an ineluctable movement toward God.

Whereas Western culture sees whole-person identification with any social bond as suspect, threatening a loss of meaning for the individual, with reference to most traditional societies the opposite is true: Why would anyone prefer to be detached from such rich, dynamic relational fields that strain towards perfection? Such cultures concur with the Church, that the higher the level of group identification, the greater the inherent good. When a person adjusts the nature and content of his self-perception to conform to an ever more inclusive level, that may be nobler and more profoundly individual. It immerses one more deeply in the Big Questions of life. The higher a corporate entity is in the scale, the more enduring and real it is. In this way the social matrix of being endows abstractions with the reality of the universe.

The meaningfulness of life's Great Questions requires affect-laden comparison and contrast, both structured into the Great Vertical Order's organizational arrangement. Horizontally, all units contrast and compete with each other. In doing this they comprise one another's external environment, a demarcation that is indispensable for reality's meaning, identity, and the elaboration of its ordered interior complexity. But at the same time these competing and contrasting mini-systems are always unified, merged vertically, by the next level upward to which they necessarily belong. Thus the Great Orders constantly bathe society in affect-infused contrasts (the horizontal) and comparisons (the vertical). This environmental immediacy is intrinsic to the Great Vertical Order: the sharp proximity of a complex but structured outside. Every solidary level constitutes and forms its constituent mini-sovereignties, serving as their exterior.

A culture chock-a-block full of affect-laden contrasts and comparisons is flooded in meaningfulness, which every action invigorates. Suffused throughout with personal identity, the entire social environment and everything in it swim in significance: days of the week, plants and animals, geographical markers (even ones no outsider might notice), how objects of daily use are located in space, colors, letters of the alphabet and numbers all signify people, events, forces in the unseen world that are intermingled profusely and indiscriminately with things belonging to the material world. All relate affectively to oneself, while at the same time all point upward to unity and goodness.

Central to the social foundation of realist metaphysics, then, is the fact that in identifying himself with the corporate family, the Church or other such groups modeled on the family, each having interested levels of increasing inclusion and greater loftiness, a person is not considered to become impoverished or deprived, to submerge his core self, or to regress to a more primitive or unconscious identity. Instead, he gains in richness and meaning, in identity, goodness, engagement with reality, nearness to Truth, and in rational as well as experiential movement toward the universal form. This social order has built into it not only epistemological realism, an upward pull drawing everyone into the larger questions of life, and metaphysical range, but also some participation, for everyone, in love of the Ultimate.

Realist Metaphysics' Confidence in Reason and the Intelligibility of the Universe

Rev. Ashley has given us a lucid exposition of the link between the concept of the unity of all nature, starting with God, and confidence in reason.[17] When in light of his analysis we consider how simply constructed the Great Vertical Order is, how easily its world is mapped out by ordinary people who constantly refer to its arrangements in their daily commitments, and how the entire society works on this one basic model, we can begin to appreciate the connection between its logical structure and its culture's affirmation of reason and sense that the universe is intelligible. While people in such a culture cannot predict or explain the internal details of groups other than their own, everyone has a clear picture of how society is put together, even domains within it with which they have no direct contact. Indeed, comprehension of the nature and significance of one's own corporate group constitutes the basis for understanding everything else, including the external environment.

No one, not even a billionaire or finance minister is exempt from the rationally structured framework built up of similar blocks, level by level – far from the Kafkaesque maze that contractually-constructed society comprises. The elemental properties of society (and by extension, of nature) are effortlessly grasped, even when the society is extremely complex, highly industrialized, and enjoying the latest modern technology. These elemental properties are: collective repetition of homologous and interdependent parts that are hierarchically arranged, and that endure and replicate themselves throughout time. Vertical regularity is directly related to horizontal, as all units mutually need and call each other forth.

Grounded in this intrinsically intelligible social order, the individual perceives a universe which is also logical and manifests the same regularity of basic forms. But as he looks outward onto nature, not only does he see a user-friendly landscape; because of its level-by-level proportional accessibility, this landscape invites him to act upon it, starting within those areas nearest him. His understanding of society's and nature's hierarchical order keeps the extremely complex in the distance; shows the more immediate reality to be comprehensible, hence do-able for whatever project he undertakes; manifests a rational continuum stretching between his place and where he may want to end up; and draws him into the whole through the prospect of movement upward with family and friends toward joint fulfillment. The universe is not only achievable through reason, but reason cannot resist being drawn into it, because while each higher level beyond him affirms the reality of the yet unknown and compels his involvement, the forms' sequencing precludes any unbridgeable gap between the steps to completion. A person placed anywhere within the system has unbroken access to the vast, over-arching horizon, howsoever distant the horizon may be that his vision places out there.

Yet the morally-bound social order fosters confidence in other dimensions of reason, too. While how we think about observable reality and order our knowledge of it in the social as well as the biological worlds proceed inductively, the particular and known building up incrementally into the general and toward the proximate unknown, the Great Vertical Order's social reality also structures the processes of deduction. After all, the here-and-now corporate family is the offspring of what have become regularities seen in the more comprehensive forms. These abstract forms are not simply the products of induction, but, taking on an active life of their own and equally true to reason, they conceive and give birth to new knowledge; herein lies their hierarchical authority. If we want to adhere to truth and goodness, we must understand and heed them, try to work within their parameters, let the emergent particulars flow from the comprehensive forms. It may be this movement from the abstract to the particular that John Paul II, along with many Thomist philosophers, considers the distinctive mark of the realist metaphysics they would restore to our culture.

Theology, Philosophy and the Decline of the Corporate Family

In the European middle ages the reality we have reviewed in our discussion of the corporate family characterized virtually all social organization. Social reality incarnated the philosophical concept of the unity of man and God through the actual institutional build-up of "The Great Chain of Being." Through membership in even the lowest of the social levels, the self could reach the all-inclusive social groupings close to God Himself, such as the universal Church and the communion of saints. Voluntarists and especially the Protestant Reformers abhorred this incrementalism and its gradients. To them an all-powerful God distant from man was no longer governed as in the same Great Vertical Order, by the same natural laws that govern us, those we comprehend.

The dualism that the Voluntarists and Reformers articulated was not restricted to theology. The dichotomous universe they depicted found its social counterpart in the gutting out of all middle range structures extending level by level from the bottom to the top of society, to the most inclusive and abstract corporate Unity. When the autonomous medieval corporate orders were replaced by the state's new science of politics so well articulated by Machiavelli, control over others who were alien to one inserted an outsider into what had hitherto been a society modeled on the corporate family. Nature, the reality of the common good, was split in two: ruler versus ruled, command versus obedience, reason versus the will, conscience policing the soul. The intermediate levels, previously governed by self-affirmed identity, internal authority flowing between top and bottom, and moral pressures, particularly moral interdependence, were now replaced by professionalized and centralized legal governance. Having to fill the terrible gap that the political dualism of power created, society needed force and formal Law, not only the mathematical laws of science to govern the biological and physical world but positive legislation set free from moral bonds and generalized authority, to govern the social order.

We can now extend Rev. Ashley's philosophical and theological dualism[18] into the corresponding social organization that accompanied it:

- first, the dualistic view of nature found its correspondence in a dualistic society without any Great Vertical Orders, hence there were no accordion-like intermediate levels from us to God, the Ultimate Good and Truth;
- second, the decline in epistemological realism expressed the social condition in which, without these vertical gradients, God, the ultimate Truth, and the most comprehensive truths and good associated with Him were indeed out of our reach, leaving us with our own subjectivity and finite truths of our own making; and
- third, the shift from the unity of nature – in social terms, the common good with natural law as its coordinational foundation – to disconnected, bric-a-brac reality only made coherent by mathematics and measurable forces, found its parallel in raw politics governing through positivist Law explicitly severed from moral values.[19]

Today the corporate family, as virtually all social organizations, is but a toy of secularized political and legal will. Those who take pride in the Rule of Law as the crown of European civilization, wishing family-based societies throughout the world would soon adopt it, should ponder how it replaced natural reality with legal reality, enabling us in the West to construct and deconstruct all social forms artificially, even the most primordial ones. Rev. Pinckaers writes:

> Charity forms bonds between us and God that are more supremely natural [than love of self], through direct participation in the spontaneity and wisdom of the Holy Spirit. . . These relationships are completely destroyed by nominalism. There is no longer any natural bond between human freedom and the freedom of God, but only a play of power . . . The essence of the first commandment is no longer love but the absolute imperative of the divine will . . . Charity itself can no longer form natural bonds between us and God. Any society uniting us will be basically artificial, like a contract or an alliance which depends upon the free decision of the free parties engaged. It will always be juridical in character . . . Consequently the notion of justice will be transformed. Having lost its foundation in nature, justice becomes the creature of society.[20]

Recall for a moment our analysis of the source of meaning in contrast and comparison, unity. The two dynamics complement each other. Meaning requires both, and both are integral to the Great Vertical Order. Dualism destroys both. In doing so it has diminished the status of human nature and lowered Western culture's metaphysical aspirations. Once dualism got a foothold in European culture, it attacked the dynamic foundations of reality we have described. Radical individualism precluded homologous units and their repetition in patterns, while radical equality precluded hierarchical ordering, hence contrast as well as comparison. Without natural verticality there could be no abstract forms to give significance downward. Without the elements of structured complexity there could be no meaning. When commenting on these consequences of dualism, scholars too rarely recognize the real forms' dependence on the Great Vertical Orders that attach the forms to us.

As a result of the intermediate levels being undermined, legal craftsmanship had to replace nature as the author of truth. This swamped the individual and his local groupings in the vast political universe of power and will. Absoluteness replaced proportion and relationality. Today we can hardly speak of being a part of "a society" or there being such a thing at all – only individual decisions, choices. The postmodernists have not driven out realist metaphysicians. They only accurately record that, there being no social reality, life offers no grist for those metaphysicians' mill.

This loss of meaning does not only consist of philosophers' influential expositions of "the death of God;" nor is it simply the consequence of intellectual trends such as those the encyclical enumerates. Rather, an analysis of the concomitant disintegration of the social foundations illuminates the social, relational nature of meaninglessness, especially realism's dependence on the principles of complex social unity, exclusive and externally contrastive homogeneity of social forms, their repetition and hierarchical order. Without the forms that make possible lower level distinctions, there is nothing to give content to higher order reality. Each thing in life becomes utterly unique and trivial, the same as every other thing. Unless the lower order can give forth weighty contrasts greater than the individual – contrasts which only real forms can elucidate – the ultimate values of which *Fides et Ratio* speaks cannot dissolve this life's differences into unity. Without the transcendent forms and the contrasts that emanate from within the Great Vertical Order, metaphysics cannot ask the Big Questions or see the Big Picture.

Science *per se* need not devalue humanity, undermining its self-confidence, but when carried out within a culture of part-selves divorced from substantive, genuinely social articulation, science interprets its models of reality in the only social terms that scientists know, those of ultimately relational meaninglessness.[21] For a culture to see the forms' reality and thus be drawn to contemplate it, people, even scientists, must have social verification of that reality in their lives. The wellspring of such recognition is direct experience in the corporate social bond and in a society replete with such forms, above all the corporate family. The highest meaning in life is non-referential membership, radical identification of the self with others in the social bond at a transcendent level.

The Encyclical's Challenge to Philosophers

In the modern, dualist social order the family continues on, hardly distinguishable as a family, in two types: first, the disembedded and unattached nuclear family, a remnant of the traditional corporate family; and second, the legally constructed or contractual family. While to Westerners these two may not seem mutually exclusive, in effect the one is sustained by socially and semantically thin moral bonds, the other by formal Law, and these two principles are irreconcilable. In lacking the corporate family's key attributes which we have outlined, these two modern kinds of family provide a useful summary of why the corporate family is essential to realist metaphysics. And they confirm that the properties of the corporate family we have reviewed are not arbitrary. Without any of these attributes the abstract, comprehensive and unitary form cannot be real, and thus cannot foster the three dimensions of realist metaphysics we have reviewed.

As for the legally-constructed family, we have already elaborated its deficiencies in our discussion of how nature was replaced by formal Law. Let us turn then, briefly, to the nuclear family which we now realize cannot meet realist metaphysics' requirements of a higher order form, particularly the form's several dimensions of transcendence, its abstraction, intricate interiority, and its ability to draw the individual's identity – and that of living society as a whole – into a higher, more comprehensive reality. It is true that the nuclear family's simplicity comprises a self-referencing interior. But most nuclear families today have no closure, making this interiority a sham. Without boundary they also lack an external environment, and therefore cannot constitute their own internal truth domains or acquire permanence. Above all, their stark simplicity precludes the key requirement of value, a combination of unity in variation, identity, and structured, substantive contrast off against complex likenesses outside. Recall that a vital aspect of the society organized on the Great Vertical Order is that it provides each family, each collective level and each autonomous order with a complex, structured external environment. Indeed, each higher level constitutes the complex environment of the subsystems within it.

A society made up of nuclear families, even healthy, intact ones not depending on law for their cohesion, comprises contrasts between individuals, but not essential contrasts between groups oriented toward patterned forms larger than the individual. In the order based on the corporate family, the primary social forms' very texture and weight, and the fact that society definitively confirms their reality in virtually every interaction in daily life, establishes being apart from thinking – so much so that thought has to constantly adjust itself to being, recognizing the latter's upper hand. Being is given. In a society of nuclear families the shoe is on the other foot: there is no social reality – no being – apart from thought. Does this not negate the fundamental condition for realist metaphysics?

How would a Thomist theologian or philosopher knowing only a society and culture made up of nuclear families fathom the heart of the Creed, "and became man"? Not in the same way as a theologian or philosopher embedded in real corporate families and transcendent Great Vertical Orders. How could a theologian or philosopher on this side of dualism possibly grasp what his medieval colleague understood by the Papacy, the Magisterium, the priesthood descended from Melchizedek, the Dominican Order, or even St. Agnes' parish? Were our counterparts from the other side of dualism here today, what would they understand of the University of Paris? The Thomistic Institute? Even, indeed, the Notre Dame football team?

Jesus was a Jew of the ancient corporate tradition. So were the evangelists and St. Paul who tell us about him. So were Plato, Aristotle, Moses and Elijah. St. Thomas wrote from within such a social foundation. Possibly John Paul II has, as well. Now we hear them exhorting us to return our society and culture to a metaphysics finely fit to that type of social organization but utterly foreign to ours.[22] They exhort us to imbue realism, and confidence in reason and the intelligibility of the universe, into a culture founded on legal reality's artificial paste-up jobs – a culture that has virtually no acquaintance with a natural social reality made up of interdependent, standard parts appearing in collective patterns and hierarchies. Jesus, Thomas and John Paul II exhort us to restore a concern for the Big Questions of life to a social void that evinces no natural commonalities across space and knows no traditive inheritance through time.

How can this be done? We face a vast "disconnect" between realist metaphysics' social requirements and our social order. We non-philosophers whom you our brothers are to transform are contractually-organized individuals. Ivory tower philosophy may be relatively autonomous of its social matrix, but philosophy as a cornerstone of our common good cannot be. How can you lift us up to participate in realist metaphysics' sublime vision? In a recent homily Rev. Ashley quoted the wisdom of the scholastics: "A thing is received according to the mode of the recipient." We join with Rev. Elders in closing his paper, "Come, Holy Spirit!"

Notes

1. I wish to begin by thanking Ralph McInerny for reading a draft of this paper and offering me suggestions.

2. I owe these observations and a great part of the underpinnings of this paper to my friend and inspiration Russell Hittinger, who, however, should bear no blame for its errors.

3. Cf. *Fides et Ratio*, §5, 47, 56, 81, 83, 92, 99, 102, 103.

4. In particular see Pinckaers, Servais, O.P., *The Sources of Christian Ethics*, trans. Sr. Mary Thomas Noble, O.P. (Washington, DC, Catholic University Press of America, 1995), pp. 229–43, 247–53, 267–73 *et passim*.

5. Pinckaers, *Sources of Christian Ethics*, pp 432–35.

6. Confucianism, the culture of corporate families par excellence, is not one known for metaphysics.

7. Benedict Ashley, O.P., *Theologies of the Body* (Braintree, MA: Pope John XXIII Medical-Moral Research and Educational Center, 1995), pp. 510–11.

8. We rule out of our concept of "social corporation" the Western business firm and government bureaucracies because they are instrumentally (hence legally) based, rather than morally. This is not true of capitalist firms and government agencies in all cultures. In light of our analysis here, the very existence of the Roman Catholic Church in the modern world is an anomaly. Now that the corporate family has disappeared from Western culture, the Church alone keeps alive there a model of living and viable corporate sociation. Most of the main attacks on her orthodoxy are associated with repudiation of her corporateness. But at least for now her loyal members remain imbued with the corporate structure's patterns. It is interesting to watch orthodox Catholic clergy and laymen defend the Church in these matters, as without being social scientists themselves many of them "instinctively" understand the basic principles of transcendent, no-exit, morally-bound sociation. Although in the context of this Thomistic Institute the corporate family that we elucidate here may suggest the European middle ages, these forms are by no means exclusive to that culture. They flourish today in many parts of the world, even providing the basis for exuberant types of capitalism.

9. That any particular family endures forever is incumbent upon each generation of living members. But even if its genealogy reaches an end, with no one to keep it "alive," no particular family ever "dies." It may disappear from the human community but not from existence.

10. Ashley, *Theologies of the Body*, p. 308. The emphasis has been added. See his fascinating analysis of interiority and transcendence in natural processes, Chapters 7 and 8.

11. Charles Peirce's tripartite classification of signs corresponds to some of the sociological analysis presented here. Cf. his *Elements of Logic*, in Collected Papers, eds. C. Hartshorne and P. Weiss, 2 vols. (Harvard University Press, Cambridge, Massachusetts, 1932), vol. 1, p. 143.

12. For understanding these questions from the analytical base of social psychology I am grateful to my friend John Turner. See his *Rediscovering the Social Group* (Oxford University Press, 1988), pp. 46–53.

13. Our knowledge of how we identify with groups into which we are placed without consent and without gain, often arbitrarily, owes a great debt to the French thinker Henri Tajfel.

14. Turner, *Rediscovering the Social Group*, p. 52

15. I am indebted to the late and extremely unusual anthropologist Roy Rappaport for helping me understand some of these ideas, both through personal correspondence and through his book *Ecology, Meaning, and Religion* (Berkeley: North Atlantic Books, 1979).

16. Darwin's explication of the open-ended dynamism and unexpected change in nature's lower levels (freedom), his confirmation of stability in levels above the species, his interest in natural classification's homologous forms, and his clarification of the real-world functions of basic morphological indicators place him directly in the epistemological tradition of the corporate family's Great Vertical Orders.

17. Ashley, *Theologies of the Body*, pp. 150, 154, 157–64, 204–5 *et passim.*

18. Ashley, *Theologies of the Body*, pp. 159–72. Rev. Pinckaers' discussion of the distortions of morality in the hands of legalists traces out a related dualism. See Pinckaers, *Sources of Christian Ethics*, pp. 230–34, 244–53, 267–72.

19. In various works the late Professor Robert Nisbet has traced the coincidence of the hollowing out of the Great Vertical Orders' intermediate structures, the centralization of political power (the polarization of society), epistemological nominalism, and the release of materialism and self-centeredness from the previous tension in which they had been held by moral bonds, a tension that had previously enabled both to make highly creative contributions to European culture. Cf. Robert Nisbet, *Quest for Community* (New York, Oxford University Press, 1953), pp. 80–191. See also his essay "State and Family," in *Social Change*, ed. R. Nisbet (New York: Harper and Row, 1972), pp. 190–210.

20. Pinckaers, Sources of *Christian Ethics*, p. 436. Underline added.

21. At the same time – and philosophers should be warned – dualism enhances universality and certainty. Without the corporate family's multi-referential epistemology, rooted in analogy and ambiguity, and without the significance and freedom that the Great Vertical Orders give to particularity, universality becomes King.

22. The Pope also calls you metaphysicians to restore in your own academic discipline confidence in reason and in the intelligibility of nature, and professional dedication to the Great Questions of life. This paper suggests that the trends in philosophy which John Paul II would have you combat, maybe including analytical philosophy, probably constitute systems of ideas particularly well suited to Western culture's currently fragmented and legalized social order. If so, how then can we explain the existence of this meeting and of the Thomist philosophers here? In terms of cultural lag? As artifacts of a dead culture? As a coming-together of refugees fed in the desert by the troglodyte Church that has somehow managed to live on in its cave? Rev. Sherwin urges me to extend the present analysis to a summary of the minimal social preconditions for realist metaphysics, perhaps preconditions for but a small band of survivors. It is beyond the ability of this paper to respond to his challenging criticism. But one encouraging ethnographical note is in order: In this paper we have insisted that an entire society has to be structured on the corporate family and Great Vertical Orders if realist metaphysics is to flourish. While the overseas Chinese hardy count as metaphysicians, their hearty cultures in various non-Chinese societies in southeast Asia abound with realist lay people. In these cases the "outside" or external "environment" which we found so indispensable in our analysis comprises the non-Chinese culture in which the overseas Chinese find themselves, in some cases not structured on Great Vertical Orders. This would suggest that an enclave of realists, such as Roman Catholics in the contemporary West, may not only survive but thrive in an unstructured, alien environment – if, that is, it can maintain strong boundaries between it and the outside. To this end the overseas Chinese enjoy numerous socio-cultural distinctions helping to maintain their boundaries, distinctions that do not separate European and American Catholics from their secular milieu.

Technology and Wisdom:
Metaphysical Stakes of the Information Society
Louis Chammings

The goal of the encyclical *Fides et Ratio* is to recall the nature and the conditions of a true Christian wisdom, which depends on reason as well as it depends on faith: "Faith and reason are like two wings on which the human spirit rises to the contemplation of truth" (FR §1). What kind of wisdom the present age requires is obviously a central question in *Fides et Ratio*. In fact, this question has been an everpresent concern of John Paul II and his immediate predecessors. Thus, it is no surprise to find within this encyclical echoes from *Redemptor hominis*, the first encyclical letter of John Paul II, and from *Gaudium et Spes* of Vatican II. Addressing the current "drama of the separation of faith and reason," John-Paul II writes :

> It should also be borne in mind that the role of philosophy itself has changed in modern culture. From universal wisdom and learning, it has been gradually reduced to one of the many fields of human knowing; indeed in some ways it has been consigned to a wholly marginal role. Other forms of rationality have acquired an ever higher profile, making philosophical learning appear all the more peripheral. These forms of rationality are directed not towards the contemplation of truth and the search for the ultimate goal and meaning of life; but instead, as "instrumental reason," they are directed – actually or potentially – towards the promotion of utilitarian ends, towards enjoyment or power (§47).

I would like to use this statement to confront the *metaphysical* implications of the powerful development of communication and information technologies which constitute the basis of our modern Information Society. More specifically, I would like to examine how far, and in which way, this so-called information society entails "another form of rationality" which deserves the qualification of "instrumental reason."

In order to clarify for purposes of our discussion the character of the current situation, I want to recall briefly a few statements from John Paul II's

Fides et Ratio. I will offer little direct commentary but let the clarion voice of John Paul II be heard unimpeded.

> The man of today seems ever to be under threat from what he produces, that is to say from the result of the work of his hands and, even more so, of the work of his intellect and the tendencies of his will (§47).

> Science would thus be poised to dominate all aspects of human life through technological progress. The undeniable triumphs of scientific research and contemporary technology have helped to propagate a scientistic outlook, which now seems boundless, given its inroads into different cultures and the radical changes it has brought. . . . This leads to the impoverishment of human thought, which no longer addresses the ultimate problems which the human being, as the *animal rationale*, has pondered constantly from the beginning of time. And since it leaves no space for the critique offered by ethical judgement, the scientistic mentality has succeeded in leading many to think that if something is technically possible it is therefore morally admissible. . . . The consequences of this are clear: in practice, the great moral decisions of humanity are subordinated to decisions taken one after another by institutional agencies. Moreover, anthropology itself is severely compromised by a one-dimensional vision of the human being, a vision which excludes the great ethical dilemmas and the existential analyses of the meaning of suffering and sacrifice, of life and death (§88).

> It remains true that a certain positivist cast of mind continues to nurture the illusion that, thanks to scientific and technical progress, man and woman may live as a demiurge, single-handedly and completely taking charge of their destiny (§91).

The solution to this crisis of positivism and its "one-dimensional" view of the human person is the recovery of a genuine philosophy – one that engages in the search for the "ultimate and overarching meaning of life." This "sapiential" dimension is required in view of the phenomenal growth in "humanity's technical capability" and concomitant blindness to the horizon of ultimate values. John Paul II warns us: "If this technology is not ordered to something greater than a merely utilitarian end, then it could soon prove inhuman and even become a potential destroyer of the human race" (§81). The search for ultimate meaning, however, requires that one can know truth. Thus, the second part of this solution is the verification, over against the claims of relativist philosophy, of our capacity to reach objective truth, the *adaequatio* of the thing and the intellect. Finally, these two aspects imply a third: "the need for a philosophy of genuinely metaphysical range, capable, that is, of transcending empirical data in order to attain something absolute, ultimate and foundational in its search for truth" (§83).

What is at stake in the Information Society?

No one today could doubt that we are living in a time of great change. The "revolution in information technologies" of the early 1970s has affected the shape of our economies and our societies. These technologies have "transformed the way we live, work, produce, consume, communicate, travel, think, enjoy, make war and peace, give birth, and die. It has also transformed, as have all major technological revolutions, the material foundations of human life, time, and space."[1] The resulting "information society" has become the very definition of the latest stage of an economically developed society, whose activities and institutions are based upon the use and development of information and communication technologies. Manuel Castells describes a city – an "informational city" – in this type of society as "an urban system with sociospatial structure and dynamics determined by a reliance of wealth, power, and culture, on knowledge and information processing in global networks, managed and organized through intensive use of information and communication technologies."[2]

Since communication as well as information is involved in the definition of the information society, there are two main dimensions to be considered: first, the social dimension, related to the communicational aspect; and second, an *intellectual* or *cognitive* dimension, related to the informational aspect. The analysis of information and communication is commonly based upon Shannon and Weaver's *Mathematical Theory of Communication.*[3] Their theory, however, is far more concerned with the conditions of transmission of messages than with their content. Hence, their concept of information is essentially related to the technical bearings of transmission. That is to say, the "semantic aspects of communication do not depend on its technological aspects."[4]

Shannon's Model Diagram

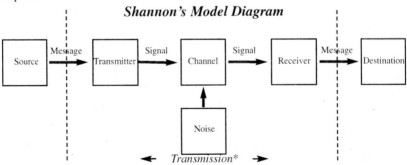

*"Transmission" here (from transmitter to receiver) is not communication itself, but only its material support.

Physically, a situation of communication is characterized by the presence of a *transmitter*, a *receiver*, and a signal sent out from the transmitter toward the receiver. This diagram must be completed by pointing out that there is someone transmitting who is the *source* of information, someone who is the *destination* receiving, and some message is what is being transmitted. The signal is transmitted through a *channel*, in which it is more or less randomly distorted by *noise*. The diagram does not indicate the important notion of *code*, which allows the message to be inscribed in the signal. The first point to be understood here is that communication is a process oriented from the transmitter to the receiver, that entails the idea of *reversibility* and the possibility of *feed-back*, the receiver becoming transmitter and *vice-versa*. The second point to underscore is that there is a splitting of the process into 1) the physical dimension of the transmission of the signal, and 2) the "informational" dimension of the communication of the message.

Man needs society not only for his material wants but also for his spiritual existence and development. As individuals, people need a marketplace for exchanging economic goods. But as persons, they need communication for exchanging "soul goods." Communication, as expressing the spiritual nature of the person, is oriented to its development. Any philosophy of communication presupposes a particular anthropology.

Central to the study of communication is the sign or symbol. According to Aristotle, "spoken words are the symbols of mental experience and written words are the symbols of spoken words."[5] Signs and symbols can be *material*, but the sense or meaning of "mental experience" is definitely *immaterial*. Now we are ready to give a definition for communication: communication is "an exchange of the content of mental experience through articulated signs or symbols." On the other hand, we can take into account the common definition in which communication is simply the "exchange of information."

Information defined analogically can mean 1) the content of mental experience, as exchangeable in communication. This definition stems from the combination of the two definitions above. It can also mean 2) what is dealt with by computers and is flowing through networks. This second meaning is the one implied in the expression "information society." Now, if we wish to express the relationship between those two meanings, we can propose that "information" in the second sense is a sign (or symbol) of "information" in the first.

To "in-form" means to give form. As a matter of fact, information is related to Aristotelian form. But we must keep in consideration the two modalities of the existence of the form: first, as the *"entitative"* form, it is the immaterial part of the existing thing; second, as the *"intentional"* form, or *"cognitive"* form, it constitutes the content of the concept abstracted from the thing through the knowing process. Considered as the immaterial content of communication, or as knowledge (sense 1), information is intentional or cognitive form. Considered as the material object of computing (sense 2), information is the sign (or symbol) of cognitive form.

Anthropological and Metaphysical Consequences

Computers and networks, including software as well as hardware, are material things. Thus, they are *materially* handling, by means of signs, something *immaterial*; namely, the cognitive forms, which are the content of mental experience. Here is the reason of their powerful and dangerous ambiguity.

My purpose here is to point out the "metaphysical" consequences of this fact through a short review of a few typical statements. But, before doing so, it is necessary to mention first the most worrying and urgent result of the current development of information and communication technologies, which is both social and economical: the widening gap between the "info-rich" and the "info-poor."

> Prevailing trends, however, cloud what could be an exhilarating moment for humankind, opening up extraordinary possibilities for material prosperity and spiritual fulfillment, with the inducement of social exclusion in parallel to social development, deepening existing patterns of sociospatial segregation. These trends are rooted in powerful processes of economic globalization and capitalist restructuring that use to their advantage the potential of new information technologies, conditioning the social trajectory of technological change. . . Thus, the emerging, informational city is by and large a dual city. . . . By dual city, I understand an urban system socially and spatially polarized between high value-making groups and functions on the one hand and devalued social groups and downgraded spaces on the other hand. This polarization induces increasing integration of the social and spatial core of the urban system, at the same time that it fragments devalued spaces and groups, and threatens them with social irrelevance.[6]

There is a strong interconnection between the scientific and technical character of our civilization, and its nominalistic mentality. As a result of this nominalism, on the one hand, the concept of "substance" is regarded as plainly meaningless; and on the other hand, the concept of matter is itself mistaken for substance. The two examples below are evidence of this confusion.

> Governments of the Industrial World, you weary giants of flesh and steel, I come from Cyberspace, the new home of Mind. On behalf of

the future, I ask you of the past to leave us alone. You are not welcome among us. You have no sovereignty where we gather. . . .Cyberspace consists of transactions, relationships, and thought itself, arrayed like a standing wave in the web of our communications. Ours is a world that is both everywhere and nowhere, but it is not where bodies live. . . . Your legal concepts of property, expression, identity, movement, and context do not apply to us. They are based on matter. There is no matter here.[7]

Thinking on this condition of immateriality, H. P. Kainz, Jr. brings together the categories of artificial intelligence and angels. He examines Aquinas' theory of separate substances and finds "some interesting analogies to contemporary computer technology." He is not hopeful that such comparisons will be able to revive interest in Angelology. Yet he supposes that those interested in the "metaphysics of the mind-body problem" will find the following comparisons "suggestive:"

Microprocessors and Angelic Self-possession
ROM and Innate Ideas
RAM and the Negative Active Potency of Separate Substances
Hard Drives and Intellectual Memory
The Operating System and the Reception of Information
Software and Habitually Acquired Species
"Downward Compatibility" and Proportional Universality
Multitasking
Modems and the Ability to Transfer Information
Networks and the Transmission of Ideas, via Hierarchies
Speed-caches and the Effect of Immateriality

The immateriality of angels does not itself render such comparisons dubious. As Kainz goes on to note, the "immateriality" of angels was an issue of considerable debate among medieval and patristic authors.

Augustine and Origen had speculated about the possibility of angelic bodies being composed of matter, albeit a more "subtle" matter. Duns Scotus gave lip-service to the received doctrine of angelic incorporeality, but challenged his readers' imagination by theorizing that angels must have some kind of "incorporeal" matter; and, consistently with this theory, Duns Scotus thought that angels must reason discursively in some fashion. If there were any kind of matter in angels – subtle or "incorporeal" – the leap from completely immaterial beings to partly material beings would be less formidable, and the analogy between angelic spontaneous instananeity and the linear, sequential operations of computers would be even closer.[8]

Pierre Lévy's prospect is different. In his view, cyberspace is the basis for the emergence of a *collective mind.* He explicitly refers to the medieval theories of *"Intellectus Agens"* coming from Al-Farabi, Ibn Sina, and Maimonides.[9]

> The concept of *collective intelligence* refers to intelligences distributed everywhere, active everywhere, valorized everywhere, coordinated and placed into synergy. In my mind, that is the best use the cyberspace can be put into. . . .Through a kind of spiralling return to the orality of origins, knowledge could once again be carried by living human collectivities rather than by separate material bases. With the difference that this time the immediate carrier of knowledge would no longer be the physical community with its carnal memory but cyberspace, the region of virtual worlds through the intermediation of which this community would recognize its objects, and itself as a collective intelligence. . . . As a remedy to the present situation, virtual worlds of *collective intelligence* will see the development of new forms of writing: animated pictograms, moving languages that will preserve traces of their interaction with navigators. By itself, the *collective memory* will organize itself, unfold itself anew for each navigator according to his interests and his previous traversings of the virtual world. The new space of signs will be sensitive, active, intelligent, at the service of its explorers. . . . The task of the collective intelligence is to discover, or to invent, the other side of writing, the other side of language, so that the manipulation of information would be distributed everywhere, coordinated everywhere, that it would no longer be the privilege of separate social organs but, on the contrary, would be naturally integrated into every human activity, as a tool in the hands of everyone. This new dimension of communication should evidently permit the mutuality of our knowledge and the reciprocity of its transmission which is the most rudimentary condition of the collective intelligence.[10]

The virtualization of cyberspace, i.e., the delocalization and dematerialization of the social space of communication, leads to some disincarnation in social relationships. In the ancient Greek theatre, the term "person" referred to a mask, the fictional projection. The person could be identified as a character played by clones or avatars, as it is the case already in network games. Cyberspace could become a new compulsory social space, like a virtual stage where everyone would have to play his part. In spite of the wide range of possibilities offered in its autonomy by the intrinsic interactivity of cyberspace, the person would then be deprived of any capability to attain truth. Appearances and reality have in this case become separated.

One of the numerous modern idolatries consists in overvaluation of images, which serve as substitutes for things. So much so that one could designate our society as "the civilization of image." For instance, computing signs are only sequences of 0 and 1 (or other symbols) which do not represent anything, and consequently are of no psychological interest for people. But images are signs similar to the things of which they are signs. They can, therefore, be substitutes for things. Ordinary things ("substances") like pizzas cannot be digitized, but pictures can be: that is the very reason why they hold the first and most strategic place in cyberspace.

Conclusion

By means of information and communication technologies, an information society materially manages the immaterial objects of the human soul. This fact is not bad in itself, but it is both powerful and dangerous. It creates by itself an urgent call for the contemporary man to reach a true wisdom including a much higher sense of reality metaphysically grounded in the "intuition of being." It is a general consequence of the nominalism permeating our scientific and technical culture that metaphysics has no place. We have become incapable of thinking correctly about real things: God, soul, and substance. Given the fact that "no God, no soul, no substance" are precisely the prerequisites of Buddhist doctrine, it should not be surprising that Buddhism is the primary challenger – the dominant alternative – to Christianity in our "civilization of image." Thus, John Paul II appeals to philosophers to

> explore more comprehensively the dimensions of the true, the good and the beautiful to which the word of God gives access. This task becomes all the more urgent if we consider the challenges which the new millennium seems to entail, and which affect in a particular way regions and cultures which have a long-standing Christian tradition. [Moreover] This attention to philosophy too should be seen as a fundamental and original contribution in service of the new evangelization (§103).

For those who wonder about the role of philosophy in serving the word of God, John Paul II reminds us that

> [p]hilosophical thought is often the only ground for understanding and dialogue with those who do not share our faith. The current ferment in philosophy demands of believing philosophers an attentive and competent commitment, able to discern the expectations, the points of openness and the key issues of this historical moment. . . . A philosophy in which there shines even a glimmer of the truth of

Christ, the one definitive answer to humanity's problems, will provide a potent underpinning for the true and planetary ethics which the world now needs (§104).

Notes

1. M. Castells, "The Informational City is a Dual City: Can It Be Reversed?" on the Web at http://web.mit.edu/sap/www/high-low/1castells.html.

2. Castells, "The Informational City."

3. University of Illinois Press, 1949.

4. From the French edition, *Théorie mathématique de la communication* (Paris: Retz, 1975), p. 37.

5. Aristotle, *On Interpretation* I.

6. Castells, "The Informational City."

7. John Perry Barlow, "A Declaration of the Independence of Cyberspace" (Davos, 1996), on-line.

8. H.P. Kainz, Jr. "Artificial Intelligence and Angelology," (Marquette University), on-line.

9. Pierre Lévy, *l'intelligence collective* (Paris: La Découverte, 1994), p. 96.

10. Pierre Lévy, *Toward Superlanguage*, translated from the French by Riikka Stewen (on-line).

Global Warming and Nuclear Power
Peter E. Hodgson

It may seem surprising to see a talk with this title in a Symposium on *Fides et Ratio*. My justification in presenting these reflections, as a physicist, is that faith and reason are intimately involved in scientific research, and science is an integral part of the, journey which has led humanity down the centuries to meet and engage truth more deeply" (§1). For "the more human beings know reality and the world, the more they know themselves in their uniqueness," so that "all that is the object of our knowledge becomes a part of our life" (§1). Furthermore, it is the duty of the Church "to serve humanity in different ways, but one way in particular imposes responsibility of a quite special kind: the diakonia of the truth" (§2). Thus the believing community is "a partner in humanity's shared struggle to arrive at truth" and this "obliges the believing community to proclaim the truths arrived at" (§2).

Although "the desire for truth is part of human nature itself" (§3) and "has driven so many enquiries, especially in the scientific field" (§25), it is not easy to satisfy that desire. It may therefore be useful to recall the methods developed in the sciences, as they may provide analogies with those employed in wider and deeper problems.

When physicists are faced with an impossibly complicated problem we start by making a model. That is, we find a much simpler system, amenable to mathematical analysis, that is in some respects similar to the problem we are tackling. Thus, if we want to understand the atomic nucleus, we compare it with a confined gas, a drop of liquid, or even a cloudy crystal ball.[1] We then analyze the model quantum mechanically, and calculate its measurable properties. Choosing appropriate values of the parameters of the model, we often find surprisingly good agreement with experimental results. A good model also has considerable productive power. We may find some disagreements that stimulate us to make the model more sophisticated. By combining several models we gradually build up our understanding of the nucleus, and this is so reliable that it provides the basis of large industries.

In a similar way we can use the interplay of faith and reason in scientific research as a model for their interplay in theology. It is often fruitful to transpose a theological problem into a corresponding scientific context; this often indicates how it may be solved. Thus, as Thomas Aquinas recognized, "nature, philosophy's proper concern, could contribute to the understanding of Divine Revelation" (§43).

Thus, if a skeptic challenges the assertion that "God is one and God is three" on arithmetical grounds, I can easily point out that this is a shallow misunderstanding. But if he goes on to ask me why I believe this statement, I find it difficult to answer. The skeptic may go on to say that in theology we accept absurdities because we are subservient to authority, whereas in science we believe as a result of a rational process. To this I can reply that the ways to God and the road of science are not so dissimilar as he thinks.[2] If indeed in science we relied purely on deductive reasoning, we still have to justify our initial premises and these require an act of faith. Furthermore, science is rarely an exercise in deductive reasoning; it is altogether a more complex process that is quite similar to the process leading to assent in theology. "There is thus a profound and indissoluble unity between the knowledge of reason and the knowledge of faith" (§16). The results of reasoning "acquire their full meaning only if they are within the larger horizon of faith" (§20).

First of all, science is itself based on very special beliefs namely that the natural world is rational, orderly, contingent and open to the human mind. They may appear quite obvious to us, but in the context of the whole of human history they form a unique set that was provided for the first time in history by Catholic theology during the High Middle Ages. This enables us to understand why science achieved its first viable birth at that time.[3] It is also the basis of the confidence of scientists that "they will find an answer. . . . They do not judge their original intuition useless simply because they have not reached their goal; rightly enough they will say that they have not yet found a satisfactory answer" (§29).

Science cannot be deduced from these beliefs about the natural world. It is a creation of the human mind that is constantly checked against our experiences. This if, for example, I am asked why I believe a particular scientific result, such as the Lorentz transformation in special relativity, I could produce a rational argument from certain very plausible premises and experimental results. This may or may not be found convincing, but it certainly does not convey the full justification of the belief. At best, it evokes a notional assent. If, however, we examine the arguments in more detail, we find that many different lines of thought converge to the same conclusion; so that if we want to deny the Lorentz transformation, we have to deny a whole range of beliefs that we would not otherwise dream of denying, as shown in the Figure (facing page).[4] A full understanding of this can induce a real assent. Theoretical physics is a very tightly-interlocking set of beliefs, and it cannot be fitted into the straightjacket of simple logical deduction. Conviction in science, as in theology, comes from what Newman called the unity of indirect reference.[5]

Newman, in his *Grammar of Assent*, was concerned to justify the faith of ordinary Catholics who may not be particularly well educated nor able to enunciate a rational argument. He found it in the convergence of numerous indications, each individually inconclusive, but cumulatively convincing. This gives real assent, in contrast to the notional assent attained by logical reasoning.

We might at this point object that there are many scientific theories such as Newtonian dynamics (and the associated Galilean transformation) that are widely supported and firmly believed, but which are now recognized to be wrong. This is to mistake the nature of scientific progress. Newton's dynamics remains valid in its domain, but Einstein showed how it must be modified for velocities comparable with that of light. The Galilean transformation is obtained as the limit of the Lorentz transformation as v/c tends to zero. In a similar way theological beliefs develop, increasing in depth and scope without rendering previous beliefs invalid.[6]

A further example of the process of coming to believe is provided by global warming. Once again this is not a simple rational argument but the accumulation of individual indications. The final conclusion is potentially of great importance for humanity. We are forced ask what actions should be taken by the State, whether the Church should concern itself with such questions and the responsibilities of scientists. Certainly, "the immense expansion of humanity's technical capacity demands a renewed and sharpened sense of ultimate values. If this technology is not ordered to something greater than a merely utilitarian end, then it would soon prove inhuman and even become potential destroyer of the human race" (§81).

Global Warming

The arguments for global warming are quite familiar. It has long been known that due to extensive burning of the fossil fuels such as wood, coal, and oil the concentration of carbon dioxide in the atmosphere is steadily increasing. This gas acts like the glass in a greenhouse: it lets the sun's rays through but blocks the secondary radiation. As a result, the earth warms up, the Antarctic icecap melts and the level of the sea rises, inundating coastal regions. While many of us would welcome a warmer climate, there may be other unpredictable climate changes.

There are other gases that contribute to the greenhouse effect, in particular methane, nitrous oxide and the chlorofluorocarbons (CFS). The last two of these are far more damaging per molecule than carbon dioxide. The concentrations of these gases are increasing annually by 0.4% for carbon dioxide, 1.2% for methane, 0.3% for nitrous oxide and 6% for CFS.

There has been much argument about the reality of global warming, and I must admit that as I have not worked in that area of research, I am not competent to form a judgment. Indeed, I have been rather skeptical for a number of reasons that I need not summarize here. However, I recently had an opportunity to discuss the matter with Sir John Houghton, who is the Chairman of the Intergovernmental Panel for Climate Change. I put all my reasons to him, and he was able to give quite convincing answers. Furthermore, the weight of scientific opinion, as given in the Report of the Intergovernmental Panel on Climate Change, is that the earth will warm by 1 to 3.5 degrees Centigrade in the next century, causing a rise in sea level of about 50 cm.[7] Thus, on the whole I am now inclined to accept that there is good reason to accept global warming as quite likely.

It will be noticed that this is a probability argument that relies greatly on informed judgment of a vast mass of data by a large number of scientists. This is quite typical of many scientific problems and completely different from what we are often told about scientific questions being answered by definitive experiments that give clear-cut answers.

There are, many more truth which are simply believed than truths which are acquired by way of personal verification. Who, for instance, could asses critically the countless scientific findings upon which modern life is based? Who could personally examine the flow of information which comes day after day from all parts of the world and which is generally accepted as true? Who in the end could forge anew the paths of experience and thought which have yielded the treasures of human wisdom and religion? This means that the human being – the one who seeks the truth – is also *the one who lives by belief'* (§31).

Anyone unconvinced by the arguments for global warming can consider the other products of burning fossil fuels which include sulphur dioxide, nitrous oxide and whole range of noxious substances. These fall as acid rain and pollute the lakes and forests so heavily that the fishes and the trees die. They pollute the air we breathe, increase respiratory diseases and shorten our lives.

Apart from these immediate consequences, a rise in the global temperature may produce far-reaching changes in the earth's climate. We may already be seeing some of these effects in the warmer weather in some countries and the floods and droughts in others. On the longer term, a rise in sea level will practically eliminate many low-lying countries such as Bangladesh and many islands in the Pacific and Indian oceans, and severely reduce the areas of many others, including Holland and England, with devastating consequences for the people living there. We have a serious moral obligation to tackle these questions before it is too late.[8]

This problem will now be considered under three headings: First, what are the possible ways to reduce global warming, and what is their relative effectiveness; second, what are Governments doing about it; and third, what is the Church doing about it.

The Ways to Reduce Global Warming

Global warming can be reduced by replacing fossil fuel power stations, and by curtailing other industrial and domestic activities. Removing fossil fuel power stations will greatly reduce the power available, so we have to learn to use less power, or find other ways of generating the needed electricity, or some combination of the two. The general experience is that in spite of exhortations to use less and to increase efficiency, the consumption of power still rises. It is, therefore, extremely difficult to reduce the demand. Exhortation is useless in the long run. An effective way is simply to increase the price, but this bears most heavily on the poor and on those living in rural areas, and would make our industries uncompetitive compared with other countries with cheap power.

The only really satisfactory way is to increase the non-fossil ways of producing power. Let us consider them in turn. Hydroelectricity is already fully developed in the major industrial countries and is limited by the availability of suitable rivers. The renewable sources, principally wind and solar, are very popular; but in spite of intensive development for many decades, they still produce a minuscule amount of power. Thus, for example, in Britain the contribution of wind power, the most promising of the renewables, to our electricity production is 0.16% This can and will be increased, but there are serious difficulties to be overcome such as the public opposition to very large numbers of windmills and the uncertain cost. It is thus very unlikely that wind can make a major contribution to energy needs in the foreseeable future.

What is left? There is nuclear power, already written off in some quarters as a has-been. But what is the reality? Nuclear reactors provide about 20% of the world's electricity. In France, they provide about 80% and in Western Europe as a whole about 50%. Since nuclear reactors produce practically no carbon dioxide, it is no surprise that countries with a large nuclear program have achieved the largest reductions in carbon dioxide emissions. Thus, since 1970, France has reduced them by 50%, Japan (32% nuclear) by 20% and the USA (20% nuclear) by 6%. The emission of noxious gases like sulphur dioxide is also dramatically reduced by going nuclear.

The British Government has set a target of a 10% cut in the period from 1990 to 2010. By 1995, a reduction of 6% had been achieved, and this is due to the increase in nuclear output by 39% from 1990 to 1994. However, if no more nuclear power stations are built, this is set to rise steeply in subsequent years as the older nuclear power stations retire, and the Government will find it impossible to reach its target. Many new gas power stations are now being built, and these emit only half the amount of carbon dioxide as coal power stations. However, this is offset by the leakage of methane, which has a global warming potential about sixty times that of carbon dioxide. The net effects of these two byproducts are about the same, and so no reduction in global warming is to be expected from the switch to gas power stations. Even if this effect is neglected, then if gas increases to 43.5% while coal declines to 2.5% we can expect a 10% reduction is carbon dioxide emissions, while if nuclear rises to 43.5% at the expense of coal there will be a reduction by 20%. Some recent estimates of the emission of carbon dioxide (in tons per gigawatt hour) from various power sources are: coal 870, oil 750, gas 500, nuclear 8, wind 7 and hydro 4.

It is thus difficult to see how global warming can be averted without nuclear power stations. Statistical analyses show that they are demonstrably safer than other energy sources. Surprisingly to many people, they emit less radioactivity than coal power stations, and the costs of decommissioning are relatively small. The problem of waste disposal has been solved: the radioactive fission fragments can be sealed in insoluble ceramic, put in stainless steel containers and buried deep in a stable geological formation. Long before any radioactivity can escape, it will have decayed naturally to a level similar to that in the surrounding rocks. The onus of demonstrating a better way to combat global warming lies on the opponents of nuclear power.

In order to stabilize the emission of carbon dioxide by the middle of the next century we need to replace 2000 fossil fuel power stations in the next forty years, equivalent to a rate of about one per week. Can we find 500 sq. km. each week to install 4000 windmills? Or perhaps we could cover 10 sq.km. of desert each week with solar panels and keep them always clean. Tidal power can produce large amounts of energy, but can we find a new Severn estuary and build a barrage costing £9 billion every five weeks? The same sort of question could be asked about nuclear power. The answer is that in the peak period of nuclear reactor construction in the 1980's, the average rate of construction was 23 per year, with a peak of 43 in 1983. A construction rate of one per week is thus quite practicable. It is a well-tried and reliable source, whereas the alternatives are mainly wishful thinking.

We may also reflect that if we do not solve the problem now, then it will soon be solved for us. We are living in a very special period in human history when oil, gas and coal are readily available. At present rates of consumption the oil will be gone in less than a hundred years, and the coal in about three hundred years. Fossil fuel burning will then cease and alternatives will have to be found. If we continue to burn the fossil fuels, we not only pollute our earth and bring on global warming, we also deprive future generations of these valuable materials, the bases of the petrochemical industries. Would it not be better to solve these problems now, instead of waiting until it is too late?

The conclusion is inescapable: the only practicable way to avoid global warming is by replacing fossil fuel burning power stations with nuclear power stations.

So what are governments doing about this?

Governmental Action

Most governments have accepted the arguments about the dangers of global warming, and several large international conferences, such as that at Rio in 1992 and that in Kyoto last December have been convened to discuss the issue. Governments have been asked to pledge to reduce carbon dioxide emissions by so many percent in a stated time. Of course, they are very reluctant to do so, because such actions may require very unpopular and costly decisions that are bitterly opposed by the industrial community.

The British Minister for the Environment, Michael Meacher, has recently stated that: "The Government recognizes that nuclear power assists the UK in limiting emissions of greenhouse gases, and provided that high standards of safety and environmental protection can be maintained and that decommissioning liabilities are fully funded, we believe that it will continue to be so."[9]

In spite, however, of the seriousness of the problem and the recognition of the contribution made by nuclear power in reducing carbon dioxide emission the public debate on the means to combat global warming is very different.

Sir John Houghton recently wrote an article on global warming in *Physics World*.[10] After describing the methods used to study global warming, he summarizes the ways to reduce carbon dioxide emission. "The key," he says, "lies in the rapid development and growth of renewable energy," and by this he means wind, biomass, solar, wave and tidal. He gives no figures for the energy produced in this way, although as mentioned above the contribution of the most promising of the renewables, namely wind, is still extremely small. He simply expresses the hope that the renewable energy sources will make up 12% of the total energy production by the year 2020.

He also mentions increasing the energy efficiency of coal power stations, improving the insulation of buildings, using cheap, long-life light sources, and making more efficient vehicles. All this is of course desirable, and improvements are being made continuously. All these measure are inherently costly and will take a long time to implement on a large scale. What is remarkable about the article is that there is no mention whatsoever of nuclear power. He certainly knows about it because in his book, *Global Warming*,[11] he remarks that "it has considerable attractiveness from the point of view of sustainable development because it does not produce greenhouse gas emissions." Furthermore, although "it is not strictly a renewable source, . . . the rate at which it uses up resources of radioactive material is small compared with the total resource available. . . . A further advantage of nuclear energy installations is that the technology is known: they can be built now and therefore contribute to the reduction of carbon dioxide emissions in the short term. The continued importance of nuclear energy is recognized in the WEC energy scenarios, which all assume growth in this energy source next century." He also wrote a similar article in the *Times Higher*,[12] again ignoring nuclear power.

Another article in *Science and Public Affairs* by Jim Skea is along much the same lines. He emphasizes the challenge to citizens and companies to use less energy and use less polluting sources. This will require Government actions: new taxes and regulations must be created, and people must be taxed to make them adopt greener lifestyles. New regulatory standards may be needed to enforce energy efficiency. "Increasing taxes on motor fuels will provide incentives for manufacturers to produce more efficient cars and for drivers to buy smaller cars and to drive less. But an ambitious transport policy will require many more measures administered through central government, planning authorities and private companies."[13] All these and many other taxes and regulations will induce wide-ranging social and economic changes. They know that the renewables cannot produce the energy we need, so everyone must be forced to use less by a barrage of regulations and taxes. The obvious way to produce the needed energy by environmentally benign nuclear power is not even mentioned.

If you start a discussion on these questions, and ask why nuclear power is not considered, one is inevitably told about the hazards of nuclear power, particularly the disposal of waste, the hazards of nuclear radiation, the decommissioning of nuclear reactors at the end of their useful life, and nuclear proliferation. These arguments have been comprehensively discussed over the years, particularly at the Sizewell Enquiry, but they are never accepted.

This is a truly bizarre situation. It seems that nuclear power has become a taboo subject, and one can only speculate on the reasons. Nuclear power has become anathema to the general public. For many, it is the symbol of the hated technological society, and any argument in its favor is instantly rejected.

Politicians, who look to the next election and not to the next generation, are very wary of nuclear power. If it is proposed to site a nuclear waste disposal facility in their constituency, an opposition pressure group is immediately formed. The politician tells the Minister for Energy that if this project goes forward, he may lose his seat at the next election. So the Minister cancels the project, even though it poses no hazards whatsoever. Quite recently NIREX has been refused permission even to make a test drilling to see whether a proposed disposal site is suitable or not. Then they are accused of not making any provision for nuclear waste disposal. No progress can be made in such situations.

As another example of what is called the nuclear debate, it has been argued that it is unwise to rely on thermal reactors because the world supplies of uranium will soon be exhausted. However, the possibility of developing fast reactors is dismissed as unnecessary, because there is plenty of uranium that will allow us to obtain our power needs from the existing thermal reactors.[14] It hardly needs a degree in nuclear physics or the skills of a master logician to see that there is something wrong with these arguments. The truth is that those who speak in this way have lost all touch with reality and are convinced only of the evil of nuclear power, which must therefore be opposed by any means.

In several European countries, completed nuclear power stations, built to the highest safety standards, have been refused permission to start generating power simply for political reasons.[15] There are continual demands for public enquiries whenever a new nuclear facility is proposed. When the report is published, it is immediately rejected and another enquiry demanded.

The result of all this is that the nuclear power program has been almost halted, and the coal power stations continue to pour their poisons into the atmosphere and to contribute to global warming.

Church Action

The Pope has frequently emphasized the need to care for the environment and has encouraged scientific study of this and related problems. Decisions vital for the future of humanity are being taken on political grounds, ignoring the long-term consequences. The Church is, or should be, above short-term political pressures, and is therefore in a strong position to speak out. As far as I know, there have not yet been any Church statements on global warming, but many Bishops' Conferences and other Church bodies have indeed spoken out on the question of nuclear power. These serve to illustrate some of the difficulties that are encountered.

The first requirement for such statements is that they should be based on a thorough knowledge of the scientific and technological facts. A survey[16] of Church statements on nuclear power shows, however, that in most cases they are gravely deficient; no one with any knowledge of the situation could take them seriously. They are worse than useless.

There are three exceptions to this that deserve more detailed comment.

The first is the comprehensive statement made by the U.S. bishops in 1981.[17] This was based on a good general knowledge, but nevertheless had several serious flaws. I published an analysis of that document,[18] but so far as I know it has had no effect.

The second statement was made by the Home Mission Division of the Methodist Church in Britain in 1981.[19] They assembled a group of about sixty scientists, technologists and engineers, and for several years they studied the problems not only of nuclear power, but also of many other technological developments including electronic computers and genetic engineering. Their report is a very valuable survey of modern problems. Their conclusions concerning nuclear power are:

> 1. Nuclear energy is an integral part of nature, just as much God's creation as sunshine and rain.
> 2. It does offer mankind a new energy source which is very large, convenient and not very costly.
> 3. Around the world the most important energy sources, oil in the rich world and wood in the poor, are becoming scarce, so that we cannot afford to set aside any energy technology with large potential which is cost effective, provided it is reasonably safe.
> 4. There are risks associated with the use of nuclear power, as with everything else, but these have been very carefully evaluated, are not very big and are not at all out of scale compared with risks of other energy sources and other ordinary hazards.

The third Church document on nuclear power was produced by the Pontifical Academy of Science. The Academy arranged a meeting of world energy experts in November 1980 and published the proceedings in a volume of 719 pages.[20] The final conclusions of the proceedings strike a note of urgency:

> We have no time to waste. Energy policies are urgently needed, involving concerted action by the responsible bodies, and this requires the support of public opinion and energy users. Unfortunately, even in the industrialized countries, the public consciousness of the problem is lacking. . . . Only coal and nuclear power – together with a strong energy conservation policy and continued gas and oil exploration – can allow us to effectively meet the additional needs for the next two decades.

This study was made the basis of the submission of the Holy See to the International Conference on Nuclear Power held in Vienna September 13-17, 1982.[21] The leader of the Vatican Delegation, Mgr. Peressin, referred to the peaceful applications of atomic energy, including food conservation, new techniques of plant breeding, medicine, hydrology and, most important of all, energy for industrial and private use. He reminded the Conference that many United Nations Agencies have stressed that the economic growth of the Third World countries seems "to be impossible without some applications of nuclear energy." Therefore, Mgr. Peressin continued, "my Delegation believes that all possible efforts should be made to extend to all countries, especially the developing ones, the benefits contained in the peaceful uses of nuclear energy."

Although I try to keep myself informed about Church statements on nuclear power, I heard about the work of the Pontifical Academy quite by accident. I was unable to obtain a copy by writing to the Academy, and eventually succeeded through the personal efforts of one of my Oxford physics students, who was at that time studying for the priesthood in Rome. As soon as I read the document I realized its importance, and urged that it be reviewed in a prominent Catholic weekly, but without success. I therefore wrote an article on it that was published in the *Clergy Review*.[22]

A conference on the Christian Dimensions of Energy Problems organized by the Catholic Union and the Commission for International Justice and Peace was held in England in April 1982. It is noteworthy that this conference took no notice of the work of the Pontifical Academy in 1980. This is unfortunately quite typical; studies are undertaken and conferences arranged by people without any knowledge of what has already been achieved. It is therefore impossible to make any progress; they are continually trying to invent the wheel. By contrast, in the scientific community, a prime requisite for serious research is a thorough knowledge of what is already known. There are scientists who are unfamiliar with the literature (often through no fault of their own) and write papers that might have been interesting two years ago, but are now quite useless. Such scientists are not taken seriously, and their papers are rejected.

The result of all this is the production of statements that are frequently worse than useless, with a small number of very competent and valuable statements that are so poorly publicized that they have little effect.

There are several reasons for this unsatisfactory state of affairs. The first and fatal mistake was to underestimate the magnitude of the scientific and technical work that must be undertaken before any realistic moral judgment can be made. In the case of nuclear power, it is essential to study in a quantitative way the world energy needs, the resources of raw materials, the economics of the different methods of energy generation, and their associated hazards and effects on the environment. The requires the cooperation of experts in many fields. Only when this is done is it possible to cut through the smokescreen of politically-motivated propaganda obscuring the whole subject and then go on to establish the true situation that must be taken as the basis of any realistic moral judgment on the best energy sources to choose. The report should be written up by the scientists and the moral theologians working together.

Without the participation of qualified scientists, the report may well contain many wise and sensible thoughts, but the cumulative impression will inevitably be that it comprises well-meaning generalities that are unlikely to have any practical result at all.

This work need not be done in every country; indeed, it is preferable that it be done on an international level. Nevertheless, it is also desirable that there is in each country a group of qualified people who keep the subject constantly under review. If this is not done, then when the report comes from the international committee, it will not be well understood and so its conclusions cannot be properly implemented.

The second mistake was to fail to ensure that the report in printed in large numbers and sent to a wide range of interested people. A vital link in this process is the weekly press and also magazines dealing with world affairs. The editors need to be aware of the status of the international committee and the importance of giving it wide publicity. They should also know some well-qualified scientists who can comment on the report and answer questions.

It is recognized that it is desirable that: "The Church must draw into the work of evangelization those Catholics who have a acknowledged competence in contemporary scientific disciplines."[23] Unfortunately these fine sentiments are seldom put into practice.

Establishing the Truth

Before any statement can be made, it is essential to establish the truth, and this is by no means easy. Global warming is one among many contemporary social problems that requires one to have a knowledge of science to understand it. To assist this understanding, many scientists have written books and articles on global warming. It may, however, be asked whether, having read this material, ordinary citizens are in a position to form an independent opinion on the reality of global warming. This is indeed very doubtful. One of the difficulties is that the whole discussion is extremely complicated, and much controversy remains. Although an overall consensus has been reached by a large body of scientists forming the Intergovernmental Panel on Climate Change, there are many other scientists who are strongly opposed. There is the additional complicating factor that huge commercial interests, and therefore pressures, may underlie reports that appear, on the surface, to be scientific and objective. It is thus difficult, if not impossible, for a scientist who does not specialize in studies directly related to global warming to form an independent judgment.

This illustrates a characteristic of scientific knowledge that is perhaps insufficiently appreciated, namely that it is only those who are thoroughly immersed in a particular field and have researched in it for years, who may be in a position to evaluate what is going on. A scientist in a nearby field is seldom able to do this, even after a period of study. This is similar to the experience of scientists that only active practitioners in a field are able to referee a paper effectively. Other scientists, however eminent, may easily miss a consideration that destroys the whole argument. These reflections should make us skeptical of the value of public declarations by groups of distinguished scientists, even if they are Nobel Prizewinners, most of whom are unlikely to have first-hand knowledge of the subject concerned. It is always flattering to be treated as an authority on everything, and the temptation to pronounce on subjects far beyond one's specialty is not always resisted. This is even more necessary when theologians speak on scientific subjects. A smattering of knowledge, such as may be obtained by taking a degree in science, followed after a few years research by a half-baked doctoral thesis, is not enough. As Duhem remarked, "in order to speak of questions where science and Catholic philosophy touch one another, one must have done ten or fifteen years of study of the pure sciences."[24]

The whole question of how one comes to believe is indeed very complicated. An instructive example of a gradual shift of belief is provided by the Copernican revolution.[25] In the Middle Ages, Aristotelian cosmology was so firmly established, and apparently confirmed by a multitude of direct experiences, that the heliocentric theory of Copernicus seemed just absurd. Copernicus' book *De Revolutionibus* made no mark on the prevailing geocentric belief as it was largely unintelligible to all but professional astronomers. This small specialized group, well aware of the large number of minor improvements that had been made in the Ptolemaic system over the previous centuries without significantly improving the fit to the unsatisfactory ancient data and which proved quite unable to fit the greatly improved data of Tycho Brahe, increasingly turned to the Copernican theory as the basis of their calculations. Many of then still rejected the heliocentric theory as a real account of celestial motions and used the Copernican theory simply as a method of calculation. The astronomers gradually improved the Copernican theory and found that it is much more tightly constrained than the Ptolemaic theory, so that it is not possible to adjust the parameters of the planetary orbits independently of each other. Furthermore, several important results, such as the retrograde motion of the planets and the phases of Venus were immediately explicable in a natural way. As so, gradually, impelled by their very practical concerns the belief of the professional astronomers changed. By around 1616, the time of the Church's first action against Galileo, the case for Copernicanism was weak; but at the time of his recantation in 1633, the tide had turned and geocentrism was almost a lost cause. According to Kuhn, "by the middle of the seventeenth century it is difficult to find an important astronomer who is not Copernican; by the end of the century it is impossible." And yet it is important to recall that not one of the arguments for Copernicanism was conclusive. Galileo's favorite argument from the tides is fallacious. Bellarmine said that if the heliocentric theory was proved correct, then it would be necessary to study carefully how it could be reconciled with Scripture, but he did not specify what he would accept as a proof. The proofs that first convinced the astronomers were only accessible to them; it is the cumulative effects of a large numbers of indications, individually not coercive, the unity of indirect reference akin to the illative sense of Newman. When eventually the definitive proof of the heliocentric theory came two hundred years later with the measurement of stellar parallax by Bessel, the battle was long over, and it is doubtful if there was any great stir among either scientists or theologians.

This illustrates the difficulty of deciding when a Church statement on such subjects should be made. If it is made too early, it may well eventually turn out to be wrong. Fortunately, for example, no Church statement was made on the clusters of childhood leukemia around nuclear plants, as these have now been shown to be due to some other cause.[26] On the other hand, if the statement is too late, it will be greeted with laughter as just another instance of the Church living in the past. There is the additional consideration that it is almost always the case that if you wait until you are sure, then it is too late to take effective action. We have, therefore, to act on arguments of probability, but be aware that we are doing so.

The Responsibilities of Scientists

If this analysis is accepted, it is obvious that the participation of scientists is essential. Correspondingly, scientists have a responsibility to put their knowledge at the service of the Church and of society in general. This was realized very clearly by the nuclear physicists in the immediate postwar years, so they were very active in founding associations of scientists, writing articles and giving lectures. This was the origin of the Federation of Atomic Scientists in the US and of the Atomic Scientists' Association in Britain.

Initially, the public was very receptive, but after a few years many newspapers had scientific correspondents, and most of the scientists thought that their work was done and withdrew from their public activities. Gradually, over the following decades, the public mood changed. The accident at Three Mile Island severely shook the public confidence. Fears of unknown radiations and memories of the devastation of Hiroshima and Nagasaki came to the fore, and were fanned by media stories of thousands of people who would die because of the accident. Although devoid of foundation, such fears, once released, could not easily be calmed. The public concern was greatly magnified by the far worse accident at Chernobyl. The public anxieties were increased by the activities of vociferous and powerful pressure groups, and so many people became hostile to nuclear power and rather wary of other scientific and technical advances. The result is that the public debate on nuclear matters has degenerated into the mindless repetition of arguments that were long ago discredited, coupled to a refusal to listen to any counter arguments.

Underlying this deplorable spectacle is a weakened sense of the importance of finding the objective truth. Thus, it is now widely accepted "that all positions are equally valid, which is one of today's most widespread symptoms of a lack of confidence in truth." Thus, "everything is reduced to opinion; and there is a sense of being adrift" (§5).

In this situation, most attempts by scientists to provide factual information are doomed to failure. If he writes an article it is seldom accepted: If he tries to correct a misconception, his letters are seldom published; and if they are published, then in the next issue they are criticized, and no opportunity is given to reply. The usual result is that a scientist soon realizes that he is wasting his time, and so no longer contributes to the public debate. I could give very many examples of this;[27] here one must suffice.

Soon after the Chernobyl accident there was a leading article in a prominent daily newspaper reporting a large increase in the death rate in the United States due to the dust from Chernobyl, complete with a large picture of Death the Reaper. It was obvious that this was extremely unlikely because such no effects had been reported from Europe, where the amount of dust deposited was much larger, though still far below that likely to cause any detectable effects. The article was however supported by statistical data apparently showing a strong correlation between the amount of dust deposited and the death rate in several areas.

Since the story seemed to be unlikely, I contacted the Atomic Energy Research Establishment at Harwell, and asked them to obtain the detailed figures for me. This took some time, and when they arrived it was clear that the figures had been obtained by statistical fudging, and that they showed no effect whatsoever. I wrote to the newspaper, but was told that it was now so long ago that everyone would have forgotten all about it and so no action could be taken to correct the story. It is, however, more than likely that they remember the association between nuclear power and Death the Reaper.

My experiences with the Church have been somewhat mixed. The editor of the *Fact and Faith* books, Lancelot Sheppard, invited me to contribute to the series, and I wrote a book entitled *Nuclear Physics in Peace and War.*[28] Subsequently, Professor Torrance invited me to contribute to the series of books, *Theology and Scientific Culture*, and I wrote *Our Nuclear Future.*[29] Several monthly journals such as *The Month, New Blackfriars* and *The Clergy Review* have published articles on nuclear power and the environment.

Other experiences have not been so good. The Catholic newspapers tend to accept the misconceptions of the secular media, and it is often impossible to present a balanced view without it being contradicted in a subsequent issue, with no opportunity for reply.

I once wrote a booklet *World Energy Needs and Resources* and sent it to a leading Catholic publisher. Subsequently, I was told that it could not be accepted because it was contrary to the statement of the English and Welsh bishops. I asked for a copy of this statement, and was told that it was to be found in a periodical called *Briefings*, which however was confidential. I therefore wrote to a few bishops known personally to me, asking about their teaching on nuclear power. Many of them thought that I was asking about nuclear weapons, but those who read my letter all said that they knew nothing about this statement, even the bishop who lectured on energy affairs. After some detective work I found out that my booklet had been sent for refereeing to a Jesuit scientist, a distinguished Catholic nuclear physicist and a lawyer. The Jesuit and the physicist recommended publication but the lawyer made the objection already mentioned. Eventually I obtained a copy of the issue of *Briefings* that contained the statement in question, and found that it was brief, trivial, unbalanced and enumerate. Who then wrote it? Not one of our bishops, or a Committee appointed by them to examine the problem, but the aforesaid lawyer, a member of an anti-nuclear group. Meanwhile I had sent my booklet to a non-catholic Christian publisher, and it was published without any difficulties.[30] This shows how simple-minded scientists are easily outmaneuvered by clever lawyers.

From such experiences one learns that it is difficult for scientists to contribute to the public debate on matters related to our specialized knowledge. It is a great mistake to assume that our contributions will be welcomed. If what we say is contrary to the agenda of some pressure group, we will have great difficulty in even obtaining a hearing. No sensible scientist would want his views to be taken on trust, but he does expect them to be given a hearing. He is familiar with what happens within scientific research: new ideas are put forward and subjected to rigorous criticism and testing until eventually the truth becomes clear. No one stands on ceremony or defers to authority; the sole object is to find out the truth. The public debate on scientific questions should also be like this. However, this sort of debate very rarely happens; usually one realizes that one is dealing with people who do not know, who do not know that they do not know, and who do not even know what knowing means.

Outside and Inside Knowledge

There is a fundamental and essential difference between the two acceptable statements on nuclear power and the remainder. Both groups of statements are written from inside Christianity, but the former are written from within science as well, while the latter by and large are not. The view from inside is always different from the view from outside. Those within science have much more chance of seeing technical matters in their true perspective, with the potentialities and dangers in proportion. In the words of C. P. Snow, we have the future in our bones, and we look forward to it with hope and confidence. So, of course, should Christians.

Viewed from outside, science apparently appears to many to be a fearful monster, giving birth to unimaginable evils that we will somehow have to fight and control. They do not understand science, so they fear science. Such people fall easy prey to every wild tale of the mass media, and lend their support to campaigns to slay the dragon. They are present in every generation. They opposed gaslight, they opposed vaccination, they drove Semmelweiss insane, they opposed steam trains, they opposed airplanes and now they oppose nuclear power.

Churchmen sometimes talk about the need for dialogue with scientists as if we were Hindus or Hottentots.[31] When will they realize that there are scientists actually inside the Church, kneeling in the pews and sharing with them the Body and Blood of Christ? Why not listen to them for a change, instead of running after the first rabid journalist and swallowing his wild stories about the strange and menacing land of science?

The chief merit of the *Methodist Study Shaping Tomorrow* and of the *Vatican Study Week* is that they got the facts right. There is little that is new in either report; they simply present in a balanced way material that is available elsewhere in much greater detail. Their specifically Christian contribution is by comparison rather meager, and this is a real weakness of the work of the Churches in such areas. There is little long-term scholarly commitment to the moral analysis of problems like global warming, the energy crisis and nuclear power. Few moral theologians devote their lives to thinking about them. The authorities of most Churches failed even to discover the essential facts and to put them into perspective, and this is no more than an essential preliminary to serious moral thinking. There is an urgent need for some moral theologians to spend years mastering the facts and thinking about them in the light of Christian principles. This very necessary theological work simply cannot be done by busy bishops on the evening before they are due to address some conference. There are some men in the Churches who are potentially able to do such work, namely the young clergy who studied science to degree standard before ordination. They know enough to understand what is going on, but not enough to make weighty contributions to the debate. They see very clearly that vague and well-meaning platitudes are no substitute for a clear moral lead. Usually their scientific knowledge rusts as they are swamped by other duties. Yet if they were specifically assigned to theological studies where their scientific knowledge would be used, and given the opportunities to learn from experts, to take higher degrees, to devote most of their lives to study, then in a few decades we would be in a position to make a serious contribution to the debates on global warming, nuclear power and similar problems that are of such vital importance for the future of humanity. Then, in the words of *Fides et Ratio*, "moral theology will be able to tackle the various problems in its competence such as peace, social justice, the family, the defence of life and the natural environment, in a more appropriate and effective way" (§98).

Notes

1. P. E. Hodgson, E. Gadioli and E. Gadioli Erba, *Introductory Nuclear Physics* (Oxford University Press, 1997).

2. S. L. Jaki, *The Road of Science and the Ways to God* (Chicago University Press, 1978).

3. S. L. Jaki, *Science and Creation* (New York: Science History Publications, 1974).

4. J. R. Lucas and P. E. Hodgson, *Spacetime and Electromagnetism* (Oxford University Press, 1990).

5. J. H. Newman, *An Essay in Aid of a Grammar of Assent* (London: Longmans Green, 1947).

6. J. H. Newman, *An Essay on the Development of Christian Doctrine* (New York: Sheed and Ward, 1960).

7. J. T. Houghton, G. J. Jenkins and J. J. Ephraums, eds., *Climate Change: The IPCC Scientific Assessment* (Cambridge University Press, 1990); J. T. Houghton, B. A. Callendar and S. K. Varney, *Climate Change*, The Supplementary Report to the IPCC Scientific Assessment (Cambridge University Press, 1992).

8. P. E. Hodgson, *Energy and Environment* (London: Bowerdean Publications, 1997); idem, *Nuclear Power, Energy and the Environment* (London: Imperial College Press, 1998); idem, "Global Warming and Nuclear

Power," *Nuclear Energy* 38 (1999), p. 147.

9. Letter from Michael Meacher to the British Nuclear Industry Forum (18 January 1988).

10. John Houghton, "Climate Change: The Challenges," *Physics World* (February 1998), p. 17.

11. John Houghton, *Global Warming: The Complete Briefing* (Oxford: Lion Publishing, 1994).

12. John Houghton, "The Two and a Half Degrees to Doomsday," Times Higher (3 December 1997), p. 21.

13. Jim Skea, "The Challenge of Climate Change," *Science and Public Affairs* (Winter 1997), p. 24.

14. P. E. Hodgson, "How Very Inconsistent!" *Nuclear Forum* (March 1991), p. 16.

15. A scandalous example is the nuclear power station at Zweitendorf in Austria.

16. P. E. Hodgson, "The Churches and Nuclear Power" (unpublished 1984); Friedhelm Solms, ed., *European Churches and the Energy Issue*, Forschungsstatte der Evangelischen Studiengemeinschaft, series A, vol. 11 (October 1980).

17. "The Moral Dimensions of Energy Policy," Bishops' Committee for Social Development. *Origins*, NC Documentary Service (23 April 1981), vol. 10: 45, p. 706.

18. P. E. Hodgson, "Reflections on the Energy Crisis," *The Month* (November 1982), p. 382.

19. Edgar Boyes, ed., *Shaping Tomorrow* (London: Home Mission Division of the Methodit Church, 1981).

20. Andre Blanc-Lapierre, ed., *Semaine D'Etude sur la theme Humanite et Energie: Besoins - Ressources - Espoirs.* Nov. 10–15 1980, Scripta varia, no. 46 (Rome: Vatican City).

21. "Statement of the Holy See to the International Conference on Nuclear Power" (Vienna, September 13–17, 1982); International Atomic Energy Authority Paper CN–42/449.

22. P. E. Hodgson, "Nuclear Power: Rome Speaks," *The Clergy Review* 78 (February 1983), p. 49.

23. Submission of the Bishop's Conference of England and Wales to the Extraordinary Synod of Bishops held in Rome (November 1985).

24. P. Duhem, quoted by S. L. Jaki, Uneasy Genius: *The Life and Work of Pierre Duhem* (The Hague: Martinus Nijhoff, 1984), p. 114.

25. Thomas S. Kuhn, *The Copernican Revolution* (Cambridge, MA: Harvard University Press, 1957); Owen Gingerich, *The Eye of Heaven: Ptolemy, Copernicus*, Kepler (New York: American Institute of Physics, 1993).

26. Sir Richard Doll, H. J. Evans and S. C. Darby, "Paternal Exposure not to Blame," *Nature* 367 (1994), p. 678.

27. P. E. Hodgson, "Reflections at La Rabida: The Responsibilities of the Nuclear Physicist for Peace," *Oxford Project for Peace Studies* 13 (1988).

28. P. E. Hodgson, *Nuclear Physics in Peace and War* (London: Burns and Oates, Hawthorn Books, 1961).

29. P. E. Hodgson, *Our Nuclear Future?* (Belfast: Christian Journals, 1983).

30. P. E. Hodgson, *World Energy Needs and Resources*, Grove Booklet on Ethics, vol. 44 (Bramcote: Grove Books, 1981).

31. Until recently the relations with the scientific community were the responsibility of the Pontifical Consilium for Non-Believers. Now, more sensibly, it is included in the Pontifical Consilium for Culture.

The Diversity of Philosophy and the Unity of its Vocation: Some Philosophical Reflections on *Fides et Ratio*
John Haldane

I

In the ordinary run of things Roman documents offer little in the way of philosophical interest. The present pontificate, by contrast, has been distinguished by the number of occasions on which John Paul II has invoked philosophical considerations in the course of addressing the Church. Three encyclicals spring to mind: *Veritatis Splendor, Evangelium Vitae* and *Fides et Ratio*. In the first two, moral philosophy is in view, and certain contemporary normative theories are criticized.[1] Although the Pope makes efforts to limit himself to general considerations and to avoid affirming any specific philosophical position, it is unsurprising to find his own colors showing, and thus the potential for controversy is not altogether avoided. Consider, for example, the following passage from *Veritatis Splendor*:

> [O]ne has to consider carefully the correct relationship between freedom and human nature, and in particular *the place of the human body in questions of natural law.* A freedom which claims to be absolute ends up treating the human body as a raw datum, devoid of any meaning and moral values until freedom has shaped it in accordance with its design. Consequently, human nature and the body appear as presuppositions or preambles, materially necessary for freedom to make its choice, yet extrinsic to the person, the subject and the human act. . . . *A doctrine which dissociates the moral act from the bodily dimensions of its exercise is contrary to the teaching of Scripture and Tradition.*[2]

The concluding reference to the teaching of scripture might suggest that the requirement to consider the body is a religious or theological one, and in that sense something extra-philosophical. Mention of the "tradition" is more ambiguous: on the one hand it might be taken to mean the Church's moral teaching as that derives from Catholic moral theology; or it may be interpreted as referring to the philosophical tradition of natural law ethics. But this disambiguation involves a contentious if not false disjunction. For until quite recently Catholic moral theology (understood as theory and not as casuistry) has largely consisted in a synthesis of natural law and scriptural interpretation.

Quite apart from the attitude of dissenters opposed to particular first order claims such as those concerning sexuality, the avowal of a particular form of rational justification of morality is somewhat controversial. It will not be enough, so far as *Veritatis Splendor* is concerned, to affirm some or other form of moral objectivism; one is expected (or is it required?) to subscribe to natural law. Moreover, while the insistence upon the relationship between right action and "human nature" may seem a formal point satisfiable in indefinitely many ways; what is said – about the human body – suggests that some styles of reasoning that describe themselves as "natural law ethics" will not do. Consider, for example, someone who argues that certain types of action are prohibited because they violate norms concerning the attainment of goods whose value is determinable by the practical rationality that we possess in virtue of our rational nature. Such a person will not yet have met the requirement set out in the quoted passage. For the "natural" in natural law refers not only to the *source* of practical rationality but to its subject matter. In the Pope's account of things ethics is essentially *about* the lives of rational animals, and our embodiment is not a further feature to which pure practical reason might then attend. If I have him aright, for John Paul II philosophical anthropology is not something to which moral rationality might turn for empirical premises, rather it is the source and precondition of morality.

Indeed, the quoted passage expresses a yet more determinate philosophical conception: that of Thomistic anti-Cartesian personalism; Christian-Aristotelianism filtered through Husserl. For my own part, I find this *committed-voice* rather more congenial than the *committee-speak* of other Church documents. Even so, I suggest that a question arises as to the appropriateness of such a level of philosophical specificity in a document addressed to the universal Church, given that Catholic moral philosophers and moral theologians who are evidently cognitivists or objectivists nevertheless differ quite widely on the nature of moral reasoning and thus on the grounding of moral prescriptions and requirements.

I raise this matter at the outset because the third of the encyclicals, *viz. Fides et Ratio* is largely and not incidentally concerned with the nature and role of philosophy, and while the Pope repeatedly assures readers that he is not seeking to accord priority to any single philosophical system – writing that "The Church has no philosophy of her own nor does she canonize any one particular philosophy in preference to others" (§49) – the suspicion arises that in truth he believes that only one approach (or family of approaches) will do.[3]

Since the text is directed to a range of constituencies beyond the formal addressees (the Bishops), it is difficult to be altogether sure about this however; and in face of that uncertainty one might not think it profitable or respectful to pursue the issue. Yet for those committed to the philosophical tradition which has the best claim to be *the* philosophy of Catholicism, *viz.* Thomistic Aristotelianism, and for those interested in the development of Catholic philosophy and in the potential for engagement with philosophers outside the Church, these matters are critical. They concern nothing less than the limits of acceptable philosophical pluralism and thus bear heavily upon the prospects for such enterprises as *ARCIC* (*Analytical Roman Catholic Inter-Philosophical Conversation*).[4] For it could be that like the other *ARCIC* (*Anglican Roman Catholic International Commission*) this exchange may run into difficulty over the authority of "the Bishop of Rome," that description now being used *de re*, and in connection with John Paul's metaphilosophical doctrine about the nature of true philosophy, or his theology of speculative and practical reason.[5]

II

The focus of my discussion is on issues raised in sections 80 to 91 of Ch VII "Current Requirements and Tasks." In the course of this – the penultimate chapter of *Fides et Ratio* – the Pope identifies three obligations for contemporary philosophy:

(i) to recover the sapiential dimension of the discipline (§81);
(ii) to establish and maintain epistemological realism (§82); and
(iii) to achieve genuinely metaphysical range (§83).

It is tempting to partition these tasks into two; grouping the second and third as aspects of a single speculative enterprise – *the establishment of realism* – and taking up the first as an exercise for practical philosophy. But that would run counter to the view of their relationship expressed in the text, and I believe counter to the proper need for an integrated conception of philosophy as dialectic and the practice of the love of wisdom.

So far as the wider philosophical world is concerned, my own feeling is that the recovery of the sapiential dimension is the place to concentrate one's efforts, and I shall make a first attempt on this task later. However, it is also necessary to say something about ii) and iii), since as the Pope observes: "this sapiential function could not be performed by a philosophy which was not itself a true and authentic knowledge, addressed to . . . [reality's] total and definitive truth, to the very being of the object which is known" (§82). So as to provide the required context for this discussion let me give a brief overview of the chapter. Earlier in the encyclical we are introduced to the universality of the philosophical impulse and to the power of its influence in shaping culture. This establishes one point of interest for the Church, but a second lies in the ancient role of philosophy as handmaiden and messenger on behalf of faith. Precisely because he values the several traditional functions of philosophy John Paul II goes on to express concern at tendencies among philosophers and theologians to limit severely the function of philosophy as discerner of objective truth. These "false trends," as one might term them (echoing the phraseology of Pius XII in *Human Generis*), are discussed in Chs. IV, V and VI. This then sets the scene for the identification of current requirements and tasks listed above.

Thus, philosophy is to establish our capacity to *"know the truth"* (*adequatio rei et intellectus*) and to achieve "genuine metaphysical range capable of transcending empirical data in order to attain something absolute, ultimate and foundational in its search for truth" (§82). These requirements exclude certain philosophical options: (i) *radical phenomenalism*; (ii) *relativism*; (iii) *eclecticism*; (iv) *historicism*; (v) *scientism*; (vi) *pragmatism*; and the more general vice to which he thinks these bad practices lead, *viz. nihilism*.

No doubt it would not have been appropriate for the Pope to give detailed descriptions of these erroneous perspectives, in part for reasons of space, but also so as to avoid needless controversy in what is a work of doctrinal instruction and not a philosophical monograph. Nevertheless, this list of errors deserves much more discussion than it receives. Both clarification and more precise characterization are needed. For one thing the syllabus includes stances that seem to be of logically different kinds some epistemological (e.g. phenomenalism), some metaphysical (e.g. scientism) and others perhaps stylistic (such as eclecticism). More to the point, however, if Catholic philosophers are to engage with the wider world, they will need to start making distinctions within these categories and that, I think, will quickly return us to the issue of tolerable pluralism.

III

Certainly not every way of going on is as good as any other, but there are differences within the broad range of those who would agree with the necessity of the second and third tasks. Let me illustrate by observing one way in which philosophers with motives akin to the Pope's own have shied away from one kind of metaphysical realism precisely because it seems to lead to *scientism*.

Before doing that, however, I think it is appropriate to offer a couple of remarks about the "syllabus of errors" cited above. The first on the list is "eclecticism: by which is meant the approach of those who, in research, teaching and argumentation, even in theology, tend to use individual ideas drawn from different philosophies without concern for their internal coherence, their place within a system, or their historical context" (§86). So described this hardly qualifies as "a current of thought" (§86, 91) or as "a position" (§90), at least as those expressions are generally used and understood. Rather it represents a form of intellectual incompetence or irresponsibility and certainly not something that one could imagine anyone seriously proposing as an alternative philosophical approach. No doubt such intellectual vice should be warned against but it seems out of place in a catalogue of contrasting philosophical approaches. There is, however, a different notion of "eclecticism" appropriately applied to certain "currents" or "positions." This connotes syntheses or blends of ideas or methods drawn from different historical approaches. Whether particular cases of this are reasonable dependent upon actual specifics, but it would ill behoove a Thomist to issue a blanket condemnation since Thomism is itself eclectic – and Karol Wojtyla's Lublin variant is highly so.

A second example of the need for "fine-tuning" is provided by the inclusion of "pragmatism" in the list of currents of thought. This might be apt were it not for the peculiar definition given of it: "An attitude of mind which in making choices, precludes theoretical considerations or judgments based on ethical principles" (§89). Certainly there is a use of the term "pragmatist" (lower case 'p') in which it contrasts with action based on principle; but once again this does not represent a philosophical position so much as the avoidance of one. On the other hand the current of thought known to philosophers by the title "Pragmatism" (upper case 'P'), and which is the subject of an entry in every philosophical dictionary or encyclopedia, is far from precluding theoretical considerations or ethical judgments. Whatever one's view of the thought of Pierce, James and Dewey, it is undoubtedly philosophical and one of its distinctive features is the philosophical emphasis given to values and norms.

What these examples suggest is that those who wish to commend *Fides et Ratio* to a philosophically educated readership will need to provide clarifying, qualifying terminological glosses. More substantial, however, is the task of determining the range of philosophical positions compatible with the encyclicals committed to epistemological and metaphysical realism. I cannot attempt this here, but I would like to touch on the issue of philosophical realism since this is an unquestionable commitment of John Paul II and one of the main issues in contemporary secular philosophy.

First, then, realism is not an "all or nothing" position. For example, one and the same philosopher might favor a realist position on causality but not on mathematics. That is to say, he or she might hold, in opposition to Hume, that causal relations obtain in nature prior to and independently of human

thought, but also maintain that truth in mathematics is not a matter of correspondence with some mind-independent reality, but rather of provability in a
constructive system, which is to say that mathematical facts are not discovered but created by thought. This raises the question of how realism either
total or partial should be understood. A very common answer equates realism
with facticity or truth, but a more metaphysical account would be in terms of
mind-independent existence.

This is not the occasion to explore the details and difficulties of these
options, but it needs to be pointed out that an exclusive and strict mind-independent criterion is liable to result in a position uncongenial to the orientation
of the encyclical. The reason is that much of what we ordinarily take to be
objective is not wholly mind-independent. Colors, tastes and other secondary
qualities are partly constituted by subjective sensibility and many common
descriptions of the "world" express schemes of classification that reflect our
interests rather than mind-independent natures. The Vatican is extensively and
exquisitely decorated in marbles of various types, but marble is not itself a
natural kind. Much but not all that is classified as "marble" is limestone in a
crystalline or granular state; and limestone is an aggregate of calcium car-
bonate and other chemical compounds. Thus, what *from the point of nature*
are importantly different substances are grouped together by us because of
their appearances – ones which themselves depend upon the form of our sensibility. Some metaphysical realists take this to be reason to say that "marble"
does not really exist. Pressed repeatedly this restrictive "natural substance"
metaphysics becomes reductive scientific realism, which is only one step
away from scientism. The Pope is right to reject the latter, but doing so coher-
ently is liable to require relaxing the requirement on realism, or at least allowing that not everything that is objective is real (in the metaphysician's strict
sense.

To repeat, my point is not to argue to a particular realist doctrine but only
to suggest that when relaying the message of *Fides et Ratio* greater understanding must to be shown in identifying philosophical positions for praise or
criticism. Quite generally, much more work needs to be done on the issue of
the range of tolerable "realisms," and none of us can afford to be triumphant
about the "tradition" or dismissive of other's ways of going on. Indeed, the
common necessity of philosophy to make progress on these issues provides an
opportunity for dialogue between Catholic philosophers and others.[6]

IV

Let me turn now to task (i) and to John Paul's call to academic philosophy
to return to the ancient concern with the pursuit of wisdom. He writes: "To be
consonant with the word of God, philosophy needs first of all to recover its

sapiential dimension as a search for the ultimate and overarching meaning of life" (§81). I think this is perhaps the most valuable positive contribution of the encyclical and one that can and should be carried beyond the world of Catholic thought. With this in mind, I would like to explore the relationship between philosophy conceived of as the practice of wisdom and the idea of philosophical spirituality as a demeanor adopted in the face of reality as one's speculative metaphysics takes it to be.

There seems little difficulty in understanding the idea of spirituality and of the spiritual life within the context of religious thought. In Christianity especially these are given definite content by reference to the indwelling of the Holy Spirit and to practices of prayer, meditation and devotion by which the soul progressively partakes in the life of God – not substantially but relationally as an adopted child might increasingly partake in the life of a family.[7]

When we turn to (non-religious) philosophy, however, a question arises whether any form of spirituality can find a home there. Yet even the most cursory reflection upon human experience and on the efforts of great writers and others to give expression to it, suggests that there is a domain of thought, feeling and action that is concerned with discerning the ultimate truth about the human condition and with cultivating an appropriate mode of being or demeanor in response to that truth. The phenomenology is compelling, the concerns are intelligible, and for some reason intelligent people persist in supposing that it must be a central part of philosophy to deal with these matters and therefore look to it to do so.

Philosophers themselves, at least academics in the dominant Anglo-American tradition, either ignore such appeals as one might the entreaties of a door to door evangelist; suggest they are confused in ways similar to those in which some metaphysicians suggest that people are mixed up when they ask about first or ultimate causes; or else, if they are inclined to grant something to the claim that questions of non-religious meaning and spirit do arise and call for attention, they point to moral theory or possibly to aesthetics as being the relevant departments to visit.

While this last option has the merit of recognizing that there is something to be catered for, it makes a mistake in consigning it to moral philosophy as this is now understood, for that is concerned essentially with rightness of conduct, and first and foremost with conduct bearing upon other moral subjects. Notwithstanding its welcome breadth, contemporary virtue ethics remains a version of moral theory and as such is concerned principally with action. Likewise, aesthetics is concerned principally with disinterested contemplation of objects of experience. Spirituality involves intellect, will and emotion and is essentially contemplative, but the process of discovering the nature of reality, evaluating its implications for the human condition and cultivating an appropriate demeanor in the face of these is not reducible to ethics, nor to aesthetics. Yet unless philosophers can show this enterprise to be confused or exclusively religious they are open to the change of neglecting something of fundamental, indeed perhaps of ultimate human importance.

V

The French classical scholar and historian of philosophy Pierre Hadot has made a series of very interesting studies of the aims and methods of the six ancient schools of philosophy, *viz. Stoicism, Epicureanism, Platonism, Aristotelianism, Cynicism* and *Pyrrhorism*, arguing that each reflects and in turn seeks to develop a permanent possibility of the human spirit. These studies have been collected and translated into English under the title *Philosophy as a Way of Life*, and I strongly recommend them.[8] I shall not even attempt to summarize, his many conclusions, but I do want to extract one or two points so as to advance my own discussion.

First, then, Hadot discerns in the various ancient traditions, but especially in the Stoics, a distinction between *"philosophy"* (*philo-sophia* conceived of as the formation of the soul, or the deep structure of character, with the addition of an orientation towards the good), and *discourse about philosophy* (understood as the investigation of the nature of things, and to a lesser extent our knowledge of them). This, of course, is related to the more familiar distinction between practical and speculative philosophy. But whereas modern, recent and contemporary thought has invested greatest effort and talent in the pursuit of speculation in the form of epistemology and metaphysics, the ancients, and again I am focusing on the Stoics, give priority to thinking about practice, and within that to the cultivation of wisdom and the development of the spiritual life. Epictetus observes that "the lecture room of the philosopher is a hospital"[9] which is to say that his work is the cure of souls. Later he writes: "How shall I free myself? have you not heard it taught that you ought to eliminate desire entirely? . . . give up everything . . . for if you once deviate from your course, you are a slave, you are a subject."[10] Hadot's reading of such texts is both informed and imaginative. It also encourages him to make three claims of great interest. First, he construes much more of the writing of antiquity as belonging to philosophy in the sense of the practice of wisdom, than has been common among historians of ancient philosophy. More precisely and more strikingly he argues that these texts concern and in some cases *are* spiritual exercises. Second, and in direct opposition to the assumption which I mentioned that the notion of spirituality is in origin a religious one, he claims that in fact Christianity appropriated this area of reflective practice from pre-existing philosophical traditions and even that it took over "as its own certain techniques of spiritual exercises as they had already been practised in antiquity."[11] Third, he implies that the historical interest of all of this is perhaps its least significant aspect. In an essay responding to Foucault's use of his earlier work Hadot writes:

> I think modern man can practice the spiritual exercises of antiquity, at the same time separating them from the philosophical [metaphysical] or mythic discourse which came along with them. The same spiritual exercises can, in fact, be justified by extremely diverse philosophical discourses. These latter are nothing but clumsy attempts, coming after the fact, to describe and justify inner experiences whose existential security is not, in the last analysis, susceptible of any attempts at theorization or systematization. . . . It is therefore not necessary to believe in the Stoic's nature or universal reason. Rather as one lives concretely according to reason. In the words of Marcus Aurelius: "Although everything happens at random, don't you, too, act at random." In this way, we can accede concretely to the universality of the cosmic perspective, and the wonderful mystery of the presence of the universe.[12]

This passage is full of promise, but a few comments are called for. First, the exercises he refers to, what Foucault called *"pratiques de soi"* (practices of the self)[13] are designed to liberate one from (inappropriate) attachment to exterior objects and the pleasures deriving from them. By regular self-examination one keeps a check on the tendency to exteriority, and by contemplating the impermanence of things one seeks to master or to possess oneself, attaining happiness in interior formation. Writing-up this examination, or better, perhaps, examining through writing is one form of spiritual exercise.

Where Hadot takes issue with Foucault is in claiming with the ancient authors (including Plotinus) that the movement toward interiorization is "inseparably linked to another movement, whereby one rises to a higher psychic level, at which one encounters another kind of exteriorization, another relationship with the 'exterior' – or what one might term the 'real.'"[14] Without necessarily wishing to reject it, one may reasonably call for further specification of this transcendent movement. A major direction of development is likely to lead to the inexpressibility of the mystical encounter with the "One," but other possibilities suggest themselves including moderate versions of Platonist ontology and even naturalistic Aristotelianism. Rather than pursue this, however, let me voice a reservation about the claim that spiritual formation may proceed independently of the truth of the accompanying philosophical discourse (metaphysics).

Presumably, even Hadot thinks there are some limits to just how wrong one can be at the speculative level while keeping on track in the practice of wisdom. Also there is reason to tie the two together as constituent components of a single enterprise, such that the content of spiritual formation is dependent upon its metaphysical compliment. The argument for this is quite straight-forward. One reason for believing that the issue of spirituality arises within philosophy is reflection on a parallel relationship between religious belief and practice. Suppose someone was persuaded by philosophical or historical arguments that the God of Christian theism exists, but that he or she then seemed wholly unmoved by this acceptance. One would be inclined to say, I think, that religiously speaking the thing (conversion) has not yet begun. For *that* belief requires the formation of a demeanor appropriate to its content. Likewise, I wish to say that a reductive materialist who really believes that his philosophy gives the ultimate truth about reality should be moved (by reason) to ask how in the face of this immensely significant belief he or she should compose themselves. It seems unintelligible to suppose that *nothing* follows for the enquirer from arriving at a fundamental view of reality be it physical-ist or theist. Not only does the question arise of how to compose one's spirit in the face of this, but the content of the metaphysical belief must condition the character of the resulting demeanor.

VI

The believer in Christian theism will be moved towards familiar Christian religious practices, and the reductive physicalist whose metaphysics is after all not so very different from that of the Old Stoics may wish to explore their spirituality. I think, therefore, that Hadot is wrong to try to loosen the link between philosophy and philosophical discourse; spirituality and metaphysics go together as I believe the writers of antiquity would agree.

The example of the Stoics and of other figures in antiquity gives some rea-son for thinking that a kind of philosophical spirituality can be fashioned on a non-theological world view. Suppose, however, that this is an illusion. That raises the following question. If it should seem after all that the necessary con-dition for the possibility of spirituality is some religious truth, and if the need and possibility of spirituality should seem compelling then might we have the beginnings of (a new version of) an (old) argument for religion?

Academic philosophy has traveled far from the concern of its founding fathers to provide a guide to life. Along the way it has lost sight of the very idea of spiritual values, and in its current phase it may have difficulty recov-ering or refashioning this idea. This very fact deserves to be examined and that examination might itself mark the beginning of a form of philosophical - *cum* -spiritual exercise: nothing less than an assessment of the value of what most academic philosophers currently practice in the name of their discipline.

Put another way and in the prophetic voice of John Paul II:

[P]hilosophy needs first of all too recover its sapiential dimension as a search for the ultimate and over-arching meaning of life. This first requirement is in fact most helpful in stimulating philosophy to conform to its proper nature. . . . In doing so it will be not only the decisive and critical factor which determines the foundations and limits of the different fields of scientific learning, but will also take its place as the ultimate framework of the unity of human knowledge and action, leading them to converge towards a final goal and meaning (§81).

Notes

1. For contrasting philosophical commentaries see A. MacIntyre, "How can we learn what *Veritatis Splendor* has to teach?" *The Thomist* 58: 2 (1994), pp. 171–95; and J. Haldane, "From Law to Virtue and Back Again: On *Veritatis Splendor*," in *The Bible in Ethics*, eds. J. W. Rogerson et. al. (Sheffield: Sheffield University Press, 1995), pp. 27–40.

2. *Veritatis Splendor* (London: Catholic Truth Society, 1997), pp. 75–77.

3. Given that it treats of philosophy in general while *Veritatis Splendor* treats of moral philosophy (and theology) in particular, one might have expected that *Fides et Ratio* would have appeared first. It is of interest, therefore, that the latter was embarked upon first in the mid-1980s.

4. See J. Haldane, "Theism" in *Atheism and Theism*, eds. J. J. C. Smart and J. J. Haldane (Oxford: Blackwell, 1996/7), pp. 164–67; idem, "Analytical Thomism," *The Monist* 80 (1997), pp. 485–86; and idem, "Thomism and the Future of Catholic Philosophy," *New Blackfriars* 80 (1999), pp. 158–71.

5. For reservations about whether the Pope's conception of the autonomy of philosophy fully recognises its self-governance, as operating by reason according to its own methods and principles, see Anthony Kenny, "The Pope as Philosopher," *The Tablet* (26 June 1999), pp. 874–75; and Jean Porter, "Letting Down the Drawbridge," *The Tablet* (3 July 1999), pp. 922–24.

6. In this connection see H. Putnam, "Aristotle after Wittgenstein," in *Words and Life*, ed. H. Putnam (Cambridge, MA: Harvard University Press, 1994), pp. 62–81; and J. Haldane "On Coming Home to (Metaphysical) Realism," *Philosophy* 71 (1996), pp. 287–96.

7. I use the analogy of participation in the life of a family rather than that of a parent given that in Christian mystical theology partaking in the life of God involves entering into the mutual Divine life of three Persons.

8. See P. Hadot, *Philosophy as a Way of Life: Spiritual Exercises from*

Socrates to Foucault, ed. A. I. Davidson (Oxford: Blackwell, 1995).

9. *The Discourses of Epictetus*, ed. C. Gill (London : Everyman, 1995), pp. 3, 23, 30.

10. *Discourses*, pp. 4, 4, 33.

11. Hadot, *Philosophy*, p. 206.

12. "Reflections on the Idea of the 'Cultivation of the Self,'" in Hadot, *Philosophy*, p. 212.

13. See M. Foucault, *History of Sexuality*, trans. R. Hurley, 4 vols. (New York, 1984), vol. 3.

14. Hadot, *Philosophy*, p. 211.

Christian Philosophy, Etienne Gilson, and *Fides et Ratio*
Steven Baldner

We naturally expect an encyclical on philosophy called *Fides et Ratio* to tell us something important about the proper relationship between theology and philosophy, and we are not disappointed in this expectation when we read Pope John Paul II's magnificent letter to the Bishops. In fact, the sixth chapter of the encyclical is devoted entirely to this topic. In the first part of chapter six, we see how theology has need of philosophy; in the second part, we see the relationship from the standpoint of philosophy, which can have, we find, three different stances toward theology. And it is here that the term "Christian philosophy" occurs in the encyclical, for the second of the three stances is that of Christian philosophy. John Paul II approves of the term, although he does so with certain qualifications, and he seems to approve of it in terms that have come from the two great French Thomists of this century, Etienne Gilson and Jacques Maritain. It is in particular the Gilsonian background to the encyclical that raises a problem that I would like to solve in this paper. Briefly the problem is that Gilson proposes both a description of and a program for Christian philosophy. The description is an excellent one, but the program has certain weaknesses. The encyclical might appear to be endorsing both the description and the program, but I hope to show that it really only endorses the description and not the program.

First, however, let me say that I agree with Henry Veatch that the old debate about Christian philosophy, a debate begun some seventy years ago between Gilson and Bréhier, is over.[1] Veatch is right to say that everyone agrees that that debate has been settled, but then, too, the war of 1812 between Canada and the United States is also, as everyone agrees, well over and settled, but the answer to the question of who won the war rather depends upon whether you read American or Canadian historians. So, for example, Fernand Van Steenberghen would have agreed with Veatch that the debate is over, but the Louvain Canon and the Hoosier Professor would each give the victor's palm to his own side of the debate.[2] Nevertheless, something important was settled by the debate, and it is this: Philosophy, whether it is called Christian or not, can only be philosophy if its principles and arguments are not dependent upon the assent of Christian faith. Everyone agrees that every philosophical principle and every philosophical argument must be fully accessible to any man, whether he is a believer or not. On the other hand, everyone also agrees that philosophers bring certain experiences, opinions, views of the world, and so forth, to the study of philosophy. A philosopher's faith is surely a part of his general understanding of the world, and it is natural and good that such faith should help to direct and to inform the philosopher's thinking, about philosophy as about many other things. On this, too, there is general agreement that the Cartesian attempt to sanitize the philosophical embryo from all non-philosophical contaminants resulted in an abortive philosophy.

To put the problem of this old debate in other terms, we could say that there is general agreement to adopt the distinction that Jacques Maritain brought to this problem long ago: the distinction between the essence or nature of philosophy and the state or practice of philosophy.[3] In its essence or nature, philosophy cannot be designated as either Christian or non-Christian, for philosophy formally considered "hinges entirely on its formal object, and since this object is wholly of the rational order, philosophy considered in itself – whether in a pagan or a Christian mind – depends on the same strictly natural or rational intrinsic criteria."[4] On the other hand, in the exercise of philosophy, in the concrete working out of any particular philosophical position, we find the work, not of an abstract essence, but of a flesh-and-blood, human individual. "To philosophize man must put his whole soul into play, in much the same manner that to run he must use his heart and lungs."[5] In putting one's whole soul into the doing of philosophy, one must give philosophical attention to what one knows to be most important; hence, one must give philosophical prominence to such questions as the existence of God, the creation of the world, the immortality of the soul, and so forth. In the working out of individual philosophical positions, as we can see in the history of philosophy, there are philosophies characterized by their focus on philosophical problems directly relevant to the faith. In this sense, it is useful to speak of Christian philosophy.

Let us turn now to Gilson's description of Christian philosophy. I quote from *L'esprit de la philosophie médiévale.*

> I call "Christian philosophy" any philosophy which, keeping well distinct the two formal orders [of revelation and of reason], considers Christian revelation as an indispensable aid to reason. Understood thus, this notion does not correspond to a simple essence that can be given an abstract definition; rather it corresponds to a concrete historical reality of which it indicates a description. It is but one kind within the genus of philosophy and denotes those systems of philosophy which would not have been what they were but for the fact that

there existed a Christian religion and for the fact that they willingly submitted to its influence. Insofar as they are concrete historical realities, these systems distinguish themselves one from another by their individual differences; insofar as they form one kind, they show common characteristics which justifies the grouping of them under one category.[6]

Here we have Gilson's description of Christian philosophy. There are three things to note about it. First, the order of reason is to be kept distinct from the order of revelation; formally, philosophy is always distinct from theology. Second, the term does not indicate a formal nature but is rather a term to designate concrete historical realities; it is a description rather than a definition. Third, the term indicates the sort of philosophy that results from the influence of Christianity; a philosophy that would not be what it is except for the influence of Christianity is a Christian philosophy. I underline these three points, because they anticipate rather closely what is said in *Fides et Ratio*. Let me quote now John Paul II:

> A second stance adopted by philosophy is often designated as *Christian philosophy*. In itself, the term is valid, but it should not be misunderstood: it in no way intends to suggest that there is an official philosophy of the Church, since the faith as such is not a philosophy [Gilson's first point]. The term seeks rather to indicate a Christian way of philosophizing, a philosophical speculation conceived in dynamic union with faith [Gilson's second point]. It does not therefore refer simply to a philosophy developed by Christian philosophers who have striven in their research not to contradict the faith. The term Christian philosophy includes those important developments of philosophical thinking which would not have happened without the direct or indirect contributions of Christian faith [Gilson's third point] (§76).

The Pope's description of Christian philosophy is the same as Gilson's. Both the Holy Father and the historian of mediaeval philosophy see the same three elements in the description. It is not a coincident, I think, that just before the description of Christian philosophy in the encyclical the name of Etienne Gilson was recommended to us, among several others, as an excellent modern example of a philosopher who understood the fruitful relationship of philosophy to the word of God.[7] It is not too much to say that John Paul II describes Christian philosophy *ad mentem Etienne Gilson*.

But it would be too much to say that John Paul II adopts what I call Gilson's *program* of Christian philosophy. Returning to Gilson's *L'esprit de la philosophie médiévale*, just after the description of Christian philosophy:

In the first place, and this is perhaps the most apparent trait of his attitude, the Christian philosopher is a man who makes a choice among
philosophical problems. By rights, he is capable of applying himself
to the totality of philosophical problems just as well as any other
philosopher; in fact, he applies himself uniquely or especially to
those problems the solution of which bears on the conduct of his religious life. The other problems, indifferent in themselves, become that
which Saint Augustine, Saint, Bernard, and Saint Bonaventure stig-
matized with the name *curiosity: vana curiositas, turpis curiositas.*
Even Christian philosophers like Saint Thomas whose interest did
extend to the whole of philosophy only did their creative work in a
relatively restrained field. Nothing could be more natural. Because
Christian revelation only teaches us about the truths that are necessary for salvation, its influence can only extend to the parts of philosophy that concern the existence of God, His nature, the origin of
our soul, its nature, and its destiny. . . . In a word, among all the
Christian philosophers who really deserve the name, the faith exercises a simplifying influence such that their originality manifests
itself especially in the area directly under the influence of the faith:
the doctrine of God, of man, and of his relations to God.[8]

This passage expresses Gilson's program of Christian philosophy, that is,
it recommends a course of action to the philosopher who wishes to pursue
Christian philosophy. In several of his works, such as *Le thomisme, Elements
of Christian Philosophy,* and *Christian Philosophy: An Introduction,* Gilson
gives us examples of this program. Consider the recently translated *Christian
Philosophy: An Introduction (Introduction à la philosophie chrétienne).* The
topics treated in this introduction to Christian philosophy make the Gilsonian
program clear: the certitude of faith as compared to the certitude of knowledge; creation; the meaning of Exodus 3. 14: "I am who I am:" the unknowability to us of God's nature; how being is known by us; the distinction
between essence and being; participation; the relation of metaphysics to the
sciences of nature.

From this list of topics and from Gilson's own remarks, we can see that
the Gilsonian program of Christian philosophy has four elements, which I will
summarize as follows. First, Christian philosophy is restricted to a narrow
range of problems. These are the problems, as we have seen, that bear directly on the faith: the existence of God, the creation of the world, the immortality of the soul, and so forth. If a Christian philosopher (such as Thomas
Aquinas) does philosophize on topics that do not bear on the faith, we can be
sure that this philosophical work is not work in Christian philosophy.

Second, Christian philosophy takes first philosophy to be metaphysics in
somewhat the same way as Descartes does. By this I mean that the philo-

sophical point of departure is in metaphysics, and in metaphysics at a rather high level. Gilson does not deny the importance of other areas of philosophy,[9] but he does insist that the correct starting point – even the way to introduce beginners – is through the metaphysical consideration of being. At the end of his *Christian Philosophy: An Introduction*, Gilson explains the purpose of the little book and in so doing explains the priority of metaphysics to the other areas of philosophy.

> These thoughts represent neither the theology of St. Thomas Aquinas nor his metaphysics, even less all the conclusions he held as true in the area of the philosophy of nature. We have said nothing here about the human person, nothing about ethics or politics. But it was not our intention to speak of them. Our only wish was to elucidate as clearly as possible a small number of literally capital truths that must be grasped if the rest of the doctrine is to be understood. All these truths depend on a certain notion of being, which was that of St. Thomas, and without which there is no Thomism truly worthy of the name.[10]

Like Descartes, Gilson regards first philosophy as pedagogically and foundationally first: once we correctly understand being, we can correctly understand substance, matter and form, causality, human nature, etc. Gilson is well aware of the Aristotelian objection that metaphysics is not to be studied by the young, and we are young until we are 50, but he counters this by arguing that the Christian philosopher has the advantage of faith.[11] The abstract intelligibility of metaphysics is rendered more concretely accessible to believers, so that, for them, it is quite appropriate to start their *Christian* philosophy with metaphysical problems such as the proofs of God's existence.

Third, Christian philosophy, according to Gilson, requires not just any metaphysics but specifically the metaphysics of *esse*. The doctrine of *esse*, understood as the doctrine that being in creatures is both distinct from essence and the first actuality, explains the fundamental fact of creation, the nature of God, the immortality of the soul, how it is that we can know that God exists, and so on. It is the one key that opens up the door to all of Christian philosophy, as Gilson understands it.

Fourth, Gilson's program of Christian philosophy requires a philosophy directed by theology.[12] The proper order of doing Christian philosophy is the theological order.[13] If, then, the *Summa theologiae* begins with a discussion of the nature of theology, with proofs for the existence of God, and with a discussion of God's nature, then that is just the way that Christian philosophy should proceed, also. A Christian philosophy remains a distinctly philosophical venture, according to Gilson, but its order, structure, and set of problems is given by theology, not by independent philosophical considerations. Such is Gilson's program of Christian philosophy. Can we find any endorsement of this program in the encyclical *Fides et Ratio*?

There are, according to John Paul II, three legitimate "stances" of philosophy toward the faith. First, there is the stance of philosophy that is *completely independent of the faith* (§75). This is the stance of any philosophy that has not in fact been exposed to Christian revelation. So, for example, the philosophy of Plato or of Aristotle is such a non-Christian philosophy. It is philosophy developed on the resources of human reason alone and without the guidance that could come from revelation. This stance of philosophy is not that of the so-called "separate" philosophy, that is, of a philosophy worked out in such a way as to reject the truth of Christian revelation. The existentialism of Jean-Paul Sartre would be an example of a separate philosophy, and there are other examples in contemporary analytic philosophy. Consider some remarks made by John Searle, who is in other respects an excellent philosopher.

> Our problem is not that somehow we have failed to come up with a convincing proof of the existence of God or that the hypothesis of an afterlife remains in serious doubt, it is rather that in our deepest reflections we cannot take such opinions seriously. When we encounter people who claim to believe such things, we may envy them the comfort and security they claim to derive from these beliefs, but at bottom we remain convinced that either they have not heard the news or they are in the grip of faith.[14]

Notice Searle's language: those who hold that God exists or that the soul is immortal *have not heard the news*, although we Christians thought that we had heard the good news, and we are in *the grip of faith* – a grip from which contemporary science can liberate us. Searle's position is an example of scientism, and it can be philosophically refuted, but John Paul II is alerting us to the fact that the philosophical stance represented by Searle's words is not a non-Christian stance but an anti-Christian stance.

The second stance is that of *Christian philosophy* (§76). The Holy Father grants that this term is legitimate, but he urges us to use the term carefully. As we have seen, the term indicates no one kind of philosophy, for the Church endorses no one concrete philosophy as an official philosophy, but rather a way of philosophizing that is in concert with the faith. Christian philosophy refers to the developments in philosophy that would not have taken place but for the influence of the faith.[15] This John Paul II elaborates upon in two ways.

> Subjectively, the Christian philosopher's faith perfects his intellect insofar as it gives him both humility and courage. Faith gives humility to free the philosopher from the presumption that is the besetting

temptation of his discipline; it also gives him the courage to attempt to solve the largest and most important of philosophical questions. Subjectively, faith keeps the philosopher in a healthy mean: the Christian philosopher will avoid the presumption and folly of thinking that his philosophy can explain everything, but he will also avoid the timidity and parsimony that would restrict the practice of philosophy to narrow, technical problems.[16]

Objectively, the faith reveals certain truths which the philosopher can aim at in his philosophizing. On revelation, for example, we know that God exists, that He is providential, that man is immortal and freely responsible for his acts, that happiness is something transcendent, and so forth. To some degree, the philosopher can understand these same truths, and he should try to do so. But no one way of understanding these truths is endorsed by the Church. In this respect, I like the image which is favored by Father Owens. The faith is a "friendly star", which shows us the destination but does not specify a way of going there.[17] We know on faith that human beings are free, volitional moral agents, but this human freedom can be explained in many ways, as one can learn by reading Augustine, Anselm, Thomas, Scotus, Descartes, Kant, Nietzsche, Whitehead, or even Searle. These accounts are not all philosophically equal, but their philosophical strengths and deficiencies are just that – philosophical – for the Church does not adjudicate in philosophical disputes.

The objective sense of Christian philosophy seems, according to the encyclical, to have two parts. Some truths, such as the truth about human free will, are solutions to problems which, once introduced into the domain of philosophy, become philosophical problems *simpliciter*. Augustine's reasons for raising the problem of free will were surely theological, but from the time of Augustine to the present the problem of free will has been a problem that can be treated in a purely and simply philosophical way. Philosophy would not have had this problem as a philosophical problem but for the faith, but once raised the problem can be solved (or not) without regard to the original theological source of the problem. On the other hand, John Paul II is also recommending problems to philosophers that will not ever be disengaged from their theological setting, for they are fundamentally theological not philosophical problems, but yet philosophers are to make philosophical, not theological, contributions to the solution of these problems. Two examples he gives are the supernatural end for man and original sin. A philosopher might be able to show, for example, the inadequacy or the imperfection of human happiness in this life, and, while maintaining the full legitimacy of a philosophical ethics, show also that philosophy prepares the way for the fuller account in theology. I can recommend no better example of the sort of thinking that the Pope wishes on this topic than R. McInerny's excellent lectures, *The Question of*

Christian Ethics.[18] On original sin, philosophers might pursue the sort of analysis that Cardinal Newman gives in his *Apologia pro vita sua*, where Newman argues that an objective, philosophical appraisal of the many follies in human history and society, leads one to a hard disjunction: either there is no God, or the human race has suffered some "terrible aboriginal calamity."[19]

Finally, on the objective sense of Christian philosophy, the encyclical makes one more point. "It could be said that a good part of modern and contemporary philosophy would not exist without this stimulus of the word of God. This conclusion retains all of its relevance, despite the disappointing fact that many thinkers in recent centuries have abandoned Christian orthodoxy" (§76). Christian philosophy can be found in philosophers who are rather clearly not Christian. Let me again use the example of John Searle. He has done more than anyone in analytic philosophy to advance a credible view of human nature on such questions as the mind-body problem, materialism, dualism, consciousness, human intelligence, intentionality, and free will. On the problem of free will, and perhaps also on the general problem of reductionism, we could say that Searle *malgré lui* is making a contribution to Christian philosophy in just the sense that the Holy Father has specified.

The third stance of philosophy toward theology is that of philosophy *in the service of theology*. In order for theology to pursue its ends, it needs a philosophical preparation and specific philosophical doctrines. Theologians cannot begin the study of theology without prior training in philosophy, and when theologians elaborate particular doctrines they naturally have recourse to philosophical truth. The theological doctrine of creation or of the Trinity, for example, cannot be elaborated in theology without some philosophical contribution on the problem of relation. When theologians fail to call upon genuine philosophy, they "run the risk of doing philosophy unwittingly and locking themselves within thought-structures poorly adapted to the understanding of the faith" (§77). A good example of the problem to which the Pope alludes is, in my opinion, the attractiveness of process philosophy to theologians who are ill prepared to see its philosophical weaknesses. The active service of philosophy to theology, which as John Paul II points out, involves a recognition by philosophers of the authority of the Magisterium, used to be expressed by the term *ancilla theologiae*. The term is no longer suitable, because it might suggest that philosophy loses its autonomy, but the important fact remains that theology needs the service of philosophy and that Christian philosophers should recognize the authority of the Magisterium.[20]

Having seen the three legitimate stances of philosophy to theology, let us return to our principal question. Does John Paul II endorse the Gilsonian program of Christian philosophy? The answer, which I think should be both obvious and correct, is no. Clearly, on the first point, the Pope is not in any way recommending a *restriction* of philosophy to certain points, and clearly on the fourth point he is not recommending a theological order to the study of philosophy. The second and the third points of the program, however, seem to be recommended by the Pope, for there are many references in the encyclical to metaphysics and to a philosophy of being. Let us consider the two most important of these.

There is, for example, in the document the recommendation that a philosophy which takes profit from the scriptures is a philosophy with a truly metaphysical range (§83-84). In sections 83 to 84, John Paul II is forcefully insistent upon the importance of metaphysics in philosophy. But what is he trying to combat? He is trying to combat the philosophical position that would *exclude* metaphysics from philosophy. If a philosopher reduces philosophy to hermeneutics or to the study of language such that transcendent, spiritual, or immaterial reality is in principle excluded, then, the Pope is telling us, we have not heeded the call manifest in scripture for a truly sapiential philosophy which naturally would culminate in metaphysical reflection. There is nothing here, however, to suggest that philosophy or Christian philosophy *is* metaphysics. Surely a danger of some contemporary philosophy has been the exclusion of the non-empirical or the immaterial. Such an exclusion is *ipso facto* an exclusion of metaphysics. John Paul II so forcefully recommends the inclusion of metaphysics precisely to combat its exclusion. There is nothing in the encyclical to endorse the Gilsonian program of reducing Christian philosophy to metaphysics.[21]

Another example occurs after the discussion of various errors that would be incompatible with a Christian philosophy when the Pope explains various problems that theology should solve with the help of philosophy.

> If the *intellectus fidei* wishes to integrate all the wealth of the theological tradition, it must turn to the philosophy of being, which should be able to propose anew the problem of being – and this in harmony with the demands and insights of the entire philosophical tradition, including philosophy of more recent times, without lapsing into sterile repetition of antiquated formulas. Set within the Christian metaphysical tradition, the philosophy of being is a dynamic philosophy which views reality in its ontological, causal and communicative structures. It is strong and enduring because it is based upon the very act of being itself, which allows a full and comprehensive openness to reality as a whole, surpassing every limit in order to reach the One who brings all things to fulfillment. In theology, which draws its principles from Revelation as a new source of knowledge, this perspective is confirmed by the intimate relationship which exists between faith and metaphysical reasoning (§97).

This passage certainly contains language that is suggestive of the

Gilsonian program. There is commendation here of the "Christian metaphysical" tradition, clearly a metaphysics based on the act of being is recommended, and there is a suggestion of a theme very dear to Gilson: the theological setting of metaphysical problems.

But what are we really being told in this passage? The immediate context of this passage makes it clear that the Pope is warning theologians against the temptation to reduce the truths of faith to a moral doctrine. He is concerned to combat a pragmatism in theology, and he does so by pointing out that revelation is given not only to elicit a moral response from us but also, and fundamentally, to tell us about certain *realities*. Christology is fundamentally about Christ, who is God and man; it is not merely a story told to encourage a certain sort of behavior. A theology that makes use of a philosophy founded in the real is a theology that can avoid such a pragmatism. A philosophy founded in the real is one that includes a metaphysics based upon the act of being. The Pope wants a philosophy that allows "a full and comprehensive openness to reality as a whole" and one which will reach "the One who brings all things to fulfillment." The Holy Father is calling for realism in philosophy[22] and for a philosophy that can reach the transcendent; he is not demanding the Thomistic doctrine of *esse*. As has been made clear several times in the encyclical, "the Church has no philosophy of her own nor does she canonize any one particular philosophy in preference to others" (§49).

My conclusion, then, is straightforward. In *Fides et Ratio*, the discussion of Christian philosophy owes much to the thought of Gilson. The description of Christian philosophy – as distinctly philosophical rather than theological, as a way of philosophizing rather than as a particular, concrete philosophy, and as philosophical developments that would not have taken place but for the influence of the faith – is a description that the encyclical adopts and recommends to us. Gilson's program of Christian philosophy, an attempt to create a philosophy that is a metaphysics of *esse*, is Gilson's own creation and is not endorsed by John Paul II. I do not for a minute wish to imply that the Pope is critical of Gilson's program but only that he does not endorse or recommend it by adopting this Gilsonian description of Christian philosophy.[23]

As an epilogue to my argument, I shall make some observations. Part of me agrees with Van Steenberghen: we would be better off if we could banish the term "Christian philosophy". The usefulness of the term is at best "in house;" among Christian philosophers the term can have some usefulness in characterizing a proper stance of philosophy with regard to the faith. The term, however, is sure to be misleading to non-Christian philosophers. I cannot imagine that analytic philosophers will make haste to buy and to read books with the words "Christian philosophy" or "Christian metaphysics" in the title. Such terms will only serve to make the discussion that John Haldane has urged Thomists to undertake all the harder to initiate.[24] We should, by all means, adopt the stance that the Pope has described as the stance of Christian philosophy, but there is no need for us to call what we are doing "Christian philosophy." Furthermore, I think that even among Christian philosophers, the term has been misleading. In being committed to the idea of a Christian philosophy, philosophers have been inclined to think that there is such a thing as a *complete and specific* Christian philosophy. Just as Platonic philosophy or Aristotelian philosophy or Cartesian philosophy might be described as complete and specific philosophical systems, so Christian philosophy has been thought, at least by Gilsonians, as a kind of complete and specific philosophical system. But this is a big mistake, I think. To take Thomas as an example, his "Christian philosophy" was just his developing or improving Aristotle's philosophy. Aristotle's philosophy is not as such a Christian philosophy, but it certainly can be used as a Christian philosophy insofar as its principles can be used to demonstrate the existence of God, the creation of the world, or the immortality of the soul, which is just what Thomas did with it. In this sense, one might consider Aristotelian philosophy to be a Christian philosophy, but it is really nothing but Aristotle's philosophy being completed and perfected by Christian philosophers. If I am right in understanding Thomas's philosophy as Aristotle's–and it is here, of course, that the principal divide occurs between Gilsonian and natural philosophy Thomists – then Thomas would not have thought of his philosophy as a Christian philosophy. Thomas's philosophy was philosophy *simpliciter*; Thomas might have regarded it as misleading to call his philosophy "Christian."

The encyclical, *Fides et Ratio*, is not so much recommending the name "Christian philosophy" as allowing its use. Surely the stance indicated by the name has been recommended to us, and I think it highly desirable that all Christian philosophers pursue Christian philosophy in the sense that they adopt the recommended stance. But I wonder whether, after all, we could do just as well without the name?

Notes

1. Henry B. Veatch, "The Problems and the Prospects of a Christian Philosophy—Then and Now," *The Monist* 75 (1992), p. 384. For the most extensive history of the debate, see Maurice Nédoncelle, *Is There a Christian Philosophy?*, trans. Illtyd Trethowan (New York: Hawthorn Books, 1960). See also Joseph Owens, *Towards a Christian Philosophy* (Washington, D.C.: The Catholic University of America Press, 1990), pp. 1–23.

2. Fernand Van Steenberghen, "Philosophie et christianisme: Épilogue d'un débat ancien," *Revue philosophique de Louvain* 86 (1988), pp. 180–91, argues that, although it is true that philosophers have been helpfully influenced by

their Christian faith, there is no such thing as a Christian philosophy. Henry Veatch, in the article cited in note one, argues that Christian philosophy is alive and well in contemporary philosophical realism.

3. Jacques Maritain, *An Essay on Christian Philosophy*, trans. E. H. Flannery (New York: Philosophical Library, 1955), pp. 11–18.

4. Maritain, *An Essay on Christian Philosophy*, p. 15.

5. Ibid., p. 17.

6. Etienne Gilson, *L'esprit de la philosophie médiévale* (Paris: Vrin, 1944), pp. 32–33.

7. "We see the same fruitful relationship between philosophy and the word of God in the courageous research pursued by more recent thinkers, among whom I gladly mention, in a Western context, figures such as John Henry Newman, Antonio Rosmini, Jacques Maritain, Étienne Gilson and Edith Stein and, in an Eastern context, eminent scholars such as Vladimir S. Soloviev, Pavel A. Florensky, Petr Chaadaev and Vladimir N. Lossky." *Fides et Ratio*, §74.

8. Gilson, *L'esprit*, pp. 33–34.

9. Gilson, however, might not allow much room for natural philosophy in his program of Christian philosophy. One of the mistakes Catholic philosophers made, according to Gilson, was to combat the materialism of the sixteenth and seventeenth centuries with the discredited science of Aristotle, rather than with the deep metaphysics of Thomas Aquinas. It is metaphysics, not natural philosophy, that is used to respond to errors about nature. See "What is Christian Philosophy" in A *Gilson Reader*, ed. Anton Pegis (Garden City, NY: Hanover House, 1957), pp. 177–91, especially p. 185.

10. Gilson, *Christian Philosophy: An Introduction*, trans. Armand Maurer (Toronto: Pontifical Institute of Mediaeval Studies, 1993), pp. 132–33.

11. In "Thomas Aquinas and our Colleagues," in A Gilson Reader, pp. 278–97, Gilson sets out to solve the following problem in interpreting Thomas. Thomas holds that ethics (including political science) and metaphysics should not be studied by youths, and the period of iuventus reaches until the late 40s. No one should study metaphysics, then, until the age of 50, but Thomas himself was not only studying metaphysics but teaching it in his 20s. How to explain this inconsistency in deeds and words? Thomas, according to Gilson, could do what he would not recommend to a philosopher because he was a theologian and not a philosopher. The theologian can handle metaphysical and ethical questions earlier than can the philosopher, but, note, he can do so in a philosophical way. Theology, thus, makes the Christian philosopher philosophically precocious.

12. The dispute between Gilson and Van Steenberghen on Christian philosophy can be expressed rather neatly on just this point. Gilson's position, as Van Steenberghen puts it, is, "Plus un maître est grand théologien, plus il est grand philosophe." Van Steenberghen's position, by contrast, is, "les bons philosophes font les bons théologiens et non pas l'inverse." Van Steenberghen, "Philosophie et christianisme," pp 184, 187.

13. John Wipple, although he may be counted as a Gilsonian, has been critical of this point in Gilson's work. Wipple seems to agree that Thomas's Christian philosophy is fundamentally the metaphysics of esse, but Wipple argues that Thomas allows for a properly philosophical order of doing metaphysics. Briefly, Wipple argues, in metaphysics we recognize esse by judgment and by *separatio* and then we argue to God as the cause of being. Metaphysics starts with ens commune but proceeds to demonstrate God as the cause of being. Theology, and the natural theology that follows the same order) starts with God and argues about His nature and works thereafter. See John Wipple, *Metaphysical Themes in Thomas Aquinas* (Washington, D.C.: The Catholic University of America Press, 1984), pp. 2–33.

14. John Searle, *The Rediscovery of the Mind* (Cambridge, MA: MIT Press, 1994), p. 90.

15. One might say that the expression here is too strong: both the Pope and Gilson characterize Christian philosophy as the sort of philosophy that would not have occurred without the influence of the faith. They might have made the weaker claim that, as a matter of historical fact, Christianity has raised certain problems for philosophers to solve. I think that it is fair, especially for Gilson, to say that the stronger claim is intended. Without the revelation of Exodus 3:14, philosophers just would not have come to the doctrine of being that is needed for a Christian philosophy. "Since God has revealed himself as He Who Is, the philosopher knows that at the origin and very heart of beings it is necessary to place the pure act of existing. The divine word absolutely transcends the philosophical notions conceived in its light; that is also why they could not be deduced from it. We do not say: Since scripture says so, the philosophical notions of being and God are in the last analysis identical with that of the act of being. In fact, scripture itself does not say this; but it does say that the proper name of God is He Who Is. Because it says this I believe it. While I thus cling to the object of faith, the intellect, made fruitful by this contact, makes deeper progress in the understanding of the primary notion of being. With one and the same movement it discovers an unforeseen depth in the philosophical meaning of the first principle and gains a kind of imperfect but true knowledge of the object of faith." Etienne Gilson, *Christian Philosophy*, pp. 31–32.

16. Ralph McInerny has considered this subjective aspect of Christian philosophy in a different way. He draws our attention to the moral life of the philosopher himself. Without moral virtue, the philosopher renders himself incapable of apprehending the real. The attempt to excise the moral from the intellectual life has resulted, McInerny points out, in a notion of the philosophical act as something completely foreign to the life that philosophers actually live. From Aristophanes to Kierkegaard, this monstrosity of a "pure" or "separated" philosophy has been rightly ridiculed. See Ralph McInerny, "Reflections on Christian Philosophy," in *One Hundred Years of Thomism: Aeterni Patris and Afterwards* (Houston: Center for Thomistic Studies, 1981), pp. 63–73.

17. Joseph Owens, *Towards a Christian Philosophy*, p. 26.

18. Ralph McInerny, *The Question of Christian Ethics* (Washington, D.C.: The Catholic University of America Press, 1993).

19. John Henry Newman, *Apologia pro vita sua* (Boston: Houghton Mifflin, 1956), pp. 278–79.

20. We must be dealing here with Christian philosophers. The Christian philosopher welcomes the service that he can provide to theology and is willingly guided by the Magisterium. There is nothing here to suggest any loss of the genuine autonomy of philosophy.

21. At the end of the encyclical, John Paul II again recommends metaphysics. "I appeal also to philosophers, and to all teachers of philosophy, asking them to have the courage to recover, in the flow of an enduringly valid philosophical tradition, the range of authentic wisdom and truth – metaphysical truth included – which is proper to philosophical enquiry" (§106). Again, the point is that metaphysics be included; the point is not to reduce Christian philosophy to metaphysics.

22. I should point out, again, that Henry Veatch has argued that philosophical realism is just what Christian philosophy should mean. See note #1.

23. My conclusion is in accord, I think, with the position of Jude P. Dougherty, who has argued that the term "Christian philosophy" is best taken as a term to describe historical or sociological realities rather than a term to indicate the intrinsic or essential nature of philosophy. Like me, Dougherty is appreciative of Gilson's vast contributions to the historical understanding of Christian philosophy. Jude P. Dougherty, "Christian Philosophy: Sociological Category or Oxymoron?" *The Monist* 75 (1992), pp. 283–90.

24. John Haldane, "What Future Has Catholic Philosophy?" Proceedings of the American Catholic Philosophical Association 71 (1997), pp. 79–90.

Contemporary Philosophy Facing *Fides et Ratio*
Angelo Campodonico

Although *Fides et Ratio* is primarily addressed to bishops and theologians, I would like to show that the connection between faith and reason is an important problem for everyone, believers and non-believers in the Christian faith. To do this implies that I shall have to address the many streams which flow into the main river of contemporary philosophy, whose diversity has influenced the encyclical itself. There are, in fact, affinities and contrasts between the subjects of contemporary philosophy and the encyclical. I would like to consider some of these subjects, attempt to highlight common points and discuss difficulties.

Faith and Reason Intertwined

I hold that there is no rationality without evidence (in a narrow or strong sense) and also there is no rationality "in practice" without trust in our reason as well as in that of others. Faith and reason are deeply intertwined in everyone. On the one hand, reason in a narrow sense means assent to evidence and well grounded truths, e.g., the truths of mathematics and particularly the main principles of logic and metaphysics (e.g., the principle of contradiction). On these first principles is grounded the classical proofs of God's existence and even hermeneutics.[1] Against contemporary hermeneuticism, widespread in postmodern thought, we must stress that even hermeneutics is grounded on the first principles of reason in addition to the phenomenological evidence of the senses.[2] Every reasonable belief is grounded on the basis of some evidence:

> Although time changes and knowledge increases, it is possible to discern a core of philosophical insight within the history of thought as a whole. Consider, for example, the principles of non-contradiction, finality and causality, as well as the concept of the person as a free and intelligent subject, with the capacity to know God, truth and goodness. Consider as well certain fundamental moral norms which are shared by all (§4).

Without evidence as its frame, faith is impossible because it lacks a firm content. We understand why natural theology (even implicit) is so important if we want to stress the rationality of the Christian faith.[3] Everybody has to achieve somehow a natural concept of God in order to be able to acknowledge the God of Revelation. This point, in my opinion, is not easily accepted by contemporary philosophy, not even by contemporary Catholic philosophy and theology (§84).

But reason is not only speculative reason in the classical sense (*intellectus et scientia episteme*). On the other hand, faith is assent to something not because its content is evident, but because we believe in someone. Testimony is the source of belief. It is noteworthy that without Christianity and its concept of faith in a strong sense there would not have been a Western philosophical approach to faith and belief as Augustine shows.[4]

Sometimes it is difficult to distinguish between evidence and faith. In fact, there are types of faith which seem to carry upon themselves a great deal of evidence. As an example let us consider our relationships with other people where we find the same type of connection as that existing between faith and evidence. On the one hand, we believe in the feelings of others, although there is no evidence of them in a strict sense, as Augustine holds. On the other hand, it is evident that we meet human beings such as we are and that they are more perfect than any other being in the world and the most worthy of respect (nowadays this evidence concerns at least normal human beings).

Faith and reason never have the same content nor do they have the same content under the same viewpoint. Without faith in others, reason would not be fed and therefore would not work (as contemporary psychology shows). Without reason (in the strong sense) and its evidence, faith could not be firm or reasonable and could not be explicated in reflection. Moreover, without reason there would be no *faith* in the capabilities of our reason. In fact, we believe more and more in reason, because reason works. Therefore faith, hope and charity (in a wide sense) are the main characteristics of reason itself as some contemporary philosophers such as Gadamer, Polanyi, Bloch, and Davidson hold.[5] Faith and reason are not unrelated. There is a "faithful reason" as well as a "reasonable faith," although there are faiths which are more or less reasonable. An example of the deep connection between faith and reason is this: we may believe a fact because we believe in those who tell us that fact, but also because we are aware of some evident truths connected with that fact. Therefore, faith and reason are the two lungs of human rationality.[6] As the encyclical *Fides et Ratio* holds:

> In believing, we entrust ourselves to the knowledge acquired by other people. This suggests an important tension. On the one hand, the knowledge acquired through belief can seem an imperfect form of

knowledge, to be perfected gradually through personal accumulation of evidence; on the other hand, belief is often humanly richer than mere evidence, because it involves an interpersonal relationship and brings into play not only a person's capacity to know but also the deeper capacity to entrust oneself to others, to enter into a relationship with them which is intimate and enduring (§32).

It is noteworthy that a great deal of contemporary philosophy (particularly continental philosophy) might quite easily accept this truth after the crisis of modern rationalism.[7]

I hold that realism, the openness of man to reality (considered in itself as well as through other people), is the common ground of a "faithful reason" and of a "reasonable faith." There is a consent (*consensus*) to being itself which is the very ground of every human question and inquiry.

World-views

World-views are grounded on evidence as well as on faiths.[8] In our world-view evidence and faith are intertwined, and they make each other strong; thus, Marxism and Liberalism might be called "faiths" in a broad sense. We do not assent reasonably to concepts of life when everything is clear, but when we think that there are enough reasons for us to assent. The virtue of *phronesis* judges here and now if a world-view is reasonable for us.

Every faith (world-view) is grounded on some reason, but not every faith is equally reasonable, because not every faith (world-view) answers the needs and goals of human existence. The value of a faith depends on will, on reasons and on the facts that we encounter. From a theological point of view, we can speak also of grace. These are the very grounds of Christian faith according to Catholic theology. Therefore, we can never judge a man upon his assent or upon his lack of assent, but we can judge and, in fact, we often judge the contents of his faith. That faith (or world-view) is reasonable which considers deeply and integrally man, his desires and demands (for happiness, justice, truth, eternity, beauty) and the evidence of reality (particularly the logico-ontological first principles and those ontological truths such as that the human person is the highest being in the hierarchy of beings intentionally open to the whole of being).[9] As *Fides et Ratio* holds:

> In this sense, metaphysics should not be seen as an alternative to anthropology, since it is metaphysics which makes it possible to ground the concept of personal dignity in virtue of their spiritual nature. In a special way, the person constitutes a privileged locus for the encounter with being, and hence with metaphysical enquiry (§83).

We can identify here some influences of contemporary continental philosophy: personalism, phenomenology, etc.

It is noteworthy that the encyclical has a Thomistic frame, but within it we may also find personalistic accents of contemporary continental philosophy. But against Kant and contemporary Kantianism we must stress that since reason is one, there is not a wide gap between theoretical reason and practical reason (our aims). That means that human desires are always grounded on ontological evidence; as Augustine stresses, we cannot look for happiness without seeking also truth and eternity.[10] Man does not only seek happiness, but reality as well and he cannot search for them without previously somehow knowing what they are.[11] He needs a true concept of himself and of his happiness. He does not want to be deceived.

As there are good faiths (in a broad sense), there are also negative faiths, in which proof is used in order to develop a narrowness of mind or a form of resentment in front of reality. This often happens in post-Christian culture. As Hannah Arendt holds:

> [T]he first disastrous result of man's coming of age is that modern man has come to resent everything given, even his own existence – to resent the very fact that he is not the creator of the universe and himself. In this fundamental resentment, he refuses to see rhyme or reason in the given world. In his resentment of all laws merely given to him, he proclaims openly that everything is permitted and believes secretly that everything is possible. And since he knows that he is a law-creating being, and that his task, according to all standards of past history, is "superhuman," he resents even his nihilistic convictions, as though they were forced upon him by some cruel joke of the devil.[12]

Two instances of a bad faith are: faith in ideologies or an exaggerated faith in science and technology. For instance: it is worthwhile to note that more than a century ago the encyclical *Rerum novarum* (1893) had foreseen the drama of twentieth century totalitarianism[13] and also that after fifty years of research the hope that computers could imitate the human mind is perhaps not so strong as it was some years ago. It is reasonable for everyone to acknowledge that in our world there are not only *problems* (which can be resolved by us), but also *mysteries* (what are in themselves reasonable but not to us). To sum up: a world-view or a concept of life is more reasonable if it acknowledges and tries to fulfill the demands of men and particularly their basic demands. But we have to stress that to fulfill does not mean to respond, here and now, in a definite way to human demands, but to acknowledge human needs (that means an exaltation of them) and to show the safe way towards their fulfillment. This is an important criterion in order to evaluate a world-view or a culture.[14]

Otherwise, because of the unity of man and his reason, it is reasonable that whoever wishes to bring his/her main demands to mature development and searches and reaches adequate responses to them can find out more than others do, not only that evidence which is peculiar to his world-view but also that which is *de iure* for everyone. Therefore, his human nature is exalted. In this case we might speak about an explicit *assent* to our everyday implicit *consent* to reality.

Philosophy and Religious Experience

If what I have just said is true, it is also reasonable to say that the assent of faith to a "Mysterious Truth" can develop also the rational capability of understanding every man's truth. If the demand for fulfillment and the religious experience are the peak of our human experience,[15] reason needs religious experience and religious faith in order not to become an instrumental, formal and ultimately nihilistic reason. In the history of Western societies this faith is the Christian faith.

The problem of the connection between philosophy and religious experience (also in a broad sense) is particularly important nowadays. In fact, we are facing a deep change of demarcations between the different disciplines and, within philosophy itself, among the different philosophical disciplines. On the one hand, there is a wide gap between religious experience and philosophy (e.g., logical positivism and some streams of analytical philosophy) On the other hand, there is a confusion of subjects and methods (a kind of gnosticism – particularly in continental philosophy). When the demarcation between religion and philosophy is not clear, it may happen that philosophy uses the kind of language of testimony and of invocation which is typical of religion.

It seems that when reason loses its fruitful connection with faith and religious experience, it fluctuates between a loss of belief in its capabilities and an exaggerated belief in those capabilities, which causes reactions of mistrust. In fact, it is philosophically reasonable that what can actually unify man and give meaning to his life and to the operations of his mind is necessarily transcendent and cannot be grasped by man through the efforts of his own reason (considered as a search for evidence), but only by a faith (which is not unreasonable and which concerns the whole man).

If a belief is conceived as certain and reasonable, even implicitly, by those who have it, if it is not only a postulate, a demand, a feeling in order to defeat fear, it attempts to justify itself when facing other concepts of life. That happens when a faith is discussed in different world-views. In fact, that is the case of the genesis and the development of Christian theology and philosophy during the first centuries, particularly of the proofs of God's existence. Nonetheless, it is true that philosophical reason seems to need the certainties of experience and particularly of religious experience in order to believe in itself, to develop its contents and perhaps, paradoxically, even in order to become free from religion itself (as has often happened during the modern period).

What Kind of Faith is the Christian Faith?

But we are not concerned with just any kind of faith. Particularly: what kind of faith is the Christian faith? It is faith in a strong sense, because it integrally concerns our freedom. Christianity seems to be not first of all a theory, a philosophy, but a unique Event, in which there implicitly lies a concept of reality which may become *partially* explicit. From this point of view we might say that to believe in Christianity can be looked upon as being fascinated by a Wise Man whom we meet and whom we can know gradually more and more. If our idea of reality is not an essentialistic one, if there is in reality a primacy of events, if, in Thomistic terms, we acknowledge the primacy of the act of existing, then the Christian faith is concerned with a Mystery, and this is not absurd. It is not *a priori* strange for one single event to bear universality. In this way we can begin answering Lessing's famous problem, which is still up to date in contemporary culture and philosophy.[16] I believe that this point remains one of the principal difficulties facing *Fides et Ratio*.

To sum up: it is reasonable to assent to truths which are meaningful for the fulfillment of fundamental human needs. From this point of view, Christian faith is not an emotional, extra-rational attitude.[17] Faith is "converted reason," reason which believes, which finds out arguments to believe: "To believe is nothing other than to think with assent."[18] Without reason, primarily the ontological dimension of our reason, faith cannot concern the totality of being (it is not true faith, faith in the strong sense). We must, therefore, study in depth the problem of the connection between the ontological and the symbolical dimension of the Christian faith.

Uniqueness of Cultures and the Analogous Concept of Culture

This concept of the uniqueness of Christianity has consequences. Although there are universal laws of reality as well as of our thought (the dimension of order, of essence, of first principles), reality is compounded by unique beings and events (the dimension of existence–act of existing).[19] We might also speak of novelty of being (*novitas essendi*).[20] This is the metaphysical background of *Fides et Ratio*. We find this idea of uniqueness also in contemporary Jewish thought (e.g., Lévinas). Christianity helps us to think of the uniqueness of events: just as the event of Christ is unique, so, in an analogous way, is Patristic thought and Aquinas's theology and philosophy.

> [I]n engaging great cultures for the first time, the Church cannot abandon what she has gained for her inculturation in the world of Greco-Latin thought. To reject this heritage would be to deny the providential plan of God who guides his Church down the paths of time and history. This criterion is valid for the Church in every age, even for the Church of the future, who will judge herself enriched by all that comes from today's engagement with Eastern cultures and will find in this inheritance fresh cues for fruitful dialogue with the cultures which will emerge as humanity moves into the future (§72).

We also hold that the role of men in society might not be the same as that of women, although they all have the same dignity. That means that the task of reason is not to level everything (that is the Enlightenment idea of reason). From this point of view every culture has equal dignity, but not the same value. Why should they? The concept of culture is analogous. That is to say, one can defend the uniqueness of a particular cultural tradition without opposing it to other cultures but by relating it to the "universality of the human spirit" (§72).

As I have stressed, the criterion for evaluating cultures is their ability to face the *integrity* of the demands of man and the *integrity* of reality in general. Both aspects are important. Many cultures deal well with reality but only by reducing the expectation for meeting human needs; or they stress such human needs and desires while ignoring the realities of this world. This kind of approach often becomes a *habitus*, sometimes a bad *habitus* (a vice). Therefore not every culture is equally important for man and for Christianity, although every culture bears some peculiar values. It is very important to stress this point in our age of multi-culturalism.

Eclecticism

Nowadays we have passed from an exaggerated belief in reason, which is possible on the ground of Christian experience and not only on Greek philosophy (Hegelism, and the great optimistic ideologies of the last two centuries, such as Marxism), to a crisis of reason, a disbelief in its capabilities of knowing reality (*nihilism*). There is a deep logic in this change. Therefore, the Church itself, which in the modern period strongly fought against optimistic-anthropocentric reason, now defends reason, its possibility to identify a common ground for every man and for every culture. I believe that we must stress this point. In particular, *Fides et Ratio* is against eclecticism in philosophy and theology. According to the encyclical, eclecticism means "the approach of those who, in research, teaching and argumentation, even in theology, tend to use individual ideas drawn from different philosophies, without concern for their internal coherence, their place within a system or their historical context" (§86). If reason does not fear reality, but loves it (assents to it) if it is faithful, if it knows that it is developing itself by facing reality, it looks for theoretical coherence. On the contrary, eclecticism with its lack of coherence may be the effect of fear in the face of reality and, therefore, of the exaggerated desire of being appreciated by contemporary culture. In this problem one might also find the root of historicism (§87). But, as Aquinas stresses, feeble arguments in defense of the Christian faith are not helpful for those who do not believe.[21]

The Roots of Nihilism and Skepticism in Contemporary Philosophy

It is not unusual for some philosophers today to negate some truths which are the very grounds of natural theology and of Christian faith. Paradoxically, it is sometimes apparent that they know they are thereby knowingly contradicting themselves (§91). The main cause of this problem is not a logical or an epistemic one, but an ontological-anthropological and an ethical one.[22] By anthropological I mean that the tendency to a "nonstop" process towards infinity in the foundation of our arguments is due to the fact that we do not acknowledge the peculiarity of the transcendental or "classic" philosophical argument.[23] Instead, there is a flattening of this kind of argument on the apodictic level which in fact is always a "nonstop" one, as Aristotle argued.[24] But coherence is grounded on ontological truth, or, in other words, on being itself. This mistrust of the abilities of philosophical reason seems to be grounded on an unjustified (explicit or implicit) presupposition: namely, that human reason cannot know *being* itself, but only the *phenomenon*. This presupposition is connected with the negation of the role of intentionality and of formal causality in our knowledge.[25] But this belief (*phenomenism*), as many philosophers such as Hegel showed, is a presupposition which involves contradiction.[26] Therefore, that kind of skepticism does not seem – at least primarily – to be epistemologically grounded. It might, however, be anthropologically and ethically grounded.

Secondly, let us look at the ethical reasons of that kind of nihilistic skepticism. Modern immanentism wrongly substituted the level of practical reason for the level of speculative reason, theoretical contradiction (which is only intentional) with practical opposition – a desire which is not fulfilled (which is a real opposition) – as happens in Hegel and Marx. But when transcendence (God) is not admitted in metaphysics, human desire becomes radically unfulfilled.[27] For those philosophers then reality is in itself contradictory.

We can find this difficulty also within the philosophical streams which reacted against modern rationalistic thought (i.e., Nietzsche and "postmodern thought"), because they are also often closed towards transcendence. The concept of "bad infinity" (a "nonstop" infinity) easily becomes a surrogate for real infinity (infinity in act), of which we seldom have experience, about which we are not accustomed to reflect and which we may consider a cause of violence and of alienation. Modern philosophers of nothingness claim that "the search is an end in itself, without hope or possibility of ever attaining the goal of truth (§46). In a post-Christian culture the philosophy of the sophists and of Heraclitus, which Aristotle strongly opposed, might acquire the character of a fight for liberation in a way they did not have previously. The search for originality and authenticity at all costs leads us to negate those theoretical and practical principles which in fact are invariably accepted by all. As Charles Taylor holds, the modern and contemporary search for authenticity requires transcendent values.[28]

To sum up: there are ontological–anthropological (that means a certain idea of man and knowledge) and ethical reasons for our difficulty in acknowledging the first principles (first evidence) on which everyday knowledge, science and ethics are grounded. In fact, we must consider also that in postmodernity the idea of an infinite God seems to set a limit on the human freedom to interpret the world and one's life (infinity of hermeneutics) and of choosing as one's own way of life (ethical relativism).[29]

Conclusion

The main difficulty for philosophical reason is to *assent* freely to those truths to which we always *consent* (as Aristotle first of all showed).[30] As T. S. Eliot wrote, "human kind cannot bear very much reality."[31] Hannah Arendt argues that

> the alternative to this resentment, which is the psychological basis of contemporary nihilism, would be a fundamental gratitude for the few elementary things that indeed are invariably given us, such as life itself, the existence of man and the world. Neo-humanists, in their understandable yearning for the stable world of the past when law and order were given entities, and in their vain efforts to reestablish such stability by making man the measure of all things human, have confused the issue, which is the choice between resentment and gratitude as basic possible modern attitudes.[32]

Without this assent to reality religious sense would not be fully developed.[33] But we cannot go back to Greek Philosophy and leave aside the event that is Christianity. Paradoxically it seems true that in the history of Western culture and philosophy the assent to Christ as both God and man can help human persons in facing reality (man and world) and in giving assent to it, fighting against fear in the face of reality.[34] Moreover, this seems to be true particularly in the age of technology and mass media (television, computer, internet, wargames) in which our feeling of reality becomes more and more feeble. Therefore, inside Western culture Christianity with its idea of an infinity in this world determines always a *prephilosophical* and therefore also a *philosophical* problem. Philosophers as such cannot ignore Christianity.

From this point of view philosophy (reflection on our experience) and particularly that philosophy which is the "philosophy of being" (strictly connected with everyday experience) cannot be used primarily as a weapon against contemporary thought in order to overcome fear but as a useful way to clarify a meaningful experience which already does not fear reality. Both the depth of the best continental philosophy and the argumentation of analytical philosophy are useful in this job of facing reality.[35]

In our time, as always, is very important that believers should help each other in seeking understanding of their faith and in facing reality. Dialogue among friends is more useful than dialectics against enemies as Plato stressed many centuries ago.[36] In *Fides et Ratio* we find agreement with this point:

> It must not be forgotten that reason too needs to be sustained in all its searching by trusting dialogue and sincere friendship. A climate of suspicion and distrust, which can beset speculative research, ignores the teaching of the ancient philosophers who proposed friendship as one of the most appropriate contexts for sound philosophical enquiry (§33).

To sum up: everyone, believer and non believer, deals with both faith and reason. The problem is which faith is *here* and *now* more reasonable and human? We are all responsible in the face of truth. Nowadays the fear of intolerance and violence widespread in our culture cannot overshadow our deep commitment to truth. If the search for truth is natural among human beings, to hinder it might sooner or later become a cause of violence.

Notes

1. Cf. A. Campodonico, "Experience of Reality, Integrity and God," in *Proceedings of the 1997 Thomistic Institute* (in press): "When our knowledge concerns accidental and individual things (and that is the case of human actions and endeavors), hermeneutics is a substitute for science. If we want to

grasp the true meaning of something, we have to gather many aspects of that subject, considering them as a whole and possibly from the point of view of the whole. For instance: Aquinas suggests in his ethics that I must look at the aim of my action, at its matter and its circumstances, if I want to know what I must do now: "malum contingit ex singularibus defectibus, bonum vero ex tota et integra causa" (*Summa theologiae* I-II. 19. 6). In this and similar cases we must ask: Is something missing? Is this the only point of view on that subject? Can I look at this problem from a wider point of view? This is actually the method of hermeneutics, that in ethics needs also moral integrity of man (practical truth). Science and hermeneutics share a common criterion: they are always based on a perfection or integrity pattern. From this point of view the classical Aristotelian science pattern is the basis of empirical science pattern and of hermeneutics' pattern too. But that pattern is not necessarily *a priori*: it develops, as I hold, through experience of reality and its order."

2. Cf. *sensibilia propria* in Aristotle, *De anima* B 418a 10–15.

3. Cf. A. Kenny, *What is Faith? Essays in the Philosophy of Religion* (Oxford University Press, Oxford 1992), pp. 33–43.

4. Cf. St. Augustine, *De fide rerum quae non videntur.*

5. On faith in a wide sense as "prejudgment" see H. Gadamer, *Wahrheit und Methode* (Tubingen: Mohr, 1965); and M. Polanyi, *Personal Knowledge. Towards a Post-critical Philosophy* (London: Routledge and Kegan Paul , 1959); on the "principle of charity" see D. Davidson, "On the Very Idea of a Conceptual Scheme," in *Proceedings of the American Philosophical Association* 47 (1973), pp. 5–20; on the "principle of hope" see E. Bloch, *Das Prinzip Hoffnung* (Frankfurt am Main: Suhrkamp, 1959).

6. Cf. *Fides et Ratio*, the Introduction.

7. Cf. M. Polanyi, *Personal Knowledge*; and C. A. J. Coady, *Testimony. A Philosophical Study* (Oxford: Clarendon Press, 1992).

8. See W. Alston, *Perceiving God. The Epistemology of Religious Experience* (Ithaca and London: Cornell University Press, 1991), p. 306.

9. On the concept of integrity see A. Campodonico, *Integritas. Metafisica ed etica in Tommaso d'Aquino* (Florence: Nardini, 1996); idem, "Experience of Reality."

10. Cf. Saint Augustine, *Confessiones* X. 20. 29; *De trinitate* XIII. 7. 10; *De civitate Dei* XIV. 25.

11. Cf. R. Spaemann, *Glück un Wohlwollen. Versuch über Ethik* (Stuttgart: Klett-Cotta, 1990).

12. H. Arendt, *The Burden of our Time* (London: Secker and Warburg, 1951), p. 438.

13. Cf. *Rerum novarum* I. 22: "to suffer and to endure is human, and although men may strive in all possible ways, they will never be able by any power or art wholly to banish such tribulations from human life. If any claim they can do this, if they promise the poor in their misery a life free from all sorrow and vexation and filled with repose and perpetual pleasures, they actually impose upon these people and perpetuate a fraud which will ultimately lead to evils greater than the present. The best course is to view human affairs as they are and, as We have stated, at the same time to seek appropriate relief for these troubles elsewhere."

14. See F. von Kutschera, *Vernunft und Glaube* (Berlin-New York: Walter de Gruyter, 1991), pp. 241–51.

15. Cf. A. Campodonico, "Experience of Reality:" "We can distinguish among some important branches of human experience: an ontological experience (of being, of reality) that culminates in a metaphysical experience of Absolute, a moral experience (of the aim of our life and of the search for that aim) that culminates in a religious experience (of salvation, or of demand for salvation) and also an aesthetic experience of beauty and art. As we can easily realize, these different kinds of experience, along with speculative and practical reason, are intertwined. In my opinion our experience is something organic on top religious experience (in its wide sense). In fact, in religious experience there is a close tie between the top of the practical use of reason (demand for salvation) and the top of the speculative use of reason (knowledge of the existence of Absolute, of God). If we do not develop experience at the religious level (and this is an ethical problem), the other kinds of experience will become contracted and our reflection on experience will not work properly."

16. Cf. Lessing, "On the Proof of the Spirit and of Power," in *Lessing's Theological Writings*, ed. Henry Chadwick (Stanford: Stanford University Press, 1956), p. 53: "First, who will deny (not I) that the reports of these miracles and prophecies are as reliable as historical truths ever can be? But if they are only as reliable as this, why are they treated as if they were infinitely more reliable? And in what way? In this way? In this way, that something quite different and much greater is founded upon them that is legitimate to found upon truths historically proved. If no historical truth can be demonstrated, then nothing can be demonstrated by means of historical truths. That is, *accidental truths of history can never become the proof of necessary truths of reason.* I do not for one moment deny that in Christ prophecies were fulfilled; I do not for one moment deny that Christ performed miracles. But since the truth of these miracles has completely ceased to be demonstrable by miracles still happening at the present time, since they are no more than a report of miracles (however incontroverted and incontrovertible they may be), I deny they can

and should bind me in the least to a faith in the other teachings of Christ. These other teachings I accept on other grounds."

17. Cf. F. Botturi, "Ragione credente e ontologia della fede," *Nova et Vetera* I (May 1999), pp. 17–26.

18. Augustine, *De Praedestinatione Sanctorum* 2. 5 (PL 44, 963); cf. *Fides et Ratio* §79.

19. Initially there is a transcendental ground of ontological experience. Here we can find, in the first place, a dimension of actuality, of event that does not depend on ourselves and that Thomistic philosophy calls "act of existing:" for something to exist or not exist is not the same. As the "act of existing" actuates everything, it means also integrity (perfection), because it is the very cause of every perfection we can find in reality. On the transcendental ground of human experience the main dimension is the act of existing which is the cause of the existence of everything. To perceive being as being makes the whole of being accessible, and that means the Absolute (whole as whole is absolute, because it does not depend on anything). In the second place reality shows a certain order, a certain harmony that we can call perfection or integrity too. This is the classical level of essence (*essentia*). This order shows itself phenomenologically as an order of reality and not as an order we ourselves create in reality. Cf. A. Campodonico, "Experience of Reality."

20. Cf. A. Campodonico, "Thinking of Creation," *Sapientia* (in press).

21. Cf. Thomas Aquinas, *Quaestiones disputatae de potentia Dei* IV. 2.

22. In fact, there is another important cause of antirealism in contemporary philosophy, particularly angloamerican: the fear of scientism and naturalism. Cf. J. Haldane, "Coming Home to (Metaphysical) Realism," *Philosophy* 71 (1996), pp. 287–96.

23. Cf. Aristotle, *Metaphysics* IV.

24. Cf. Aristotle, *Post. Anaytics*; and P. Pagani, *Il tema della "fondazione ultima" in alcuni aspetti del dibattito contemporaneo* (Milano: Franco Angeli, 1999).

25. "It is very important . . . to make clear that formal causation is not a kind of efficient causation, or a rival to it . . . Efficient causation is the vehicle for the communication of form; form is what structures the object, the thought and the movement between them." Cf. J. Haldane, "A Return to Form in the Philosophy of Mind," *Ratio* XI (1998), p. 269 *passim*.

26. Cf. G.W. Hegel, *Encyclopedia of Philosophy* (New York: Philosophical Library, 1959), Introduction, §10.

27. Cf. C. Vigna, "Contraddizione pratica, desiderio, coerenza," ed. C. Vigna, *L'etica e il suo altro* (Milano: Franco Angeli, 1994), p. 29.

28. Cf. C. Taylor, *The Malaise of Modernity* (Canadian Broadcasting Corporation, 1991).

29. Cf. F. Nietzsche, *The gay science*, trans. Walter Kaufman (New York: Random House, 1974), §110, 111, 115.

30. Cf. Aristotle, *Metaphysics* IV.

31. T. S. Eliot, *Four Quartets* (New York: Harcourt Brace Jovanovich, 1971), I. 44–45.

32. H. Arendt, *The Burden of our Time* (London: Secker and Warburg, 1951), p. 438.

33. Cf. L. Giussani, *The Religious Sense*, trans. J. Zucchi (Montreal and London: Queen's University Press, 1997).

34. "[I]t is necessary not to abandon the passion for ultimate truth, the eagerness to search for it or the audacity to forge new paths in the search. It is a faith which stirs reason to move beyond all isolation and willingly to run risks so that it may attain whatever is beautiful, good and true. Faith thus become the convinced and convincing advocate of reason." *Fides et Ratio*, §56.

35. Cf. J. Haldane, "Thomism and the Future of Catholic Philosophy," *New Blackfriars* 80 (April 1999), pp. 158–71; "Analytical Thomism," J. Haldane, *The Monist* 80: 4 (1997), pp. 485–86; R. Pouivet, *Après Wittgenstein, Saint Thomas* (Paris: PUF, 1997).

36. Cf. Plato, *Letter* VII.

The Problem of Nihilism in *Fides et Ratio*
Vittorio Possenti

In this encyclical, which deals with the necessary and fruitful encounter between faith and reason, the theme of nihilism, though not developed at great length, is of crucial importance. The fact that this is the first time a major document of the Church has touched on the topic (which was shelved by the second Vatican Council) confers a dramatic quality on *Fides et Ratio*, which deals with man's permanence in or escape from nihilism. By addressing the subject, the papal Letter produces two powerful effects: it places itself at the center of the spiritual situation of the present age, and it offers a determination of nihilism that has hitherto been lacking in the world's culture (an assertion that I attempt to motivate below). There is so far little awareness that the encyclical has contributed something new to the subject; and the reason for this is deeply rooted: the fields of philosophy and culture which still exist in the shadow of nihilism are incapable of perceiving its baleful influence, and even less capable of escaping from it.

Almost half a century ago, when nihilism had long been a familiar topic and was in fact considered rather an old hat, E. Jünger held that a substantial definition of it was still wanting.

> A good definition of nihilism would be comparable to the identification of the cause of cancer. It would not in itself be a recovery, but it would certainly be the precondition for one, provided that men work to that end. It is in fact a process that occupies largely the history.[1]

It is hardly reassuring that still today in a period when the term "nihilism" has been used in all possible senses (as a term of condemnation or even as a mark of benediction) the question remains confused. This situation is very similar to what Sartre diagnosed as happening as a result of the increasingly copious and indiscriminate use of the term "existentialism:" namely that it no longer had any meaning, since all too many and heterogeneous currents prided themselves on being existentialist. The word became a conventional term put to the most varied uses and serving to deck out very different silhouettes.

So it remains difficult to imagine how nihilism can be overcome. In my opinion, one factor of this outcome is the lack of a prior philosophical investigation of the subject, so that often the philosophical and the theological approaches overlap and cause confusion; or else the theological approach is taken up very prematurely without an adequate method for tackling the problem, i.e., without the conceptual infrastructure indispensable to deal with the arduous ontological problems entailed by the theological approach.

Absorbed by age-old confrontation with the modern cultures of action, especially Marxism, Christian thought has tended to overlook nihilism, and in this it has been remiss with the result of a considerable delay on this matter. It has been aware of the challenge, it has feared nihilism above all on the moral plane, has sought to exorcise it by keeping it at a distance, yet has rarely looked it steadily in the face. The major Christian thinkers have partly laid the foundations for an understanding of the character of nihilism, but without going far enough. One consequence of this failure is that the dominant philosophical line has been that embodied by other thinkers, especially Nietzsche and Heidegger. The documents of the Church's teaching (social encyclicals and pastoral letters) have often dealt with consumerism, almost never with nihilism. Now, by investigating this issue more carefully, we see that nihilism is one of the causes of consumerism and the hedonism related to it. This leads to an important shift of perspective from the centrality of consumerism to that of nihilism, considered a far more radical and disquieting phenomenon.

What is Nihilism?

Fides et ratio takes a first step towards correcting this accumulated delay by offering that determination of nihilism, that modern philosophy has been seeking with unusual assiduity for 150 years though without much success.[2] To understand this event we need to grasp, in the encyclical's pithy phrasing, the way in which it presents the essence of nihilism. The problem is firstly touched on in §46.

> As a result of the crisis of rationalism, what has appeared finally is nihilism. As a philosophy of nothingness, it has a certain attraction for people of our times. Its adherents claim that the search is an end in itself, without any hope or possibility of ever attaining the goal of truth. In the nihilist interpretation, life is only no more than an occasion for sensations and experiences in which the ephemeral has pride of place. Nihilism is at the root of the widespread mentality which claims that a definitive commitment should no longer be made, because everything is fleeting and provisional.

Subsequently the encyclical returns to the question at §81 and §91, but especially in §90. Making reference to the horizon common to many philosophies, which have taken leave of the sense of being, the encyclical refers to the nihilist outlook,

> which is at once the denial of all foundations and the negation of all objective truth. Quite apart from the fact that it conflicts with the demands and the contents of the word of God, nihilism is denial of humanity of man and of the very identity of the human being. It should never be forgotten that the neglect of being inevitably leads to losing touch with objective truth, and therefore with the very ground of human dignity (§90).

The era of nihilism brings the end of the age of certainties, replaced by the absence of meaning.

The two formulations complement each other. While the first, acute in grasping the origins of nihilism in rationalism and its crisis, presents some symptomatic features that are not always necessarily connected with nihilism (the reference to the ephemeral), the second seizes on the nature of nihilism, especially theoretical (or alethic) nihilism, which is often both preliminary to and more original than moral nihilism. Four characteristics are presented as integrating the very nature of nihilism: 1) crisis in the concept of truth, 2) neglect or oblivion of being, 3) breakdown of real or objective knowledge, 4) negation of man's humanity: we might say that nihilism arises when the light of the speculative intellect is no longer directed on being, so that men and things are no longer ordered according to their nature and value of being.[3]

The original speculative core, to which many forms of nihilism (first of all theoretical nihilism and subsequently, and with specific modes, practical nihilism) can be traced, can be found in a compact, negative structure, within which some events combine to reinforce each other, and in which as many negations are clearly perceptible:

> a) a profound existential rift between man and reality, of which gnoseological antirealism is the most decisive theoretic expression;
> b) oblivion/concealment of being, so that the aim always and continually sought by philosophy is not (any longer) the knowledge of being, which it considers to be permanently blocked or obstructed. The knowledge that escapes philosophy may, perhaps, be replaced by the scientific knowledge or by the will to power;
> c) victory of nominalism over realism within the framework of a widespread antirealism, in which generally the concern with being is abandoned for a concern with the text, in the passage from a metaphysical ontology to an "indirect" ontology of some other kind. The fundamental language of philosophy is no longer seen as that of metaphysics but that of the sciences, or in the hermeneutic axis

addressed towards the understanding of texts and hence at most within a second degree of immediacy;

    d) the attempt to do without the concept of truth or to transform it by attacking the very idea of truth as *adaequatio* between thought (or statement) and being: truth is born of consensus and not of a consonance between intellect and objective reality (§56).

In the compact core of nihilism there also takes place a sort of annihilation or dissolution of the object, considered by idealism as an unconscious product of the Self.[4]

The probings of *Fides et ratio*, compared with some intuitions of Nietzsche and Heidegger, but transported into a different horizon of thought, help to conceive the post-metaphysical and post-Christian essence of nihilism. It includes a strong antinomianism (*antinomos*), a notable sign of which is the widespread rejection and at times even the hatred of the *lex naturalis*; as well as a comprehension that is no longer revelatory (phanic and theophanic), but mute of being and the cosmos. Man, engaged in surviving in a hostile cosmos, develops within himself an anti-contemplative spirit and a corresponding innerworldly activism. If the eclipse of the "phanic" or revelatory nature of being and an anti-contemplative attitude refer to each other, the search, so common today, for a barrier against nihilism, identified in ethics, risks becoming a diversion. Ethics cannot last long when the realm of truth and meaning is compromised. With clear insight Nietzsche grasped that the death of ethics would follow upon the "death of God," if only because (I would add) it is a "secret agent" in the service of the Almighty.

Objectively bound up with these fundamental definitions of nihilism, beyond the intentions of the author, is Nietzsche's dazzling statement: "Nihilism: the end is lacking, the answer to the question 'why?' is lacking!"[5] Reality exists, being is a given, yet everything is without meaning, since it is rigorously impossible to discover any meaning when the ideas of purpose, of intelligibility, of reason of being (*raison d'être*), have failed. Nihilism appears to us here as the loss or total concealment of meaning, and most probably the refusal of the original, primordial Logos as everywhere present in the whole (*en archè logos en; in principio erat Verbum*). If right from the beginning there is Logos, this implies that being, life, nature be intelligible, in principle open to the human reason. And reason cannot proceed from an obscure, original abyss of irrationality.

The above mentioned assumptions, anything but isolated, hold in their grasp, for example, the generative insights that underpin the monumental work of Weber, a lucid yet disenchanted disciple of Nietzsche; for, unlike him, Weber felt no confidence in future philosophy as creation and place of manifestation of the superman (*Übermensch*). The nihilistic character of the work of Weber emerges in many of his formulations. Especially eloquent among them is his statement that culture "is a finite section of the infinite, meaningless world-becoming, to which is attributed sense and significance from man's point of view."[6] This formulation confirms that a feature of nihilism is the lack of meaning (the answer to the question "why?" is missing, the purpose is missing), and its reduction to an act of will on the part of the subject, who to survive and not fall into the absurd posits meaning as a challenge to an existence devoured by becoming and which appears to be hostile, mute, absolutely non-revelatory. The Weberian idea of the modern era as directed by a powerful "instrumental rationality" is highly dependent on nihilistic presuppositions and mainly on Nietzsche's determination of nihilism as lack of end/purpose. If ends cannot be known by reason nor placed in hierarchy, then a science of ends will be impossible, and only a science of means, in sight of purposes which will be only decided by desire or by factual power actually in force, is allowed. The "instrumental rationality" exactly consists in irrationality of ends accompanied by technical decisions about means.

The nihilistic content of the core, in which the rift between man and reality, oblivion of being, and the crisis of the idea of the truth all combine, is high because, bearing on the origin, its effects are transmitted indefinitely in many directions. One of them is the question of essence, to which the philosophical tradition attributed great importance for the comprehension of existence and the whole. There is a nihilism that holds the concept of essence to be inconsequential, a mere linguistic convention, *flatus vocis*. I term this attitude nihilism of the essences. To it is directed the ideology (in itself nihilistic) of technological scientism, whose advanced wing today is in the biological-genetic sector. The source from which this specific form of nihilism is nurtured lies in an emphatic raising of becoming alone, conjoined with the a priori negation of the necessary stratum of being and the assumption that essences are mere lexical conventions, something that depends fundamentally on the choices of man and on the never firm determinations of his freedom.

The gnoseological-ontological antirealism here takes the form of unreality of the essences/natures. Given that this negation is postulated and therefore illusory, it appears to the scrutiny of the intellect to be condemned to failure and also dangerous, since many undesirable results can flow from the attempts to violate the inviolable. For this reason *Fides et ratio* shows itself clear sighted in its invitation not to stop at the way language expresses and understands reality, but to go further and verify the ability of reason to discover essences. This would make it possible to establish a limit to the drive towards the omnipotence of technology, which can "attempt essences" but not transform them. The essences represent the "unavailable." To the oblivion of being and of essences corresponds with geometrical precision nihilism as the will to power of technology.

Coordinate with the position defined as "nihilism of the essences" is the attack on the idea of *substance*, in an attempt to resolve it into that of function, as in the case of Kelsen. An inner necessity links theoretical nihilism as oblivion of being with the abandonment of the concept of substance, as it is the first and fundamental expression of real being: only individuals or individual substances exist.

If now, without losing sight of the speculative diagnosis, we pass to the practical field, we can speak of an ethical nihilism, understood as an attack on values, an attempt at their dissolution, relativism. The moral nihilism that today constitutes perhaps the most evident component of the theme of nihilism, by the frequency with which it is evoked in culture, possesses some practical roots (as well as much else). To us it seems to originate from the primacy of the negative over the positive, of eros over agape, of the indirect-negative over the direct-positive. This nihilism, in which it is postulated that the positive stems from the negative, is paradigmatically matched by Nietzsche's idea that the morality of love, of forgiveness, of mercy, is born not from a positive heroic impulse of the person, but emerges as an unconfessable disguise of a harsh feeling of resentment against life, strength, and joy.[7]

It is not difficult to connect with this picture another remarkable meaning of ethical nihilism, which stems from a weak, plural reason, skeptical and resigned to decline. The "soft" form of moral nihilism which seems to prevail in the contemporary West, is rather like a form of "do it yourself" and originates in the metamorphosis of the criterion of autonomy, on which modernity had staked its best cards. Maintaining that the supreme principle of morality is autonomy as the self-legislation of the reason, Kant[8] had before his mind a single moral law and a single, universal, and immutable self-legislation of the reason. But what can be said today, when the one has become many? When the moral law has crumbled into the unlimited plurality of the empirical self-legislations of single individuals? Within this new spiritual climate both prohibiting and prescribing become meaningless.

To express our own conviction fully, in many forms of speculative nihilism a leading part is played by an intimately anti-realistic logico-dialectical formalism. Empty and sterile in real terms, it is devoid of all sense of being: an absolute logicism reduces it to nullity. Its decisive origin can perhaps be found in the concealment of real being of which the great and delusive machine of Hegelian dialectic is pregnant: on this basis, being, that which is richest and most fully determinate, is seen in the *Science of Logic* as the emptiest, poorest, the most indeterminate, the pure nothing. Rarely in the history of philosophy has there been a form of oblivion of being of equal intensity. Meanwhile it will remain as a constantly revived question whether it is ever possible to grasp reality while remaining enclosed within a grid of merely logical concepts. In logicist nihilism there circulates to a greater or lesser degree a feeling of contempt for reality: it appears perhaps too humble to the eyes of the doctors of logic for them to pause to consider it.

Nihilism and analogia entis

The diagnosis that links nihilism to the removal of being, hence to oblivion of being and to the loss of contact with objective truth, while it goes to the roots, leaves much unexpressed. Dwelling in its space, it is now required to grasp the unspoken, starting from the element by which the dismissal of being relates to another notable core of ideas, which we shall formulate as follows: oblivion of being includes the oblivion and ultimately the rejection of the *analogia entis* and of onto-theology. The separation from these is often driven by a more or less conscious desire to deconstruct the concept of God as an obstacle to the radicality of the philosophical duty, and to deny the identity between God and Being. The criticism of the onto-theology and the analogy, now become almost a commonplace in many schools, is generally conducted by drawing on Heidegger. Moreover, there is little awareness of a crucial point: namely, if a thought like his, which rests on the finiteness and the insuperable transcendental circle of temporality, does not seem inadequate to pass judgment (whether positively or critically) on the infinite, on whatever lies beyond that circle. To attack onto-theology and the *analogia entis* on this basis is like biting granite.

Heidegger's criticism is contained in numerous writings, among them, *Identity and Difference* and especially *The Onto-theo-logical Constitution of Metaphysics*. They maintain the proposition that God is conceived by onto-theology as the supreme being and as *causa sui*. It is not an adequate solution to attribute this (colossal) misunderstanding to Heidegger's inadequate knowledge of history of philosophy, which yet played its part (where and when did the more reputable natural theologies conceive the God who enters into philosophy as *causa sui*?). In reality two positions that cannot co-exist are being maintained here: on the one hand, the limitation of onto-theology is identified in having conceived God as *ens* and not as *esse*; on the other it is held to be impossible to posit the identity between God and being (*esse*). In this regard important are the passages of the *Beiträge zur Philosophie* where God is determined as unfailing need of being (*Notschaft des Seyns*), as if possessed by an obscure hunger; and also in those parts where the –equation *Deus=Esse* is denied with a clarity that leaves nothing to be desired:

> Being and God are not identical and I would never seek to think the essence of God through being. Some know that I come from theology and that I have preserved an old love for it, and understand a little about the subject. If I were to write a theology – and at times I feel the urge to do so – the term "being" would not appear in it. Faith has

no need of being. If it uses the term, it is already no longer faith... I
hold that being can never be thought as the essence and foundation of
God.[9]

In these words are expressed two aversions: one anti-Hellenic and one
anti-biblical, for in the Bible the attribution of being to God is common. This
is part of the idea that he is original Perfection: he is neither a God that makes
himself, that feels hunger for being, nor a future God, analogous to the "last
God" introduced in Heigegger's *Beiträge zur Philosophie*. The denial that
faith is faith if has recourse to being, vividly reveals the risk of ontophobia in
Heidegger's thinking. In no onto-theology has the problem of the difference
between *esse* and *ens* been explored with such profundity as in that of the
Seinsphilosophie, which asserts the validity of the identity of *Deus* with *Esse*,
and hence God's infinite distance from beings, his value as the Unique and
Other. Only by conceiving of God as *Esse* can one perceive the difference
between being as *esse* and being as *ens*. This grandiose development escaped
Heidegger, who here, too, failed to get rid of the oblivion of being.

Attempts to Break out from Nihilism

If technological scientism – for which "to be/being" in the highest sense
does not signify "to be forever/always being" but only "to remain in the presence, ready for every transformation" – reveals itself as an important trait of
nihilism, it does not seem to us that the existentialist philosophies, those of
freedom or the transcendental ones, are capable of achieving the desired
escape from it. Often existentialism hangs existence to an act of freedom and
ultimately to the abyss of freedom (the term is symptomatic), that is in the last
resort to a decision. The existentialist, understanding that one cannot dwell
endlessly in relativism and nihilism, decides to emerge from it by an act of
freedom. The problem does not consist in escaping from relativism or
nihilism, but in the way we do it.

Perhaps the most inward character of existentialism is its awareness that
at the bottom of all knowledge and of ourselves we discover the abyss, that-
which-is-not-founded. It is so radical that it threatens the Absolute itself, so
that in the last analysis all truth and meaning rest on the unfounded abyss of
freedom, human or divine, as the case may be, but the original structure of the
reality is not altered. If all meaning comes from the obscure and principle (i.e.,
that has reference to the principle) act of freedom, then all meaning is founded on a decision and ultimately there is no such thing as meaning but only
decision. Despite differences of personal intention, existentialism of this kind,

which contains a misunderstanding of the essence of freedom and of the ultimate nature of being, does not seem capable of checking the progress of nihilism.

If we look at it from the aspect of transcendental philosophy, which taken as a whole has constituted the ontology of the moderns, we find it contains many things worthy of respect but not being. One finds things and men, *onta* and human subjects, and certainly the "anthropological difference" between the inanimate *onta* and living, thinking men. In fact subjectivity is raised so high that modern transcendental doctrine could hardly have been born outside the all-embracing doctrine of anthropocentrism, in which, according to Barth, man is the universal subject and Christ at best the predicate. Such a philosophy could have been a philosophy of consciousness and of freedom, and it was both of these things together. Yet it failed to produce that openness of the soul to the whole, without which it is impossible to break out of nihilism. The openness of the soul, expressed in the ancient adage *anima est quodammodo omnia*, here signifies openness to being and to experience, in the possible acceptance of that infinite openness produced in us by the Revelation. Nietzsche had profound reasons for seeking with unflagging energy to abolish the soul as ontological and theological sensorium. Oblivion of being and of the soul and dissolution of ethics go hand in hand.

Two great and vital currents seem available to help us to break out of nihilism: *the philosophy of being and the biblical tradition*. Without mixing itself with questions which are left to discussion among different philosophical currents, the encyclical suggests that one of the major limits of modern philosophy lies in having put being in brackets, in not having been able to present itself as philosophy of being.[10] Consequently it has encountered greater difficulties in rediscovering the proper wisdom that is peculiar to philosophical thought, going toward the fragmentation of knowledge (cf. §83 and 97), the latter a pivot of the whole discussion). With reference to metaphysics, we are justified in evoking by contrast that area of contemporary philosophy that defines itself as post-Metaphysical, in allusion to the irreversible devaluation of the foundations of the true and valid which it sees in Western culture.

Concluding words

Among the several concluding remarks that could be presented, I'll retain only a few matters:

1) The Western secularized culture is rather deeply affected by nihilism: this culture spreads and circulates a new "common sense" according to which

the universe is deprived of any sense and, if God exists, he remains totally hidden to our mind. As very seldom contemporary philosophy goes beyond the border of the finite, an anguish, correlated to man's closing in the finiteness, affects the subjects living in the postmodern spiritual climate. In the realm of culture and of philosophical quest, the main challenge arising from nihilism concerns the very continuation of philosophy. With nihilism could occur not only a transformation of philosophy as provoked by linguistic and hermeneutic turn, but the very end of philosophy as an enterprise aimed at the knowledge of truth and at a form of wisdom. In fact, with the advent of nihilism the sapiential dimension inherent to philosophy is progressively dissolved, while disappears the perspective according to which philosophy is seen as a vocation and an existential practice with deep resonances in personal life.

At the end of this dialectics, starting from the removal of knowledge of being, reason becomes more and more a prisoner to itself: some Kantian ideas concerning the "transcendental illusion" of reason could have prepared this attitude. Nihilism seems to be an internal parasite of reason and metaphysics, especially strong at the end of this century, when "one of our greatest threats is the temptation to despair" (§ 91).

2) Breaking free from nihilism could be a kind of rebirth for philosophy; and for theology a resumption of its sapiential, contemplative, dogmatic function, now less deeply felt because of the weight of various factors, including: the still onerous influence of Heideggerianism in theology; a certain exegetical-philological positivism in the approach to the Bible, which beyond all its good intentions produces fragmentation in the understanding of God's plan. For this breakout to take place, a resumption of the dialogue between philosophy and Revelation is desirable.

But it is unclear whether in the West, "the land of broken symbols" (P. Tillich), the two will ever communicate intensely again. Yet many, including Jaspers, continue to hope: "The Bible and biblical tradition are one of the bases of our philosophy. . . . The philosophical enquiry in the West – whether it is acknowledged or not – is always conducted with the Bible, even when it is directed against the Bible."[11] Here it is possible to suggest the fundamental meaning of open philosophy which is the matrix of the encyclical: open philosophy is that which, conscious of its limits verified through a rational and controllable process, remains on the watch for a possible Revelation, a word spoken by the Transcendent in history; and which does not preclude the possibility that a new impulse might come from it, a contribution enabling it to better attain its end. It seems that two legitimate processes go hand in hand: the process, commonly conceded, that it is reason which questions the

Revelation; and that one which questions reason on behalf of the Revelation, verifying whether it cannot provide a contribution to restart the philosophical quest and reveal new horizons.

3) An open philosophy of this kind would be presented neither as a philosophical religion, whose grave limits are well known, nor yet as a generically religious philosophy. A name that would not be inappropriate, through historically charged with multiple meanings, might be "Christian philosophy," since it would be open not only to the religious phenomenon but specifically to the Revelation of Christianity. It would then be possible to resume the labor of the concept in philosophy and in theology. By recreating a virtuous circle between philosophy and Revelation we would make progress towards overcoming a state of reciprocal extraneousness that has been notable: whether because theology has sought to summarize into itself the vertex and totality of knowledge; or because the same has happened to the advantage of philosophy, which especially in the case of idealism is charged with theological purposes captured in the system.

The absorption of one discipline into another or, by contrast, their reciprocal indifference, has led to the exiguous dialogue of culture and philosophy with the Bible which, while not exhausting the totality of the Revelation, remains the great code of the European East and West. It is a solemn river that gathers the waters of a thousand streams: voices, doubts, praises, lamentations, protests, questions, answers. It is the book of the dialogue between man and God, the *acta* of God's initiative towards man. We read Hesiod, Plato, Sophocles, Cicero, Virgil, not Genesis, Luke, Paul, Clement. Why Homer and not John? Here what is called for is a far-reaching revolution in the model of education that has existed for many centuries now in Europe, and which was based first of all on the Greek and Latin humanities, with a subsequent broadening of the curriculum to science and technology, while still leaving the biblical code at a distance.[12]

The integration of the paradigm presupposes the construction of a different relationship with Scripture and Revelation, a frequentation of them not limited to historico-critical method, which is certainly important but in some instances unproductive and problematic. So it is possible to glimpse the need for a concern with and use of the Bible in philosophy, rather along the method followed by some Jewish thinkers, at least in the sense that the Bible should not be understood as a document enclosed in the past.

4) The very essence of Christianity is threatened by nihilism, and the struggle against it could be a founding dimension of the present situation of Christianity. On a *theologal* (not simply theological) level the inner and con-

cealed meaning of nihilism could be the man's limitation to this world, with the cutting of his desires directed toward the infinite, toward God. This is a strong challenge for Christianity and Revelation, because their ultimate meaning is not merely *salvation*, which implies liberation from sin, but mainly and firstly to become similar to God, i.e., *deification* (*deificatio* in Latin, *theiosis* in Greek). With nihilism Christianity is no longer understood as a faith which is centered around the deification of man as a gift of God.

Notes

1. E. Jünger, "Oltre la linea," in *Oltre la linea*, eds. E. Jünger-M. Heidegger (Milan: Adelphi, 1989), p. 57. Retracing the dense and uneven debate on nihilism, to which Italian philosophy has contributed on various occasions, it is difficult to escape the assumption that the term "nihilism" is undergoing an increasing semantic extenuation: if many, all too many, phenomena of the spirit are branded as nihilism, it becomes a catch-all term, like an elastic that can be pulled in any direction. Its growing extension is matched by a large vagueness of comprehension and definition. A first step in avoiding this situation suggests that we should consider nihilism as an event with several faces, which postulates a hermeneutics on several levels and which suggests to the philosopher an attitude which excludes all attempts at being exhaustive and all-inclusive. There are notable presences of nihilism in art, in the life of the spirit, in religion, and even perhaps in mysticism, if it is true that for certain mystics the Nothing is taken as the purest and highest name of God. These few references already reveal the evocative charge and also the semantic equivocalness of the term.

2. For an analysis of the nature and the widespread presence of nihilism, cf. V. Possenti, *Terza navigazione, Nichilismo e metafisica* (Rome: Armando, 1998). In the understanding of the nature of nihilism we should recognize the inescapable propaedeutic step to be taken before we can begin to cure its illness: clearly it is impossible to free oneself from an event of whose nature one is ignorant.

3. As anticipated, some other hints to nihilism are integrated in *Fides et ratio*, §81 and 91. In the latter reference is made to a few postmodern currents, according to which "the time of certainties is irrevocably past, and the human being must now learn to live in a horizon of total absence of meaning, where everything is provisional and ephemeral. In their destructive critique of every certitude, several authors have failed to make a crucial distinction and have called into question the certitudes of faith."

4. If the doctrine that overcomes the opposition between thought and object is

anti-nihilistic, this comes about by very different paths in idealism and realism. The latter maintains the intentional identity of intellect and object, in the
wake of Aristotle's teaching, and the ontico-real primacy of the object (all the
light comes from the object), instead of the primacy of the transcendental pro-
ductivity of the Self which posits the non-Self. A notable nihilism of the
object as external and extra-psychic is present in Freud, especially in the interpretation of dreams, understood as an absolutely and integrally inner fact, an
exclusive production of the individual: "The dream is an absolutely asocial
psychic product . . . having arisen inside a person as a compromise between
the psychic forces in conflict, it remains incomprehensible even to this person
himself." The psychoanalytic interpretation of dreams as wholly inner products risks having been one of the most tenacious myths of the 20th century.
An aspect of the anti-nihilism is its value as a metaphysic of exteriority and
hence of the real density of the object, not however presenting itself as the
negation of the subject, since the highest form of existence is personal existence, in which the philosophy of being recognizes a maximum of ontological profundity and mystery.

5. *Frammenti postumi*, Opere di F. Nietzsche, 23 vols. (Milano: Adelphi,
1979), vol. 8: 2, p. 12. In the same fragment Nietzsche develops the idea that
the height of nihilism consists in the inexistence of truth.

6. M. Weber, *Il metodo delle scienze storico-sociali* (Milan: Mondadori,
1980), p. 96.

7. According to Nietzsche, resentment (*ressentiment*) serves as the unconfessable motive that underlies the morality of love, mercy, forgiveness. He
claims that these feelings connote the "revolt of slaves in morality," which
begins "when *ressentiment* itself becomes a creator and generates values; the
ressentiment of such creatures [the weak] to whom the true reaction, that of
action, is denied and who console themselves only with an imaginary
revenge." Nietzsche, *Genealogia della morale* (Milan: Adelphi, 1988), p.
251. If the force of resentment is strong in several modern ethics, as Max
Scheler pointed out in his well known studies, the "consentment" (*consente-
ment*) to being and life should be a basic, existential position of man, and one
of the highlights of the Christian transcendental faith.

8. Cf. Kant, Grundlegung zur Metaphysik der Sitten.

9. Heidegger, *Seminare*, Gesamtausgabe, 79 vols. to date (Frankfurt a. M.:
Klostermann, 1986), vol. 15, p. 437. On these aspects see V. Possenti,
Approssimazioni all'essere (Padua: Il Poligrafo, 1995), pp. 99–106.

10. On philosophy of being see in *Fides et ratio* §44, 66, 76, 97. The boldness
of reason (cf. §48) is at its best when it dares to rise to the truth of being (cf.
§5). The high importance recognized to this philosophy in itself and as an

indispensable, essential aid in developing theology represents one of the more impressive innovations in the papal Letter: the matter is discussed in my book *Filosofia e Rivelazione* (Rome: Città Nuova, 1999), pp. 32–38.

11. K. Jaspers, *La foi philosophique* (Paris: Plon, 1952), p. 129.

12. In *Le poète et la Bible* (Paris: Gallimard, 1999), which contains Claudel's writings on the Bible, we find the following: "Isn't it monstrous, in purely cultural terms, that the Bible has no place in our university education when we wear out our poor young people with the insipidities of Horace and force them to admire, however unwillingly, Plutarch's great men, who for the most part are nothing but indecent puppets?" Quoted from *Avvenire* (January 24, 1999), p. 19.

The Scientific Revolution and Contemporary Discourse on Faith and Reason
William E. Carroll

> Aristotelian physics made sense of the world and strengthened the
> hands of the men of God and all those striving to redeem civilization,
> culture, and truth from barbarism. There was only one problem. It
> was wrong.[1]

In early June of this year, when Pope John Paul II addressed a meeting of
Polish academics at the new University of Copernicus in Torun, he observed
that Copernican astronomy, especially its defense in the Seventeenth Century
by scientists such as Galileo, reminds us of an "ever-present tension between
reason and faith." The Pope noted that although Copernicus saw his new
astronomical system as "giving rise to even greater amazement at the Creator
of the world and the power of human reason, many people took it as a means
of setting reason against faith." Coincident with the rise of modern science in
the Seventeenth and Eighteenth Centuries, there was, according to the Pope,
a tragic split between reason and faith. "Particularly, beginning in the
Enlightenment period, an extreme and one-sided rationalism led to the radi-
calization of positions in the realm of the natural sciences and in that of philosophy. The resulting split between faith and reason caused irreparable dam-
age not only to religion but also to culture."[2] The Pope called upon his audi-
ence to work for "a reconciliation between faith and reason,"[3] and remarked
that, "it is quite important to remember constantly that authentic freedom of
scientific research cannot prescind from the criterion of truth and goodness."
Interpretations of modernity, including the understanding of the relationship between faith and reason, depend in important ways on analyses of the
Scientific Revolution of the Seventeenth Century. In particular, the materialism, mechanism, and reductionism so often associated with modern science
has its roots in a faulty philosophy of nature supported by an interpretation of
the history of science.[4] The understanding of the rise of modern science as
involving a rejection of Aristotelian science[5] has led many to ignore the profound truths about nature, human nature, and God which are found in

Aristotelian and Thomistic thought. There are related interpretations of the
Scientific Revolution which see it as an emancipation of science from the
clutches of theology: interpretations which provide considerable support for
view that reason and faith are bitter enemies, or for the view recently dubbed
NOMA by Stephen J. Gould.[6] According to Gould, reason and faith properly
exercise "non-overlapping magisteria," and it was Galileo who led the way
for the modern recognition of these distinct magisteria.

As we look at the importance of the history of science in contemporary
discourse on faith and reason, I want to begin with a conclusion: the developments in the natural sciences in the Seventeenth Century, most apparent in the
field of physics, do not so much represent a rejection of the *principles* of
Aristotelian physics[7] as they mark a great advance in our understanding of the
ways in which mathematics can be applied to the study of physical reality. The
sciences of Galileo and Newton, strikingly original as they are, remain fully
consistent with a general Aristotelian science of nature. There is, of course,
much more to the developments of science in the Seventeenth Century than
the role played by mathematics as applied to motion. Nevertheless, by keeping this focus we will have an opportunity to pursue with appropriate sophistication an understanding of the Scientific Revolution.

Let us turn to a characteristic rendering of what we might call the master
narrative of the Scientific Revolution. Herbert Butterfield, writing more than
forty years ago in a book entitled *The Origins of Modern Science* (1957),
remarked that because the Scientific Revolution:

> overturned the authority in science not only of the Middle Ages but
> of the ancient world, . . . since it ended not only in the eclipse of
> scholastic philosophy but in the destruction of Aristotelian physics, it
> outshines everything since the rise of Christianity and reduces the
> Renaissance and Reformation to the rank of mere episodes, mere
> internal displacements, within the system of medieval Christendom.
> Since it changed the character of men's habitual operations even in
> the conduct of the non-material sciences, while transforming the
> whole diagram of the physical universe and the very texture of
> human life itself, it looms so large as the real origin of the modern
> world and of the modern mentality that our customary periodisation
> of European history has become an anachronism and an encum-
> brance.[8]

Although we may be less enthusiastic than Butterfield in his characterization of the importance of the Scientific Revolution, we ought to recognize in
his comments the prevailing view of the Scientific Revolution as the overthrow of Aristotelian science. We may well accept Thomas Kuhn's descrip-

tion of this Revolution as a "paradigm shift" and thus react skeptically to claims which conclude that Aristotle's science was false and modern science true, but nevertheless the master narrative remains intact, since, in Kuhn's terms, there is an incommensurability between the old and the new paradigms.

The master narrative tells the story of how Galileo and Newton overturned the antiquated Aristotelian view of the universe and established the principles of modern science. The very first principle of the new physics is the principle of inertia: "Every body perseveres in its state of rest or of uniform motion in a straight line, unless it is compelled to change that state by forces impressed upon it." Alfred North Whitehead called the principle of inertia "the first article of the creed of science, and like the Church's creed it is more than a mere statement of belief; it is a paean of triumph over defeated heretics."[9] The defeated heretics, Whitehead explains, are "the Aristotelians who for two thousand years imposed on dynamics the search for a physical cause of motion."[10]

Contemporary commentary on the relationship between theology and the natural sciences has been heavily influenced by the orthodox interpretation of the Scientific Revolution as a radical rupture in the history of science. Anthony Kenny, for example, denies the probative force of Aquinas's proofs for the existence of God because these proofs are based on the principles of Aristotelian science, a science which the modern world has shown to be false.[11] Kenny also thinks Aquinas's ethical theory suffers because Aquinas's account of appetites in man and in animals depends upon an "archaic physics," now known to be false. Any notion of the natural agency of inanimate matter cannot be reconciled with the principle of inertia. Newtonian mechanics, according to Kenny, rules out any appeal to a teleological account of *all* of nature.[12] Kenny observes that, for Aquinas, "all action, including the most elemental actions of completely inanimate bodies, was . . . fundamentally teleological. This part of Aquinas's system is something which must be discarded if we are to make any use of his philosophy at the present time."[13] Mortimer Adler, in *How to Think About God* (1980), makes essentially the same point:

> In the realm of motion, the modern discovery of the principle of inertia requires us to reject as false Aristotle's view that the continuing motion of a body set in motion needs a continuing efficient cause. . . . The view held by mediaeval theologians, and some of their modern followers, concerning the continuing existence of contingent beings in the natural world, closely resembles the Aristotelian view concerning the continuing movement of a body set in motion. . . . I hold that something akin to the principle of inertia applies in the realm of existence, and leads us to reject the mediaeval view that the continu-

ing existence of individual things needs the continuing action of an
efficient cause. . . . [S]o individual things of nature, which are
brought into existence by natural causes, continue in existence without the action of any efficient cause of their continuing existence; and
their existence continues until the action of counteracting natural
causes results in their perishing, or ceasing to be. . . . It is the natural
tendency of everything that exists to persevere in existence – by inertia, which is to say, without the action of an efficient cause that acts
to cause its continuing existence.[14]

One particularly influential contemporary theologian, Wolfhart
Pannenberg, claims that the acceptance of the principle of inertia in the
Seventeenth Century represents not only a radical break in the history of science but is also a fundamental problem for the Christian doctrine of creation.
According to Pannenberg, the principle of inertia lies behind a denial of the
radical contingency of the world: a contingency central to the doctrine of creation.[15] For Pannenberg, it is not until the ascendancy of field theory in contemporary physics that we can discern a complementarity between the claims
of physics and the theological concept of creation.[16] Ultimately, Pannenberg
argues that the "Spirit of God" is a kind of "field" which environs the entire
cosmos and engenders a creative unification of all of reality.

Pannenberg observes that, especially with Descartes, the principle of inertia "leads to an emancipation of the natural processes from their dependence
on God, . . . [even though] the general framework of Descartes' ideas on the
creation of the world and on its [the world's] need for continuous preservation
by God was still quite traditional."[17] It was Descartes who referred to inertia
as "the first law of nature."[18] Descartes did take the law of inertia to be a manifestation of the immutability of God, but the seeds are sown, according to
Pannenberg, for the eventual affirmation of the autonomy of the world and its
processes.[19] It was Newton's understanding of inertia in terms of a force that
is inherent in bodies, along with the reduction of force to a body and its mass,
that contributed in a decisive way "in the course of the eighteenth century to
the removal of God from the explanation of nature."[20]

> The emancipation from the creator God entailed in the principle of
> inertia did not apply only to natural bodies and beings which at the
> same time continued to undergo influences from outside themselves.
> Even more serious was the consequence that the system of the natu-
> ral universe had to be conceived now as an interplay between finite
> bodies and forces without further need for recourse to God.[21]

The source of Pannenberg's understanding of the importance of the principle of inertia for the Christian doctrine of creation is the work of another

German thinker, Hans Blumenberg. In two major books, *The Legitimacy of the Modern Age* and *The Genesis of the Copernican World*, Blumenberg ranges widely in philosophy, the natural sciences, theology, political thought, and literature as he examines the transition from the medieval to the modern world. For Blumenberg, the novelty of modernity is to be found in what he calls the "reoccupation" of prior explanations of man, nature, and God.

Let me offer an example of what Blumenberg means. The modern commitment to human autonomy and self-assertion (*Selbsterhaltung*) is, for Blumenberg, a response to the claims of divine omnipotence, of the absolute power of God, characteristic of Nominalist thought. Such affirmation of divine omnipotence necessarily entailed a denial of an intelligible order of nature discoverable by human reason. The utter contingency of a world dependent upon the absolute will of God is, according to Blumenberg, "a disappearance of order [*Ordnungsschwund*]" which causes doubt "regarding the existence of a structure of reality that can be related to man" and makes the traditional conception of human activity bound up in the ancient and medieval cosmos no longer workable.[22] Blumenberg notes: "The modern age has regarded self-preservation (*conservatio sui*) as a fundamental category of everything in existence and has found this borne out all the way from the principle of inertia in physics to the biological structure of drives and the laws of state building."[23]

Blumenberg thinks that the early modern mechanistic explanation of nature, with its commitment to "absolute matter," re-occupies the position of the late medieval Nominalist mode of explanation based on an absolute divine will.[24] Self-assertion and human autonomy are the broader cultural correlatives of a fundamentally new principle of explanation – and, for Blumenberg, it is the principle of inertia which lies at the core of this new view of things. With the principle of inertia, there is in all things, in all matter, that is, an inherent force of self-preservation (a *vis insita*). Consequently, a "transcendent conservation [*Fremderhaltung*] of nature becomes indeed superfluous. In a similar way, the transfer of movement renders the assumption of a divine cooperation in the activities of creatures superfluous. Thus deism must be seen as the consequence of the principle of inertia in modern physics."[25]

The incompatibility between the principle of inertia and the doctrine of creation, which Blumenberg and Pannenberg see as a characteristic feature of the modern age, rests upon a misunderstanding of creation. In their analysis, creation is really a kind of change, and the creator functions as one more agent not fundamentally different from other agents in the world of change. Both will speak of God as a transcendent agent, but God's creative actions in the world are causes which differ only in degree from other efficient causes. God's role as unmoved mover, for example, is necessary for medieval Aristotelian physics because the science of nature requires God's agency in order to explain motion. Thus, Blumenberg and Pannenberg think that an appeal to God's agency is irrelevant – or at least is seen to be irrelevant – in a world operating according to the principle of inertia. As Blumenberg says, God's function as conserver of the natural world is rendered superfluous. No longer is the continuing existence of any given state of affairs in need of explanation, but only the occurrence of any change of this state.

An important error in this analysis, as I have suggested, is to consider creation as a kind of change. You will remember that throughout his discussion of creation Aquinas was always careful to point out that creation is not a change; rather, it is a metaphysical dependence in the order of being.[26] This metaphysical dependence is the same throughout the being's existence as it is at its beginning. The traditional doctrine of creation remains unaffected by any conclusion in the natural sciences, since creation is a metaphysical notion not a physical one.

Blumenberg's and Pannenberg's analysis of the impact of the principle of inertia on the doctrine of creation has its roots in their acceptance of the standard interpretation of the Scientific Revolution as a rejection of Aristotelian physics.

If there is a fundamental incompatibility, or incommensurability, between Aristotelian science and modern science, then any theological or philosophical reflection rooted in or employing principles from Aristotelian science must either be rejected or radically reformulated. Often I participate in conferences on the relationship between religion and science in which speakers refer to the "Newtonian settlement" as the basis for modern philosophy and theology.[27] This "settlement" tends to rule out appeals to Aristotelian and Thomistic natural philosophy since, so the argument goes, such a philosophy of nature has been rendered false[28] by modern science. This helps to explain why in the Seventeenth and Eighteenth Centuries it was apparent to many that only a mechanistic philosophy of nature could meet the evidence of modern science. Indeed, early proponents of mechanism, especially in the Seventeenth Century, saw in it a way to reconcile their belief in God with the insights of Newtonian science. More frequently today process thought is urged as providing the necessary philosophical complement to the natural sciences. Form and matter, substance and accident, teleology and the like are thus all seen as part of a view of the world which, thanks to the Scientific Revolution, we know is wrong.

Nowhere is the rejection of Aristotelian physics more evident, so the master narrative of the Scientific Revolution would have it, than in the principle of inertia, which, so it seems, directly contradicts the fundamental Aristotelian principle that everything that is moved is moved by another.[29] If we turn to the principle of inertia and examine it in some detail we can find evidence against the view that to accept modern science one must reject Aristotelian natural philosophy.[30]

Newton's famous three laws of motion appear early in the *Principia*. He begins with a series of definitions concerning mass, forces, and the like; then states the three laws and deduces corollaries from them. These laws, corollaries, and definitions are expressed in expository prose without those mathematical equations with which we have become familiar. In the preface, Newton reminds the reader of that in this work he will "subject the phenomena of nature to the laws of mathematics." At another place, he observes that he only provides "a mathematical notion of . . . forces, without considering their physical causes."[31] He tells us that he is considering "forces not physically, but mathematically."[32] At the beginning of Book III, the section called the "System of the World," Newton notes: "In the preceding books, I have laid down principles not philosophical but mathematical."[33] When he turns to discuss various explanations of planetary movement, he notes the ancient view of the planets' being imbedded in solid orbs. Newton thinks that Descartes and Kepler postulated celestial vortices as a way to account for such motion, and then he comments: "From the first law of motion it is very certain that some force is required. [But] [o]ur purpose is to bring out its quantity and properties and to investigate mathematically its effects on moving bodies."[34]

Although Newton was convinced of the tremendous power of mathematics to discover and describe accurately certain fundamental characteristics of the world, we must not think that Newton was some 17th century Pythagorean for whom the mathematical description of reality is *the* only truly scientific account of nature. Newton warns against such an attribution when he remarks:

> those violate the accuracy of language, which ought to be kept precise, who interpret these words [time, space, place, and motion] for the measured quantities. Nor do those less defile the purity of mathematical and philosophical truths, who confound real quantities with their relations and sensible measures.[35]

Immediately prior to his enunciation of the principle of inertia, Newton provides a definition of centripetal force in which he hypothesizes what would happen in projectile motion "if the resistance of the air is taken away." In this discussion Newton moves *from* the world of ordinary experience to imagine the limiting case of motion: *viz.*, that at which the projectile would proceed in its motion forever. Newton describes what obtains in a limiting case, and, thus, he presupposes the concept of limit in the derivation of that case. Newton's notion of limit is drawn from mathematical modes of reasoning. It is precisely such a mathematical concept of limit which is at the root of the principle of inertia. The principle is an *inference* drawn from the mathematical-physical approach to a limit. In other words, as the resistance of the medium approaches zero, the distance traveled approaches infinity.[36]

As William Wallace has pointed out, there is no explicit discussion in the *Principia* about the need for an extrinsic cause for motion, apart from what Newton says about God as universal mover. Nevertheless, in some reflections on mechanics at the end of the *Optics*, Newton observes:

> The *vis inertiae* is a passive principle by which bodies persist in their motion or rest, receive motion in proportion to the force impressing it, and resist as much as they are resisted. By this principle alone there never could be any motion in the world. Some other principle was necessary for putting bodies in motion; and now they are in motion, some other principle is necessary for conserving motion.[37]

As an idealized, quasi-mathematical concept, the principle of inertia involves an abstraction from the extrinsic forces acting on real bodies moving in a physical environment. The principle also involves an abstraction from any kind of physical causality. Accordingly, the principle of inertia, regardless of its truth, says nothing in support of nor in contradiction to Aristotle's principle in physics that everything that is moved is moved by another. Only if one assumes that the principle of inertia is a law of nature and not simply a principle in mathematical physics would one have a problem with its relationship to Aristotelian physics.

The principle of inertia considers bodies simply as three-dimensional realities devoid of natures. Newton's first law of motion cannot be a "law of nature," least of all the *prima lex naturae* that Descartes thought necessary in his universe of geometrical space. Only in such a Cartesian world of "nude bodies," each with a fixed "quantity of matter" and a fixed "quantity of motion," can there be such a first law of nature.[38] The Cartesian world, however, is not Newton's world, and Descartes' notion of inertia is not Newton's.

If the real world is actually a world of natures, of qualitative distinctions, and of intrinsic principles of spontaneous behavior, there would be no problem in abstracting from such a world to consider only the quantitative features of things. The scientific study of such abstracted reality we should recognize as mathematical physics, the principles of which are different from those of other sciences.

The application of mathematics to the study of motion necessarily involves an abstract world. And an abstract world is not a false world; but nor is it identical with the world of nature. Newton knew full well that when, for example, he defined "mass" as "the quantity of matter" and "momentum" as the "quantity of motion," that he was proceeding in the realm of mathematical physics. We should take a clue from the title of his work: *Mathematical Principles of Natural Philosophy* [*Philosophiae Naturalis Principia Mathematica*], which differs significantly from Descartes' title, *Principles of Philosophy*. Along with James Weisheipl and William Wallace, whose analyses (as I have indicated) have influenced my work significantly, we should recognize that in Newton there is not so much a rejection of the principles of Aristotelian physics as a great expansion of and sophistication in the science of mathematical physics.[39]

Whether it be Thomas Aquinas in the thirteenth century or Galileo in the seventeenth, no major thinker in the Middle Ages or the Renaissance was unaware of the importance of understanding the connections uniting and the differences separating mathematics and the natural sciences. Natural bodies are not constituted, are not made what they are, by their quantitative dimensions; and, thus, mathematical measures are not the principles of explanation in physics: since the principles of explanation in physics must provide the explanation for what constitutes the body as such. To explain the nature of a tree or a molecule requires knowing what makes a tree be a tree, or a molecule be a molecule. The science of nature, in all its branches, is an autonomous science having its own proper principles, and is, thus, distinct from and not dependent upon mathematics. In the Aristotelian tradition, although mathematics and physics are both theoretical sciences they differ in what they study. Physics – again, what we would call the natural sciences, or perhaps what we should call a broad, general science of nature which includes all the natural sciences – [physics] studies the world of matter-in-motion (*ens mobile*): what is perceptible; what we can see, or smell, or taste, or touch, or hear; the world of concrete physical reality as it undergoes generation and destruction, changes of place, shape, and the like. Mathematics, on the other hand, has as its object the quantitative features of the world of physical reality – those quantitative dimensions which exist in physical objects but which can be considered separate from them. The geometer, for example, studies spheres, not spherical basketballs. The human mind has the ability to separate intellectually geometric forms from physical matter and to know these forms in their separated state, but the sphere which a geometer studies does not truly exist prior to a spherical body. For Albert and Thomas, the mathematician studies quantities which, although necessarily existing in sensible matter, can be understood without such sensible matter. Many of the advances in science since the time of Aristotle – Euclid's systematization of geometry, Archimedes' discoveries in mechanics, the astronomy of Ptolemy, and advances in optics – lent support to the Platonic view that mathematics affords the only truly scientific explanation of natural phenomena. Yet, in the middle of the thirteenth century, Albert the Great in his commentary on Aristotle's

Metaphysics attacked "the error of Plato, who said that natural things are founded on mathematical [things], and mathematical being [is] founded on divine [being], just as the third cause is dependent on the second, and the second on the first; and so [Plato] said that the principles of natural being are mathematical, which is completely false."[40] The "error of Plato," according to Albert, is not simply an illegitimate emphasis upon the importance of mathematics, but is, rather, a defective understanding of metaphysics and epistemology. In his commentary on the pseudo-Aristotelian *Liber de causis*, Albert lists four main errors of the Platonists: 1) they allow for motions without the contact of some efficient cause; 2) they identify principles of knowing with principles of being, so that once they have postulated an exemplar they think they have explained the cause of the thing; 3) they postulate subsistent numbers as the *per se* principles of physical things; 4) they make solids, surfaces, and lines flow from a point to constitute a *corpus mathematicum*, to which they add a *corpus naturale*, as though it were an additional *forma*.[41] Albert, following Aristotle, affirms that the proper principles of the natural sciences are not mathematical. The natural sciences (i.e., physics) are not subordinate to an allegedly "higher" science of mathematics. "Dimensions are not principles of bodies according to any *esse* [any thing which makes the body what it is], rather they [dimensions] are consequent upon the fact that they [bodies] are concrete physical bodies having proper principles like matter and form, and that the form giving the existence is in this matter."[42]

As Thomas Aquinas points out,[43] the natural sciences study what exists in matter and in motion *precisely* as these things exist in matter and motion. Man cannot be studied, as man, distinct from flesh and bones. Man cannot be understood without his materiality. Mathematics studies those dimensions and quantities which *exist* in sensible matter, but which can be *known* separate from sensible matter. Man, through a special process of abstraction on the part of his intellect, has the capacity to understand shapes and numbers independently from the material bodies in which they exists. Mathematics and the natural sciences can be distinguished in terms of their respective objects of study, as well as in terms of the different ways in which the objects are known.[44]

Mathematics does not provide a *deeper* explanation of the world of nature than does physics; nor does mathematics provide the true principles of scientific inquiry for the natural sciences. Thus, the natural sciences have an autonomy appropriately their own.[45]

Although mathematics and physics are autonomous and distinct sciences, one may apply mathematical principles to the study of natural phenomena. Such applications occur in neither the science of mathematics, nor in physics. They constitute mixed sciences: types of knowledge that are intermediate between what we today might term "pure" mathematics and a more general science of nature. Aristotle, in the second book of the *Physics*, recognizes the legitimacy of such intermediate sciences, what he considers to be *in some sense* branches of mathematics which come nearest to the study of nature: optics, harmonics, and astronomy. Referring to such a mixed science, Aquinas writes: "it does not belong to the mathematician to treat of motion, although mathematical principles can be applied to motion. . . . The measurements of motions are studies in the intermediate sciences between mathematics and natural science."[46]

The application of mathematical principles to the study of natural phenomena is never a substitute for the science of physics which has as its object the study of physical bodies in their full reality. Principles of mathematics, although applicable to the study of natural phenomena, cannot explain the causes and true nature of natural phenomena.

It seems to me that we can best understand the history of science in the fourteenth through the seventeenth centuries – and, indeed, beyond to our own time – if we recognize that some of the greatest accomplishments in the sciences have taken place in mathematical physics – that intermediate science between mathematics and physics. The careful distinctions drawn by Albert the Great and Thomas Aquinas frequently have been lost in the midst of the great advances mathematical physicists have achieved: the confusion is already in Descartes, who, as we have seen, called inertia the first law of nature, rather than recognizing it, as Newton did, as a mathematical principle of natural philosophy.

Once we understand the nature of mathematics, physics, and the intermediate sciences – an understanding present in the thought of Aristotle, and made explicit especially by Thomas Aquinas – then, I think, we can see a fundamental continuity in the history of science from the time of Aristotle to the present. Although ancient and mediaeval thinkers were not very concerned with what is called "mathematical physics," and they surely did not expect such a fruitful expansion of the role of mathematics in describing the world of nature, still, they did recognize the validity of the use of mathematics in investigating nature. Such a perspective on the Scientific Revolution frees us from the false view that one must chose between Aristotle and the great advances of modern science. We would also be emancipated from the false exaggeration of the importance of mathematics, an exaggeration which has encouraged many to force all the sciences – natural and social – into the Procustean bed of mathematics, belittling or tending to ignore what cannot be timed, weighed, measured, or counted.[47]

The philosophical baggage of a mechanistic and materialistic natural philosophy which is often associated with modern science is the product of philosophical traditions in the Seventeenth Century and beyond. Mechanism and materialism represent a radical rejection of Aristotelian and Thomistic natural philosophy, but mechanism and materialism remain excess baggage, *not required* in order to accept the advances in our understanding of the world which are the legacy of Galileo and Newton. Although many historians, philosophers, and theologians see modern science as providing, ultimately, a challenge to the God of traditional religion, such a judgment rests on questionable interpretations of the Scientific Revolution as well as on a failure to appreciate the theological and philosophical heritage of the Middle Ages.

Remember the Pope's remarks to the Polish academicians last June, that "authentic freedom of scientific research cannot prescind from the criterion of truth and goodness." Modern science seen as a rejection of Aristotelian physics is often viewed as being opposed to any notion of the good discoverable in nature. Or, at most, science must remain, as Stephen Gould claims, irrelevant to questions about "God, meaning, and morality."[48] I suppose it is not strange that once purpose, meaning, and finality are excluded from nature, then the postmodern denial of truth in science should find a hearty welcome.

Misinterpretations of the Scientific Revolution may have also tempted some in the Thomistic tradition to retreat from the arena of natural philosophy to bask in the seemingly safer and ethereal realm of metaphysics. The history of science can help us distinguish among the advances of modern science, the mechanistic and materialist natural philosophy which has accompanied these advances, and the principles of Thomistic natural philosophy which can lead to a deeper and more complete understanding of nature, human nature, and God.[49]

Notes

1. Charles Gillispie, *The Edge of Objectivity: An Essay in the History of Scientific Ideas* (Princeton University Press, 1960), p. 13. Gillispie is the general editor of the *Dictionary of Scientific Biography* (1980).

2. Pope John Paul II, "Address at Meeting with Rectors of Academic Institutions: Torun, Monday, 7 June 1999," Vatican Web Site.

3. This theme is apparent in *Fides et Ratio*, §48: "Deprived of reason, faith has stressed feeling and experience, and so run[s] the risk of no longer being a universal proposition. It is an illusion to think that faith, tied to weak reasoning, might be more penetrating; on the contrary, faith then runs the grave risk of withering into myth or superstition. By the same token, reason which is unrelated to an adult faith is not prompted to turn its gaze to the newness and radicality of being. This is why I make this strong and insistent appeal... that faith and philosophy recover the profound unity which allows them to stand in harmony with their nature without compromising their mutual autonomy." The Pope locates in the late Middle Ages an increasingly "fateful sep-

aration" between faith and reason which ultimately led some to espouse the cause of "rational knowledge sundered from faith and meant to take the place of faith." The Pope argues that such a separation led to an "ever deeper mistrust of reason itself." Gradually "[i]n the field of scientific research," the Pope writes, "a positivistic mentality took hold which not only abandoned the Christian vision of the world, but more especially rejected every appeal to a metaphysical or moral vision." The Pope sees nihilism as the ultimate outcome of this "crisis of rationalism." "As a philosophy of nothingness, it has a certain attraction for people of our time. Its adherents claim that the search is an end in itself, without any hope or possibility of ever attaining the goal of truth. In the nihilist interpretation, life is no more than an occasion for sensations and experiences in which the ephemeral has pride of place. Nihilism is at the root of the widespread mentality which claims that a definitive commitment should no longer be made, because everything is fleeting and provisional." *Fides et Ratio*, §48.

4. More than twenty-five years ago, the French biologist Jacques Monod remarked: "Anything can be reduced to simple, obvious, mechanical interactions. The cell is a machine; the animal is a machine; man is a machine." Jacques Monod, *Chance and Necessity: An Essay on the Natural Philosophy of Biology* (New York: Knopf, 1974), p. ix. Or consider the well-known comment by Richard Dawkins, author of *The Selfish Gene*, who claims that a human being is not a cause but an effect, and that life and mind are merely the outcome of genes that "swarm in huge colonies, safe inside gigantic lumbering robots." Richard Dawkins, *The Selfish Gene* (New York: Oxford University Press, 1976), p. 21. In another work Dawkins is not afraid to draw the following conclusion: "The universe we observe has precisely the properties we should expect if there is, at bottom, no design, no purpose, no evil and no good, nothing but blind pitiless indifference. . . . DNA neither knows nor cares. DNA just is. And we dance to its music." Dawkins, *River Out of Eden: A Darwinian View of Life* (New York: Basic Books, 1995), p. 133. Sir Francis Crick, co-discoverer of the double-helix structure of the DNA molecule, writes at the beginning of *The Astonishing Hypothesis*: "The Astonishing Hypothesis is that 'You,' your joys and your sorrows, your memories and your ambitions, your sense of personal identity and your free will, are in fact no more than the behavior of a vast assembly of nerve cells and their associated molecules." (New York: Scribner, 1994).

5. The commonly accepted narrative of the Scientific Revolution, whether we accept Pierre Duhem's claim for a radical change in fourteenth century Paris or Anneliese Maier's argument that the principle of inertia, set forth in the seventeenth century, is fundamentally at odds with the Aristotelian principle that everything that is moved is moved by another, sees a fundamental dis-

continuity in the history of science which heralds the birth of modern science. Recently several historians of science have suggested that we ought to move beyond the categories of continuity and discontinuity in examining the history of science, in general, and the Scientific Revolution, in particular. This view is especially apparent in the increased interest in the social history of science, and is associated with broader questions concerning the sociology of knowledge. See Steven Shapin, *The Scientific Revolution* (University of Chicago Press, 1996). For an excellent survey of various interpretations of the Scientific Revolution, see H. Floris Cohen's *The Scientific Revolution: A Historiographical Survey* (1994). David Lindberg's introductory essay on conceptions of the Scientific Revolution in *Reappraisals of the Scientific Revolution,* eds. D. Lindberg and R. Westman (1990) is also excellent.

6. Stephen J. Gould, *Rocks of Ages: Science and Religion in the Fullness of Life* (New York: Ballantine Publishing Group, 1999).

7. Here it is important to distinguish between the principles which inform Aristotle's science of nature, principles set out in his *Physics, Posterior Analytics, On the Generation of Animals, De Anima,* and the like, and particular conclusions which Aristotle reached, such as that Earth is immobile and at the center of the universe; or other conclusions he supported in cosmology in *De Caelo.*

8. H. Butterfield, *The Origins of Modern Science,* rev. ed. (New York: The Free Press, 1965), pp. 7–8.

9. A. N. Whitehead, *Essays in Science and Philosophy* (New York: Philosophical Library, 1968), pp. 234–35. This analysis depends significantly on the work of James Weisheipl, especially as found in *Nature and Motion in the Middle Ages,* ed. William Carroll (Washington, D.C.: The Catholic University of America Press, 1985).

10. Whitehead, *Essays,* p. 235.

11. "[I]t seems that Newton's law [of inertia] wrecks the argument of the First Way. For at any given time, the rectilinear uniform motion of a body can be explained by the principle of inertia in terms of the body's own previous motion without any appeal to any other agent. And there seems [to be] no *a priori* reason why this explanatory process should not go backwards for ever. Newton's law will not explain how motion began; but how do we know that motion had a beginning?" Anthony Kenny, *The Five Ways: St. Thomas Aquinas's Proofs of God's Existence* (New York: Schocken Books, 1969), p. 28.

12. "[T]he operations of the laws of inertia and gravity and the natural activities of sulphur or uranium are not teleological activities at all. If we today are to seek, as Aquinas did, to locate animal desire and human willing in a hier-

archy of different kinds of tendencies towards good, then we must put at the bottom level of the hierarchy not the natural agency of inanimate matter, but the non-conscious teleological activities to be found in the plant world." Anthony Kenny, *Aquinas on Mind* (London: Routledge, 1993), p. 61.

13. Kenny, *Aquinas on Mind,* p. 61. Alasdair MacIntyre, despite his sympathies for Aristotle and Aquinas, argues for the *necessity* of providing a new foundation for ethics, different from the natural philosophy of Aristotle and Aquinas, by pointing to the encounter between impetus theory and the inertial physics of Galileo and Newton, which encounter he calls a classic case of "systematically different and *incomparable* observational languages, key concepts, and theoretical structures [which] were framed in terms of rival and *incomparable* standards . . . [such that] there was no shared common measure [between the two physical systems]." Alasdair MacIntyre, *Three Rival Versions of Moral Enquiry* (Notre Dame, IN: University of Notre Dame Press, 1990), p. 118. Italics added.

14. M. Adler, *How to Think About God* (New York: Macmillan, 1980), pp. 123–25.

15. Pannenberg: "any contemporary discussion regarding theology and science should first focus on the question of what modern science, and especially modern physics, can say about the contingency of the world as a whole and every part in it." Wolfhart Pannenberg, "The Doctrine of Creation and Modern Science," *Zygon* 23.1 (1988), p. 9. For an excellent analysis of Pannenberg's position on contingency, see Robert John Russell, "Contingency in Physics and Cosmology: A Critique of the Theology of Wolfhart Pannenberg," *Zygon* 23.1 (1988), pp. 23–43. This entire issue of *Zygon* is dedicated to the work of Pannenberg.

16. In an introduction to Pannenberg's *Toward a Theology of Nature*, Ted Peters describes Pannenberg's position in the following way: "The relationship between uniform laws of nature and the contingency of particular events provides the formal point of departure for Pannenberg's theological analysis of modern science. . . . One area to which he has devoted considerable attention is the concept of the force field in physics. The work of Michael Faraday and his successors such as Albert Einstein draws particular interest. The achievement of the field concept is that it reverses the previous view that forces are solely the unmediated result of bodies in motion, that action-at-a-distance is precluded. To Faraday, in contrast, the body is a manifestation of force field; and a force field is an independent reality prior to the body. Body and mass become secondary phenomena, concentrations of dynamic force at particular places and points in the field. Action-at-a-distance is possible.

This is theologically significant for a number of reasons. First, the problem with the post-Newtonian reduction of forces to mass in motion is that the resulting picture of the universe precludes any divine force. If God does not have a body, and if all forces require a prior body, then God cannot have force. This problem is eliminated with contemporary field theory.

This is theologically significant for a second reason. Dynamic field theories from Faraday to Einstein claim a priority for the whole over the parts. The value of this is that God and the whole are correlate categories. God, as the all-determining reality, must be conceived to be the unifying ground of the whole universe if the divine is to be conceived as creator and redeemer of the world. By appealing to the divinely granted whole of reality, Pannenberg believes he can make the effective presence of God in every single event intelligible. To increase this intelligibility, Pannenberg points out that the field concept was originally a metaphysical concept going back to the pre-Socratics. By the time the Stoics got hold of it, the field had become associated with the *pneuma*, the divine Spirit.

This brings us to the third reason that field theory in physics is theologically significant: it provides a possible means for conceiving of the divine Spirit as active in the natural world. Even more – and this may be one of the most courageous of his conceptual hypotheses – Pannenberg employs the notion of a dynamic field to describe the workings of the Spirit within the trinitarian life proper. The essence of divinity is spirit, he says; and it is due to the Holy Spirit *as* a dynamic force field that the Son is generated from the Father and that the two, Father and Son, are bound together in love." Ted Peters, "Introduction," in Wolfhart Pannenberg, *Toward a Theology of Nature*, ed. Ted Peters (Louisville, KY: Westminster Press, 1993), pp. 13–14.

Keith Ward summarizes Pannenberg's position in this way: "Wolfhart Pannenberg has suggested that one might think of the Spirit of God as such a 'total field' which environs the cosmos . . . the idea of Spirit as a 'universal field of energy' which engenders a process of creative unification, leading organisms to transcend themselves towards increasingly complexity and structure [*Toward a Theology of Nature*, p. 140]. He appeals to the work of Teilhard in developing this view, and also to Polanyi's idea of a morphogenic field, which may be an explanatory factor individual development. The model suggests very well the way in which God's influence would not be either intermittent or confined to some initial act of origination. It would set the origin, the limits, and the goal of the process, being a constant presence and influence at every point." Keith Ward, *Religion and Creation* (Oxford: Clarendon Press, 1996), pp. 298–99.

17. W. Pannenberg, *Metaphysics and the Idea of God*, trans. Philip Clayton (Grand Rapids, MI.: W. B. Eerdmans, 1990), p. 30.

18. Descartes, *Principles of Philosophy* (Part II, 37), trans. J. Cottingham, *The Philosophical Writings of Descartes*, (New York and Cambridge: Cambridge

University Press, 1984) Vol. I, p. 240.

19. "The entire conception of God's creative activity was deeply challenged in the seventeenth century because of the principle of inertia. The German philosopher Hans Blumenberg has repeatedly put his finger on this remarkable event, an event of far-reaching importance in the history of modern times. *The principle of inertia as formulated by Descartes means that no longer is the continuous existence of any given state of affairs in need of explanation but only the occurrence of any changes of this status* [my emphasis]. This consequence seems to be inevitable, if inertia in contrast to Descartes is understood as a force of self-preservation inherent in the body, a *vis insita*. On this basis, a transcendent conservation (*Fremderhaltung*) of nature becomes superfluous. In a similar way the mechanical interpretation of the changes occurring to the bodies in terms of a transfer of movement renders the assumption of a divine cooperation in the activities of the creatures superfluous. Thus deism must be seen as the consequence of the introduction of the principle of inertia in modern physics." Pannenberg, *Metaphysics*, p. 35

20. Pannenberg, *Metaphysics*, p. 31.

21. "When, almost one hundred years after Spinoza, Immanuel Kant again used the contingency of all finite reality as a starting point for developing his idea of God, he found himself confined to the puzzlement such contingency presented to human reason; he no longer could claim a direct dependence of contingent reality on God for its preservation." Pannenberg, *Metaphysics*, p. 20.

22. Blumenberg, *The Legitimacy of the Modern Age*, trans. Robert Wallace (Cambridge, MA: MIT Press, 1971), p. 137. Robert Wallace edited a special edition of *Annals of Scholarship* (1987) dedicated to analyses of Blumenberg's work. For a recent survey of Blumenberg's thought, see Elías José Palti, "In Memoriam: Hans Blumenberg (1920–1996). An Unended Quest," *Journal of the History of Ideas* 58.3 (July 1997), pp. 503–24.

23. Blumenberg, *Legitimacy*, p. 143.

24. Ibid., pp. 145–79. Some historians of science see a connection between the emphasis on the absolute power of God, characteristic of Nominalist thought, and the corresponding importance of divine sovereignty in the theologies of Luther and Calvin, and the development of a mechanistic conception of nature. With all causal agency located in God, it makes sense to view the world of nature as entirely passive or inert, only subject to extrinsic/external forces. Gary Deason writes: "The world as Newton described it appeared to be the product of God's action on mindless, inchoate matter. . . . Were it not for God's gracious bestowal of active forces such as gravity, the world would have languished inert and purposeless. As the key to the meaning and struc-

ture of the new mechanical world, gravity became the mark of power and grace. In the decades after Newton's *Principia*, theologians and religious popularizers latched onto the grace of gravity as a valuable weapon in the ongoing fight against atheism. . . . The Reformers faced a crisis in faith brought about by what they believed was a misconception of divine grace. Addressing the needs of the believer, they effected a theological revolution by focusing on the absolute sovereignty of grace and the assurance of salvation that they thought belief in it would bring. The mechanists faced the very different problem of developing a plausible conception of nature in the light of recent discoveries of mathematical laws of nature. They employed the sovereignty of God to impose laws of nature on the corpuscles of ancient atomism, making atomism into a viable worldview and laying the conceptual basis for mathematical physics. In the process, however, God changed character. The sovereign Redeemer of Luther and Calvin became the sovereign Ruler of the world machine. The Reformers' search for assurance of salvation gave way to the assurance of scientific explanation. The radical sovereignty of God between the Reformation and the Enlightenment followed the course of many concepts in the complex history of religion and science." Deason, "Reformation Theology and the Mechanistic Conception of Nature," in *God and Nature: Historical Essays on the Encounter Between Christianity and Science*, eds. David Lindberg and Ronald Numbers (Berkeley: The University of California Press, 1986), pp. 167-191, at pp. 185, 187. Michael Buckley, in *At the Origins of Modern Atheism* (Yale, 1987), argues that the attempt to use science as a justification for belief – especially evident in the seventeenth century – paves the way for modern atheism.

25. Pannenberg, *Metaphysics*, p. 35.

26. See Steven E. Baldner and William E. Carroll, *Aquinas on Creation* (Toronto: Pontifical Institute of Mediaeval Studies, 1997).

27. It is important to note that those who speak of such a "settlement" also argue that contemporary science, especially relativity theory and quantum mechanics, have altered this settlement so radically that theologians and philosophers must adjust their understanding of nature, human nature, and God to take into consideration the new scientific perspective(s).

28. For those who dislike the notion of "truth" and "falsity" in discussions of claims about the world, the argument is simply that the new paradigm has replaced an old one.

29. One could, of course, discuss the denial of final causality in nature or the reduction of qualities to quantity, but these are more specifically developments in natural philosophy. It is the principle of inertia which is the key doctrine to examine.

30. My analysis of the principle of inertia relies upon the excellent work of William A. Wallace and James A. Weisheipl. William Wallace's early work on the principle of inertia is "Newtonian Antinomies Against the *Prima Via*," *The Thomist* 19 (April 1956), pp. 151–92. See also, James Weisheipl, "Galileo and the Principle of Inertia," in *Nature and Motion in the Middle Ages*, ed. William E. Carroll (Washington, D.C.: The Catholic University of America Press, 1985), pp. 49–73.

31. Newton, *Principia* I, Definition VIII, trans. by Florian Cajori (University of California Press, 1971), pp. 4–5.

32. Ibid., I, pp. 5–6.

33. Ibid., III, p. 397.

34. Ibid., III, p. 550.

35. Ibid., I, p. 11.

36. This is a key insight in William Wallace's analysis, cited in note 30 above.

37. Newton, *Opticks* III.1 ([4th edition, 1750] New York: Dover, 1952), p. 397.

38. This is the point that Weisheipl makes in the essay cited in note 30. We must remember that "quantity" can be studied 1) in metaphysics as a category of being; 2) in physics as a property of substance (and according to its [quantity's] proper nature; and 3) in mathematics as it has certain properties that lack any order to substance – hence as "nude quantity."

39. Many historians of science in this century have concentrated on the role of mathematics in the Scientific Revolution. E. A. Burtt and Alexandre Koyré, for example, accepted the central importance of the principle of inertia in identifying the revolutionary character of seventeenth century science, but they located the development and the enunciation of the principle in the context of a mathematization of nature. In what has become a classic text, *The Metaphysical Foundations of Modern Science*, E. A. Burtt summarizes this position: "We have observed that the heart of the new scientific metaphysics is to be found in the ascription of ultimate reality and causal efficacy to the world of mathematics, which world is identified with the realm of material bodies moving in space and time. Expressed more fully . . ., the real world in which man lives is no longer regarded as a world of substances possessed of as many ultimate qualities as can be experienced in them, but has become a world of atoms (now electrons), equipped with none but mathematical characteristics, and moving according to laws fully statable in mathematical form." E. A. Burtt, *The Metaphysical Foundations of Modern Physical Science* (Atlantic Heights, NJ: Humanities Press, 1980), p. 303. In what is perhaps his most famous book, *From the Closed World to the Infinite*

Universe (Baltimore: Johns Hopkins, 1957), Alexandre Koyré argues that the Scientific Revolution is, at its core, a fundamental metaphysical shift away from a finite Aristotelian universe of qualitative distinctions to a universe of infinite geometrical space in which physical reality is exhaustively captured in mathematical terms. Newton's principle of inertia is, for Koyré, inconceivable without this change in metaphysics. Only in an infinite universe could one conceive of uniform motion in a straight line forever.

40. Albert, *Lib. I Metaph.* tr. 1, c. 1 (Borgnet 6, p. 2b).

41. Albert, *Liber de causis* I, tr. 1, c. 4 (Borgnet 10, 368b–69a).

42. Albert, *Lib. I Metaph.* tr. 1, c. 1 (Borgnet 6, pp. 2b–3a).

43. Aquinas's most important work in this respect can be found in his commentary on Boethius' *De Trinitate*, questions 4 and 5 and in his commentary on the second book of Aristotle's *Physics*.

44. Aquinas locates the fundamental error of the Platonists in their failure to understand the way in which the intellect functions in the acquisition of knowledge. Because the intellect is able to consider a nature, or an essence, or a quantitative dimension without thinking of the respective individuals whose nature it is, Platonists think that the nature or essence or quantitative dimension must truly exist separate from the individuals. Platonists confuse the order of intelligibility and the order of existence. Simply because the object of thought – a triangle, or a square, or a sphere – is, in itself, intelligible, Platonists conclude that such an object of thought must have a substantial existence. Here is how Albert the Great puts it: "This [in my judgment] has been the entire cause of the controversy between Plato and Aristotle, that he [Plato] wished to utilize arguments of a logical order, and deduced from them principles of the real world. Aristotle, however, does not do this, but looks for principles of real things from within the natures of thins." Albert, *In II Sent.* 1, a. 4, ad 4 (Borgnet 27, 15a).

45. The importance of mathematics in the thought of Galileo and Newton led, has led some scholars such as E. A. Burtt and Alexandre Koyré, to see the Scientific Revolution as a radical shift in metaphysics: a return, if you will, to the heritage of Plato and a rejection of Aristotle. Such an interpretation misses an important point in the mediaeval understanding of the relationship between mathematics and physics.

46. Thomas Aquinas, *In Boethium De trinitate*, q. 5, a. 3, ad 5 [*The Division and Methods of the Sciences*, trans. Armand Maurer (Pontifical Institute of Mediaeval Studies, 1963), p. 36]. See also, *In II Phys.* lec. 3, n. 8. "So there are three levels of sciences concerning natural and mathematical entities. Some are purely natural and treat of the properties of natural things as such, like physics . . . . Others are purely mathematical and treat of quantities

absolutely, as geometry considers magnitude and arithmetic number. Still others are intermediate, and these apply mathematical principles to natural things; for instance, music, astronomy, and the like. These sciences, however, have a closer affinity to mathematics, because in their thinking that which is physical is, as it were, material, whereas that which is mathematical is, as it were, formal. For example, music considers sounds, not inasmuch as they are sounds, but inasmuch as they are proportionable according to numbers; and the same holds in other sciences. Thus they demonstrate their conclusions concerning natural things, but by means of mathematics." (Maurer, pp. 37-38) For an insightful discussion of this treatise, see Stephen L. Brock, "Autonomia e gerarchia delle scienze in Tommaso d'Aquino. La difficoltà dellla sapienza," in *Unità e autonomia del sapere. Il dibattito del XIII secolo*, ed. Rafael Martínez (Roma: Armando Editore, 1994), pp. 71–96.

47. One of the great achievements of Albert the Great and Thomas Aquinas was their clear demonstration of the autonomy of the natural sciences: an autonomy, by the way, with respect to theology and to faith, as well as with respect to mathematics. They had no doubt that the physical universe is intelligible and that it is, therefore, an appropriate object of scientific investigation. The natural scientist explains change in its many forms: generation and destruction, locomotion, alteration, and the like. A science of generation and destruction, locomotion, and alteration must provide explanations in terms of the proper causes for these changes. The principles used in these explanations are not mathematical. And it does not matter whether we are speaking of productive, practical, or theoretical science. How can points, lines, surfaces, numbers, or equations – principles of mathematics – how can these cause the construction of houses or the writing of a poem? How can points, lines, surfaces, numbers or equations cause men to fashion constitutions, to engage in commerce or to live virtuously? How can points, lines, surfaces, numbers or equations cause the birth of an animal, the growth of an acorn into an oak tree, the movement of either planets or subatomic particles? As Albert and Thomas clearly understood, scientific explanations – explanations in terms of causes – employ the principles appropriate to each science. Although mathematics is clearer and more certain than the natural sciences, we must resist the temptation to regard mathematics either as the only true science or as a substitute for the natural sciences.

48. S. Gould, *Rocks of Ages* (New York: Ballantine, 1999), p. 193.

49. Much work needs to be done by those in the Thomistic tradition to incorporate the discoveries of modern science into a broader philosophy of nature. Three authors who have worked in this area are: Benedict Ashley, *Theologies of the Body* (St. Louis, MO: Pope John Center, 1985); Richard Connell, *Substance and Modern Science* (Houston: Center for Thomistic Studies,

University of St. Thomas, 1988); and William Wallace, *From a Realist Point of View* (Washington, D.C.: The Catholic University of America Press, 1979) and *The Modeling of Nature* (Washington, D.C.: The Catholic University of America Press, 1996).

Fides et Ratio: Exorcizing the Ghost of Descartes
John Hittinger

In *Fides et Ratio* Pope John Paul II invites us to consider both the ways of faith and the ways of reason in overcoming the crisis of our time – the crisis of meaning and truth which has issued in human degradation – called "nihilism." This crisis of modernity has led people to face the untenable options of "a destructive will to power or to a solitude without hope" (§90). The roots of this crisis lie deep in historical decision and philosophical reflection in the encounter of human beings with their own conscience, question of being, and God. The contemporary crisis recapitulates in the depths of the soul of modern man the foundational and originating questions of modern philosophy. In brief, the crisis is spawned by a hyper-rationalist mentality which separated itself from the wisdom of faith, claiming for itself more than the legitimate autonomy of the ancients, but a self-sufficiency, closed in and hostile to faith (§75). The modern philosophy required the abandonment of a living faith, a faith that provides guideposts that beckon along the way and transform the interiority of the search. And by the great irony of history, the result has led to an abandonment of reason. Thus, by the same dynamic, working in reverse, a recovery of reason – a bold philosophical reason – is in some way connected to a revitalization of faith: "each without the other is impoverished and enfeebled" (§48).

There are many ways to approach this rich text of John Paul II, the philosopher Pope. I propose to read this encyclical as a venture in the philosophic quarrel of the ancients and moderns, which quarrel has been engaged by such seminal thinkers as Jacques Maritain and Leo Strauss.[1] Specifically, I propose to trace certain themes in *Fides et Ratio* which we must come to identify as "Cartesian." We must then come to understand the nature of Descartes' quarrel with pre-modern philosophy and the problematic character of its resolution; this should help us to appreciate what positive gains were made by Descartes and what important things were lost. An authentic "postmodern" position must continue to hold these gains and losses in tension and perspective. That is, John Paul II's critique of modernity seeks to rescue the advances and aspirations of the modern age and yet to understand them in a larger perspective in which the wisdom of the ancients and medievals can be re-appropriated and provide some ways out of the present crisis. In order to explore John Paul II's account of the philosophic crisis of the modern age, I propose to do the following: first, gather together the various signs of the times which indicate the crisis of modern philosophy and culture; second, match up such signs with their philosophic roots in the modern project as found in Descartes' *Discourse on Method*; third, review the important critique of Descartes made by Jacques Maritain, one of five Western thinkers put forward by John Paul II as an exemplar of the successful integration of *fides et ratio*.

Signs of the Times: The Crisis of Modernity

John Paul II approaches the crisis of modern philosophy in terms that Nietzsche revealed long ago – the crisis of nihilism. Modern man has lost a sense of the meaning of life and the cosmos. The very search for meaning is made "difficult and fruitless" because of the fragmentation of knowledge and the proliferation of theories (§81). Many can remain content within a purely utilitarian point of view "locked in the confines of immanence" with an indifference to the very question of transcendence and "ultimate and overarching meaning" (§81). John Paul II is concerned for the younger generation who find themselves at a loss in contemporary culture:

> For it is undeniable that this time of rapid and complex change can leave especially the younger generation, to whom the future belongs and on whom it depends, with a sense that they have no valid points of reference. The need for a foundation for personal and communal life becomes all the more pressing at a time when we are faced with the patent inadequacy of perspectives in which the ephemeral is affirmed as a value and the possibility of discovering the real meaning of life is cast into doubt. This is why many people stumble through life to the very edge of the abyss without knowing where they are going. At times, this happens because those whose vocation it is to give cultural expression to their thinking no longer look to truth, preferring quick success to the toil of patient enquiry into what makes life worth living. With its enduring appeal to the search for truth, philosophy has the great responsibility of forming thought and culture; and now it must strive resolutely to recover its original vocation (§6).

For the sake of the young, if for not for the older generations, John Paul II considers it a time to take stock of modern philosophy. If the path of modern philosophy has led to nihilism, is it not time to reconsider some of its fundamental principles, specifically its very self-conscious rejection of the ancient philosophy? John Paul II discusses at least three points in which modern philosophy has resolved its quarrel with the ancients in ways which now have become problematic in their connection to nihilism. The three points are: (1) the emphasis upon subjectivity; (2) the method of separation and reduction; (3) the project of mastery of nature. Each of these items contributes some share to the nihilism of the present age. Perhaps then we could see better the need for: (a) a rediscovery of being, (b) a refashioning of an integrative and expansive approach to knowledge, and (c) a reaffirmation of a moral and contemplative good beyond mastery and utility. In other words, a serious look at the crisis of the modern age recommends to us a reconsideration of ancient philosophy as a constructive task.

It is part of John Paul II's great achievement to combine the old and the new, he has done so philosophically as well as theologically. The discovery of subjectivity he acknowledges to be an advance of modern philosophy[2] which "clearly has the great merit of focusing attention upon man. From this starting-point, human reason with its many questions has developed further its yearning to know more and to know it ever more deeply" (§5). But he adds that this advance has been "one sided," thereby obscuring other important truths:

> Yet the positive results achieved must not obscure the fact that reason, in its one-sided concern to investigate human subjectivity, seems to have forgotten that men and women are always called to direct their steps towards a truth which transcends them. . . . It has happened therefore that reason, rather than voicing the human orientation towards truth, has wilted under the weight of so much knowledge and little by little has lost the capacity to lift its gaze to the heights, not daring to rise to the truth of being. Abandoning the investigation of being, modern philosophical research has concentrated instead upon human knowing. Rather than make use of the human capacity to know the truth, modern philosophy has preferred to accentuate the ways in which this capacity is limited and conditioned.

Or again John Paul II says that some moderns have simply abandoned the search for truth as they make their "sole aim the attainment of subjective certainty or a pragmatic sense of utility" (§47). John Paul II uses the same language again saying that this modern turn leads to an "obscuring" of "the dignity of reason" equipped as it is to know truth and the absolute (§47). The crisis of modern philosophy is due in part therefore to loss of a sense of being, and a sense of the absolute in whose mystery we live and move and have our being. John Paul II does not of course deny that human mind suffers from limit and condition. But modern philosophy has so emphasized this aspect, that the very quest for being is atrophied – it does not "dare to rise to the truth of being" (§5). Using the poetry of Gerard Manley Hopkins we may say that the moderns have discovered how much our knowledge "wears man's smudge [&] shares man's smell; the soil/ Is bare now, nor can foot feel, being shod." And thus does the modern soul despair of the richness of transcendent meaning and objective truth. They do not see that "for all this, nature is never spent:/ There lives the dearest freshness deep down things," which nature and freshness reason could discover. Nor do can they see anymore that morning of faith which comes because the "Holy Ghost over the bent/ World broods with warm breast [&] with ah! bright wings."[3] They look not to the wings of the spirit, neither reason energized by nature and its deep freshness nor the bright and warmth effects of faith. It is the loss of the élan of knowledge, the weariness with reason, which John Paul II seeks to counter and revive: "Faith and reason are like two wings on which the human spirit rises to the contemplation of truth; and God has placed in the human heart a desire to know the truth – in a word, to know himself – so that, by knowing and loving God, men and women may also come to the fullness of truth about themselves" (§1).

The second point concerning modernity, needing fundamental reconsideration, accompanies the first. It is the separation of thought from faith and a reduction of the richness of human experience. Philosophy rightly seeks its own "autonomy" or distinction from theology and so too are the various disciplines to be distinguished each from the other. Each seeks an authentic "autonomy" in the sense of following a proper method and tracing distinct lines of causality and intelligibility:

> If by the autonomy of earthly affairs we mean that created things and societies themselves enjoy their own laws and values which must be gradually deciphered, put to use, and regulated by men, then it is entirely right to demand that autonomy . . . all things are endowed with their own stability, truth, goodness, proper laws and order. Man must respect these as he isolates them by the appropriate methods of the individual sciences or arts."[4]

Thus, philosophy is rightly distinguished from faith and seeks to follow its own methods and demand its own evidence and proof. But in modern philosophy the quest for distinction has becomes separation. John Paul II calls this position a form of rationalism – the philosopher seeks to be "separate from and absolutely independent of the contents of faith" (§76). Complete independence or self sufficiency are other terms used by John Paul II to describe this approach of modern philosophy. It is an exaggerated sense of autonomy. It is a "false autonomy," say the Council Fathers, which seeks to cut off temporal and secular affairs from their deeper roots and ultimate goals, to suppose that created things do not depend on God and that man can use them without any reference to their Creator. Nihilism follows as a consequence of this separation, for without the Creator the creature disappears. One finds in modern method a dogmatic separation; a reductive approach which excludes the very possibility of faith. This is done because faith is considered to be a threat to the autonomy of the mind.

The third factor in the crisis of modernity may well be the most decisive. It is the capstone; the other two themes, the focus on subjectivity and the reductive method, are often mentioned as dynamically connected to the quest for mastery over nature. The modern age is characterized by great technological progress. The technical advances grant what seems to be "a quasi-divine power over nature and even over human beings" (§46). The desire for mastery most engenders the crisis of meaning. Nihilism results from the denial of limitation, ethical principle, and a higher being. The technological mentality moves away from "contemplative truth," abandons the search for ultimate goal, and substitutes instead an "instrumental" conception of reason which promises to procure for man "enjoyment or power" (§47). In his first encyclical John Paul II mentioned this problem as indicating the crisis of our time, and he refers to that very text here in *Fides et Ratio.*[5] The deep fear of technology bringing with it a wide spread tyranny or degradation is one of the deepest signs of the times and an indication of the crisis of modernity. Philosophy must recover a "sapiential dimension" so that the "immense expansion of humanity's technical capability – [be] ordered to something greater lest inhuman and destroyer of human race" (§81). The great evil of this century, a century of technological progress, causes a sense of despair in reason (§91). We now have an opportunity for recovering the sapiential dimension precisely because we have come see the illusion of "technical progress making us a demiurge, single handedly and completely taking charge of destiny."[6]

These three themes resound throughout *Fides et Ratio*: the turn to subjectivity, a reductive and separatist method, and mastery of nature. It does not take too much reflection to detect here the presence of Descartes. John Paul II does not mention him by name, but this constellation of philosophical themes puts us on the trail of Descartes; and it is John Paul II's mission to exorcise his ghost. The spirit of Descartes – subjectivity, rationalist separation, and mastery – continues to haunt modern and contemporary philosophy; now one, now another element may be denounced or shaken off by this or that thinker claiming to be "postmodern." Descartes is a favorite object of critique by postmodern philosophers; and yet they continue to employ one or the other theme. But it is rare indeed to find a bold thinker who would throw them all off at once. John Paul II urges us to do just that and begin anew in our philosophical quest for first things. In an official document of the Church, it would be not be fitting to name names, but rather to sketch trends and identify principles. But we may surmise that John Paul II has Descartes in sight from looking at names he does mention favorably. Jacques Maritain is held up as an exemplar of a thinker who well integrated faith and reason (§74). We know that Jacques Maritain sketched out his philosophical project of recovery of Aristotle and Aquinas in explicit contrast with Descartes and modern philosophy. This is evident from his great work *Degrees of Knowledge*, to his treatments of Descartes in *Three Reformers*, and *The Dream of Descartes*.[7]

In addition to thematic analysis and the indirect link through Jacques Maritain, we have direct indications of John Paul II's concern with the ghost of Descartes in his more informal work entitled *Crossing the Threshold of Hope*. We find a striking similarity in the use of the three themes of modernity in the sections entitled "If God exists, why is he hiding" and "What has become of the History of Salvation?"[8] John Paul II claims that the very demand for the total evidence of God stems from a way of philosophy "that is purely rationalistic, one that is characteristic of modern philosophy – the history of which begins with Descartes, who split thought from existence and identified existence with thought itself."[9] John Paul II detects an impatience with mystery. The term rationalism embraces the first two of the themes mentioned above: the turn to subjectivity and the reductive method. The turn to subjectivity evinces a rebellion against our creaturely status and an attempt to overcome the distance between God and man. Picking up on this theme a few pages later John Paul II claims that they very idea of salvation history is forgotten, obscured if you will, because of Descartes; while he does not claim that Descartes lacked faith or even sought to destroy it, at least we can say that Descartes created a "climate in which, in the modern era, such estrangement became possible."[10] What is this era, and what characterizes the climate hostile to faith? The new era is characterized by a "great anthropocentric shift" in which subjectivity and reduction prevail – the *cogito* as the motto of modern rationalism signifies the plan for subjectivity and separation – the Cartesian method.[11] John Paul II says that the trajectory of modern philosophy, Anglo and Continental – is but an expansion of the fundamental Cartesian position. John Paul II finds its root in the *cogito*: "by making subjective consciousness absolute, Descartes moves instead toward pure consciousness of the Absolute, which is pure thought." That is, compared to Thomas's philosophy of existence and God as *Ipsum esse subsistens,* Descartes unfolds "autonomous thought. Human thought must measure existence and banish mystery. Objectivity is lost in favor of human consciousness. Hence, John Paul II says Descartes put us "on the threshold of modern immanentism and subjectivism."[12] The transcendence of truth and of God are lost. As we have seen, these themes echo throughout *Fides et Ratio.* Now John Paul II does not name

Descartes and the theme of mastery, but it follows close behind his treatment of Descartes as "father of rationalism." That is, the rationalism of subjectivity and reduction, is the rationalism of mastery. Thus in the following section of *Crossing the Threshold*, "The Centrality of Salvation," John Paul II says that the Enlightenment mentality does not need God's love. No one needs his intervention, he says, in a world that is "self-sufficient, transparent to human knowledge, free of mystery thanks to scientific research, that is evermore an inexhaustible mine of raw materials for man – the demigod of modern technology."[13] It is clear that John Paul II's *Fides et Ratio* seeks to reopen the quarrel with modern rationalism, with the Enlightenment mentality, which has banned faith and which is rooted squarely in Descartes. It would be worthwhile therefore to make a brief survey of Descartes' own account of this new philosophy, which created the climate for loss of faith.

Revisiting the Quarrel of Ancients and Moderns: Descartes' Discourse on Method

Descartes' *Discourse* is one of the founding documents for modern philosophy. Descartes surveys his training in the ancients and self-consciously proclaims the need for a new method, indeed a new goal for philosophy and all learning. With good reason then does Albert Borgmann, *Crossing the Postmodern Divide*, name the *Discourse* as one of three key works, the others being Francis Bacon's *New Atlantis* and John Locke's *Second Treatise of Government.*[14] Bergmann rightly notes that any attempt to get through the "post" of postmodern must first understand what is distinctively modern.

Just the briefest review of Descartes' *Discourse on Method* will show us that the problematic of *Fides et Ratio* involves the way of philosophizing initiated by Descartes. The question of Descartes' deepest intention as an author, and the question of his relationship to the faith of the Catholic Church, is beyond the scope of this brief paper.[15] But we can show how Descartes did indeed create the intellectual climate for the eventual loss of faith.[16]

René Descartes outlined the philosophy which gave a charter to the growth of modern technological society in his *Discourse on Method*. Rejecting the ancient philosophy for its lack of effective control, Descartes says that he wishes to found a new practical philosophy; by "knowing the force and actions of the fire, water, air and stars, the heavens, and all other bodies that surround us, just as we understand the various skills of our craftsmen, we could make ourselves the masters and possessors of nature."[17] Surely John Paul II looks out at Europe and the West and sees that we are now approaching the fulfilled dream of Descartes' modern project. Descartes promised as the fruit of his new philosophy, "an infinity of devices that would enable us to enjoy without pain the fruits of the earth and all the goods one

finds in it, but also principally the maintenance of health."[18] John Paul II sees
rather a society "completely centered upon the cult of action and production
and caught up in the heady enthusiasm of consumerism and pleasure seeking."[19] Technology has fulfilled its dream, only to find a life now emptied of
higher purpose or deeper meaning. Faith suffers in such a climate "free of
mystery thanks to scientific research, that is evermore an inexhaustible mine
of raw materials for man – the demigod of modern technology."[20] The Pope
seems to indicate his awareness too of the source deeper than Descartes,
namely Machiavelli, who counseled the mastery of fortune and chance and
providence itself.

Furthermore, is faith also not cast into oblivion in light of the other great
criterion for the modern philosophy – mathematical certitude? In order to
reach this goal, Descartes recognized the need to reform the entirety of education and the social role of the intellectual in society such that expertise
would be more readily developed and experts be revered as great benefactors
who are free to pursue their study. He evaluated the curriculum of studies in
terms of certitude and utility: he sought "a clear and assured knowledge useful for life."[21] Poetry, theology, philosophy, ethics and a few other disciplines
were cast aside in light of these new criteria of certitude and utility. In fact,
the disciplines that would lay the basis for the experts, scientific studies,
would have to be built from the ground up. On the basis of mathematical science, Descartes proposed his famous new method for the conduct of inquiry.
It would begin with a universal doubt of anything not clear and distinct; again,
traditional opinion would be swept aside in all areas in order to make room
for the useful and certain knowledge of science. The certitude of science
would be assured by the use of simple nature and forms such as principles of
mechanics. In its streamlined form, the method for arriving at knowledge
would follow the analytical method, breaking apart a problem into its simplest
terms and then building up to greater level of complexity. Descartes' project
and method have been tremendously successful.

But its success is marred by an ambiguity about its goal or purpose. For
when Descartes turned to human production he praised projects that followed
a rational and effective plan, whatever their end. For he admits that in the
political order he must admire Sparta even if its ends or purposes were not
sound. At least they were organized effectively. The crack in the system
appears here. For the end is not subject to the same clarity as the method. The
end is left ambiguous since it is not within the competence of the new science
to determine it; as Richard Kennington puts it, "the utility goal can never be
brought within the charmed circle of certitude."[22] Descartes simply adopts the
lowest common denominator by appealing to that which is most universally
desired: health and life and convenience of living. To cite Kennington again,
"the benefits are as universally available to humanity as they are devoid of

exacting duties or self-sacrifice."[23] But this begs the question about the nature of the good life. The technical skills appear to be neutral to an end, but, in fact, they point to one end and encourage us to judge in terms of a utilitarian and hedonistic ethic.

The criterion for the new knowledge is certitude which entails a skepticism towards traditional modes of opinion and grants to the expert a special status. The method is not only inherently set against tradition and opinion, it requires a reductive approach to the material in the name of "objectivity." And it further requires specialization and a narrow or partial vision in the name of competence. Most of all, the Cartesian project is problematic because of the ambiguity about the end or purpose. On the one hand, the expert must appear neutral; for the question of end or purpose is beyond his competence. This is the contradiction at the heart of the project. Every technique is put to use for some end, but then end is not determined by a technique. The expert easily assumes an end for technique by appealing to what people want. Thus, on second look, the expert appears as a humanitarian who simply appeals to universal human desires and passions. The expert is therefore unproblematic. But when it is seen that the method requires a reductive approach and that it encourages the lowering of human goals, it becomes problematic in the extreme. The reductive approach to human affairs is potentially dehumanizing and degrading. It may well lead to the "abolition of man."[24] Man no longer dares to know the truth of being, says John Paul II. This ghost of Descartes needs to be exorcized by a return to and recovery of the pre-modern traditions of the ancient Greeks and medievals. A climate must be restored in which we dare to seek the truth of being. Thus we shall finish our presentation with a turn to the philosophy of Jacques Maritain. Maritain took upon himself the task of working through the modern philosophy and finding those places at which the perennial philosophy of Thomas Aquinas, and Aristotle, could assist us in restoring a sound philosophy of being.

Maritain on Descartes' Fides et ratio

Maritain provides a thorough and detailed critique of Descartes in *The Dream of Descartes*. It is beyond the scope of this brief paper to explore the long list of texts of Descartes in which Maritain finds the deep betrayal of Catholic intelligence made in the name of the modern project. Fortunately, there are variations of his critique to be found in his more popular work, *Three Reformers,* as well as in his *Saint Thomas Aquinas.*[25] Maritain's general accounts of the Cartesian origins of the crisis of modernity match the basic account of the crisis of our time provided by John Paul II in *Fides et Ratio.* That is, Maritain says that the Cartesian heritage has bequeathed to us a distorted philosophy because of (1) idealism, (2) rationalism, (3) dualism.[26]

These three problems bequeathed to us by Descartes correspond to the themes of *Fides et Ratio* identified above: subjectivism, methodological reduction, and mastery of nature. Idealism is the separation of thought from being, the very root of modernity identified by John Paul II in *Crossing the Threshold of Hope*. Indeed, Richard Kennington has argued that Descartes' *Meditations* is metaphysically neutral, that is, the precise nature of being human or the scope of nature and being themselves are secondary to the utility of our understanding of nature. Maritain pursues the problem in terms of the basic orientation of the mind to things. It is the angelic mode of knowing which can proceed as if independent from things, in a fully intuitive mode, with eventual power over natural forces. Although Maritain and John Paul II seem to think that the mind's orientation to being is the root issue for understanding the relationship of faith and reason – it is the second item, rationalism, which must be of more immediate concern. Maritain's account of this notion of rationalism is quite thorough and shows the reason why our intellectual climate is so hostile to faith. In his chapter entitled "The Revelation of Science," Maritain points out the reductive method of Descartes imposes mathematical intelligibility on all knowledge.[27] The pre-modern tradition recognized that human knowing is diverse and requires various methods or modalities. It would foolish to demand the same level of certitude in all matters (See Aristotle's *Ethics*, *Metaphysics*[28]). The mind has an expansive range of objects of thought, but not every object can be made to conform to the same method without suffering a distortion or obscuring of its true being. Thomas also discusses the divisions and methods of the sciences and he speaks rather of "modes" not methods of science, to indicate the need for the human mind to approach the levels of science in diverse, analogous ways.

The third consequence of Cartesian philosophy, dualism, stems from the split between consciousness and body. It allows the body to be exploited by technical means serving the enjoyment of a detached consciousness. John Paul II argues that dualism has obscured the importance of virtue as a habit of personal choice and self-mastery.[29] Maritain previously saw the impending nihilism. Man has been "split asunder" and "nothing in human life is any longer made to man's measure, to the rhythm of the human heart." Man is at the center of a world "inhuman in every respect."[30] Maritain and John Paul II both see the greatest sign of the time to be this fear of technology. It is the confusion brought about by the originating principle of modern philosophy in Machiavelli and Descartes – the mastery of fortune and nature. The first work of renewal requires a return to moral self-mastery as taught by the ancients and medieval. Perhaps C. S. Lewis was not far off when he said that we need is something like repentance if we are to find our way out of the modern crisis.[31] For grace (*fides*) not only presupposes and perfects nature (*ratio*); but grace also restores and heals nature. Reason will be restored by faith. Perhaps the deepest lesson we learn from John Paul II II, Maritain, and Lewis is that the nihilistic spirit of modernity, the ghost of Descartes, can only be cast out by prayer and fasting.

Notes

1. See Jacques Maritain, "Integral Humanism and the Crisis of Modern Times," *Scholasticism and Politics* (New York: Macmillan, 1940), pp. 11–32; idem, *Integral Humanism: Temporal and Spiritual Problems of New Christendom,* trans. Joseph W. Evans (Notre Dame, IN: University of Notre Dame Press, 1973); Leo Strauss, *Natural Right and History* (Chicago: University of Chicago Press, 1953); idem, *What is Political Philosophy?* (New York: The Free Press, 1959).

2. See Charles Taylor, *Sources of the Self: The Making of Modern Identity* (Cambridge: Harvard University Press, 1989).

3. G. M. Hopkins, "God's Grandeur," in *Gerard Manley Hopkins: A Selection of His Poems and Prose,* ed. W. H. Gardner (New York: Penguin, 1953), p. 27.

4. *Gaudium et spes,* §36.

5. *Redemptor Hominis,* §15.

6. "[P]ropter reperta scientifica et technica, homo veluti demiurgus assequi ex se solo possit sibique obtinere plenum suam in *fortunam dominatum*" *Fides et Ratio,* §91 (Emphases added).

7. Jacques Maritain, *Three Reformers* (New York: Apollo, 1970); idem, *The Dream of Descartes,* trans. Labelle L. Andison (London: Editions Poetry, 1946).

8. John Paul II, *Crossing the Threshold of Hope,* ed. Vittorio Messori (New York: Alfred A. Knopf, 1994), pp. 37–41, 50–53.

9. *Crossing the Threshold,* p. 38.

10. Ibid., p. 52.

11. Ibid., p. 51.

12. Ibid., p. 51; Cf. *Fides et Ratio,* §81.

13. *Crossing the Threshold,* p. 55.

14. Albert Borgmann, *Crossing the Postmodern Divide* (Chicago: University of Chicago, 1995), pp. 22–26.

15. I wish to thank Cyrille Michon for raising the issue of Descartes' knowledge and commitment to Catholic principles, as indicated in Descartes'

"Notes directed against a certain programme" (Cf. *Discourse on Method*, The Philosophical Works of Descartes, ed. and trans. E. S. Haldrane and G. R. T. Ross [Cambridge: University Press, 1972] vol. 1, pp. 438–39). In this text he provides a role for the faith to give a negative influence, that is, reason may used to disprove contradictions to itself. It may be close to but does not really reflect the Thomistic view. Cf. *Fides et Ratio*, §76.

16. I shall be drawing on many points which I learned from Richard Kennington, my professor at the Catholic University of America, from class and from his published articles: Richard Kennington, "René Descartes," in *History of Political Philosophy*, eds. Leo Strauss and Joseph Cropsey, 3rd ed. (Chicago: University of Chicago Press, 1987), pp. 421–39; Richard Kennington, "Descartes and the Mastery of Nature," in *Organism, Medicine, and Metaphysics*, ed. S. F. Spicker (Dordrecht, Holland: D. Reidel, 1978), pp. 201–23. I take responsibility for this interpretation as applied to John Paul II and the problem of Catholic philosophy in the contemporary context. Some material is drawn from my articles "The Moral Status Of The Expert In Contemporary Society," *The World and I* 4:8 (August 1989), pp. 560–85; and idem, "Why Locke Rejected an Ethics of Virtue and Turned to an Ethic of Utility," *American Catholic Philosophical Quarterly* 64 (1990), pp. 267–76.

17. Descartes, *Discourse on Method*, The Philosophical Works of Descartes, ed. and trans. E. S. Haldrane and G. R. T. Ross (Cambridge: University Press, 1972), vol. 1, p. 119 (§6).

18. Descartes, *Discourse on Method* VI, p. 83.

19. John Paul II, *Reconciliation and Penance*, §18.

20. John Paul II, *Crossing the Threshold*, p. 55.

21. Descartes, *Discourse on Method*, p. 83.

22. Kennington, "René Descartes," p. 212.

23. Ibid., p. 221.

24. Cf. C. S. Lewis, *The Abolition of Man* (New York: Macmillan, 1947), pp. 80–91; Michael D. Aeschliman, *The Restitution of Man: C. S. Lewis and the Case Against Scientism* (Grand Rapids: Eerdmans, 1983); Peter Kreeft, *C. S. Lewis for the Third Millenium* (San Francisco: Ignatius Press, 1994).

26. Maritain, *Dream of Descartes*; idem, *Three Reformers*; idem, *Saint Thomas Aquinas*, trans. J. F. Scanlan (New York: Sheed & Ward, 1931); idem, *Peasant of the Garonne*, trans. M. Cuddihy and E. Hughes (New York: Holt, 1968); see also work by Peter Redpath, *Cartesian Nightmare: An Introduction to Transcendental Sophistry* (Amsterdam and Atlanta: Rodolpi, 1997).

27. This is from his most thorough critique in *Dream of Descartes*, pp.

130–50. In *Saint Thomas Aquinas* (pp. 58-59), Maritain works the trilogy of Agnosticism ("by cultivating a more or less refined doubt which is an outrage both to the perception of the senses and the principles of reason, that is to say the very things on which all our knowledge depends"), naturalism ("The mind at the same time refuses to recognize the rights of primary Truth and repudiates the supernatural order, considering it impossible – and such a denial is a blow at all the interior life of grace"), and individualism/angelism ("the mind allows itself to be deceived by the mirage of a mythical conception of human nature, which attributes to that nature conditions peculiar to pure spirit, assumes that nature to be in each of us as perfect and complete as the angelic nature in the angel and therefore claims for us, as being in justice our due, along with complete domination over nature, the superior autonomy, the full self sufficiency, the *αvτάoxελα* appropriate to pure forms"). In *Three Reformers* (pp. 55ff) he emphasizes that the root of "angelism" is something that embraces all three in many respects.

27. Maritain, *The Dream of Descartes,* pp. 37–42.

28. Aristotle, *Ethics* I. 3 1094b20–27; idem, *Metaphysics* II. 3 995a5–20.

29. John Paul II, *Reflections on Humanae Vitae* (Boston: Daughters of St. Paul, 1984), pp. 36–38.

30. Maritain, *Dream of Descartes*, p. 146.

31. C. S. Lewis, *Abolition of Man* (New York: Macmillan, 1947), p. 89.

Conceptions of Reason
Christopher Martin

Wittgenstein once suggested that one could write a book of philosophy consisting solely of jokes. I bring this in, not merely so that at least one paper at the Thomistic Institute might begin with the name "Wittgenstein," but to marvel at his perspicacity, since he was perhaps the least likely of his generation to produce such a book. Though perhaps Ayer was just as unlikely to produce a good book of philosophy consisting solely of jokes, for different reasons: Wittgenstein because he knew little about jokes, Ayer because he knew little about philosophy.

I mention this because I think this may come near to being a philosophical paper consisting mainly of digressions – if it can be done for a novel, as it was in the case of *Tristram Shandy*, why not for a philosophical paper? To tell the truth my main themes have already been covered by other papers. Like Prof. McInerny, I want to look at first principles, implicit philosophy; like Prof. Dougherty, I want to investigate the ambiguities involved in notions such as "faith" and "reason," rather than try to deal with the relations between these notions, as if they were wholly fixed and univocal, and all that needed dealing with were their mutual dealings.

I want to start in a rather provincial way, with some quotations from the great ghost that stalks through English-speaking philosophy, that of David Hume. (One advantage of Scottish parochialism in this context is that it enables one to say that Hume is not, as so many seem to think, the world's greatest philosopher, not even perhaps Scotland's greatest philosopher: if we can accept the plausible hypothesis that Duns Scotus was indeed born in Duns, we can argue that Hume is probably no more than Berwickshire's second greatest philosopher. The jibe has added point when one remembers that Berwickshire, on the English borders of Scotland, is such a wretched little county that it has lacked its capital, or county town, the City of Berwick, since the English captured it in the fourteenth century and with typical bad faith failed to restore it in the peace treaty.) Speaking of reason, Hume has some interesting things to say (I quote more or less from memory): "reason is and should be the slave of the passions;" that "the ordinary way of reasoning" is quite separate from what we affirm in moral judgments; and that it is "not contrary to reason" to prefer the destruction of the whole world to the scratching of one's little finger. This last remark would perhaps inspire any normal person to say; well, if your conception of reason entails that conclusion, you'd better get a different conception of reason. Would the encyclical, would St. Thomas, endorse this naive reaction?

Naturally one feels that both ought to, but the position is more complex than that. In the first place, the phrases quoted from Hume relate more to practical reason than to speculative reason – though we could have a nice little argument about *scientia speculativa de practicis*, if we wanted – while the encyclical seems to relate more obviously to speculative reason. This perhaps doesn't matter. I could easily have quoted a number of Humean principles about speculative reason, such as his genealogical validation of ideas, or such as his distinction between "matters of fact" and "relations of ideas," which he intends should rule out the whole of scholastic theology and metaphysics, as fit only to be consigned to the flames. Or I could say that the reason why this encyclical does not deal with practical reason is that this task was performed already by *Veritatis Splendor*. I hope everyone agrees that to a philosopher of average talents and tidy mind it is a cause for annoyance that *Veritatis Splendor* should have come out before *Fides et Ratio*, when it is so clear that *Veritatis Splendor* is no more than an application (admittedly in a very important field) of the principles laid down in *Fides et Ratio*. It is amusing how much the enemies of the Church and of God's law were upset by *Veritatis splendor* and how little they cared about *Fides et Ratio*, when clearly the later encyclical provides the justification for everything that was attacked in the earlier.

A more serious reaction, perhaps, would be to notice that the doing of philosophy is itself a practice, and must therefore be governed by the principles of good practice which are enshrined in the Ten Commandments and elsewhere in Revelation, which are taught by the Church, and which the greatest of pagan philosophers struggled to articulate (and in so many cases succeeded). A person who tries to live by these moral norms would not have agreed with Hume that it is not contrary to reason to prefer the destruction of the whole world to the scratching of one's little finger. I am strengthened in holding this claim by the fact that *Fides et Ratio* speaks explicitly of the ethics of intellectual pursuits when it rejects, for example, "false modesty" among philosophers. (Though, in my first serious digression, I would like to suggest that the relation between the highest human practical wisdom and divine or supernatural practical wisdom may not be as close as we tend sometimes to think. This suggestion is strengthened by the consideration that it is a principle of human practical wisdom that I am not going to live forever. Or, if we decide to deny it the title of "first principle," we can surely say that it is a major step forward in young people's lives when they realize that this is true. However, it also seems that one of the most basic principles for Christians to grasp, the basis of all Christian practical wisdom, that I am going to live for ever. Where does that leave us in reconciling faith and reason at a practical level?)

Or perhaps the answer to the problem about the relations of *Veritatis Splendor* to *Fides et Ratio* should be: *Veritatis Splendor* deals with errors in practical reasoning, but does not deal with practical reasoning as such. But there is an obvious reply to this, which I think is at first sight correct: that *Fides et Ratio* deals with aberrations in speculative reason, but does not deal with the nature and perfection of speculative reason as such. I am bolstered in this reaction by the fact that Prof. McInerny has found it necessary to work carefully through the text, attempting to derive from it some features of the perfection of speculative reasoning as such. If the encyclical bore an account of the perfection of reason on its face, such an investigation would not be necessary.

This leads me to my main point. "Faith and reason," we say; but, to plagiarize a more famous pair of questions, "Whose faith? Which reason?" I will leave faith on one side and speak of reason. "Whose reason?" we ask, and the only answer I can definitely give at this stage is: not Hume's. I brought in Hume not merely because he enables me to make a couple of jokes about Berwickshire, but because there is little doubt that a very large number of Hume's basic principles of "reason," whether of practical or of speculative reason, are shared by our contemporaries in English-speaking universities (and some others) throughout the world: our contemporaries, our fellow-philosophers, in some sense, our colleagues. And some of us have been so affected by our company that we begin to feel that at least some of their methods and perhaps some of their attitudes can or should be taken on board by us.

So this is going to turn into another piece on the question "Is analytical Thomism possible, or even recommendable?" Perhaps I am the only person present who felt any kind of annoyance or irritation at the (slightly late) arrival of Prof. Haldane, since I had hoped that in his absence that I might be able to get away with making some rather naive comments without magisterial correction.

First, I want to say that some of the methods and attitudes of analytical philosophy are to me entirely admirable. A preference for writing clearly and simply, limiting oneself, as I once recommended to a Spanish colleague, to one abstract noun *per* sentence, is one which I share and would recommend to any young person starting philosophy. And I must say that when I try to read contemporary French or German philosophy, I am reinforced in my view, and come to believe that obscurity is often adopted as a mere simulacrum for profundity. St. Thomas is clear as well as deep. Depth is something we cannot all achieve, but clarity is, and it strikes me that it is something of a moral duty to strive for it.

This example, many will remark, is trivial. I am not so sure, but we can let it pass. What is wrong with analytical philosophy is that some people regard it as in some ways the antithesis of Thomism? I am going to assert, without any argument, that what is principally wrong with analytical philosophy is its historical origin in a highly Humeanised milieu – that, in fact, what is wrong with analytical philosophy is its first principles of reason, shared with Berwickshire's second greatest philosopher, indeed inherited from him. Accept that as a hypothesis, which at least brings the debate on analytical philosophy within the scope of the discussion of the first principles of reason as mentioned in *Fides et Ratio*.

My point here would be that analytical philosophy possesses resources within itself to overthrow its false first principles. Quine's brilliant overthrow of the Humean distinction between analytic and empirical truths in *Two dogmas of Empiricism* would be a case in point. So would the demonstration by Kripke that the metaphysics presupposed by our ordinary language – and Kripke, at least, knows enough to know that "our ordinary language" does not mean "English" – is a metaphysics of substance, i.e., substances which have essences. The whole basis of empiricism is overthrown by the reflections of analytical philosophers using techniques that first arose in a thoroughly empiricist milieu. That no one seems to have bothered to take on board the implications of the work of Quine and Kripke on these questions is regrettable but has more to do with the ethics of the practice of doing philosophy, of which we spoke earlier. If analytical philosophy has the resources to overturn the false first principles of reason with which it is born, that is all we can demand, surely. We cannot also demand that it should turn its practitioners into philosophical saints capable of welcoming this overthrow and seeking to work further on a new basis. After all, it is Christ who saves us from sin, not Aristotle (let alone Quine). Aristotle, or even Quine to some extent, may be able to save us from confusion and obscurity, but we could very well be damned no matter how clearly we think.

A similar point can be made about the Humean principles of practical reason with which I started. It is not necessary to have much, or indeed any cargo of Thomistic knowledge on board to overturn the fact-value distinction: the resources of analytical philosophy are quite sufficient, as the work of Prior, Foot and Hursthouse have shown. (Though, indeed, the former pair do know something about Thomas, and the last knows a lot about Aristotle: but no one would call them Thomists or Aristotelians.)

If the false first principles of Americo-British analytical philosophy can be overthrown adequately by the use of the methods of the same philosophy, we can clearly make a distinction between the methods and the false first principles. At first sight, then, it should be absolutely harmless for a Thomist to adopt at least some of the methods and attitudes of analytical philosophy: she or he will not thereby be committed to the false principles with which analytical philosophy began, and indeed may be more successful in arguing against them. The techniques and resources of analytical philosophy, then, can be quite easily detached from the principles of false reason with which they are associated, and put at the disposal of true reason.

But is this enough? Given that analytical methods may be innocuous, and may even be of value in overthrowing falsehood, is this enough to show that a true analytical Thomism is possible or even valuable? About this positive point I have less to say, but let us take a case related to what we have already said. Once the false principles of reason are undermined, are the resources of analytical philosophy sufficient to arrive at true principles? Perhaps the example of Kripke, already cited, can be used again – on either side. There is no doubt in my mind that the work of the middle Kripke can be a starting place for the establishment of true first principles of reason. There is equally no doubt that no one has ever tried to do it. My question is, if Thomists do not try to do it, who will? It seems pretty obvious that the work done in *Naming and Necessity and Identity and Necessity* was so alien to the false principles of reason on which most of Americo-British philosophy is based, that no one wanted to follow it up, not even Kripke. Well, if not Thomists, who? And if this task is not carried out by Thomists, what right have Thomists to claim that they have at least attempted to dialogue with their misguided peers in a way which those colleagues will appreciate and understand? And if Kripke's work needs or deserves continuing, how should it be continued if not, to some extent, by his methods? And if Thomists are not willing to do this, should we not read *Fides et ratio* a little more carefully?

The theoretical structure of Thomist thought – as opposed to what St. Thomas actually does, or what his followers actually do, which is often different, as it should be – that structure seems to have no resources for establishing first principles. We heard why the other day: it is obvious that no one can argue deductively to first principles. Aristotle and St. Thomas appear to offer little explicit guidance here. How does one argue to first principles? Dialectically, inductively, even rhetorically, or *ad hominem*; by *reductio ad absurdum*. Now, what criticisms are most often made by old-fashioned Thomists against analytical philosophy? Perhaps that they ignore the power of inductive argument, but instead argue dialectically, inductively, even rhetorically, or *ad hominem*; by *reductio ad absurdum*.

I think with that I rest my case, such as it is.

The Angst of Reason
Rémi Brague

The main move in the encyclical, *Fides et Ratio*, is a powerful turning of the tables. The "*et*" in the title is in fact a hinge. Apologetics traditionally conceived of its role as being a defense of faith against an overly obtrusive reason. Such a task had to be done. It was accomplished by the first Vatican Council, more than a century ago. The Pope reminds us of this achievement (§52–53). But what is at stake at present is no longer staving off reason by showing that it has not a clear consciousness of its own limits. On the contrary, reason itself must be defended against its own devils. Faith becomes the advocate of reason (§56).

The all-pervading tone is uneasiness. At first sight, this somehow contrasts with the famous first words of the newly elected Pope: "be not afraid." However, the ultimate aim is the same: courage asserts itself in the teeth of what is fearful. In order to be courageous, and not simply foolhardy, you have to feel how scared you could be. By this token, there is no contrast. On the contrary, the encyclical applies the same battle cry to the realm of intellectual pursuits.

In what follows, I will first summarize the diagnosis, and complement it by delineating the types of dangers that await reason. I will remind us of the rationalistic nature of Christianity and the Christian nature of rationality. Then, I will elaborate a plea for the metaphysical dimension of reason. Finally, I will say some words on the implicit concept of Truth that underlies our enterprise.

The Diagnosis

The Pope ventures a diagnosis on the present disease of reason. He does that from several outlooks. Some are traditional, some more original. Among the former, for example, he mentions reason that does not look upwards anymore and rejects any transcendence. He calls this by the name of "bent reason" (*ratio incurvata*), a variation on Bernard of Clairvaux's *anima incurvata*[1] (§5). Behind this lurks the attempt at a self-sufficiency of man, the alleged "humanism."

Furthermore, the vice of philosophical pride is mentioned twice. Curiously, the phrase is to be read in Voltaire: "l'orgueil philosophique / Aigrit de nos beaux jours la douceur pacifique."[2] Reason should not be overbearing (§4, §76). A whole school of apologetics took this as its point of departure: humiliating reason by the tools of skepticism in order to make place for faith. Montaigne's endeavor is to be replaced on the backdrop of a whole tradition of Christian skepticism, and Pascal somehow flirts with it: "humiliez-vous, raison impuissante."[3] Even Kant alluded to this procedure in the famous formula in the second preface to his first Critique: "*das Wissen aufheben, um zum Glauben Platz zu bekommen.*"[4] It is important to note that, with the encyclical, the bells are tolling for this style of apologetics.

For the Pope stresses heavily the opposite vice of pusillanimity. On the one hand, the critique of pusillanimity is hoary. This is the ancient, Aristotelian vice of mikroyucia.[5] Descartes called this: lowliness or vicious humility.[6] What is new is its application to intellectual pursuits, which is only adumbrated in Socrates' dismissal of the temptation of misologia in Plato's *Phaedo.*[7] It is all the more so in a Christian context: *sapere aude* was rather the catchword of Enlightenment.[8]

Be that as it may, the Pope harps upon the idea of an overly modesty of reason. The theme crops up no less than four times: we should not content ourselves with partial and provisional truths and give up the hope of reaching ultimate meaning (§5); we should not yield to the diffidence against reason that arose at the end of the Middle Ages (§45); we should not set our sights too low in philosophical reflection (§56); we should overcome our crisis of confidence towards reason's capabilities (§84).

There is no contradiction between the critique of pride and the critique of false humility, for claiming to be able to set one's limits is the peak of pride. Little wonder that, on the contrary, the Pope should see in authentic humility the source of courage (§76).

Historical Pathology of Reason

Let me now replace this on a broader setting. In order to do that, I will have to sketch a typology of the various dangers that lie in ambush around reason. I will do that on the basis of the history of ideas. This approach receives some legitimacy from the fact that the Pope himself makes use of a historical frame, very broad in nature, that takes its bearings from the commonly accepted distinction between ancient, medieval and modern times, nay even condones the characterization of our present time as postmodern. He suggests, for instance, that modern reason sinned more seriously than its antique or medieval versions (§49) – a statement towards which I have some reservations. Nevertheless, the diagnosis itself has a modern ring as when the concept of nihilism is brought to bear three times (§46; §81; §90); an idea that was brought to the fore by Nietzsche.

The crisis of the Ancient World may have been a crisis of reason, too.[9] Classical reason was supposed to spread light and to be itself a light that cannot fade. Its devils were outer fiends. They were, for instance, other powers of the soul: the senses, as in Plato's *Phaedo*, passions or imagination as in the Stoa or Spinoza. Those enemies could be placed in an evolutionary scheme. What was to be blamed were the prejudices either of individual childhood, as in Descartes, or of the early ages of the whole of mankind, what the rhetoric of the Enlightenment called "the powers of darkness and prejudice."

More recent reason has inner fiends, too. The idea has several aspects. The first one, more moderate, is static. Reason is supposed not so much to yield to its enemies but to somehow switch itself off. This can be expressed through the images of drowsiness. As a trained philosopher Pope John Paul II belongs to the phenomenological school. Now, the founder of this school, Husserl, explained in a famous lecture given in Vienna in 1935 that the most serious danger for "Europe" – Husserl means thereby an inner teleology of reason – is tiredness (*Müdigkeit*).[10] There is a somewhat more refined version of the idea in the encyclical. According to the Pope, the present-day disease of reason is despair – the "temptation to despair" (§91), a phrase coined by the French novelist Georges Bernanos.[11] Despair is more than simple tiredness. It has a temporal dimension. Postmodern man despairs because he has given up the idea of progress. But this idea originated in Enlightenment reason.

This leads us to a deeper, more radical assessment of the problem. Reason does not only fade, it puts itself out. Let us look at a famous etching by a man of the Enlightenment, the spanish painter Goya (1746-1828) – drawn, by the way, exactly two centuries ago. A man is sitting at a table, asleep and reclining on his elbow. From the background strange animals emerge. A feline creature is sitting behind his chair, another one right behind his back. Flying creatures that can be bats or birds overshadow him. The birds evoke birds of prey. One is about to land on the sleeper's shoulder. The legend is: "the sleep of reason produces monsters (*el sueño de la razón produce monstruos*)."[12] We are not given any answer to the question as to how it is that reason can fall asleep and have nightmares. Now, the picture is more complex than it looks like at first blush. On the one hand, the sleeping man might be the painter himself. On the table lie sheets of paper and what looks to be a painter's brush. The sleeper is not a brute, but a civilized white male, clad in correct garments. On the other hand, the nightmarish birds that assault him resemble very much owls, the very bird that functions as a symbol of Athena, the goddess of reason. The title itself is ambiguous, for the spanish *sueño* may mean "sleep" and "dream" as well. We do not know whether the danger is to be looked for in reason's dozing off or in its very inability really to lose consciousness.

The idea that reason can be endangered by itself receives a powerful treatment in Kant's transcendental dialectics in the first Critique. Reason can get caught in its own snares, be "hoist by its own petard." Kant's revolution somehow brushes the classical ranking of psychological faculties against the grain. He rehabilitates the lower faculties of the soul, such as perceptual knowledge or imagination. He even very forcefully pleads for the senses.[13] The lower faculties are no longer fetters or traps. On the contrary, they are helpful banisters that prevent it from falling prey to itself. Nietzsche's idea of a "faithfulness towards the Earth" is – strange bedfellows – a remote consequence of Kant's discovery.

The idea of a dialectic of the Enlightenment was first expressed by Adorno and Horkheimer in their famous book.[14] It can be understood as the historicized version of Kant's transcendental dialectics. If reason undermines itself, the historical project of a full rationalization of life is doomed to failure. Modernity that set out to fulfill this project and that always conceived of itself as an experiment does not meet its own claims. It parasitically feeds on what it cannot reproduce – an idea that is to be read in Péguy.[15]

Christian Rationalism

The Pope pleads for what he calls an alliance between "parrhesia of faith and audacity of reason" (§48). I will begin with the second point, reason. I do that not for the sake of rhetoric only, but because I feel impelled by the thing itself, for, according to the Pope, it seems that despair in reason is more serious than giving up Christian faith. He mentions: "a positivistic mentality . . . which *not only* abandoned the Christian vision of the world, but *more especially* rejected every appeal to a metaphysical and moral vision" (§46). We witness the same stance some pages further in a different context: "quite apart from the fact that it conflicts with the demands and the content of the word of God, nihilism is a denial of the humanity and of the very identity of the human being" (§90). There are obviously two layers: first comes metaphysics, morals, or man, second faith. The danger is not only atheism, but man's destruction. To quote a phrase made famous by Foucault but that originally stems from André Malraux, God's death must be followed by Man's death.[16] As a matter of course, the claim is that lack of faith endangers man's humanity. But the logical move must be noted. It shows that Christianity does not preach for itself, which it would unmistakably do if it were an ideology. It defends man. Its task is that of a servant; it is the deacon of Truth (§2).

Now, defending reason is not a strategic ploy, but belongs to the very essence of Christianity. Chesterton's Father Brown, when he is asked how he succeeded in unmasking a fake priest, answers: "you attacked reason, it's bad theology."[17] Jews and Christians are rationalists. At the Beginning, at the

Principle of everything, there was and is the Logos. The first words of the Fourth Gospel echo the first words of Genesis. God is a rationalist, too. This pervades the whole Bible, but there is a passage in which this becomes explicit. Isaiah has God say:

> For this is the word of the Lord, who created the heavens – he is God!
> – who formed the earth and made it; he established it firmly; he did
> not create it a chaos [*tohu*], he formed it to be inhabited: I am the
> Lord, and there is no other. I have never spoken in secrecy, in some
> place in the land of darkness; I have never said to the children of
> Jacob, 'Seek me in the void' [*tohu*]. I, the Lord, speak the truth,
> declare what is right (Isaiah 45. 19-20).

We witness here what we could call the triangle of rationalities. Reason manifests itself under three guises: as the order and meaningfulness of the created world over against the primeval chaos, as clarity of verbal expression against a trouble thirst for esoteric experience, and as righteousness of behavior against crooked ways.[18]

Little wonder that the human response to such a God should be a "sacrifice of the intellect," which does not mean that we should jettison reason but, on the contrary, that reason is worthy to be the subject of the supreme worship. This sacrifice is brought by the intellect, it is a "rational worship" (Romans 12. 1).

We are not only rationalists, we may be the only ones who are. We may be the last consequent rationalists left. Once again I will quote Chesterton's Father Brown: "I know that people charge the Church with lowering reason, but it is just the other way. Alone on earth, the Church makes reason really supreme. Alone on earth, the Church affirms that God Himself is bound by reason."[19] Alleged "rationalists" are not. According to them, reason comes from the Irrational. Reason is, for instance, explained away as a behavior determined by natural selection of the fittest: a being endowed with reason has more trumps in such a struggle. For us, all those phenomena, or, to be precise, all those hypotheses, come after *Logos*. *Logos* alone is at the beginning, is the principle. The ultimate principle is not a *big bang* that is, as the very name has it, a meaningless noise.

The intelligibility of Being is commonly taken for granted and left unexplained. It should become again the center of philosophical reflection. We need an up-to-date version of German idealistic and/or romantic *Naturphilosophie* that could at least give an account of the very rationality of nature, a *logos* of the *logos*, so to speak. To be sure, Christian faith does not claim to refute the scientific hypotheses that have just been mentioned and displace them with better ones. Neither does it expect to provide this philosophy of nature. The affirmation of an ultimate rationality of Being does not furnish science with any answer. But it gives it the very ground that it treads. Nietzsche saw this with a perfect lucidity: even if we are the staunchest supporters of the Enlightenment, we are still too pious; our belief in reason is still the aftermath of a Faith kindled by Plato.[20] As for Nietzsche, he wanted us to cast off the last moorings that link us up to this faith. But can we?

Do We Need Truth?

We must now face a radical objection. Could we do without reason, and without truth? Why should we not imagine a "happy (*gaio*) nihilism," to borrow the felicitous phrase probably coined by the Italian philosopher Augusto Del Noce? In the last resort, there isn't anything, but this does not matter. This is an Epicurean stance, properly speaking. This may hold water as long as we stick to the present time: since we exist anyway, since we already belong to the whole show, why shouldn't we make ourselves comfortable? In order to do that, you need some practical savvy, but no metaphysics. On the contrary, we should listen to Nietzsche's contention: the very fact that we say that life has a meaning – the core affirmation of any metaphysics – presupposes that life needs something different from, and superior to, itself. Hence, it debases and condemns life while wanting to salvage it.

Let me first answer with a pun that can be done in French only. In my mother tongue, the word for "meaning," *sens*, has several senses. One is "meaning," but other ones are "perception" and "direction." Now, life is not only being alive ζωή, but having a life story, a βιος – the subject matter of what we accordingly call a biography. Life is a motion of sorts, too. It spreads from one individual of a species to its offspring. It evolves from one simpler level of organization to another more complex one. In human beings it accumulates its own experience through psychological and social memory (language and writing, etc.) and grows like a snowball. Now, even if we granted, for the sake of argument, that life has no *sens* as "meaning," the question would remain as to whether we can do without a *sens* as 'direction." We do not understand such a *sens* by soaring above concrete realities, but on the contrary by a sort of inserting ourselves into their stream, or, to use an image by Plotinus, by dancing to their rhythm.

We are supposed to accept life as such, without asking whether it measures up to some external standard. But the question must arise: do we really love life? I will bring to bear on the question a distinction that Augustine makes in a passage from the *Confessions* that the Pope quotes in another context (§25). The passage I would like to use comes right afterwards.[21] It was commented upon by Heidegger, in a lecture course that was published some years ago.[22] The question is exegetical in nature: how is it that the Scripture, more precisely John, can say that some people hate Truth? Augustine distinguishes two aspects of Truth. Truth can be *lucens* and it can be *redarguens*. We love *lucens* truth, whereas we hate *redarguens* truth. *Lucens* does not mean only shining, but light shedding. Truth does not only shine in itself, thereby manifesting itself. It casts its glow on other things and enables us to become cognizant of them. *Redarguens* means what "argues' against us, but at the same time, as the very root *arg* suggests, it is some sort of light. I suggest it could be rendered as "lucidity." Now, lucidity is not very pleasant, because it reveals many shades, not to say dust and cobwebs, in the nooks and corners of our soul.

Now, if we really loved Truth, we would wish other people, nay everybody, to be able to pry into our soul and expose its content. The first love of Truth is thirst for knowledge. The second one is honesty towards oneself. The Pope alludes to this function when he mentions that, among the reasons that thwart our access to Truth, there is the fact that we fear its demands (§28). The first love for truth, for truth *lucens*, unmasks itself as love for the knowledge that we can have. Hence, it is in the last resort *self*-love. We do not like Truth, we like what truth enables us to know. To apply a classical Augustinian distinction, we use (*uti*) Truth, whereas we should enjoy (*frui*) it.

In the same way, love for life may mean two very different things. There is the *lucens* love for life, such as it is expressed by the set phrase in Homeric Greek: "to live and see the sunlight" (ζωειν και φαπς ηλιοιο).[23] Life is bathing and basking in the light of presence. We naively love our life, such as we can experience it. We like to be alive because this enables us to do and enjoy many pleasant things, from the basest to the highest and most dignified. But to what extent do we love life as such? There must be an equivalent of the *redarguens* kind of life. We love our own life, i.e., we love ourselves. We can be sure that we love life as such in so far as we foster life outside of ourselves.

The trouble comes to a head when what is at stake is not merely living on, but transmitting life, i.e., "creating" a life that is not there, making the present encroach upon the future. This question is not academic; it lies at the bottom of several crucial problems that all have to do with the long run: demography, ecology, education. Everybody knows Keynes' quip: "in the long run, we are all dead."[24] But this cop-out is the word of a homosexual who *per definitionem* is childless. As a matter of course, you can live without truth. To be precise you can survive without it. Without Truth, however, you cannot love life, i.e. foster life. Playing one's part on the scene properly can be done – since it must be done, anyway. The trouble begins when the question is whether one has a right to bring other players onto the scene. Are we allowed to foist life off on other people, whom we cannot ask about their wishes?

We cannot do that unless we are sure that life is a gift, that life is good in itself. If we are not, taking Schopenhauer or Buddha seriously becomes not only a possibility but a sacred duty. If we are, the question is whether we can do that without something like implicit or explicit faith. This has direct consequences on the idea of truth. For some people, the Pope reminds us, Truth is nothing more than the result of consensus (§56). Now, obviously, such a consensus must obtain among people who are alive at the same time. Thus, the truth that they decide will have to be imposed upon future generations. Clearly, those generations will be able to change by building a new consensus that will make new decisions. But they will have to do that on the basis of the "truth" of the former generation. Democracy will boil down to absolute lack of democracy. There must be something like an objective truth to be handled down to generations still to arise, if they are not to be left prey to the whims of their forebears.[25]

Conclusion: Truth as Ocean

Modern consciousness has misgivings with that kind of Truth, because it mistakenly conceives it as a set of ready-made objects. It therefore values research higher than possession of truth. We remember Lessing's well-known parable: if God were to present us with Truth in one hand and unceasing striving for Truth in the other one, we should have to choose the latter.[26] But Christian tradition possesses an idea that is worth retrieving, for it could prove more palatable for modern mentality. Truth is something *in* which we are, a space more than a thing.

This is the implicit concept of truth conveyed through the splendid image that closes ch. 2: launching oneself onto the infinite ocean of truth (§23). This is an implicit quotation of the Greek Church Fathers, who spoke of the infinite ocean (απειρον πελαγὸς) of the Godhead,[27] a phrase that entered the Latin West through commentaries written on Ps.Dionysius by people like Eriugena or Hugo of Saint-Victor.[28] Surprisingly, the phrase is diametrically opposed to John Locke's appeal to modesty in metaphysics: we should not "let loose our thoughts into the vast Ocean of Being."[29] God is thereby conceived of as a field, not as an object. God cannot be reached, but – *sit venia verbo* – sailed or surfed upon. The Good Friday liturgical sequence that the Pope quotes, takes up the Augustinian theme of the *cor inquietum* (§24). But the same Augustine strikes another chord elsewhere that must complement the first one: "He is hidden, so that we might look for Him in order to find Him; but He is boundless, so that we might look for Him even when we have found Him" (*Ut inveniendus quaeratur, occultus est; ut inventus quaeratur immensus est*).[30]

Notes

1. First in Persius, *Saturae* II. 61; see Bernard of Clairvaux, *In Cantica Canticorum* XXIV. II. 6–7 (PL 183. 897ad).

2. Voltaire, *À Horace* (1772).

3. Pascal, *Pensées*, Br. 434, t. 2, p. 347 and see Br. 282, p. 205.

4. Kant, *Kritik der reinen Vernunft* (Leipzig: F. Meiner, 1919), p. xxx.

5. Aristotle, *Nicomachean Ethics* IV. 3. 1129b9–11; 1125a19–27.

6. Descartes, *Traité des Passions* III. 159; *AT* XI, p. 450.

7. Plato, *Phaedo* 89cd.

8. Kant, *Was ist Aufklärung?* (Gottinger: Vandenhoeck Ruprecht, 1967), first paragraph.

9. M. Zambrano, *La agonía de Europa* (Buenos Aires: Sudamericana, 1945), pp. 105–6 [non vidi].

10. Husserl, "Die Krisis des europäischen Menschentums und die Philosophie" (Vienna Lecture 1935), Husserliana, 26 vols. (Haag: M. Nijhoff, 1950-), vol. 4, p. 348.

11. Bernanos, *Sous le soleil de Satan* (1926), Title of the 1st part.

12. Goya, *Los caprichos*, n. 43 (around 1799).

13. Kant, *Anthropologie in Pragmatischer Hinsicht*, Werke, ed. W. Weischedel (Darmstadt: Wissenschaftliche Buchgesellschaft, 1983 [1964]), VI, §8–10, pp. 432–36.

14. T.W. Adorno and M. Horkheimer, *Dialektik der Aufklärung. Philosophische Fragmente* (Amsterdam: Querido, 1947).

15. See Péguy, *De la situation faite au parti intellectuel dans le monde moderne devant les accidents de la gloire temporelle,* Oeuvres, 3 vols. (Paris: Gallimard and Pléiade, 1907), vol. 2, p. 725.

16. A. Malraux, *La tentation de l'Occident* (Paris: Livre de poche, 1926), p. 128.

17. G. K. Chesterton, "The Blue Cross," in *The Amazing Adventures of Father Brown* (New York: Dell, 1958).

18. See my *La Sagesse du Monde. Histoire de l'expérience humaine de l'univers* (Paris, Fayard, 1999), p. 59f.

19. Chesterton, "The Blue Cross."

20. Nietzsche, *Die fröhliche Wissenschaft*, Werke, 24 vols., eds. Giorgio Colli und Mazzino Montinari (Berlin: de Gruyter, 1967-), Abt. 5, Bd. 2, §344; *KSA* V, pp. 574–77.

21. Augustine, *Confessiones* X. XXIII. 34.

22. Heidegger, *Phänomenologie des religiösen Lebens*, Gesamtausgabe, eds. M. Jung, T. Regehky, C. Strube, 68 vols. (Frankfurt am Main: Klostermann, 1995), vol. 60, pp. 199–201.

23. Homer, *Ilias* 24. 558; *Odyssey* 4. 540 *et al.*

24. J. M. Keynes, *A Tract on Monetary Reform* (London: Macmillan, 1923), ch. 3.

25. For a forceful illustration of this point, see C. S. Lewis, *The Abolition of Man* (London: Oxford University Press, 1944), ch. 3.

26. Lessing, *Eine Duplik* 1 (end), Werke, ed. H.G. Göpfert (Darmstadt: Wissenschaftliche Buchgesellschaft, 1911), vol. 8, p. 33.

27. St. Basil, *Contra Eunomium* I. 16 (*PG* 29. 468); St. Gregory Nazianzen, *Oratio* 38; (*PG*, 36. 317); Dionysius, *Celestial Hierarchy* IX. 3, ed. M. de Gandillac, *SC* 58 (Paris: Cerf, 1958), p. 135.

28. John Scotus Eriugena, *Expositiones super Hierarchiam caelestem* (*PL* 122. 218a); Hugo of Saint-Victor, *In Hierarchiam caelestem* (*PL* 175. 1093d–94a, etc.).

29. John Locke, *An Essay Concerning Human Understanding* I. 1. 7. This metaphor was pointed out to me by J. Hittinger.

30. Augustine, *In Johannis Evangelium* 63. 1, *CCSL* 36, p. 485.

The Third Millenium and the Philosophical Life
Or, "Celsus, Don't Despair"
Michael Sherwin, O.P.

In an extraordinary passage in *Fides et Ratio* (§38), the Pope counters an argument advanced by Celsus against the Christian faith – that Christians were "illiterate and uncouth." Remarkably, a Pope from the twilight of the Second Millenium engages in debate with a pagan philosopher from the dawn of the First Millenium. This fact merits attention. By citing Celsus and Origen's response to Celsus, John Paul II is calling our attention to that early encounter between Christian theology and pagan philosophy. One of the issues over which Celsus and Origen argued was the nature of the philosophical life. Which life really leads to wisdom and human fulfillment: the way of life pursued by the pagan philosophers or the way of life pursued by the Christians? By calling this debate to our attention, the Pope, I would like to suggest, is inviting us to locate discussions concerning faith and philosophy in the larger context of the classical search for the way of life that leads to wisdom and fulfillment. The Pope does so, I believe, for two reasons: first, because it is on this level that people live their lives; people are seeking fulfillment. They seek to be happy. Second, the Pope is convinced that when people bring their search for happiness to reflective consciousness, it is then that they become open to responding to God's grace and to receiving the proclamation of the Gospel. In other words, by promoting the philosophical life, one is promoting the New Evangelization.

In the Pope's judgment, however, there is something that threatens this New Evangelization: despair, despair of reason's ability to know the truth about the human person. This despair is essentially the abandonment of the philosophical life. It marks a collective loss of faith in the quest for the truth. In the Pope's view, philosophical despair is not benign. It does not lead to tranquility or to intellectual humility. It leads, instead, to blind faith in the will to power; and when blind faith in the will to power becomes dominant, the roads that lead to life in Christ become obscured.[1] In the Pope's judgment, therefore, one of our tasks is to rekindle in people's hearts belief in philosophy, belief that the quest for truth is possible.[2] Interestingly, the Pope is encouraging non-Christian and secular philosophers not to despair of their craft. The image that comes to mind is of Celsus and the Pope in the boxing ring together; and Celsus, instead of sparring with the Pope, has fallen on the floor in self-inflicted philosophical despair and the Pope is leaning over him with a towel, trying to revive him. Our task is to participate in this revival, and to do so in two principal ways: first, by promoting true philosophy, through conveying its basic truths and its method of inquiry; second, by living the witness of a Christian life. To put flesh on this thesis, let us first look more closely at Celsus, the *philosophia* that he pursued as his ideal, and Origen's response to it.

The Early Church and the Philosophical Life

Scholars know little about the identity of Celsus, except that he was a Middle Platonist philosopher of the second century who, during the reign of Marcus Aurelius (161-180), wrote a pamphlet attacking Christianity.[3] Celsus entitled his work, provocatively, *alèthès logos*, which is customarily translated as the "True Doctrine," but can, of course, literally be translated as the "True Word," the "True Logos." In Celsus' view, Christians have severed themselves from the ancient wisdom of philosophy; they are not living the "true logos." For Celsus, the error of the Christians concerns not only what they think, but how they live. Celsus recognizes that Christians strive to follow Jesus, but in Celsus' view, Jesus was an ignorant charlatan who led those more ignorant than himself into an immoral way of living.[4]

As one can imagine, Origen was not at all happy with Celsus' view of Jesus or with his view of the Christian life. Origen responded to Celsus vigorously and at great length.[5] What interests us, however, is that in spite of their vast differences, Origen and Celsus share several assumptions in common. For both of them, philosophy was not merely a theoretical tool or a body of doctrine, it was a way of life. It was a style of life and a way of being whose goal was to direct one toward and place one in harmony with true wisdom. This was the common view held by most pagan philosophers during the Hellenistic period.[6] Integral to the view that philosophy was a way of life, was the conviction that there was such a thing as wisdom.[7] The goal of the philosophical life was to attain wisdom, to be in harmony with it. "Philosophy," Pierre Hadot explains,

took on the form of an exercise of the thought, will, and the totality of one's being, the goal of which was to achieve a state practically inaccessible to mankind: wisdom. Philosophy was a method of spiritual progress which demanded a radical conversion and transformation of the individual's way of being.[8]

Many of the early Christian apologists accepted this ideal of philosophy; indeed, they embraced it. They argued, however, that only in Christ is this ideal fulfilled. In other words, these early Christian thinkers respected *philosophia* as a life dedicated to searching for wisdom and to striving to live that wisdom.[9] They argued, however, that the ancient schools of philosophy had failed in their endeavor. The wisdom they contained was partial and did not lead to the healing, peace and happiness that the philosophers sought. For Justin Martyr (d. 162–167), Clement of Alexandria, as well as for Origen, the Gospel is the "true philosophy," because Jesus is the true Wisdom.[10] He is the Logos itself made visible in human form; as such Jesus is the pattern of the true philosophical life.[11] Celsus had claimed to know the true logos, but, Origen counters, in reality Jesus is the "True Logos."[12] Only in Christ do we fully discover the way to wisdom and only in Christ do we have the power to live this wisdom.

The Philosophical Life and Despair: the Example of the Weimar Republic

In the centuries that have passed since the days of the Early Church, the meaning of the word "philosophy" has clearly changed, and it would not be helpful, as the Pope notes, to start calling the Christian faith a philosophy.[13] Yet, when we read what John Paul II says about the human person's search for wisdom, we discover that the Pope is describing human culture in classical terms. He affirms that all people search for wisdom, for the meaning of their lives, and that every human life and every human culture is essentially a response to the question of meaning.[14] In other words, John Paul II affirms that every life in its own way is a philosophical life: it is a search for wisdom and a lived response to the question meaning. "The human being," John Paul II tells us, "is by nature a philosopher."[15]

Like the early apologists, however, John Paul II proclaims that only in Christ, the eternal Logos, does the philosophical search find its fulfillment.[16] From this perspective, John Paul II shares with the apologists the view that philosophy and the philosophical life are of propaedeutic value.[17] Only those who seek, find. Only those who believe that a search for truth is possible, can encounter a Truth that calls them to loving union with itself. From this perspective the principal threat to the New Evangelization is not non-Christian or secular philosophy, but the despair of philosophy. (One could perhaps more accurately say that he regards secular philosophies as a threat only to the extent that they constitute a form of despair.) Thus, the Pope states, "now, at the end of this century, one of our greatest threats is the temptation to despair."[18]

Here I believe the Pope's biography becomes important. Karol Wojtyla lived firsthand the terrors of the Nazis occupation of Poland.[19] The American Catholic philosopher/novelist Walker Percy observed that "Buchenwald was only four miles from Weimar."[20] How those four miles were traversed is a question that continues to haunt us at the end of the Millenium. Indeed, I would like to suggest that concern for this question has been a guiding factor throughout John Paul II's work.

What was there in the fabric of German life during the Weimar Republic that gave rise to Nazism? The answer to this question is beyond the scope of this short reflection. But the path from Weimar to Buchenwald can perhaps be sketched by looking at the experience of someone who lived through those days. The psychiatrist Karl Stern was raised in a Jewish family fully assimilated into secular German culture. Looking back at the Weimar years, Stern describes himself as one who "had known the life of 'freedom,' the perfect libertinism of European youth of the twenties, and the hangover of nothingness and spiritual despair."[21] After his conversion to Catholicism, Stern wrote an autobiography in which he explains that his "spiritual despair" led to a search for meaning. By the time the twenties had turned into the thirties, Stern had drifted from Orthodox Judaism, to secular Zionism, and back again to Orthodoxy. It was a journey that took him through the philosophical currents of his day and was tinged with a rejection of the beliefs and mores of the older generation. A parallel restlessness existed among non-Jews. Stern saw spring up around him a generation of young people who were alienated from their parents, restless and searching.[22] Children raised in secularized homes, whether of Jewish or Christian ancestry, were left with an inner void. The hangover of nothingness, it would seem, was giving way to a search for a cure-all far stronger than a raw egg: Germany's youth were searching for meaning and were going to extreme lengths to find it. Troubled and angry, they sought a goal to live for and a community with which to pursue it, and many found this with the Nazis.

Weimar Revisited: Despair at the End of the Millennium

The desire to understand the relationship between Weimar and the Nazis is not merely of historical interest. A number of thinkers hold the view that certain features of contemporary culture are strikingly similar to features present in German culture during the Weimar Republic. Nicholas Boyle, for example, describes Weimar Germany in the following terms:

> Germany . . . entered the post-modern and post-bourgeois era a generation before the other industrialized European states. In the 1920's,

stripped of empire and bourgeoisie, Germans were dropped into the world market and left to find an identity for themselves.[23]

After painting this description of pre-war Germany, Boyle turns his attention to the present.

> After the collapse of the Cold War balance of power, the dilemmas of Weimar Germany have been revealed to be general. The need to compete in a world market is undermining social and political certainties everywhere. The most serious threat to world peace seems once again to come from violent sectarian ideologies. And once again it seems doubtful whether the intellectuals of Europe and North America can mount any counter-offensive or whether the Post-Modernists are not unwittingly collaborating with forces that will destroy them. . . . The decline of the Weimar intelligentsia into Fascism may be seen as the first case of the failure of a Post-Modernist movement to meet the political challenge of globalization.[24]

In *Evangelium Vitae, Centesimus Annus* as well as *Fides et Ratio*, John Paul II offers descriptions of contemporary culture that are reminiscent of the cultural and spiritual upheaval of the Weimar years in Germany.[25] The notion that we are currently sowing the seeds for some future holocaust is a disturbing prospect. Yet, in John Paul II's view, this need not be the outcome. There is no historical necessity that we too must walk those four miles to Buchenwald. The peoples of the world are free to choose a different course. The challenge for the Christian is to help our contemporaries choose that other way.

How to help others choose the way that leads to eternal life is a theme that recurs in John Paul II's work. In *Centesimus Annus* and *Evangelium Vitae* John Paul II focuses on the task of promoting true culture. In *Fides et Ratio* the focus is upon promoting true philosophy: the vocation of the philosopher, John Paul II explains, is to share philosophy's basic truths and method of inquiry so that our contemporaries can undertake a search for the truth. In each of these encyclicals, however, John Paul II notes that merely "thinking it right" will not be enough. We must live it right: thought and action together.[26] Philosophy and the Christian life are what John Paul II is calling us to in order to help our contemporaries walk the way that leads to the tree of wisdom.

In section 74 of *Fides et Ratio*, the Pope invites us to look at the spiritual journeys of philosophers who have promoted the philosophical life. By looking briefly at the life of one of these thinkers, we shall have a better sense of how philosophy and the Christian life work together to promote confidence in the search for truth. We shall look at the experience of Edith Stein.

True Philosophy and the Christian Life: the Case of Edith Stein

By the time Edith Stein was fifteen years old, she had lost her faith in God, but her desire to know the truth remained.[27] In college she undertook the study of philosophy. In God's providence she became a student of Husserl. Here is how she describes Husserl's early method:

> The main reason the *Logical Investigations* had made such an impact was that they seemed to mark a radical break with critical idealism, both of the Kantian and neo-Kantian types. The book had been considered as representing a "new form of scholasticism," because it transferred the attention away from the subject and back onto the object. Once again perception was treated as something receptive, governed by its objects, rather than constitutive and regulative of the objects as in critical philosophy. All the young phenomenologists were committed realists.[28]

This method of receptivity before the real, led Stein to be receptive to the religious experiences of others. Thus, when she started to attend Max Scheler's seminars on "the Nature of the Holy," she was profoundly moved.

> This was my first encounter with this hitherto totally unknown world. It did not lead me as yet to the Faith. But it did open for me a region of "phenomena" which I could then no longer bypass blindly. With good reason we were repeatedly enjoined to observe all things without prejudice, to discard all possible "blinders." The barriers of rationalistic prejudices with which I had unwittingly grown up fell, and the world of faith unfolded before me. Persons with whom I associated daily, whom I esteemed and admired, lived in it. At the least, they deserved my giving it some serious reflection.[29]

From the realism she had learned from the early Husserl, Stein was able to see the religious experience of others as phenomena from which she might be able to learn some new truth. This is precisely the realist philosophy that the Pope desires to promote. He does so, I would like to suggest, precisely because of the effect it has had on people such as Edith Stein and on others like her.

But, we should recognize that more was happening among Husserl's students than merely philosophy. There was the presence of God's grace and there was the presence of committed Christians who were influencing these students through the witness of their lives. Stein herself offers many examples of these Christian witnesses: an important one was the calm hope and resignation exhibited by a Lutheran friend when her husband was killed: this hope-filled response was new to Stein and left her deeply impressed and puzzled.

It was my first encounter with the Cross and the divine power that it bestows on those who carry it. For the first time, I was seeing with my very eyes the Church, born from its Redeemer's sufferings, triumphant over the sting of death. That was the moment my unbelief collapsed, and Christ shone forth in the mystery of the Cross.[30]

The summit, however, of these witnesses occurred in Stein's accidental encounter with Teresa of Avila, when Stein stumbled upon her autobiography in the home of a friend. She stayed upon all night reading it, and by dawn when she finished the book, she had the faith of the Church.[31] Stein became a Catholic because in that encounter with the life of Teresa she encountered a truth, which, through the gift of grace, she was able to receive. Thus, in Stein's own life we see the two elements that the Pope believes promote the philosophical search for truth and a subsequent openness to the Gospel: (a) realist philosophy and (b) the witness of a Christian life.

What Stein did after her conversion is also significant. Her response to the rise of the Nazis was to enter the Carmelites, the Order that, perhaps more than any other, recognizes the Christian life to a journey of discovery: an ascent up the mount of truth, an ascent into the mystery of Christ's cross. Although the logic of despair and of the will to power was to surround her and lead to her death at Auschwitz, Edith Stein's fidelity to the truth about human life – the truth about the cross and resurrection – continues to speak to us. She lived the life of the Logos, and did so in confidence and peace. By doing so, she says to Celsus and to all of us, don't despair: in God's grace, the search for truth leads to eternal life.

Notes

1. Cf. *Fides et Ratio* (henceforth FR) §90: "The positions we have examined lead in turn to a more general conception which appears today as the common framework of many philosophies which have rejected the meaningfulness of being. I am referring to the nihilist interpretation, which is at once the denial of all foundations and the negation of all objective truth. . . . It should never be forgotten that the neglect of being inevitably leads to losing touch with objective truth and therefore with the very ground of human dignity. This in turn makes it possible to erase from the countenance of man and woman the marks of their likeness to God, and thus to lead them little by little either to a destructive will to power or to a solitude without hope. Once the truth is denied to human beings, it is pure illusion to try to set them free. Truth and freedom either go together hand in hand or together they perish in misery."

2. *FR* §56: "in the light of faith which finds in Jesus Christ this ultimate meaning, I cannot but encourage philosophers – be they Christian or not – to trust in the power of human reason and not to set themselves goals that are too modest in their philosophizing. The lesson of history in this millennium now drawing to a close shows that this is the path to follow: it is necessary not to abandon the passion for ultimate truth, the eagerness to search for it or the audacity to forge new paths in the search." §102: "There is today no more urgent preparation for the performance of these tasks than this: to lead people to discover both their capacity to know the truth and their yearning for the ultimate and definitive meaning of life."

3. Henri Crouzel, *Origen*, trans. A. S. Worrall (San Francisco: Harper and Row, 1989), p. 47. Crouzel describes this pamphlet as the "first attack launched against Christianity on the intellectual plane."

4. Marcel Borret, "Introduction Générale, Tables et Index," in *Contre Celse*, SC 5 (Paris: Editions du Cerf, 1976), pp. 33–121.

5. The text of the *Alèthès Logos* has only come down to us through the extensive quotations of it that Origen makes in the *Contra Celsum*. On the character and accuracy of Origen's method of quoting Celsus' text, see Marcel Borret, "Introduction Générale." For an analysis of Origen's *Contra Celsum*, see, in addition to Borret, Henry Chadwick, "Introduction" in Origen, *Contra Celsum*, trans. Henry Chadwick (Cambridge: Cambridge University Press, 1980); Eugene V. Gallagher, *Divine Man or Magician? Celsus and Origen on Jesus* (Chico, CA: Scholars Press, 1982); Robert John Hauck, *The More Divine Proof: Prophecy and Inspiration in Celsus and Origen* (Atlanta, GA: Scholars Press, 1989); Jeffrey A. Oschwald, "The Self-Evident Truth: Scripture and Apology in the *Contra Celsum* of Origen" (Ph.D. diss., University of Notre Dame, 1993); Louis William Roberts, "Philosophical Method in Origen's *Contra Celsum*" (Ph.D. diss., State University of New York at Buffalo, 1971).

6. Pierre Hadot, "Présentation au Collège International de Philosophie," (unpublished manuscript), p. 3, cited by Arnold I. Davidson in his Introduction to Hadot's *Philosophy as a Way of Life*, ed. Arnold I. Davidson (Oxford: Blackwell, 1995), pp. 30–31. See also, Hadot's statement in the same volume: "During this period, philosophy was a *way of life*. . . . philosophy was a mode of existing-in-the-world, which had to be practiced at each instant, and the goal of which was to transform the whole of the individual's life." Ibid., p. 265. I wish to thank Brian Daley, S.J. for introducing my to Hadot's work.

7. Cf. Arnold I. Davidson, "Introduction," p. 25.

8. Pierre Hadot, *Philosophy*, p. 265.

9. See, for example, Justin Martyr in *Dialogue with Trypho*: "Philosophy is indeed one's greatest possession, and is most precious in the sight of God, to whom it alone leads us and to whom it unites us, and they in truth are holy men who have applied themselves to philosophy" (ch. 2 [*PG*, 6.475]); "Man cannot have prudence without philosophy and straight thinking. Thus, every man should be devoted to philosophy and should consider it the greatest and most noble pursuit; all other pursuits are only of second or third-rate value, unless they are connected with philosophy. . . . Philosophy, . . . is the knowledge of that which exists, and a clear understanding of the truth; and happiness is the reward of such knowledge and understanding" (ch. 3 [*PG*, 6.479–82]). The translation is from *Writings of Saint Justin Martyr*, trans. Thomas B. Falls (New York: Christian Heritage, 1948). For analysis of the meaning of *philosophia* for both pagans and early Christians, an analysis that collects most of the relevant texts, see A. N. Malingrey, *"Philosophia," Étude d'un groupe de mots dans la littérature grecque, des Présocratiques au IVᵉ siècle ap. J.-C.* (Paris: C. Klincksieck, 1961). Cf. Hadot, *Philosophy*, p. 141, n. 17.

10. Clement of Alexandria, *Stromata* 1. 18. 90. 1 (*SC* 30.115); *FR* §38.

11. Justin Martyr, *Second Apology* 10 and 13 (*PG*: 6.459–62; 466–67); *Dialogue with Trypho* 8 (*PG*: 6.491–94); Hadot, *Philosophy*, p. 128; *FR* §38. Although Origen is highly critical of many of the doctrines held by the pagan philosophers, he respects their ideal and makes it his own. As Crouzel notes, "Origen holds in high esteem the moral ideal of the philosopher characterized by the love of truth and the quest for it." Henri Crouzel, *Origen*, trans. A. S. Worrall (San Francisco: Harper and Row, 1989), p. 157. Elsewhere, Crouzel describes Origen's attitude as follows: *"Origène est sensible à l'ideal hellénique du philosophe et en assimile tout ce qu'il peut. Il emploie fréquemment le mot dans un sens chrétien . . . Cet idéal moral et religieux, joint au travail et à la recherche intellectualle, Origène le fait sien."* Henri Crouzel, *Origène et la Philosophie* (Paris: Aubier, 1962), pp. 69–70. At the same time, however, he affirms that Greek philosophy fails to attain its end. Only the "divine philosophy," only the "philosophy of the patriarchs" fully imparts the true wisdom of the Logos. Cf. *Contra Celsum* 3.4.15–17; *SC* 136.20.

12. *Contra Celsum* 8.1.4–16 (*SC* 150. 180).

13. *FR* §76: "the Christian faith as such is not a philosophy."

14. *FR* §30: "All men and women, as I have noted, are in some sense philosophers and have their own philosophical conceptions with which they direct their lives. In one way or other, they shape a comprehensive vision and an answer to the question of life's meaning; and in the light of this they interpret their own life's course and regulate their behavior." *FR* §70: "When they are

deeply rooted in experience, cultures show forth the human being's characteristic openness to the universal and the transcendent. Therefore they offer
different paths to the truth, which assuredly serve men and women well in
revealing values which can make their life ever more human." *Centesimus
Annus* (henceforth *CA*) §24: "Man is understood in a more complete way
when he is situated within the sphere of culture through his language, history,
and the position he takes towards the fundamental events of life, such as birth,
love, work and death. At the heart of every culture lies the attitude man takes
to the greatest mystery: the mystery of God. Different cultures are basically
different ways of facing the question of the meaning of personal existence."
CA §50: "From this open search for truth, which is renewed in every generation, *the culture of a nation* derives its character."

15. *FR* §64. Cf. *FR* §27: "people seek in different ways to shape a 'philosophy' of their own – in personal convictions and experiences, in traditions of
family and culture, or in journeys in search of life's meaning under the guidance of a master. What inspires all of these is the desire to reach the certitude
of truth and the certitude of its absolute value;" *FR* §30: "The truths of philosophy, it should be said, are not restricted only to the sometimes ephemeral
teachings of professional philosophers. All men and women, as I have noted,
are in some sense philosophers and have their own philosophical conceptions
with which they direct their lives. In one way or other, they shape a comprehensive vision and an answer to the question of life's meaning; and in the light
of this they interpret their own life's course and regulate their behavior;" *FR*
§33: "From all that I have said to this point it emerges that men and women
are on a journey of discovery."

16. *FR* §34: "[Jesus] is the *eternal Word* in whom all things were created, and
he is the *incarnate Word* who in his entire person reveals the Father (cf. Jn 1.
14 and 18). What human reason seeks 'without knowing it' (cf. Acts 17. 23)
can be found only through Christ: what is revealed in him is 'the full truth'
(cf. Jn 1. 14–16) of everything which was created in him and through him and
which therefore in him finds its fulfillment (cf. Col 1. 17)." See also *FR* §99
and *Redemptoris Hominis* 8: "The truth is that only in the mystery of the
Incarnate Word does the mystery of man take on light. For Adam, the first
man, was a type of him who was to come, Christ the Lord. Christ, the new
Adam, in the very revelation of the mystery of the Father and of his love, fully
reveals man to himself and brings to light his most high calling" (cited in *FR*
§60).

17. *FR* §67: "Recalling the teaching of Saint Paul (cf. Rom 1. 19–20), the First
Vatican Council pointed to the existence of truths which are naturally, and
thus philosophically, knowable; and an acceptance of God's Revelation necessarily presupposes knowledge of these truths. . . . From all these truths, the

mind is led to acknowledge the existence of a truly propaedeutic path to faith, one which can lead to the acceptance of Revelation without in any way compromising the principles and autonomy of the mind itself."

18. *FR* §91.

19. See Darcy O'Brien, *The Hidden Pope: the Untold Story of a Lifelong Friendship that is Changing the Relationship between Catholics and Jews. The Journey of John Paul II and Jerzy Kluger* (New York: Daybreak Books, 1998), pp. 164–71, 185–95, 202–18; Tad Szulc, *Pope John Paul II: the Biography* (New York: Scribner, 1995), pp. 124–32; Carl Bernstein and Marco Politi, *His Holiness: John Paul II and the Hidden History of Our Time* (New York: Doubleday, 1996), pp. 225–30.

20. Walker Percy, *The Second Coming* (New York: Farrar, Straus, Giroux, 1980), p. 132.

21. Karl Stern, *The Pillar of Fire* (New York: Harcourt, Brace and Company, 1951), p. 222. Stern says these words in describing himself and his future bride: "Whatever our views may be, we had come from roots far apart; she from an over-sophisticated academic tradition, I from the merchant's house in the small town; she from a liberal Lutheran, I from an 'enlightened' Jewish background. We both had been instilled with Goethean humanism but our revolts against the bourgeois tradition had taken entirely different routes. We both had known the life of 'freedom,' the perfect libertinism of European youth of the twenties, and the hangover of nothingness and spiritual despair."

22. Karl Stern, *The Pillar of Fire*, pp. 47–48, 160–61.

23. Nicholas Boyle, *Who Are We Now: Christian Humanism and the Global Market from Hegel to Heaney* (Notre Dame, IN: University of Notre Dame Press, 1998), pp. 125–26.

24. Nicholas Boyle, *Who Are We Now*, p. 126. Karl Stern noticed as early as the late 1940's that a number of his colleagues in the medical profession were already expressing views, such as the legitimacy of killing the chronically mentally ill, that were chillingly close to those expressed in Germany during the Weimar Republic and subsequently taken up by the Nazis with great efficiency. Karl Stern, *The Pillar of Fire*, pp. 125–27. Flannery O'Connor was also sensitive to this growing attitude, describing it as flowing from a compassion that is cut off from Christian faith. Concern about the implications of faithless compassion is a theme throughout her fiction. In 1960 she expressed her views on this subject clearly in an essay introducing a biography of a young girl who had died of cancer: "Ivan Karamazov cannot believe, as long as one child is in torment; Camus' hero cannot accept the divinity of Christ, because of the massacre of the innocents. In this popular pity, we mark our gain in sensibility and our loss of vision. If other ages felt less, they saw more,

even though they saw with the blind, prophetically, unsentimental eye of acceptance, which is to say, of faith. In the absence of this faith now, we govern by tenderness. It is a tenderness which, long since cut off from the person of Christ, is wrapped in theory. When tenderness is detached from the source of tenderness, its logical outcome is terror. It ends in forced-labor camps and in the fumes of the gas chamber." Flannery O'Connor, "Introduction to *A Memoir of Mary Ann*," reprinted in *Mystery and Manners*, eds. Sally and Robert Fitzgerald (New York: Farrar, Straus and Giroux, 1969), p. 227. This concern was also a theme in the work of Walker Percy. It is present in the passage from the *Second Coming* cited above; Percy investigates it at length in *The Thanatos Syndrome* and offers a non-fiction account of his views in "Why Are You A Catholic," in *Signposts in a Strange Land*, ed. Patrick Samway (New York: Farrar, Straus and Giroux, 1991), pp. 304–15. For an analysis of Percy's views, see Patricia Lewis Poteat, "Pilgrim's Progress; or, A Few Night Thoughts on Tenderness and the Will to Power," in *Walker Percy: Novelist and Philosopher*, eds. Jan Nordby Gretlund and Lark-Heinz Westarp (Jackson, MS: University Press of Mississippi, 1991), pp. 210–24; Sue Mitchell Crowley, "*The Thanatos Syndrome*: Walker Percy's Tribute to Flannery O'Connor," in *Walker Percy: Novelist and Philosopher*, pp. 225–37. See also Deal W. Hudson, *Happiness and the Limits of Satisfaction* (Lanham, MD: Rowman and Littlefield, 1996), pp. 42–45.

25. *Evangelium Vitae* (henceforth *EV*) §4, 12–17; *CA* §24, 41; *FR* §46–47, 55, 81, 90–91.

26. *FR* §32; 105. John Paul II develops this theme more explicitly in his earlier encyclicals: *CA* §57–58; *EV* §80–100.

27. The nature of Stein's loss of faith during her early years is not entirely clear. Waltraud Herbstrith asserts in her biography of Stein that "Edith Stein acknowledged years later that from thirteen to twenty-one she could not believe in the existence of a personal God." Waltraud Herbstrith, *Edith Stein, A Biography*, trans. Bernard Bonowitz (San Francisco: Harper and Row, 1985), p. 5; but Herbstrith does not offer a source for this assertion. Stein does state in her autobiography that at the age of fifteen, when living in the home of non-practicing relatives, that "deliberately and consciously, I gave up praying." Edith Stein, *Life in a Jewish Family: 1891–1916: An Autobiography*, ed. L. Gelber and Romaeus Leuven, trans. Josephine Koeppel (Washington, D.C.: I.C.S. Publications, 1986), p. 148. Stein's niece, however, wisely cautions that an adolescent's decision not to pray does not necessarily mean that the adolescent is an atheist. Susanne M. Batzdorff, *Aunt Edith: the Jewish Heritage of a Catholic Saint* (Springfield, IL: Templegate, 1998), p. 67. What is clear

is that Edith Stein herself affirms that during her years as a college student she was without faith in God. See, for example, Edith Stein, *Life in a Jewish Family*, p. 195..

28. Edith Stein, *Aus dem Leben einer jüdischen Famile Kindheit und Jugend*, Edith Steins Werke, 8 vols. (Louvain: Nauwelaerts/Freiburg: Herder, 1965), vol. 7, p. 174, as cited by Waltraud Herbstrith, *Edith Stein*, p. 18. See Edith Stein, *Life in a Jewish Family*, p. 250.

29. Edith Stein, *Life in a Jewish Family*, p. 260. Cited in Waltraud Herbstrith, *Edith Stein*, p. 19.

30. Edith Stein in a letter to Fr. Hirschmann, S.J. cited by Waltraud Herbstrith, *Edith Stein*, pp. 24–25. The friend was Anna Reinach; her husband, the phenomenologist, Adolf Reinach, was killed in the First World War. For an account of Stein's friendship and professional relationship with the Reinachs, see Edith Stein, *Life in a Jewish Family*, pp. 247–300, 377–85.

31. See Waltraud Herbstrith, *Edith Stein*, pp. 30–32.

Fides et Ratio and the
Graceful Redemption of Philosophy
Jennifer Hockenbery

I am so thankful to be here. Especially since I am something of an inter-loper, having three strikes against me at this conference of Thomists. First, I am catholic only with a small "c." Second, I am a student of Augustine, and I am rather ignorant of Aquinas. Third, given a choice, I prefer to climb about on Plato's divided line, rather than swim through Aristotle's *Metaphysics*. But with these three strikes against me, rather than being "out" I have been invit-ed in. And in being invited in, I have been allowed to learn a great deal. So you as a group have served as a human example of the divine graciousness that will be the theme of my quodlibet.

You might wonder why I, a young Protestant female philosopher with Augustinian leanings, wanted to attend this seminar. I wanted to come, and I wanted to come badly, because I loved this encyclical. I loved this encyclical for the same reason I first fell in love with the writings of Saint Augustine. I loved it because in its pages I saw the hope of redeeming philosophy. By this I mean that I saw here a program to restore to philosophers the real hope of finding the truth. The core of this program is that we cannot hope to find truth using reason alone. That project has failed. But the Pope claims, like Augustine before him, that by using faith and reason together, we might advance in our understanding. And I claim that what allows the Pope, as it allowed Augustine, to be hopeful as a philosopher using faith and reason, is an epistemology of grace. I mean by an epistemology of grace the idea that the truth, the object of the search of philosophy, is interested in being found. An epistemology of grace states that God, who is the truth, wants us to know and helps us in our path towards wisdom. With such an epistemology, philos-ophy can really be what its etymology reveals – not an erotic love for wisdom, but a friendship with wisdom.[1]

To put forth my argument that it is an epistemology of grace that allows for philosophy's redemption, I have divided the paper into four parts. First, I must show that philosophy does in fact need redemption, for some contem-porary philosophers would argue against that first point. Second, I want to examine the Pope's two-fold project for the redemption of philosophy which includes recovering philosophy's original vocation and discovering the need for faith and reason. Third, I hope to demonstrate that this two-fold project is grounded in a belief in grace. And finally, I will discuss why a belief in grace is philosophically acceptable.

Does Philosophy Need Redemption?

Throughout this week we have been discussing the "crisis of meaning" that the Pope claims is occurring. This is a crisis for everyone, for all people by nature desire to know, as Aristotle instructs us. We, as human beings, crave understanding of ourselves. We crave to know more about our world. And we crave to know more about God who is the Truth. The crisis of meaning occurs when we begin to lack hope that there is any real wisdom for us to find, or when we worry that even if such wisdom exists it is beyond our ability to discover it. This lack of hope, this despair, is the sickness of nihilism. It is a sickness that whispers to its victim that the very thing the human soul most longs for is unattainable if not altogether non-existent. It is a sickness that whispers that the pursuit of truth is "quixotic, absurd and dangerously arrogant."[2]

And if this fear that we shall never rest in the truth is a crisis for everyone, it is much more a crisis for the professional philosopher who has devoted much of her working life to the search for truth. As Larry Cahoone writes in his book, aptly titled *The Ends of Philosophy*, this is a crisis that has every professional philosopher on trial just as Socrates once was. He writes, "For if philosophy cannot do or be what it claims, if it cannot serve the ends for which we choose to practice it, then our lives are threatened, too, not with death, which must befall everyone, but with *waste*, a fate Socrates would have thought considerably worse than hemlock."[3]

If we professional philosophers cannot find a way to save philosophy as a real and hopeful pursuit of truth, we admit that we are earning our keep by playing a game with no goal. And worse, we are seducing others, our students and our readers, to this goal-less game. We are wasting our time and theirs. We ought to be out doing something of more value. Or, if there is no real meaning, we ought to at least do something more lucrative.

So, philosophy needs redemption. This is especially true for those of us in the profession. But as the Pope claims, this is true also for all of humanity, for whether we recognize it or not, each of us is restless until we can rest in the truth.

The Path to Redemption – Recovering Philosophy's Original Vocation

Philosophy's original definition has changed over the years, as has been mentioned several times in these papers. Once philosophy was the love of wisdom. It was the love of the wisdom of ourselves, our world, and God. Indeed, philosophy in its ancient sense seems to have an almost mystical goal of spiritual union with the divine. Today, philosophy's definition is rather narrow. It is an autonomous, independent, and rational pursuit of answers to a set of very specific questions. It is a field that claims to be different and independent from physics, psychology, history, anthropology, and theology. Although we must admit that questions of cosmology, of the soul, of human progress, of human nature, and of God all used to be at the heart of philosophy.

The Pope calls us to remember philosophy's "original vocation" – to recall philosophy's "sapiential dimension". This means that we are to remember that philosophy is about the love of wisdom – the wisdom of ourselves, our world, and of God who is wisdom.

To give us a sense of what this original vocation looked like in the ancient world, I would like to read Augustine's description of his conversion to philosophy. In reading this, we see what philosophy meant in antiquity. The passage is a famous one from the *Confessions*. At the time of the conversion, Augustine had done quite well for himself by Roman standards. He had a concubine whom he loved, and he had a son. He was doing exceedingly well in school, as his parents had hoped. And he wanted to continue to do well in the academy. So he studied, and as he studied one night his homework assignment was to read Cicero's *Hortensius* – a dialogue about the merits of philosophy. And suddenly Augustine was converted. He was transformed. He writes about the occasion,

> This book changed my affections. It changed my prayers to you Lord. It produced in me new promises and desires. Suddenly every empty hope became worthless to me, and I longed for Immortal Wisdom with an incredible rage of fire in my heart, and I began to awaken in order to return to you . . . How I burned, my God, how I burned to return from the earth to you, although I knew not what you might do with me! With you is indeed wisdom. The love of wisdom has the name in Greek of philosophy. With this love I was inflamed.[4]

What is apparent about philosophy in its original sense is that philosophy was above all else passionate. Augustine is on fire, he is raging, he is inflamed. Nothing else matters to him but finding wisdom. Philosophy is about the greatest love a human has, the love of wisdom. Augustine explains this love erotically, claiming in the *Soliloquies* that he wants to hold Wisdom naked under the sheets. He says that he would give up his friends, his wealth, his leisure time, even his life itself to have her. He asks in *On Free Will*, "If men exclaim that they are happy when they embrace the beautiful bodies, deeply longed for, of their wives, shall we doubt that we will be happy in the embrace of truth?"[5] Truth is more desirable than a beautiful woman, and we all know how Augustine felt about beautiful women.

It is an interesting aside to mention that in Augustine's passion for truth, the first place he turns is to the Bible. Also, Augustine mentions that not only were his affections changed by philosophy, but also his prayers. For Augustine, there was no distinction between philosophy and religion. He would use any and every thing he could to find the truth he loved.

So, I think that recovering philosophy's original vocation means recovering the passion for truth, in its most absolute sense. We must recover the passion the Pope claims seems to be missing in modern philosophy. Perhaps this is because in modern philosophy we are no longer looking for the wisdom that will fulfill us, complete us, make us happy, and soothe our souls. This is why the ancients did philosophy. As Augustine claims there was only one reason to do philosophy in antiquity, to search for the *beata vita* – the blessed or happy life.[6] We do not have to take Augustine's word for this; we can turn to other ancient writers. Plato claims through Diotima in the *Symposium* that the goal of philosophy makes all of the rest of life's goals – gold, success, beautiful young men – pale in comparison.[7] Epicurus says that philosophy is our only hope to find happiness.[8] Cicero, skeptic though he was, agrees and says that we will remain wretched unless we seek the art of healing the soul which is philosophy.[9]

This is the ancient attitude of philosophers, that we must seek to know the self, the world, and God in order to find satisfaction and happiness. It is this attitude that must be recovered if philosophy is going to be redeemed.

The Role of Faith and Reason

But perhaps the reason that philosophers have lost the passion of the original project is because the goal of wisdom seems impossible. We have used our rational faculties and we have not found truth. We take our Descartes' *Mediations* into our room at night and we think and we think and we think. And at the end of the night, not only do we not know truth, we do not even know if the room exists, if our chair exists, if we are really wearing our dressing gown and sitting in front of the fire. After all our meditating we actually feel farther from truth than we did before. Of course, Descartes believed he had found knowledge of God and the external world, but for most philosophers the rationalist project leaves us desperate, sure only of our own momentary existence proven in the *cogito ergo sum*. We cannot prove God's existence, we cannot prove the existence of external objects, and we certainly cannot find the wisdom that is the key to the happy life. So our first inflamed passion begins to die, as we fall into skepticism and nihilism. Reason only seems to prove that reason cannot bring us to the truth.

And we cannot return to simple faith. Unlike Tertullian, moderns, and really people of every age, cannot believe because it is absurd. We have been hurt to many times by such faith. We have trusted one scientist only to have her facts disproved the next week. We have trusted a political leader only to later see we have been deceived. We cannot find wisdom in belief.

So the Pope says that we must not use faith or reason. We must use faith and reason. Our only hope is to start with premises that are believed but not proven. We must then continue to think, to use reason and phenomenological experience to test our faith and explore it further. Faith needs reason to keep it from error. Reason needs faith to keep it from skepticism. Using both together we can get closer to our original philosophical goal of greater understanding of ourselves and our world.

The Need for Grace

Using faith and reason together is pragmatic. Indeed, it is our usual way of inquiry. Daily we trust certain authorities – our parents, our teachers, our newspapers. We do not try to verify everything for ourselves. We could not survive if we did. But we do continue to use reason and experience as well. If experience and reason contradicts the authority, we re-examine that authority and then re-examine our experience until we can come to some conclusion.

Augustine, in his own crisis of skepticism, realized that faith and reason were part of everyday life. He realized that he had to trust his parents' claim that they were his parents. He had to trust his teachers' and books' claims about places he had not visited and events that preceded his birth. And he also had to use his rational faculties to correct errors he had previously believed.

But while this is pragmatic and necessary for daily life, there is no promise that this method will really lead us to true wisdom. While Augustine knew he had to use faith and reason in everyday life he refused to use faith in his philosophical quest for truth. He would rather claim to know nothing absolutely, than believe something about wisdom only to later find he was wrong. He had been embarrassed by his commitment to the Manichees, and promised that in philosophy he would not entrust himself without certainty.

What changed Augustine's mind, and allowed him to use faith and reason not just in daily life but in philosophy, was an experience of grace. This passage is also a famous one from the *Confessions*. Augustine describes the scene saying that he, philosophically skeptical though he was, had begun to study himself according to the Platonic command. In his study he becomes aware of a light above him. It is not a corporal light, but the light of truth. Unlike the Platonic sun, this light does not merely shine upon him while he begins to see clearly. Instead, this light lifts Augustine up. It picks him up, and beats back his weakness so that he can see clearly. And moreover, after he asks an impetuous question about whether truth exists, the light even speaks to him saying, "I am that which is." Suddenly, Augustine can no longer doubt the existence of truth.

On this day, Augustine learned that the truth not only existed, but that the truth was gracefully, personally, and lovingly interested in him being able to see the truth. It was this encounter with grace that allowed Augustine to trust faith and reason, because he realized that the truth wanted to be known. Indeed, as Kierkegaard wrote many centuries later in the *Philosophical Fragments*, the truth wants to be understood by us as much as any lover wants to be understood by his beloved. If the truth wants to be known, we using our faculties of faith and reason, are given access to the truth. Augustine explains it this way,

> We have a promise, who shall annul it? If God is on our side, who is against us? Ask and you shall receive. Seek and you shall find. Knock and the door shall be opened to you. Everyone that asks will receive, that seeks will find, that knocks will have the door opened to him. These are your promises and who needs fear deception when the Truth promises?[10]

The message is, if God is gracious and wants us to find wisdom, surely we will find it. This message is interwoven throughout *Fides et Ratio*. Phrases such as "as the source of love, God desires to make himself known," "knowledge expresses a truth based upon the very fact of God who reveals himself, a truth which is most certain, since God neither deceives nor wishes to deceive," "God has willed to reveal himself in history" abound in the document, for only if the truth wants to be known can faith and reason help us find it. Perhaps most important in the document are the words that remind us of the Incarnation. In Jesus, we learn that God wants us to understand truth so much that the truth became flesh to walk among us, speaking words with a human tongue so that our human ears could understand. Truth came in the flesh so we could touch it, taste it, see it, feel it. How can we despair that we will never find truth when we have a God who does that?

The Philosophical Acceptability of Grace

This is all well and good. We see how much hope is offered to philosophers if the truth is gracefully interested in teaching them. But can we really believe in such grace? I think we can, using the method of reason and faith together. First using reason and phenomenological experience alone we have evidence that we were created by a Being that wishes us to know. For example, physicists tell us that the universe is made up of tiny vibrating particles and empty space. And yet we are constructed in such a way that we do not see a buzzing chaos of sense data; instead, we see people, trees, animals, stars and other things that obey scientific laws that we can discover. This ability seems to point to a creator who wanted us to be able to know about our world. Another example, brought forth in Louis Chammings's paper on communication is the miraculous fact that I have immaterial ideas in my head and you have immaterial ideas in yours, and yet I can give you my idea, my "beetle in the box," simply by sending vibrations through the air which strike your ear. This, too, seems to present a case for a Creator that wishes us to be able to learn from and about each other. And as a final example, there is the rarer and yet universal case of a time when we are trying to understand something, a math problem perhaps. After lots of study and effort we sometimes still cannot figure out the solution. And then, suddenly, with no further effort on our part, the solution strikes us. Such experiences point to the possibility that not only were our brains constructed to know, but that continually in our lives, we are being taught by something higher than ourselves.

But these are just inferences. These examples may point to the idea that truth is gracefully interested in being known, but they cannot prove it. And a person could well ask why, if truth wants to be known, are we so frequently in error? The answer perhaps comes from our faith. As the Pope writes,

> According to the apostle, it was part of the original plan of creation that reason should without difficulty reach beyond the sensory data to the origin of all things: the Creator. But because of the disobedience by which man and woman chose to set themselves in full and absolute autonomy in relation to the One who had created them, this real access to God the Creator diminished . . . All men and women were caught up in this primal disobedience, which so wounded reason that from then on its part to full truth would be strewn with obstacles. From that time onward the human capacity to know the truth was impaired by an aversion to the One who is the source and origin of truth (§22).

Faith in the authority of Scripture, tells us something which is not at odds with what reason and experience discover – that while the Creator wished us to know truth fully by reason alone, by our own sinfulness we are unable to see that truth clearly. Further the faith makes the claim that the truth, not willing to let the unruly student be dismissed, continues to try to teach – coming to us on our own terms in the Incarnation, and also by the Incarnation washing away our error so that we might again see more clearly.

To conclude, the faith tells us, and reason infers that truth is gracefully interested in the seeker of truth. Because the truth wants to be known and is working with us to teach us even as we seek to learn, we can have real hope in the original project of philosophy, to know ourselves and our world and to come to a more happy and satisfying life lived in the light of Truth.

As one final remark, if we accept the epistemology of grace, I think we can and must study everything we can. We no longer need to fear studying other traditions and philosophies – the Pope suggests starting with those of India. We can study all the sciences. We can study other theologies. I think, and I may get some disagreements, we can even study Nietzsche. If the truth wants to be known, we need not fear getting stuck in deception. As long as we use reason and experience to explore a teaching, we know that the truth will be helping us to see error when there is error and truth when there is truth. It may take long periods of study, but with the help of the graceful God, philosophy can result in better understanding.

So I would like to end with the same quote used by Rev. Michael Sherwin, from Edith Stein. "In God's grace the search for Truth [that is philosophy] leads to eternal life [that is salvation]." As Augustine says if the truth is on our side, no one is against us. So let us go forth in the friendship with God to search for the wisdom that will bring rest to our restless hearts.

Notes

1 See Carl Vaught, "Faith and Philosophy," *Monist* 75 (July 1992), pp. 325–26.

2. See Lawrence Cahoone, *The Ends of Philosophy* (Albany: State University of New York Press, 1995), p. 2.

3. Cahoone, *Ends*, pp. 4–5.

4. Augustine, *Confessions,* III. 4

5. Augustine, *De Libero Arbitrio*, 2.13.35.

6. See Augustine, *Sermon* 150.4

7. See Plato, *Symposium* 211d.

8. See Epicurus, *Letter to Menoeceus* 122.

9. See Cicero, *Tusculan Disputations* 3.3.6.

10. Augustine, *Confessions* XII.1.

Consolatio Philosophiae:
Philosophy Consoling and Consoled
Steven C. Snyder

What is distinctive in the biblical text is the conviction that there is a profound and indissoluble unity between the knowledge of reason and the knowledge of faith (*Fides et Ratio*, §16).

On the Feast of the Triumph of the Cross (1998), John Paul II issued the encyclical *Fides et Ratio*, Faith and Reason, arising from two thousand years of Christian reflection on the relation of faith and reason. The message of *Fides et Ratio* is that the new evangelization requires also a renewed reconciliation, a renewed harmonizing of the teachings of the two books, the book of natural wisdom and the book of revealed wisdom. This reconciliation, *Fides et Ratio* makes clear, cannot be imposed by theology onto philosophy, or vice versa. Philosophy and theology are each autonomous sciences, given their own powers and domains by God; the two must be united as in a marriage and not subsumed one to the other as in a conquest. Each must find its way back to the other.

I wish to focus on one such journey of reconciliation which is part of the rich heritage of Western thought. Boethius' *Consolation of Philosophy* is a journey made, I believe, in the spirit of harmonizing faith and reason as discussed in *Fides et Ratio*. I choose Boethius' text because it presents a view of philosophy's relation to revelation that is implicit but not emphasized in *Fides et Ratio*. And I choose the *Consolation of Philosophy* also because it presents such a compelling question: how can it be that in this work the great Christian author Boethius, the author of the theological tractates, the great defender of the divinity and humanity of our Lord and Savior made Flesh, makes not one mention of Christ, not one mention of the God of Abraham, not one mention of the cross? When we face death and fear it, whence comes our consolation? Is it from philosophy, or is it from Jesus Christ?

There is no doubt that for the Boethius of the theological tractates salvation is through Jesus Christ, and so ultimately is consolation through Christ. But a study of the *Consolation of Philosophy* can be used to illustrate an important fact about the intellectual journey of one who is both philosopher and Christian: philosophy[1] is open to the wisdom of faith because philosophy's longing is for faith, even though philosophy cannot know that the faith is that for which she longs. Put another way, my thesis is that the "of" in *Consolation of Philosophy* is both objective and subjective genitive: the title means both that philosophy consoles and philosophy is consoled.[2]

The right reason of philosophy, through her metaphysical journey, first consoles and heals the man buffeted by the caprices and evils of the world; but in this very act of consoling she comes to know herself as needing consolation. *Qua* philosopher she knows only her need, her longing for harmonizing wisdom; *qua* Christian a philosopher like Boethius knows that that consolation which can fulfill philosophic longing is to be found in revealed Christian wisdom. Philosophy, by her natural powers, can conclude that is reasonable – not demonstratively requisite but reasonable – for reason to hold that there is a supernatural wisdom beyond natural reason which resolves the mystery that philosophy can see but cannot herself by reason's own natural powers hope to resolve.

Let us journey for a time with Boethius in the *Consolation of Philosophy*. Boethius was a Roman born around A.D. 480 and executed under the Arian Ostrogothic King Theoderic by order of the Senate as a subverter and traitor around 525, that is, at about 44 years of age.[3] The maxim "to whom much is given much is expected" was no abstract doctrine to the noble Boethius; it was a principle animating his life. Knowledge of Greek was dying in the Latin West. Boethius, expert in Greek, set himself to translating and expounding in Latin all the works of Plato and Aristotle, so that subsequent generations would not be bereft of their wisdom. His monumental task was cut short by premature death, but the little he did translate from Aristotle's logical works were treasured as a rich legacy by Latin scholars until new translators came along six hundred years later. The Church was threatened with formidable Christological and Trinitarian heresies in his day; Boethius responded with five theological tractates of unquestioned orthodoxy which went far towards establishing the theological terminology of the Latin Church. Boethius the political man, the Senator and Consul, was not deaf to the cries of the poor but gave freely of his substance in their times of need.

In his life Boethius strove to harmonize.[4] His life seems to have been dedicated to finding the common ground, the common value, the common truth in disparate arenas: his research sought harmony between Plato and Aristotle, his theological writing sought harmony between Orthodox Greek and Latin Christian Christologies; and his public life sought to harmonize the moral integrity and learning of the philosophers with the legitimate needs of government and the people. Boethius was a natural harmonizer.

Boethius the orthodox Christian, Senator, and philosopher was unjustly imprisoned and finally tortured and executed for treason and sorcery. At the beginning of the *Consolation* we find Boethius wickedly imprisoned, lamenting most grievously his unjust fate. Solzhenitsyn in the beginning of the *Gulag Archipelago* captures the despair of the prisoner unjustly accused:

> Arrest! Need it be said that it is a breaking point in your life, a bolt of lightning which has scored a direct hit on you? That it is an unassimilable spiritual earthquake not every person can cope with, as a result of which people often slip into insanity.[5]

Immediately, Solzhenitsyn identifies the cause of this "spiritual earthquake," giving the same reason given by Lady Philosophy to Boethius to explain his grief:

> The Universe has as many different centers as there are living beings in it. Each of us is a center of the Universe, and that Universe is shattered when they hiss at you: "You are under arrest." If *you* are arrested, can anything else remain unshattered by this cataclysm?[6]

The disease that is the source of so much grief, Lady Philosophy argues, is that Boethius, or Solzhenitsyn's *you*, has forgotten his own identity. No man, no creature, is the center of the Universe; God, the creator of all things, is the center of the Universe, and of each individual creature's being. Convincing Boethius of this truth is the way Philosophy consoles; by this wisdom Philosophy replaces grief with the joy that comes from knowing the highest truths.[7]

The arguments that Lady Philosophy uses begin in ethics and culminate in metaphysics.[8] The man who is "shattered" by the injustice done him is grieving for a lost good. But what is the good for man? After the manner of the *Nicomachean Ethics* (Bk. One), Lady Philosophy argues that it is not some temporal good that can be lost with changing fortune but must be the supreme, completely fulfilling, unchangeable good. Her argument progresses until she can conclude that the good of all creation is God, and God is especially the good of man. Man's happiness is "to acquire divinity, become gods . . . *omnis igitur beatus deus* . . . by participation."[9] "O happy race of men," Lady Philosophy sings, "If the love that rules the stars/ May also rule your hearts."[10]

But Philosophy must demonstrate that God is indeed the "love that rules the stars" and the entire created universe. Philosophy's metaphysical arguments are several and extended, but the primary argument is a customarily Platonic way of arguing, that the grades of imperfect goods we experience in the universe can only be accounted for by the existence of a single, perfect, complete goodness which is the complete cause of their being, conjoined with no other cause; and this ultimate cause is God.[11] The point I wish to focus on is Philosophy's necessary demonstration that God is the cause of all of being. There is no being that is not God or caused by God. And since God is the very meaning of Goodness, we can just as well say that all is caused by Love. There is no being that is not caused by God; there is no reality that is not under the constant care of infinite Divine Love.

The consolation Philosophy offers by necessary demonstrations is indeed great: fear not, for all is under God's care; grieve not, for all that happens happens because God knows that it will bring us closer to His Likeness; hate not, for the wicked have a sort of disease of the mind; lament not, for death ushers the good closer to God and terminates wickedness before it can completely consume its host; and hope confidently, since providence "from [its] lofty watch-tower" arranges what perfect knowledge knows is best and fitting for each of his beloved creatures.[12]

A great legacy this, from a long-dead man and an every-young Lady. But it is only part of the dialogue:

> Lady, [Boethius says,] you who lead the way to the true light, what your speech has so far poured into my mind has clearly been both divine, contemplated on its own, and invincible because of our arguments, and you have told me things which, although lately forgotten because of the pain of my injuries, I was not previously totally ignorant of. *But this itself is the greatest cause of my grief,* that, although there does exist a good ruler of the universe, evil can exist at all and even pass unpunished . . . and . . . when wickedness flourishes and is in control, virtue . . . is even thrown down.[13]

In the last two books of the *Consolation*, Lady Philosophy moves to resolve Boethius' *aporia*. She shows that virtue is never thrown down, that the vicious are truly the weakest and most ineffectual of men because their very wickedness keeps them from achieving the happiness they truly want. In Book V Philosophy rises to the height of examining the compatibility of divine foreknowledge and human free will, to show that human free will can exist without jeopardizing the self-sufficiency of divine knowledge.

Now, it is customary to stop the analysis here, with Boethius' answer to the question of the possibility of human free will given divine foreknowledge. But there is a more fundamental question that Boethius has raised: given his demonstration that God is the creator and first efficient cause of all creaturely being, how can there be divine *causality* and true human agency, true human free will? Providence is not just a knowing, it is a disposing, a causing. If God is the cause of everything, how can man, or any creature, be the cause of anything? The problem of moral evil is, for all its existential import for salvation history, philosophically a subset or derivative of the greater question of how the infinite divine leaves room for finite creatureliness.

With this question Philosophy has brought herself to the limits of Philosophy's ability to know. This limit is not one of degree, it is by nature, and it arises from the finitude and creatureliness of reason itself. Philosophy has arrived at an *aporia* that is insoluble by natural reason. On the one hand, I have free will and am thus truly the first efficient cause of my action, the originating cause that is wholly new. My action has being, and my free will is its cause. If free will is not, man is not. On the other hand, divine causality means that God is the first efficient cause of every being, including my choice. Since God is the first, totally self-sufficient cause of every existent, then God is the cause of my being, of the being of my action, of the being of the circumstances of my action, of the being of my deliberations, and of the being of the movement itself of my will, for each of these is indeed a being, either substantial or accidental. It is not that God contributes some being, and I contribute some being. God is the efficient cause of all being. If Divine Causality is not, God is not. The deliberations of Philosophy herself have brought her to inescapable dilemma: to deny either statement of the pair, *viz.* "My will is the efficient cause of my action" and "God is the efficient cause of my action," is impossible, for each is a necessary conclusion arrived at by the autonomous science of philosophy. But it is beyond the power of reason to harmonize these two truths, to put them both together and understand how they both can both be true. Philosophy's necessary arguments for the causality of the creature on the one hand and of the creator on the other have led to mystery.[14]

Philosophy reaches mystery, and so realizes that although she is autonomous in principles and methods, she is not without dependence on another, higher wisdom if her longing for truth is to be achieved. "Mystery" does not mean "stop thinking philosophically." Reason can continue to reflect on the mystery, because its parts are individually open to philosophic understanding: free will, God's existence, and causality among creatures can all be understood in greater depth. Ultimately, however, philosophy cannot achieve the harmonizing or synthesizing of these "parts" of truth. That harmony is what remains ultimately impossible to reason and naturally mysterious. The metaphysical reflections, for example, of philosophers from Parmenides through Thomas Aquinas, and Boethius himself was noteworthy among these, show the increasing depth of understanding possible as we reflect on the relation of creature to creator. Boethius' discussion of participation in the *Consolation* and the *Quomodo substantiae (De hebdomadibus)* sheds great philosophic light on our question.[15] But finally Parmenides is right: how there can be any being other than the divine being is mysterious to reason (although he was wrong that there is, therefore, no beings other than Being Itself).

Reason cannot account for the mystery of "creatureliness." My point is not that philosophy could perhaps someday resolve the mystery with further study; and it is not that reason is denied an answer because it is denied data. My point is that philosophy by nature, by philosophy's methods and conclusions, has encountered reality "beyond philosophy." It has encountered natural, and not properly theological, mystery.

Let us consider this notion of mystery by comparing it with paradox and contradiction. All three words refer to reason's recognition that it has arrived at two assertions that seemingly both cannot be true. In a paradox, e.g., I am there and I am not there, reason by her own natural powers can discern how both assertions can be true (e.g., I am there in spirit but not in body). In a contradiction reason by her own, natural powers can discern that both assertions cannot be true, e.g., this figure is a square and this figure is a circle. But in a mystery reason discerns by her own natural powers that both assertions must necessarily be true even though it is impossible for reason to understand how both can be true. Reason discerns that it will take a wisdom higher than reason to comprehend the unity of the two truths; for reason herself they remain two truths whose unity is unfathomable. Reason discerns that it is reasonable for reason to affirm that a wisdom higher than reason exists which can harmonize the two truths and see them in their unity.[16] "At the summit of its searching, reason acknowledges that it cannot do without what faith presents" (*Fides et Ratio*, §42)

At the end of the *Consolation of Philosophy*, philosophy has consoled Boethius. But philosophy, and the philosopher within Boethius, is left with mystery and thus is left in need of consolation. Reason's natural desire for ultimate, harmonized truth cannot be achieved by reason; philosophy is left with a natural, self-generated longing for what she cannot herself achieve, wisdom beyond reason. *Fides et Ratio* says,

> The desire for knowledge is so great and it works in such a way that the human heart, despite its experience of insurmountable limitation, yearns for the infinite riches which lie beyond, knowing that there is to be found the satisfying answer to every question as yet unanswered (§17).

What place, then, does the *Consolation of Philosophy* have in the works of Boethius, the Christian philosopher? Boethius is in jail because of his political life, and he engaged in politics by the prompting of philosophy, so that the rulers might be philosophers. It is upon philosophy, therefore, that he calls for his consolation, and philosophy does console him to a point.[17] But by her own power of reasoning philosophy penetrates to a mystery deeper than natural reason can fathom, and it is at that point that the philosopher recognizes the need for a higher wisdom than natural reason. That wisdom is the wisdom of Christianity, the wisdom of Christ, the wisdom of Boethius' *opuscula sacra*. Boethius does writes a Christian consolation, but not a theological consolation. He has already written those. He writes the work he had not yet written, of the philosophic soul's inchoate longing for the wisdom that revelation knows to be Christ.

There is no implicit or potential knowledge of Christ in philosophy, such that philosophy could hope to deduce or even guess at the wisdom which would fulfill her longing for the ultimate harmonizing of truth.[18] The philosopher who is Christian, however, sees by the faith he holds from the Holy Spirit that faith does fulfill his philosophic longings better than any other explanation the philosopher has ever heard. Questions still remain, but the answers so far as they are understood are satisfying in ways that other answers are not, even though philosophy *qua* philosophy grasps these answers only as matters of opinion. They are reasonable to philosophy, not reasoned to by philosophy.[19]

There are, I propose, several such "natural philosophic mysteries," some of which are raised in Boethius' *Consolation of Philosophy* and some of which are not. Let me give some very briefly stated examples. In Aristotelian-Thomistic philosophy, for example, it can be demonstrated that the human soul is immortal but also that the soul is naturally ordered to union with the body. How can reason reconcile these two demonstrated conclusions? Also, we by nature are ordered to knowledge of all of being, to the answering of every "why?" (the receptive intellective power is the power that becomes *all things*), and yet we by nature cannot know God, the ultimate being and "answer." Can we have been made with a natural desire that by our nature cannot be fulfilled? Also, there is injustice in the world and yet there is a creator of a world with injustice in it. This creates a dilemma or mystery not so much of divine causality of evil as of divine toleration of any evil at all. Philosophy has much it can say to shed light on these propositions and their relations to one another, but ultimately they each represent an area of philosophic mystery, two demonstratively true propositions which reason knows must be reconcilable but which reason by nature cannot harmonize. Reason therefore reasonably holds that there is a higher wisdom than reason by which the harmony is accomplished.

The philosopher examines the teachings of the religions of the world not with the eyes of faith but as opinions which merit his consideration. The philosopher cannot help but note that the Christian religion alone among religions of the world acknowledges these mysteries as the philosopher sees them, affirming in each case both assertions that constitute the mystery and promising their reconciliation. To the rational mystery of creator and creature, Christianity gives witness to Christ, two unmixed natures, creator and creature, united in one person. To the mysteries of the separated human soul and the limits of its knowledge, Christianity reveals the resurrection of the body and the beatific vision. To the mystery of evil in the world, Christianity testifies to the way of the cross and the Lord's resurrection and ascension. For the philosopher, Christian revelation is only opinion. But they are opinions, I would argue, that are speak in a way that other religions do not to the philosopher's conclusions and experience of philosophic mystery.

Conclusion

What I give is a possible explanation of why the historical person, Boethius, wrote such a consolation of philosophy. Other explanations are possible, especially that Boethius wanted to make one more contribution to philosophy. Perhaps this was his way of showing the reconciliation of Platonic and Aristotelian philosophy to which his larger project of translation and commentary was dedicated. There is nothing anti-Christian in the text, and one might argue that Boethius' fears were natural human fears that could be naturally resolved. Such a reason to write philosophy would certainly be a legitimate use of philosophy by the man of faith, as I think *Fides et Ratio* shows. If one were to take the position, however, that Boethius meant philosophy's consolation to be the only consolation possible or to be a completely sufficient consolation for the human condition, then Boethius would in the last months of his life be denying his Christianity.[20] However, it seems to me that the text does not support this exaggerated assertion about philosophy's consolation.

Philosophy is an autonomous science because it has its own proper principles and methods. It is a natural wisdom ordered to a higher wisdom, revealed truth. The *Consolation of Philosophy* is a philosophical text, but I am arguing that Boethius' text shows us that philosophic wisdom can know its own insufficiency, its own need for a wisdom higher than itself. Philosophy consoles but in the end knows itself to be in need of consolation. The demonstrations of divine causality and of human causality (free will) bring philosophy to natural mystery, two conclusions which must be true and so must be harmonized, but whose harmony is beyond philosophy's natural power to conceive. Reason reasonably concludes to the existence of a wisdom higher than reason. Philosophy is both consoling and consoled. The harmony and union of creator and creature, longed for by philosophy but unimaginable by her, is witnessed in the Incarnation and shared in most intimately by us in the Beatific Vision. The subsuming of evil under the plan of divine love is realized in the Resurrection and shared in by our resurrection, body and soul. These revealed truths are not known by philosophy, but they are her consolation in the person of the Christian philosopher. "Reason cannot eliminate the mystery of love which the cross represents, while the cross can give to reason the ultimate answer which it seeks" (*Fides et Ratio*, §23). Although

Philosophy does not know it of herself, it is known to the man who lives in grace that the philosophical man in each of us may find consolation in the Triumph of the Cross.

Notes

1 "Philosophy" here should be taken as Plato, Aristotle, Boethius, Thomas Aquinas, *et al.* mean it, that is, philosophy capable of causal arguments which can demonstrate some truths about material and immaterial reality. Thus, the term as used here is narrower than its common use and corresponds roughly to what I take *Fides et Ratio* to be indicating is a realist philosophy, which can know truths about both material and immaterial reality.

2. In the summer of 1978, the late John M. Crossett, pointed out to me the possibility of understanding *Philosophiae* in the title of Boethius' work as both objective and subjective genitive. I also owe to him the distinction of "paradox," "contradiction," and "mystery" employed below.

3. See Owen Chadwick, *Boethius: The Consolations of Music, Logic, Theology, and Philosophy* (Oxford: Clarendon Press, 1981), pp. 1–68.

4. Ralph M. McInerny, *Boethius and Aquinas* (Washington, D.C.: The Catholic University of America Press, 1990), p. 16.

5. Alksandr I. Sozhenitsyn, *The Gulag Archipelago: 1918–1956*, trans. Thomas P. Whitney (New York: Harper and Row, 1974), p. 3.

6. Sozhenitsyn, *The Gulag Archipelago*, p. 3.

7. This point is very persuasively made by D. F. Duclow: "men find consolation in a turn to the divine center. As this vision becomes clearer and more forceful Boethius is progressively healed." Donald F. Duclow, "Perspective and Therapy in Boethius' *Consolation of Philosophy*," *The Journal of Medicine and Philosophy* 4 (1979), p. 343.

8. For a discussion of the consolations by philosophy, which have the ultimate goal of reconciling Boethius to the order of things, see John Haldane, "*De Consolatione Philosophiae*," in *Philosophy, Religion, and the Spiritual Life*, ed. Michael McGhee (Cambridge: Cambridge University Press, 1992), pp. 31–45. Haldane notes that there are "several forms of philosophical consolation, and it is important to see that while these overlap (to some extent), they also draw upon two distinct traditions, *Stoicism* and *neo-Platonism*, and differ in their metaphysical commitments and practical implications" (p. 36, author's emphasis). Given Haldane's identification of Boethius' initial error as "a double error: identifying the self with the embodying organism, and reality with the sensible world" (p. 35), perhaps there is not conflict but progression (dialectical to demonstrative) from Stoic to neo-Platonic arguments.

9. Boethius, *Consolation of Philosophy* III, pr. 10. 80–90; cf. I, pr. 4. 143–45. This and all subsequent quotations are taken from the Loeb Boethius. *The Theological Tractates [and] The Consolation of Philosophy,* trans. H.F. Stewart and E. K. Rand, rev. S. J. Tester (Cambridge, MA: Harvard University Press, 1973).

10. *Consolation* II, m. 7. 27–30. On the neo-Platonic background of this notion, see C. J. De Vogel, *"Amor Quo Caelum Regitur,"* *Vivarium* 1 (1963), pp. 2–34.

11. *Consolation* III, pr. 10.

12. *Consolation* IV, pr. 6.

13. *Consolation* IV, pr. 1. 5–19 (my emphasis).

14. Gerard Verbeke refers to the limitations of philosophic knowledge in discussing the problem of "the coexistence of the finite and the infinite" and points out that "[i]n his commentary on Aristotle's *Peri Hermeneias,* Thomas Aquinas wonders if divine causality, which is integral, is not incompatible with human liberty." Cf. G. Verbeke, "Philosophy and Theology," in *New Themes in Christian Philosophy,* ed. Ralph M. McInerny (Notre Dame, IN: University of Notre Dame Press, 1968), pp. 129–51. In his discussion which follows, Verbeke notes that "Gods causality belongs to another order; it cannot express itself by means of categories which translate the relations [*viz.* necessary or contingent] of the finite beings among themselves." This distinction seems the same as what I mean as a "the radical difference in kind" between the rationality of philosophy and the wisdom of God. Because God's wisdom does not deny the rationality He Himself has made, philosophy is possible; but philosophical rationality sees its own limits and its dependence for the ultimate synthesis and harmonizing of even philosophic truth on a wisdom higher than reason. This is the distinction between the two kinds of revealed truths in Thomas Aquinas's *Summa theologiae* (I. 1. 1). I would suggest that one possible reason the greatest pagan minds mixed even their properly philosophical reflections on God with "much error" was because the mind naturally recoils from mystery when it has no reason to hope for mystery's resolution. Perhaps that is one reason that Aristotle was so unclear on the immortality of the human soul, because he could not account for the soul's happiness and fulfillment by its natural powers alone. Cf. *Fides et Ratio,* §73. For the discussion of divine causality and human liberty referred to by Verbeke, see Thomas Aquinas, *In Libros Peri Hermeneias Expositio,* Bk. I, lect. 14, nn. 8–24, esp. 17–18. Note that Thomas refers in this text to the distinction of Divine and created being in order to refute those who say philosophy can demonstrate the impossibility of true secondary causality; he does not, for all that, explain philosophically the mystery of creation. Cf. also *Fides et Ratio* §12 and 13.

15. See McInerny, *Boethius and Aquinas*, pp. 199–247.

16. In his discussion of divine foreknowledge and human free will, Boethius refers to Intelligence (e.g., *Consolation* V, pr. 5. 13–18), and this is what I am calling "Divine Wisdom." He speaks of Intelligence as beyond the limits of human reason, as God's being is beyond the limits of human being. My position is that as the dialogue progresses we learn something more about reason and intelligence: that reason knows itself to have encountered by its natural powers mystery, and reason has a reasonable hope that divine intelligence can provide consolation for philosophy by harmonizing what philosophy knows she herself by her natural powers cannot harmonize but which must finally be harmonized, namely divine and creaturely causality.

17. Andrew Belsey notes the appropriateness of Boethius' turning to philosophy to get him out of a fix she got him into (since it is philosophy who concludes that societies will be well governed only when philosophers are rulers). In general, Belsey's thought-provoking study brings out well the notion of tension in the *Consolation of Philosophy*, although I think many of the tensions Belsey finds are ones arising from his own conception of philosophy rather than from Boethius'. A. Belsey, "Boethius and the *Consolation of Philosophy*, Or, How to Be a Good Philosopher," *Ratio* 4 (1991), pp. 1–15.

18. Haldane argues that the consolation philosophy offers is that of "uniting oneself with the real, of coming to be at one with things – not, as mystics have often claimed, at one with everything, the totality itself being conceived of, in Parmenidean style as a unity, but united with each thing as one contemplates it for what it is." J. Haldane, "*De Consolatione Philosophiae*," p. 43. I certainly agree that intellectual fulfillment in this life can be explained in this way. But philosophy can be aware of our natural desire for a much higher degree of fulfillment. Our intellects are only fulfilled when we grasp the *non*-Parmenidean All, God as God, face to face, and grasp also his creatures' relation to him.

19. "Of itself, philosophy is able to recognize the human being's ceaselessly self-transcendent orientation toward the truth; and, with the assistance of faith, it is capable of accepting the 'foolishness' of the cross. . . . Here [*viz.*, in the preaching of Christ crucified and risen] we see not only the border between reason and faith, but also the space where the two may meet." *Fides et Ratio*, §23.

20. There seems no evidence of apostacy by Boethius, and the local Christian cult that developed after his death makes the conclusion implausible and unjustified, it seems to me.

Faith, Reason, and Logic
Roger Pouivet

As everybody knows, Pope John Paul II is Polish. In his encyclical, *Fides et Ratio*, he renews the recommendations of Pope Leon XIII in favor of Thomas Aquinas's philosophy and theology. He quotes a number of Thomists, among them Jacques Maritain and Etienne Gilson; but, perhaps curiously, the Polish Pope does not speak about a very interesting group of Polish Thomists, often referred to as the Cracow Circle. The fact that the philosophical background of John Paul II is mainly phenomenological, and that the members of the Cracow Circle were not phenomenologists, constitutes only an anecdotal explanation of this omission. Probably the main reason for it is simply that the encyclical is not meant to be a philosophical study, and the Pope isn't trying to give an overview of a philosophical topic to be published in an encyclopedia; he is merely concerned to convey the doctrine of the Church. Nevertheless, I think that it may prove interesting to examine the Cracow Circle's Thomistic stand on the subject of faith and reason. I shall maintain that it reflects a serious confusion between rationality and logic, despite my view that the Cracow Circle numbered among its members several excellent, and important, philosophers. I will first talk briefly about the Cracow Circle, because I am not sure that it is very well known. I will then present a critique of the general project of this group, although I will be unable to enter into much detail.

The Cracow Circle is part of the so-called Lvov-Warsaw School. The Lvov-Warsaw School was initiated by the Polish philosopher Kazimierz Twardowski at the end of the nineteenth century. Twardowski was strongly influenced by, and was in fact a former student of, Brentano. Like many Austrian philosophers, Brentano considered it essential to study Aristotle and Thomas Aquinas. Jan Lukasiewicz studied with Twardowski in Lvov. The method they developed was built around anti-irrationalism, rigorous argumentation, the formulation of precise concepts and a thorough knowledge of the history of philosophy, especially Aristotelian philosophy.

When Poland was rebuilt after the First World War, Lukasiewicz began to teach at the University of Warsaw, where it had become possible to lecture in Polish, and not, as previously, only in Russian. Lukasiewicz transported the methodology of the Lvov Department of Philosophy to Warsaw, with an added commitment to the essential role of logic.

The Lvov-Warsaw School was the major influence within Polish philosophy between the two world wars, and its influence persisted even after political circumstances became inimicable to philosophy. Among the distinguished philosophers of this school are Tadeusz Kotarbinski, who was closely studied by the English philosopher Peter Geach, and Alfred Tarski, who is perhaps the best known philosopher in this group. I think also that Quine's sojourn in Warsaw during this period had a very strong influence on his thought and that through him the ideas of the Lvov-Warsaw School were subtly osmosed into a large part of so-called analytic philosophy.

During the thirties, a new trend developed within the Lvov-Warsaw School, due to the special influence of Lukasiewicz. Lukasiewicz was a Roman Catholic. He thought that the anti-metaphysical materialism of Carnap and the Vienna Circle had nothing to do with the application of logic to the investigation of traditional metaphysical problems. He also strongly rejected the Kantian anti-realistic influence and its main consequences. Lukasiewicz's project was not the rejection of metaphysics, but its revision. In his way of applying logical methods to questions of metaphysics he was rather close to Leibniz. Of course, this is a very scholastic approach. But Lukasiewicz believed that the contemporary logic of his time provided new techniques for dealing with metaphysical problems. He encouraged the work of two young priests, Jan Salamucha and Josef Bochenski, the well-known Blackfriars, and two young logicians, strongly Catholic, Jan Drewnowski and B. Sobocinski. Together, during the Third Polish Conference of Philosophy in Cracow, held in 1936, they officially founded the Cracow Circle.

In a unpublished paper entitled "Tradycja myli katolickiej a ciso [*The Tradition of Catholic Thought and Exactness*]," Rev. Bochenski said:

> From the beginning, Catholic thought has been characterised by a tendency for a maximum precision. If modern formal logic has tools which, for their exactness, overcome physics and mathematics, then Catholic Philosophy should use those tools, achieving in such a way St. Thomas Aquinas, who developed his system on an axiomatic basis.

The program of the Cracow Circle is here clearly stated: to be Catholic philosophers in the spirit of Aquinas, but to use the modern tools given by post-Fregean logic. In a particular way, the philosophers of the Cracow Circle wanted to conjoin *faith, reason* and *logic*.

It must be said that such a program was not welcomed by the Catholic authorities in Poland in the thirties, especially by philosophers and theologians of the Catholic universities of Lublin and of Cracow. Indeed, the program was conceived of as a *virus logisticum* with respect to Catholic thought. Drewnowski felt obliged to say: "The effect of that misunderstanding is, generally speaking, a very low scientific level of the contemporary philosophy elaborated by the Catholics, in comparison with the leading position in St. Thomas's times."

Jan Salamucha's paper on the *ex motu* proof for the existence of God provides a good example of what the members of the Cracow Circle were trying to do. He formalized Aquinas's proof using quantificational logic and the theory of relations. The intent is very clear: to improve traditional proofs and to show that and how they can be expressed in the language of contemporary logic. As Thomists, the work of the Cracow Circle focused mainly on *a posteriori* proofs, like the *ex motu* proof. We may remark that the much more recent work of Alvin Plantinga on the ontological proof and the problem of evil, even if not inspired by Thomistic thought, is in very much the same spirit.

During the war, the activity of the Cracow Circle of course stopped. Salamucha, like many professors of the Jagellionian University, was killed by the Nazis and Rev. Bochenski fought in the Polish army. After the war, Sobocinski rejoined Bochenski at the University of Notre Dame, in the United States, and worked as a "pure" logician. And after the war, of course, nothing like the Cracow Circle could possibly exist in Poland.

I do not think that when John Paul II criticizes "rationalism" in his encyclical, *Fides et Ratio*, his target includes the kind of reconstruction of traditional proofs and arguments proposed by the members of the Cracow Circle. He is concerned rather with scientism (as described in the §88 of the encyclical) and also, I suppose, with the Hegelian-inspired idealism which seeks to transform faith and its contentincluding the Mystery of the death and resurrection of the Christinto rationally conceivable dialectical structures (§46). The Cracow Circle's program in the philosophy of religion clearly concerns the relation between faith and reason; but nothing indicates that Bochenski, Drewnowski or Salamucha thought that it was possible or necessary to provide a logical foundation for religious faith. Remember, (they were Thomists!) Ryszard Puciato said, "it is not possible to formalize the internal structure of being, because logic grasps only the external relations of being." It could hardly have been the goal of the Polish analytical Thomists to formalize the internal structure of being, especially if this were to imply trying to give a formal account of the existence of God. On the contrary, they simply tried to present traditional proofs in a way that would give them greater strength. Logic, for them, was conceived as an *ancilla theologiae*.

What seems to me problematic in the program of the Cracow Circle is the identification of *rigor* with *logical formalism*. My criticism is akin to that which Wittgenstein directed against the Cantorian theory of sets. Wittgenstein remarked that even if Cantor's theory provides a relevant calculus, it doesn't explain at all what the Cantorian means when he speaks about the infinite. Successful formalizations do not necessarily protect us from conceptual confusion; a calculus may work even in the presence of such confusion. For me, this means that *analytical* cannot be identified with *formal.*

While this should not deter anyone from attempting to parse traditional proofs in the best possible logical form, using contemporary tools, it implies that by "reason," in the expression "faith and reason," we have to understand something different than a simple formalization of arguments. A formal argument is never a reason to believe something. Logic says absolutely nothing about the *reasons* we have for believing in the truth of any proposition; and even a logical rule like *modus ponens* cannot force someone to *accept* that a given proposition follows from certain premises.

I explained earlier that the Cracow Circle developed under the influence of the Lvov-Warsaw School, and most especially of Lukasiewicz. A central commitment of that School was the anti-psychologism initiated by Frege. It would take a long time to discuss this question fully, but I think that propositions are human intentional thoughts, and that we can therefore not subscribe to an unbounded anti-psychologism. Why must we adopt a rule like *modus ponens?* Logical analysis doesn't answer this. The reason why we place confidence in such rules is not that they have been proven logically, but that they are basic, entrenched instruments of our thought. In fact, even Lukasiewicz recognized that logical reasons do not provide the strongest motive for believing something; and perhaps Wittgenstein meant to indicate something of the kind when he declared that we follow a rule *blindly.*

I am not here preaching anti-rationalism or *fideism,* whose condemnation by the Church is renewed in the encyclical (§52). I simply think that the error of the Cracow Circle was to conceive of the philosophy of religion as a field independent from philosophical psychology of the sort that can be found in the works of Aquinas and that has been taken very seriously in recent times by Anscombe, Geach, Kenny, McInerny and Haldane, among others.

I have no time to enter into much detail concerning the relation between the proofs of the existence of God, belief and will. And this is a very difficult question especially in the philosophy and theology of Aquinas. I can simply say that even if a proof does not of course depend of our assent the conclusion follows the premises without any supplementary act of belief the logic in itself says nothing concerning the reasons we have to believe in certain premises or to believe in the truth of conclusions that follows logically these premises. This is what a purely logical examination of traditional proofs leaves aside; but it is not certain that those proofs can be rightly understood if this aspect is not taken into account. This question of the credibility of the premises is epistemological and requires a good philosophical psychology. Perhaps is it the weakness of the Cracow Circle account to segregate, at least so it seems, questions of logic and questions of epistemology? More generally, as Geach has put it: "*Credo et intelligam*; without an initial venture of faith the mysteries remain permanently opaque; once that venture has been made, they more and more enlighten and strengthen the mind that contemplates them."[1] The members of the Cracow Circle would surely have agreed concerning the role that must be played by something else than logical rules, especially by one could be called the "noetic of faith," in a Christian religious life. Nevertheless, the way in which they studied traditional proofs focusing upon their logical features *independently of the way such proofs must be understood in the larger context of religious life* lends itself to a caricature of religious belief in the existence of God. It is not clear that the way the traditional proofs work can be properly explained without any reference to a psychological philosophy of faith (and even of the intervention of grace). Nicholas Wolterstorff says: "God wills that we do what we ought to do. When a theist believes nonrationally, he acts in violation of the very will of the very God in whom he believes unless it be the case that there are extenuating circumstances."[2] For Wolterstorff, it seems that our duty is to believe rationally because we *are* rational creatures. So, God wants us to believe rationally; but if rationality were to be reduced to logic, there would be no *epistemological* place for the virtue of faith (which is not a logical attitude), and surely God does not want that. Perhaps chapter 6 of the First Book of the *Summa contra Gentiles* ("That to give assent to the truths of faith is not foolishness even though they are above reason") could also be understanding in this way. Rationality cannot be limited to the respect of logical rules in the demonstration of the *preambles of faith*. The members of the Cracow Circle never said that such preambles are exclusively a question of pure logic, but it seems to me that they were tempted to isolate the question of the proofs from the question of the rationality of religious belief in a broader sense. They were led to a sort of *formalism* in the question of religious rationality.

This is the deep difficulty in the philosophical project of the Cracow Circle. A logical study of the traditional proofs, or of analogy, is surely a very good thing. But such a study cannot be completely detached from a broader approach, including the question of faith and its relation to reason it is, I think, what the encyclical reminds us. Perhaps the difficulty of the Cracow Circle account of the traditional proofs is that it separates theses proofs from the central question of the relation between *fides* and *ratio*. The rationality of belief is an *epistemological* subject whose treatment must include a philosophy of human spirituality; it is not matter that can be treated by purely *logical* means.

Notes

1. P. Geach, *The Virtues* (Cambridge: Cambridge University Press, 1971), p. 41.

2. N. Wolterstorff, "Can Belief in God be Rational?" in *Faith and Rationality*, eds. A. Plantinga and N. Woterstorff (Notre Dame, IN: University of Notre Dame Press, 1993), p. 156.

Faith and Reason: Aquinas's Two Strategies
Cyrille Michon

Fides et Ratio is an encyclical concerned mainly with philosophy. It is not a philosophical text, and it contains no discursive argument. But it enunciates and defends many theses, concerning the powers of reason, and so of philosophy, which are not broadly accepted nowadays. They are very similar, if not identical, with Aquinas's views, which are also not broadly accepted. This seems to be a problem for both, and for one who engages himself in philosophy while trying to be faithful to the Catholic Magisterium.

The encyclical contains at least three modes of speech. One is descriptive of the present situation in philosophy and theology, and of the history of the links between faith and reason. One is parenetic and gives advice, most of them positive: encouragements to philosophers, scientists and theologians. And one is evaluative and gives an appreciation of the different forms taken by those speculative disciplines. To my mind, the second mode of speech is the most original. I would just like to single out the emphasis laid on the climate of friendship the Holy Father asks philosophers, and specially Christian philosophers, to create in their debates (§33),[1] because this is precisely what Ralph McInerny allows us to do during these days. But the third mode of speech is certainly the most important: description leads to evaluation, and counsels derive from it. It is also the most delicate, because an authoritative voice seems to enter the field of free rational inquiry.

I would like to comment on the two uses of reason related to faith that are recommended by the Pope, which are also those defended by Aquinas. And so I would like to discuss in some way the presence of Thomism in the encyclical. I will focus on what I have called Aquinas's two strategies. This will need a first step in which I try to summarize what he says about faith that seems to me to be relevant in that perspective. I will then make some comments on *Fides et Ratio* and Aquinas.

I

"What we believe we owe to authority, what we know (understand) we owe to reason."[2] Augustine's slogan is hardly avoidable. Though he welcomes the distinction,[3] it is not on this Augustinian formula that Aquinas dwells in order to define what it is to believe. It is a pity because, first, this is a crucial distinction: that of the bases on which something is accepted. We *know* 'that p' in virtue of the meaning of 'p,' or of *what* 'p' says, and, eventually, of our direct, sensible knowledge of the world and/or of other known propositions. But we *believe* 'that p' on the basis of *who* says 'that p.' It is the identity of the sayer, not the content of what is said, which is now the ground for accepting 'p.' As such, the distinction is not one between religious belief, or faith, and reason, but it opposes two propositional attitudes, belief and knowledge. And religious belief can only be seen as a subspecies of belief so defined. But, when he engages himself in the task of defining religious belief, Aquinas does not go that way, and religious belief does not appear as a kind of belief.

In fact, Aquinas has tried to justify two well known definitions of religious belief: one of the act of *credere*, and one of the *habitus*, and in that case virtue, of faith, *fides*. Following another Augustinian formula he defines *credere*, as *cum assentione cogitare*.[4] This definition presupposes a distinction between the act of cogitating or, more precisely, of *considering*[5] some (propositional) content and the act of *assenting* to it. On the basis of the distinction between consideration of a content and assent to it, he distributes different propositional attitudes:[6] (1) In doubting, the intellect considers a content, but is not inclined to assent or to dissent.[7] (2) The intellect may be more inclined to assent than to dissent, without being totally determined, and this can be (2.1) because it has only light motives, which is the case of suspicion, or (2.2) because of the fear that the other part of the contradiction be the good (true) one, which is the case of opinion.[8] (3) The intellect can also be totally determined to one part of the contradiction, but the determination can be provoked (3.1) by the content to which one assent, or (3.2) by the will. In the first case, the assent can be prompted (3.1.1) immediately, by the very fact of understanding the terms out of which it is composed, as in the evidence of the first principles ("the whole is greater than the part"), and Thomas calls it intelligence (*intellectus*), or (3.1.2) mediately, if the content considered as to be refered to others which will function as premises for this content as consequence. Such a disposition is called science. Finally (3.2), the assent is not prompted by consideration of the content alone, nor with consideration of other contents. The investigation of reason goes on without finding sufficient motives. If assent is given this must be because of a motion of the will. And Thomas adds that the will moves because one finds some convenience or utility in such an assent. We have here the act of *credere*, sharply distinguished from all others.[9]

Nothing in the definition points towards a religious content, that of Christian revelation, nor towards any divine intervention in the process of believing. Nonetheless, Thomas seems to say that *credere* so defined in a purely psychological way is the act of religious belief. Perhaps he would maintain that non-religious beliefs can always be counted as instances of what he calls "opinion." That would have as a consequence that there would be no assent totally determined to a false content, e.g. Noah's firm opinion that the rain has ceased, while it is still raining. And it would also imply that no opinion (in Thomas's sense) could be motivated by will, e.g., there could be no such thing as Noah's opinion that the rain has ceased being caused by his desire that it be the case. Perhaps we should take those criteria (total determination and motivation by the will) as forming a conjunction which is in itself defining (necessary and sufficient) but whose elements are not when taken separately. But this would go against Thomas's own words.

That Thomas has been speaking of the religious act of believing is shown by what follows: he then introduces *fides*, as the *habitus* whose acts are acts of *credere*.[10] Thomas knows that there are grounds for calling "faith" a disposition to believe others with reference to non-religious contents. This "human faith" is indispensable to social life, and is manifested in promises, testimonies and so on. But that is not what he will call "faith." Faith is defined in Hebrews (11:1): *substantia rerum sperandarum, argumentum non apparentium*, and Thomas adds that this is a *completissima diffinitio*,[11] though an obscure one.[12] This time, the content of what is believed is part of the definition, and it can be shown that those hoped things are the matter of Christian revelation. Thomas shows also how the distinct notes of the definition make faith being different of science and intelligence (which do not bear on what is not appearing), of opinion and doubt (which do not rely on any kind of *argumentum*), and from human or common faith, which does not bear on what one hopes.

But this definition still does not mention any necessary divine intervention and does not make it clear, for example, that faith as a virtue is also a gift and that man is unable to believe without God's grace. Thomas could answer that those precisions are true but unnecessary to single out faith from the other propositional dispositions, as they were not necessary to single out the act of *credere* from the other propositional acts. It seems to me that he nevertheless introduces those characteristics when it is useful. In particular, he must add that in faith (disposition or acts) the assent we give to the particular content is due to a certain light, *lumen quoddam*, which is the *habitus fidei*, divinely infused in our minds.[13] This *habitus*, or *lumen fidei*, coming from God, as a *sigillatio primae veritatis in mente*, does not move *per viam intellectus* but more *per viam voluntatis*: it does not make us *see* the truth, as in intellectual evidence, but it makes us *assent* to it, *voluntarie*, without compelling our will. We can thus gather all the elements which seem to be necessary for a complete and clear definition of faith: this is a virtuous disposition to assent to a propositional content referring to things, hoped for in which the intellect is moved by the will, and the will by God's grace.[14] I do not want to quarrel Aquinas here but only underline some difficulties that appear when the first Augustinian distinction is lost of sight, and when the habitus of faith and its proper act of *credere* are not referred to the genre "belief" more than to the genre "knowledge" or "science."[15]

We must admit two components of faith, and a twofold divine origin of faith:[16] 1) The objective component is the content of Revelation, which comes from God through the prophets, and is accessible to all; it is public and not reserved to the happy few. It has been called, after Aquinas, the *fides quae* (*creditur*). 2) The subjective component is the *habitus* which makes the believer believe this content, and it comes from God who infuses it in each particular believer, so that it is a private gift, and not given to all but to some. This is what Aquinas calls faith, and what has also been called the *fides qua* (*creditur*). Thomas compares this light of faith to the knowledge of principles: both are infused, but the second in all human beings, the first in some only. And he compares the *fides quae*, the contents proposed to our acceptance, to the sensible evidences: *fides* is *ex auditu*. Both elements are needed, in human knowledge, sensible experience and light of first principles, in faith, the content revealed and the infused habitus. Considerations of the Christian existence, of the faith as virtue, as informed by charity, as an encounter between man and God, or between man and Christ, are certainly all the more important, from our and from God's point of view. But it is inescapable that there is no sense in the idea of the light of faith given to someone, without a content to be believed. Faith, in the subjective sense, is said to be man's response to God's revelation faith in the objective sense. The *fides qua* presupposes the *fides quae*.

This content can be, and has been, summed up in formulas. They are the articles of faith. The shortest list consists in two parts: God's existence and His Providence, or the divinity and Christ's humanity.[17] We recognize here the Greek terms of *theologia* and *oikonomia*. Of course, the well known symbols of the faith proposed by the Church to our profession can also be considered as a perfect summary of the *fides quae*.[18] But we can also include all dogmatic definitions, and all the content of the Scripture. To all those contents we can assent by the *virtue* of faith. But in order to assent, we must be able to consider, and understand *prima facie* what those articles *mean*. So faith presupposes reason. Only a rational being can be a believer. Only one who understands the content of the *fides quae* can receive the habitus of the *fides qua*. What may be controversial is the space left to reason which is apart from being a capacity to understand the revealed words and articles. We have seen that in faith, the basis on which the content on the *fides quae* is accepted is authority. Were it not authority, there would be no more faith. That is why faith disappears with vision, and that is why, for Aquinas, there is no faith where we have science. Believed (*creditum*) is opposed to seen (*visum*) as well as to known (*scitum*).[19]

II

Here we come to the announced two strategies. In a famous quodlibetal question disputed during Aquinas's second parisian teaching in 1271, being asked whether the theologian should use only authority in theological disputes, Thomas answers with making a distinction between two kinds of disputes. One kind of dispute, addressed to non-believers, is given the scope of answering *an sit*. It must establish the fact of the matter, *quia est*. The master can and even must use all authorities available. But when disputing with a non-believer, one may use only those authorities accepted by both sides. Some accept the whole Bible, some only one of the two Testaments, and some no textual authority at all so that only natural reason can be used.[20] The second kind of dispute, one found in theological schools where the master addresses those who already believe, pursues an understanding of what is believed, an *intellectus fidei*. Authorities are of no use here, they would leave the interlocutors empty.[21] This *intellectus* is reached through the second work of reason we examined earlier. I would now suggest that the two strategies here fit very well with the two comprehensive syntheses of the Catholic faith Thomas wrote.

Aquinas argues that reason is not only presupposed by faith in order to understand the content of Revelation, but that we can also assent to part of the content of Revelation on the basis of reason alone, i.e., certain revealed truths can be known by unaided natural reason. Using mainly Aristotle's achievements, Thomas maintains that part of the *fides quae* can be accepted by the work of natural reason without the virtue of faith. This part of Revelation can be *known* and not *believed*. And for Aquinas, this part is not small: it includes the existence of God, many of His attributes, the spirituality and immortality of the human soul, and a large part of what the Bible says of divine Providence and commandments, in particular the content of the Decalogue. What is not included among these naturally knowable truths are the mysteries of the faith: the Trinity, Incarnation, redemption and sacraments.[22] These articles of faith cannot be established on the basis of reason alone. Only one who accepts the Revelation, and so only one who has been given the *fides qua*, can assent to those articles.[23] But, faced with the content of those articles, reason is not confined merely to accepting them. Two roles for reason are still in place.

The first one is the refutation of all argument that would contradict the content of faith. Because truth is one, there can be no opposition between that

grasped by faith and that grasped by reason.[24] So, an argument that runs contrary to the truths of faith must be unsound, and reason must be able to show
it. This does not mean that reason should be able to establish the denial of the
argument's conclusion, but that it could discover the logical failure in the
inference, or the falsity in the premises, and so the non-necessity of this conclusion. Thomas's position on the question of the eternity of the world is a
case in point: reason cannot establish the truth believed by faith (i.e., that the
world has a beginning), for it is not a necessary but a contingent truth. It can,
however, show that every argument to the contrary is inconclusive.

Additionally, though not in this last case, reason can also give probable
arguments in favor of what is believed.[25] The second use of reason is that of
giving probable arguments and offering analogies, discovering harmonies, the
content of what is believed more acceptable to natural reason. The best example is that of Augustine in the *De Trinitate*. Both uses of reason, offensive and
defensive, so to say, stay within the scope of the first kind of dispute, which
aims at establishing the truth of the matter.

If we recall the first one, concerned with natural truths, we have what
Aquina called the three uses of philosophy in the sacred doctrine.[26] They are
at work in the *Summa contra Gentiles*, also known as the *Book on the Truth
of the Catholic Faith Against the Errors of the Infidels.*[27] And in fact, Thomas
is only concerned with questions intrinsically related to matters of faith. The
book tries to establish the truth and to refute all the errors that have been committed on those points (I. 2, §2). In a text very similar to the one quoted from
the *Quodlibets*, Thomas explains that he will use all kinds of authorities, but
that some interlocutors, the Muslims, do not accept any kind of authority, and
so they will only accept purely rational argumentation (*ibid.* §3). The plan of
the book is clear: Thomas will first establish all the truths that can be reached
by reason alone, and then those that cannot (I. 9, §3). The first part includes
the first three books, and, if Thomas is true to himself, it implies that the content of books I-III is apt to be known rather than believed. I have no space here
to discuss Thomas's fidelity to his plan,[28] but I can offer the following observations: Book III, on Providence, goes very far in attributing to natural reason
the power to establish the necessity of grace for man to reach his end, which
cannot be a natural end, and even the necessity of glory in the afterlife. Not
only that, but Thomas also establishes this necessity for angels (whose existence is not demonstrated but shown to be very convenient).[29] And in moral
matters, he not only argues in favor of the content of the Decalogue, but he
also defends on purely natural grounds the legitimacy and usefulness of religious vows.[30]

The second part of the the *Summa contra Gentiles*, book IV, concerns
establishing the truths contained in Christian Revelation which are unaccessi-
ble to natural reason alone. As previously announced, it will proceed from

authorities, but a brief examination suffices to reveal that Thomas is not only quoting authorities in order to establish those truths. A significant part of Book IV is concerned with the refutation of heresies by rational arguments taking authorities as premises, and as far as possible, authorities that are accepted by the adversary. The bulk of book IV, however, is concerned with arguments for the convenience or "suitability" of revealed truths using established arguments, especially those of the councils, or building new explanations of, for example, the attributes given to Christ according to His two natures (qq. 27–44), the links between the Holy Spirit and the human soul (qq. 20–22), the reasons for not following the Greeks in their restrictive understanding of how to celebrate the Eucharist (qq. 67–69), or the putative qualities of resurrected bodies (qq. 82–89). In so doing, book IV does not engage in the second kind of dispute. The purpose was to establish the truth of the Catholic faith. And it was announced that authority would be used, where reason cannot find the way. But Thomas also said that reason would still be used in order to refute errors and to give probable arguments (I. 9, §3). I take it that book IV still aims at establishing the truth, though reason cannot do more than refute errors or give probable arguments.

Of course, probable arguments in favor of articles of faith also contribute to an understanding of what is believed. This is why a rational argument given in the context of the first kind of dispute may also serve for the second kind. But the difference is one of scope, and I would suggest that the *Summa theologiae* fits more with the second. This last Thomistic synthesis of Christian doctrine is explicitly addressed to beginners in theology, and so to believers.[31] The purpose of the *Summa* is to give them an understanding of what they believe, and not to establish what they believe already. As a matter of fact, the structure of an article in the *Summa*, as we know, firmly distinguishes the argument taken from authority in the *sed contra* from the rational argument in the *corpus*. That is to say, no authority is given as a basis for assent in the body of the article. There, only rational argumentation is in place, and the conclusions of the responses are justified along the lines of this argumentation. This is not to say that the rational argumentation is free from all authorities, but that authorities are invoked implicitly when the argument concerns an article of faith. The premises may be accepted on the basis of authority, but not the conclusions, and so the arguments are not and cannot be arguments of authority. Drawing conclusions from articles which can only be held by faith, reason can establish some necessary consequences, or some necessary links between the articles of faith, in short, different *rationes fidei*, as Anselm called them.[32]

This occurs many times, for example, in the questions on the Trinity in the first part, in the different questions on the gifts of the Holy Spirit in the second part, and in most of the questions of the *Tertia pars*. Though the differences of order between this *Summa* and the *Summa contra Gentiles* may

appear very slight, they are nonetheless significant: the double mode of truth
is no more the main principle of organization, not even a secondary principle.
Of course, Thomas's discourse and arguments are almost the same from one
Summa to the other on many points,[33] but the difference is one of scope and
involves the two kinds of disputes. Revealed truths that are accessible to reason are rationally demonstrated in both *Summas*, e.g., the existence of God.
But in the later *Summa*, it is not a question of *establishing* the otherwise
believed truth that God exists; rather, it is more an exercise of *understanding*
faith which tells us that God exists and that God's existence can be reached
by natural reason. We could say that the *Summa contra Gentiles* uses philosophy (and Aristotelian metaphysics) as a preamble to faith, and as part of theology in order to establish the truth of the Catholic faith.[34] But the *Summa
Theologiae* uses reason (and Aristotelian metaphysics) in order to reach the
intellectus fidei, and this seems to be more a *philosophy of faith*.

If we limit ourselves to the work of reason in order to establish or to
understand the content of faith, we can assimilate Aquinas's two strategies to
the two forms of theology accessible to us. Aquinas often distinguishes two
different modes of the knowledge of God, or of theology in the broad sense
of *sermo de deo*. The first one proceeds from the created world to God, and
the second one proceeds from God to us. This can be directly, as in the case
of the beatific vision, or indirectly, as in the case of divine revelation through
the prophets. We could call the first theology, "natural theology," because it
needs natural reason alone, the second one "glorious theology," because it
needs the light of glory, and the third one "gracious theology," because it
needs the gift of grace.[35] In our present situation, only the first and third theology are available to us. The principal, twofold distinction is thus sufficient,
N. Kretzmann calls them "theology from the bottom up" (natural theology)
and "theology from the top down" (gracious theology). But both theologies
are also forms of rational argument about the most fundamental aspects of
reality. That is why we could also take them as two uses of philosophy, one
strictly limited to natural premises, the other admitting also supernatural
premises. Both argue along the same lines, and with the same philosophical
background, in Thomas's case Aristotelian philosophy.[36]

III

Now, both strategies and theologies are extensively recommended by
Fides et Ratio, whose insistence on the necessity of metaphysics cannot be
underestimated.[37] I remarked at the beginning that this is a very controverted
statement. I would like to ask three questions related to this perfect agreement
between Aquinas and the encyclical, and disagreement of both with so many

others. I will restrict myself to considerations concerning metaphysics within the first strategy, that of "natural theology," because it is presupposed by "gracious theology."

The first question concerns the Thomism of the encyclical. We noted that *Fides et Ratio* does not develop any kind of philosophical argument, and so the question is more that of the coherence with, and the positive evaluation of, St. Thomas's attitude and teachings. The encyclical mentions Thomas's teaching explicitly three times.[38] The last one (§78) offers Aquinas as the best example of the synthesis of faith and reason which respects the legitimate autonomy of both. The first one (§43–45), during the historical survey of the links between faith and reason, gives a place of preeminence to St. Thomas, underlines the same feature, but is much more precise on the role of Aquinas for the use of pagan philosophy in Christian theology; that is to say, one grounded on a conception of nature as accomplished by grace, and of faith as presupposing an exercise of thought, and leading to a form of supernatural knowledge. It also refers to the two kinds of wisdoms, philosophical and theological, distinguished according to the double mode of truth but united by the unity of Truth. This is a true Thomistic point, though not exclusively. Another not exclusively Thomistic point is Aquinas's realism and philosophy of being, to which I will return. Lastly, in the chapter on the interventions of the Magisterium in the philosophical domain, the subsection entitled "The Church's interests for philosophy" (§57–63) recalls the different advice given by this Magisterium in favor of St. Thomas, and more specially of St. Thomas's *philosophy*. It mentions Aquinas's attitude concerning the relation between faith and reason and recalls briefly the role played by this advice in the field of historical studies, in the editions of Aquinas's works, and on the renewal of Thomism and neo-Thomism. Nevertheless, there is a mention of *other forms of Christian philosophies*, without precise references, but with the label of "the great tradition of the Christian thought in the unity of faith and reason" (§59).

At this point, we could conclude that the encyclical makes more references to Aquinas than to any other, though it does not exclude philosophers and theologians coming form other traditions of thought. Aquinas's theses in the fields of philosophy and theology are not canonized, so to say, but his conception on the relation between faith and reason is. However, this conception cannot be totally independent of other philosophical views. And the encyclical not only affirms at length the necessity of the study of philosophy, in the *praeparatio fidei* (§61), but it defends[39] 1) the preeminence of philosophy among the different forms of knowledge, because of its sapiential function, 2) an epistemic realism or doctrine ot objective truth as end of knowledge, and 3) the idea of the metaphysics of being, which can be taken for another formulation of epistemic realism but refers to the ability of the human mind to reach some parts of Revelation such as the existence of God, the immortality and freedom of man, the objectivity and universality of moral values.

If we add to this the fact that philosophy is presented as needed by theology in its investigation of Revelation itself, it appears that Aquinas's two strategies, or two ways of uniting faith and reason, are explicitly reassumed. Of course, epistemic realism and a broad notion of metaphysics are not enough to characterize Aquinas's philosophy. Even Descartes's philosophy would be well adapted to *Fides et Ratio*'s requirements. At that level of description, there is no great difference between Aquinas and Descartes. Both consider that philosophy can reach a part or the revealed truths, and both give to philosophical argumentation a significant place within theology, though they have not developed it at equal length. It would not be so easy to characterize other philosophers among those mentioned explicitly or implicitly by the *Fides et Ratio*. And the fact is that those two theses, on the powers of natural reason in natural and in gracious theology, are now largely denied, outside and inside Christian thought. So I leave here the question of the Thomism of the encyclical, for a more intriguing one: how can the Magisterium enjoin the philosophers to accept any particular thesis, or, from the other point of view: how can a philosopher accept any particular thesis on the basis of authority?

Almost no non-Christian thinkers accept today the thesis of the natural human capacity to reach those truths as God's existence, and the soul's immortality. It is neither possible nor necessary here to give an overview because the encyclical recognizes it (§55 and §61). I think, therefore, that it should be considered as an uncontroversial statement that a great majority of philosophers do not accept Aquinas's and Decartes's conception of the powers of natural reason. Now, for a Christian philosopher, even though, as Christian, he holds as true the assertions of God's existence and of individual immortality, those assertions may not appear philosophically well grounded. Without holding them as false on the basis of rational arguments which would put him in a *double truth* situation, he can profess, and many do profess, *philosophical agnosticism*, while professing also a *firm faith* in those two articles. The first attitude is based on rational considerations only, the second one on authority. Now, there is a problem with the exercise of authority in the way those truths should be reached when this way is natural reason. The rationally agnostic but firmly faithful Christian philosopher could obey the injunction not to profess his philosophical agnosticism. But how could he obey the injunction of reaching rationally, or of accepting on rational grounds only, those truths? How can he accept any kind of rational demonstration, or even any kind of rational understanding, of what he is rationally doubting? And if that is not possible, what sense can it have to make this injunction?

In fact, the encyclical teaches (and so enjoins the reader to believe and profess), that this reaching is possible, but does not say how. The agnostic Christian philosopher is in the following situation: he firmly believes 'that p' (e.g. there is a God), he finds no rational grounds for 'p,' but, following the Magisterium's teaching, he firmly believes that there are such grounds and that, as a rational being, he is able to find them. Should he not ask the Magisterium, who affirms those two points, to show him those grounds? The answer is in the text (§76): it is not the Magisterium's task to tell which argument, nor which philosophy (as a large body of coherent concepts, descriptions and arguments), give the grounds. It only says that there are such grounds, not which are such. And this can be firmly held by faith, without compromising the legitimate autonomy of reason and philosophy.[40] It is only if the Magisterium said that *this* particular argument should be accepted as demonstrative, or as rationally sufficient, that it would introduce authority into philosophy and destroy it.

The Magisterium can only exert authority regarding the acceptance (and public profession) of truths not naturally knowable and so ask for faith. The demand is respectful of natural reason and of the autonomy of philosophy: assent on the basis of authority is faith. What is implied in such a conception is only that faith includes as part of its content that faith and reason cannot oppose themselves. Thus, the Magisterium cannot teach something known as false on rational grounds and neither can reason establish something contrary to what the Magisterium teaches in matters of faith. It is a second-order thesis on the content of faith and the exercise of reason. And this is exactly Aquinas' conception.[41] What is affirmed here is 1) the uniqueness of truth, which can be reached by the way of faith or by the way of reason; 2) the truth of the content of faith; 3) the truth of what reason reaches when it reaches science; and 4) the ability of reason to reach science in those philosophical questions which are put in doubt by the agnostic Christian philosopher.

The agnostic Christian philosopher is not in a situation of contradiction, as long as he truly believes the teaching of *Fides et Ratio* and Aquinas on faith and reason. Many agnostic Christian philosophers are not really looking for rational grounds that would lead them out of agnosticism. They may think that this is an impossible task, and so, according to the Magisterium, they must be wrong. They may think that, even if possible, this task is not the most urgent one. And they may be practically right or wrong. I suggest that the reason why they are not looking for those grounds is that they have no real hope of finding them. That is why the main feature of the encyclical is its parenetic discourse, encouraging philosophers to work in view of those truths.

And this leads to my third and last question: what is the way out of philosophical agnosticism? I can make only a few remarks. First, for the reasons just given, *Fides et Ratio* does not show the way out, though it emphasizes the second order thesis that there is such a way, and it encourages philosophers to find it. Second, the encyclical does not trace the kind of philosophical achievement that could lead one out of agnosticism. Of course, Thomism is presented as such. But it is not said that Thomism gives *the* best arguments. As we noted earlier, Aquinas's doctrine on faith and reason, a second order doctrine, is assumed by John Paul II. But Aquinas's first order doctrines (e.g. his metaphysics, and more specifically his proofs for God's existence) are not even mentioned. Acceptance, refusal or discussion of them are left to the autonomy of philosophy, as long as the content of faith is not compromised. Speaking of the great metaphysical achievements of the Indian tradition, the Pope may be even trying to enlarge the idea of the "natural capacity of reason." Our occidental tradition has given a precise sense of the reason *capax Dei*: it means that one is able to give some kind of logical demonstration that God exists. But there may be other, non-demonstrative forms of rational approaches to God. That is not to say, that the occidental understanding is false but to insist on the possibility of different achievements, corresponding to different cultures. God may be reached by reason in different ways.

I would suggest the following as a radical modification of Aquinas's program that would still be in accordance with his second order views on faith and reason. According to Aristotelian philosophy, a conclusive argument should have a syllogistical form: if the premises are true and the inference valid, the conclusion follows. For the sake of argument, I will restrict myself to the paradigm of the proofs for God's existence. If the inferences are valid and their premises true, so the conclusion is scientific. Few people have denied the logical soundness of the proofs, but many have contested one or more premises. I would insist on the conclusions. How can they be scientific and still denied by so many, even among philosophers? This is not characteristic of science as we know it. We could evade this objection by saying that Aquinas's conception of science is not ours. But that would not be a good move, for I assume that in Aquinas's mind scientific demonstration is such that no one who grasps the premises and the logical links can still doubt the conclusion. However, forgetting those who absolutely deny the value of the proofs, I think that one can accept the premises, the logical soundness, and still have some doubts on the efficacy of the proofs.

In other words, the label "scientific" seems to be too strong. Can we not see in the so-called demonstrations of God's existence, or of the intellect's subsistence, inferences to the best explanation available (of movement, of order in nature, of existence of contingent things, and of human rationality as distinct from animal abilities), rather than deductive demonstrations, as Barbara-syllogisms are meant to be.[42] This would be more in accordance with a conception of philosophy as distinct from empirical sciences. Philosophy alone is dedicated to the study of our natural beliefs and concepts, of their logical links. This would make philosophy a descriptive discipline more than a demonstrative one, having no particular thesis of its own but helping to maintain, against different speculative constructions, some of our basic natural convictions, including natural beliefs (in the exterior world or in God's existence), which can be found in different cultures.

I will not defend such a Wittgensteinian, perhaps a Thomistic-Wittgensteinian, conception of philosophy. I would just suggest that such a deflationary approach could still satisfy the Encyclical's requirements. After all, to say that God's existence and human freedom and immortality can be *reached* by natural reason, is not to say that those truths, held by faith, are also *deductively demonstrable*. It could be sufficient to say that we have good reasons to accept them, that they are intrinsically intelligible, and give a good explanation or description of well-known phenomena.[43] Another line of approach, and alteration of Aquinas's views would be, for example, to say with many philosophers today, that the philosophical problem is less with God's existence than the intrinsic intelligibility of the attributes by which we describe him (omnipotence, omniscience, goodness, etc.). Aquinas affirms that before the study of God's attributes, we must establish his existence.[44] This is certainly too strong a requirement, inherited from the peripatetic tradition (Avicenna), which asks for the proof of the existence of the subject of science before investigating its nature. Can we not study God's attributes without any proof of his existence, but in order to show their intelligibility? Many atheist arguments proceed precisely by trying to show an inconsistency in one or more divine attributes. The refutation of atheist arguments does not need to presuppose God's existence.

Those are, I think, amendments to Aquinas's conception of philosophical argumentation which are still in agreement with his views on faith and reason. I think they could also be maintained with many substantial theses of his philosophy and theology. But I also think that other aspects of his thought can no longer be maintained. If I am right, this is a subject left to philosophical discussion. *Fides et Ratio* assumes Aquinas's conception of the links between faith and reason, but leaves it to us to decide which philosophy will do the best job, even though it gives Aquinas's work as an example. Speaking in a second order way of faith and reason, Aquinas has expressed the Magisterium's teaching, and no coherent Christian philosopher could avoid it. But it is not the Magisterium's duty to tell which first order philosophical theses, which philosophy to choose. Moreover, it could not be its duty for conceptual reasons: one does not choose his way in philosophy on the basis of authority (that would not be philosophy anymore), although one can be told to stop on this or that way; or to accept this or that content. In particular, it is left to the philosophers to decide whether Thomistic metaphysics, and, more broadly, Aristotelian philosophy, is still viable, with some alterations. Should I add that this seems to me to be a great challenge?

Notes

1 "It must not be forgotten that reason too needs to be sustained in all its searching by trusting dialogue and sincere friendship. A climate of suspicion and distrust, which can beset speculative research, ignores the teaching of the ancient philosophers who proposed friendship as one of the most appropriate contexts for sound philosophical enquiry."

2. *De utilitate credendi* XII. 25 (quod intelligimus); *Retractationes* I. XIV. 25 (quod scimus).

3. I know of only one occurrence of Augustine's formula in Aquinas: *Super Boetium De Trinitate*, q. 3. But the link between faith and authority is made very often, and in Augustinian words.

4. *De Praedestinatione sanctorum* II.

5. *Cogitare* is the term used by Augustine whom Thomas follows in *Quaest. de ver.*, q. 14, a. 1; but, distinguishing *cogitatio* from *scientia* and from *intellectus* in *Summa theologiae* II-II, q. 1, a. 2, he defines it as a *consideratio* with *inquisitio* of the intellect. *Consideratio* is so a more neutral term, which may be used in defining science as well as belief, for example.

6. The main references on which these divisions rely are *In III Sent.*, d. 23, q. 1, a. 1-5; *Quest. de ver.*, q. 14, a. 1–2; *Super Boet. De Trin*, q. 3, a. 1; *Summa Theologiae* II-II, q. 1–4; *In Hebr.* 11, 1.

7. Thomas does not make any distinction between dissenting from p, and assenting to not-p.

8. To my knowledge, the distinction between *suspicio* and *opinio* is made only in *Summa Theologiae* II-II, q. 2, a. 1.

9. The firmness of assent distinguishes belief (*credere*) from doubt, opinion and suspicion. The going on of cogitation (*cogitatio non formata*) distinguihes it from science, where cogitation stops and gives place to assent (*cogitatio formata*), and from intelligence, where assent arises without following any cogitation. In the *Quaest de ver.*, Thomas says that in *credere*, cogitation and assent are *ex aequo*, whereas in science, cogitation leads to assent through the way of resolution (*per viam resolutionis*).

10. This the case in the *Quaestiones de veritate*, and in the *Summa theologiae*.

11. *Quaest. de ver.*, q. 14, a. 2.

12. This in said in the commentary on the Hebrews Epistle, which is the latest text of the series. Thomas has progressively come to admit the unclarity of this definition, cf. C. Spicq, OP, "L'exégèse de Hebr., XI, 1, par s. Thomas d'Aquin," *Recherche Sciences Philosophique et Théologique* 31 (1947), pp. 229–36.

13. *Super Boethium De Trinitate*, q. 3, a. 1, ad 4.

14. This is precisely the definition of faith given in *Summa Theologiae* II-II, q. 2, a. 9. Believing is an act of the intellect assenting to the divine truth by command of the will moved by God through grace. But the context is no more that of the search for a definition, only the question of the meritorious aspect of the act of faith. I do not know whether Aquinas would so accept to distinguish two kinds of beliefs: one which could have any content, and could also be false, and one which could only have a revealed truth as content. Neither if he would say that this distinction is equivalent to that between the acts of *credere* and *opinari*.

15. In fact, in the texts quoted of *Summa Theologiae* II-II, q. 2, Thomas puts together faith and science because of the firmness of assent. It is psychological criterion which is given supremacy over the epistemological one (the ground of the assent).

16. *Super Boethium*, q. 3, a. 1, ad 4.

17. *Summa Theologiae* II-II, q. 1, aa. 7 and 8.

18. *Summa Theologiae* II-II, q. 1, a. 6 on the very notion of "article", a. 8 on their division.

19. It is this opposition, much more than the opposition between *credere* and *opinari* which is at work here, thus confirming the importance of Augustine's distinction.

20. *Quodl.* IV, q. 9, a. 3: "disputatio autem ad duplicem finem potest ordinari. quaedam enim disputatio ordinatur ad removendum dubitationem an ita sit; et in tali disputatione theologica maxime utendum est auctoritatibus, quas recipiunt illi cum quibus disputatur; puta, si cum iudaeis disputatur, oportet inducere auctoritates veteris testamenti: si cum manichaeis, qui vetus testamentum respuunt, oportet uti solum auctoritatibus novi testamenti: si autem cum schismaticis, qui recipiunt vetus et novum testamentum, non autem doctrinam sanctorum nostrorum, sicut sunt graeci, oportet cum eis disputare ex auctoritatibus novi vel veteris testamenti, et illorum doctorum quod ipsi recipiunt. Si autem nullam auctoritatem recipiunt, oportet ad eos convincendos, ad rationes naturales confugere."

21. *Quodl.* IV, q. 9, a. 3: "Quaedam vero disputatio est magistralis in scholis non ad removendum errorem, sed ad instruendum auditores ut inducantur ad

intellectum veritatis quam intendit: et tunc oportet rationibus inniti investigantibus veritatis radicem, et facientibus scire quomodo sit verum quod dicitur: alioquin si nudis auctoritatibus magister quaestionem determinet, certificabitur quidem auditor quod ita est, sed nihil scientiae vel intellectus acquiret et vacuus abscedet."

22. See lower the presentations given by the *Summa contra Gentiles*.

23. In *Summa Theologiae* I, q. 1, a. 8, he says of the Creed's first article: "multa per fidem tenemus de deo quae naturali ratione investigare philosophi non potuerunt, puta circa providentiam eius et omnipotentiam, et quod ipse solus sit colendus. Quae omnia continentur sub articulo unitatis dei."

24. See *Summa contra Gentiles* I. 7.

25. *In I Sent.*, prol., q. 1, a. 5; *In III Sent.*, d. 24, a. 3, qla 3; *Super Boethium De Trinitate*, q. 2, a. 1; *Summa contra Gentiles* I. 8; *Summa Theologiae* I, q. 1, a. 8; II-II, q. 2, a. 10; III, q. 55, a. 5, ad 3.

26. "We can use philosophy in sacred doctrine in three ways: First, in order to demonstrate the preambles of faith, which we must necessarily know in faith. Such are the truths about God that are proved by natural reason, for example that God exists, that he is one, and other truths of this sort about God or creatures proved in philosophy and presupposed by faith. Second, by throwing light on the contents of faith by analogies, as Augustine uses many analogies drawn from philosophical doctrines in order to elucidate the Trinity. Third, in order to refute assertions contrary to the faith, either by showing them to be false or lacking in necessity." *Super Boethium De Trinitate* 2. 3 (*The Division and Methods of the Sciences*, trans. A. Maurer [Toronto: Pontifical Institute of Mediaeval Studies, 1953], p. 49).

27. This is the *incipit* in many traditions of the text, the title "Summa contra gentiles" comes from some *explicit*. See Gauthier in Saint Thomas d'Aquin, *Somme contre les Gentils* (Editions Universitaires, Paris, 1992), Introduction, pp. 109–12.

28. I have tried to do it in my introduction to Thomas d'Aquin, *Somme contre les Gentils* I: *Dieu* (Paris: GF Flammarion, 1999), pp. 27–33.

29. *Summa contra Gentiles* II, 46 says that it was convenient for the perfection of the universe that some intellectual creatures existed, but ch. 91 is more affirmative in asserting that there must exist intellectual creatures separated from all bodies.

30. Cf. *Summa contra Gentiles* III, 134–38.

31. See the prologue.

32. This is a main theme for the notion of theology as science, e. g. *Summa Theologiae* I, q. 1, a. 2.

33. Thomas's evolution is mainly relative to his better knowledge of Aristotle's Ethics in the *Summa Theologiae*, and so to a more philosophical approach of moral life.

34. The notion of *praeambula fidei*, not frequent in Aquinas, appears in the *Super Boethium De Trinitate*, q. 2, a. 3: "sic ergo in sacra doctrina philosophia possumus tripliciter uti. Primo ad demonstrandum ea quae sunt praeambula fidei, quae necesse est in fide scire, ut ea quae naturalibus rationibus de deo probantur, ut deum esse, deum esse unum et alia huiusmodi vel de deo vel de creaturis in philosophia probata, quae fides supponit." In the *Summa Theologiae* II-II, q. 2, a. 1, ad 2, he says: "rationes demonstrativae inductae ad ea quae sunt fidei, praeambula tamen ad articulos, etsi diminuant rationem fidei, quia faciunt esse apparens id quod proponitur; non tamen diminuunt rationem caritatis, per quam voluntas est prompta ad ea credendum etiam si non apparerent. Et ideo non diminuitur ratio meriti."

35. See for example this threefold division in *Summa contra Gentiles* IV. 1.

36. In the text of the *Super Boethium* quoted earlier, Thomas distinguishes three uses of philosophy in theology, but the third one is that of refutation, it is not a strategy of its own, but it goes with the two others. The text goes on that way: "[Possumus philosophia uti] Secundo ad notificandum per aliquas similitudines ea quae sunt fidei, sicut augustinus in libro de trinitate utitur multis similitudinibus ex doctrinis philosophicis sumptis ad manifestandum trinitatem. Tertio ad resistendum his quae contra fidem dicuntur sive ostendendo ea esse falsa sive ostendendo ea non esse necessaria." Aquinas, *Super Boethium*, q. 2, a. 3.

37. There are at least 22 mentions of "metaphysics" (in a substantive or adjective form) in the encyclical, 9 of which appear in *Fides et Ratio* §83. Sometimes "metaphysical" characterize one aspect or one domain of reality, or one kind of knowledge, or power to know, unrestricted to the empirical (§22; §72: metaphysics in Indian conceptions of reality; §105: the metaphysical dimension of truth), and more often, the philosophical discipline called "metaphysics" (§55: the so-called "end of metaphysics"; and §61; 72; 83; 88; 95; 97; 98; 106).

38. In *Fides et Ratio* §13 Aquinas is quoted, from the *Sequence for the Solemnity of the Body and Blood of the Lord*. In §74, he is listed among other medieval doctors.

39. The three following features of philosophy, mentioned in different places in the Encyclical, are grouped to constitute the three *postulata* formulated by the Pope at the end. Cf. *Fides et Ratio*, §81–83.

40. Autonomy is also a very often used expression in *Fides et Ratio*. I have numbered 17 occurrences, almost all of them in a positive sense: autonomy is

characterized as legitime (nn.80 and 98 are exceptions, but they criticize a bad use of autonomy more than autonomy itself). Autonomy is applied to reason (§16; 67; 79), philosophy (§45; 48; 49; 75; 85; 108), science (§45, 106), theology (§75), faith (§48), and to the creature (§15). The principles of autonomy characteristic of modern thought are mentioned §77, in order to explain why the expression "ancilla theologiae" would not be well received.

41. As given in the *Summa contra Gentiles* I. 3–8, for example.

42. R. Swinburne has often defended this line of argument.

43. It does not seem to me that what the Catechism says on man as *capax Dei*, in its first chapter, asks for more than that.

44. For example, in the *Summa contra Gentiles* I. 9, §5

The Boldness of Reason and the Obedience of Faith
Alejandro Llano

In the past few years, I do not recall having read anything as stimulating as the encyclical *Fides et ratio*, published a couple of months ago by John Paul II. Its obvious conceptual and historical rigor proves to be no obstacle to the decisiveness with which it takes on one of the most nagging and problematic issues of contemporary thought – the roots of which dig deep into the first centuries of our Christian era – which in one way or another, draws us back to the ancient Greek dialectic between *mythos* and *logos*.

Surprisingly, however, two among the first pervasive critiques made of this document leave in doubt the novelty of its contributions and the relevance of its message. "This Encyclical says nothing new," so goes the first impression I was able to gather, especially from Catholics well acquainted with Church doctrine on the relationship between faith and reason. The observation was meant to express, clearly, something more than the usual passivity with which believers often receive a document from the Magisterium. The last thing they expect is some substantial change in the Catholic position on issues which affect faith and morals. Lurking in the background, however, was a certain disappointment at not finding in the text any new perspective or fresh insight. But such a feeling of *déjà vu* could be deceiving. As we shall soon see, the encyclical *Fides et ratio* corresponds to a new state of mind, characterized by cultural relativism and the resulting skepticism about a universally valid truth. Such an attitude was absent during the First Vatican Council and when the encyclical *Aeterni Patris* was written. Nevertheless, at the moment when *Veritatis splendor* was being penned, this mindset was already very much in place. Granted that we're dealing with different problems, their corresponding solutions, understandably, could not be but diverse; despite the fact that the baseline teaching has not, or in truth, cannot at all change.

The second reaction comes from a non-Catholic, and has a name, a place and a date It comes from Paolo Flores D'Arcais, in his article entitled "*Aut fides aut ratio*," published in *MicroMega* (1998). Aside from other talking points that I shall comment on later, the author maintains that official Catholic culture – of which the Encyclical is a burning example – has nothing at all to say to the contemporary person. In this case as well there is a trivial reading of the position at hand; that the Church's judgment of the present cultural situation does not coincide with the world-view of the contemporary human being, riven and distraught by intellectual exhaustion and moral uncertainty, to the point that she becomes unable to accept a message as sharp and uncompromising as the one contained in the *Fides et ratio*. Flores D'Arcais, of course, would like to say something less flattering, and if you would allow me, more caustic. He claims that the Catholic view on the present moment of the *Vernunftsgeschichte* has been unredeemably surpassed, inasmuch as it displays a childishness unacceptable to the radically critical and unbelieving attitude proper of today's mature and discerning intelligentsia. Now then, this is precisely the conflict that confers cultural relevance to a set of propositions which hopes to form part of the solution, instead of wearisomely repeating the terms, however biased, of the problem itself.

These two views, taken almost randomly from a wide range of reactions provoked by the Encyclical, turn out to be most useful in measuring the thickness of the postmodern skull, through which the *Fides et ratio* has to drill in order to reach its interlocutors' minds and hearts. They serve no other purpose. As Professor Fernando Inciarte of the University of Münster has pointed out, this papal document takes on an issue of very ancient vintage, but in a refreshingly new light. Thanks to economic globalization and the immediacy of telecommunications, we seem to live in an ever-shrinking world. Yet such universalization demands, at the same time, the fragmentation of the *Lebensformen*, as multiculturalism requires and is plain to see in any of the big cities of the West. And multiculturalism, in turn, seems to imply the relativization of truth and life's loss of meaning. The objective of the Encyclical, however, is not so much that of solving, once and for all, the very subtle conceptual problem of the relationship between faith and reason, between Philosophy and Theology, but rather, that of summoning the intellectual and religious resources necessary in order to recover the universal meaning of truth and its deep impact on the life of each person.

This is certainly a daunting task, one in which the margin for error is extremely narrow, yet we have to proceed – as one reads in the text – "amid the pressures of an immanentist habit of mind and the constrictions of a technocratic logic" (§15). Max Weber had already foretold that the human being of the late twentieth century would be some sort of *specialist without a soul, a living being without a heart*. Philosophers such as Husserl and sociologists such as Daniel Bell have not done anything other than confirm this observation. Conspicuously absent in this fractured horizon is human reason in its full array, that is, what used to be called *Metaphysics*. And to try to defend the actual validity of sapiential realism is definitely no trivial, commonplace or irrelevant enterprise.

John Paul II describes this situation in the following terms: "We see among the men and women of our time, and not just in some philosophers, attitudes of widespread distrust of the human being's great capacity for knowledge. With a false modesty, people rest content with partial and provisional truths, no longer seeking to ask radical questions about the meaning and ultimate foundation of human, personal and social existence. In short, the hope that philosophy might be able to provide definitive answers to these questions has dwindled" (§5); "and now, at the end of this century, one of our greatest threats is the temptation to despair" (§91). Before this panorama of relativism and skepticism, Karol Wojtyla is convinced – and he tries to convince us through this Encyclical – that today´s most urgent task is "to lead people to discover both their capacity to know the truth and their yearning for the ultimate and definitive meaning of life" (§102).

Max Weber himself had foreseen that aside from the *polytheism of values*, that splintering of ends and conditions that nowadays affects us, the end of the "brief century" or the twentieth century would be characterized by the phenomenon of the *crisis of meaning*. Section 81 of the Encyclical describes this cultural moment with extraordinary lucidness: "Perspectives on life and the world, often of a scientific temper, have so proliferated that we face an increasing fragmentation of knowledge. This makes the search for meaning difficult and often fruitless. Indeed, still more dramatically, in this maelstrom of data and facts in which we live and which seem to comprise the very fabric of life, many people wonder whether it still makes sense to ask about meaning. The array of theories which vie to give an answer, and the different ways of viewing and of interpreting the world and human life, serve only to aggravate this radical doubt, which can easily lead to skepticism, indifference or to various forms of nihilism" (§81).

As far as I can tell, this is the first time that the Magisterium of the Catholic Church has engaged in a theological reflection over the role of Philosophy in the contemporary world, something akin to a "Theology of Philosophy." And this is no doubt something new, even from the viewpoint of the Academe. (In due course, Alasdair MacIntyre called our attention to a meaningful precedent, *Veritatis splendor*, a document of sublime reflexiveness, which undertakes the task of developing some sort of "Theology of Moral Research," wherein the spiritual lives of the researchers themselves acquire an unprecedented importance, as manifested above all in the hermeneutics of the Gospel episode featuring the rich, young man, which serves as the existential backdrop for the doctrinal content of that decisive discourse). In our case, what is most surprising is that such a theological meditation leads us to underscore, with a dogged insistence, the need for Philosophy to be true to its own nature, as the human love of wisdom, instead of caving in to the siren calls of a diminished Rationalism and a Fideism incapable of looking beyond its own navel. The very essence of Christianity – which rests on the mystery of the Incarnation, and on the intellectual and vital assent to Jesus Christ, the Word made Flesh – nurtures in its bosom, as a necessary condition, a trusting recourse to human reason, exercised with autonomy and rigor, to that study of reality in its roots or *Philosophy*, in other words. The paradoxical nature of this enterprise – a defense of the value of reason starting from the horizon of faith – attains a fullness of meaning and coherence when one realizes that the ultimate source of this rational daring is none other than the receptive attitude of obedience to God's manifestation of Himself through the gift of creation and through the Uncreated Gift of the Spirit of Jesus.

There are three reasons, to my mind, for which our present epoch constitutes an opportune moment, a *kairos*, for composing an uncanny "ode to Philosophy." In the first place, we find ourselves in that decline of nihilistic skepticism, that final stage which one of the great systems of reason has forced upon itself. It would be interesting to note that in a world sullied by relativism, the Catholic Church is, nowadays, the only institution that defends the irreplaceable role of Philosophy, which aspires for a universal and definitive validity. On the other hand, a Philosophy that is purely formal or functional, dwarfed by its own technicalities and asphyxiated by an erudition that barely clears a ridiculous, minimalist bar, becomes the reason why "the human spirit is often invaded by a kind of ambiguous thinking which leads it to an ever deepening introversion, locked within the confines of its own immanence without referent of any kind to the transcendent. A philosophy which no longer asks the question of the meaning of life – the Pope continues – would be in grave danger of reducing reason to merely accessory functions, with no real passion for the search for truth" (§81).

One of the gravest consequences of Philosophy's loss of its *sapiential dimension* in our time is the growing tendency – fostered by a simplistic and erroneous interpretation of the Second Vatican Council – for Theology to prescind of its support on rational Metaphysics and Anthropology. In my opinion, this constitutes the second motive for which Pope John Paul II considered it urgent to reaffirm the need for cooperation between Philosophy and Theology, in order to orient properly that desire for truth which inhabits the heart not only of Christians, but of every human being. Only a naturalist mode of thinking could have led to the conclusion that the strength of Theology relies on the weakness of Philosophy, or the other way around. The Naturalism called to fore would be responsible for the crude image of the different sciences, which have come to occupy the place of privilege formerly reserved for others, to the effect, as it were, of some sort of principle of the impenetrability of bodies taking over the realm of Epistemology. This naïve and trivial detail brings alongside it terrible consequences for the culture of Christian wisdom. "I cannot fail to note with surprise and displeasure," John Paul II remarks, "that this lack of interest in the study of philosophy is shared by not a few theologians" (§61). The deformative and "anti-pastoral" effects of this disinterest are serious and known to all. That's why the Roman Pontiff categorically insists: "I wish to repeat clearly that the study of philosophy is fundamental and indispensable to the structure of theological studies." (§62). But then, the kind of Philosophy to which Theology takes recourse, could not simply be an *ad hoc* or improvised system, one that limited itself to rhetorically express or illustrate the same conclusions at which a presumably pure theological reflection had previously arrived. The Encyclical is also very clear on this point: "The Church has no philosophy of her own nor does she canonize any one particular philosophy in preference to others. The underlying reason for this reluctance is that, even when it engages theology, philosophy must remain faithful to its own principles and methods. Otherwise there would be no guarantee that it would remain oriented to truth and that it was moving towards truth by way of a process governed by reason. A philosophy which did not proceed in the light of reason according to its own principles and methods would serve little purpose. At the deepest level, the autonomy which philosophy enjoys is rooted in the fact that reason is by its nature oriented to truth and is equipped moreover with the means necessary to arrive at truth. A philosophy conscious of this as its "constitutive status" cannot but respect the demands and the data of revealed truth" (§49). On the other hand, an *ersatz* Philosophy which onesidedly based itself on Theology would be begging the question. Furthermore, it would invert the classic Catholic position according to which grace does not destroy nature nor substitute it, but rather, elevates and perfects it. Even the ancillary role which corresponds to Philosophy with regard to Theology would be rendered impossible if Philosophy were not to distinguish itself from Theology. Only in the measure that Philosophy distinguishes itself, without separating itself, from Theology, could Philosophy lend Theology its necessary assistance.

> Theology in fact [the Encyclical teaches] has always needed and still needs philosophy's contribution. As a work of critical reason in the light of faith, theology presupposes and requires in all its research a reason formed and educated to concept and argument. Moreover, theology needs philosophy as a partner in dialogue in order to confirm the intelligibility and universal truth of its claims (§77).

A third reason for which, I believe, *Fides et ratio* is relevant to our present cultural state is "the lure of rationalism" (cf. §54). That is to say, the exclusivist ambition of reason that considers itself self-sufficient and not needful of a rational gift, a clarifying present, which faith offers to whomsoever pays its obeisance, to her who remains with an attentive ear to a voice which, despite its mysterious origin, is no less luminous and revealing. The anthropocentric narrow-mindedness of Rationalism converts it into some sort of serpent that swallows its own tail. In the end, what this shows is a fear of facing up to that which we supposedly control; as if the control which we ourselves exercise had some magical power to neatly discern the rational from the irrational. This feeble narrow-mindedness, so common among the followers of Scientism and Pragmatism in their prime, draws a stark contrast with the greatness of heart of the Humanist who thus calls out: "I ask *everyone* to look more deeply at man, whom Christ has saved in the mystery of his love, and at the human being's unceasing search for truth and meaning. Different philosophical systems have lured people into believing that they are their own absolute master, able to decide their own destiny and future in complete autonomy, trusting only in themselves and their own powers. But this can never be the grandeur of the human being, who can find fulfillment only in choosing to enter the truth, to make a home under the shade of Wisdom and dwell there. Only within this horizon of truth will people understand their freedom in its fullness and their call to know and love God as the supreme realization of their true self" (§107). One may think that a calling of this kind enters into contradiction with the demands for autonomy which Philosophy implies. Nothing is farther from the truth. Precisely because it is autonomous and is no way shackled from without, Philosophy is able to open itself to a higher light, without sacrificing its own methodology or rational nature. When Philosophy goes out of itself and receives data and stimuli from Revelation which does not contradict, but rather extends and empowers rational truth from within, it fulfills its highest calling in the service of truth and in its openness to the Transcendent. A *sensu contrario*, a Philosophy which declares itself to be programatically agnostic, one which as a matter of principle denies the possibility of accepting a message that comes from the deepest nucleus of the mystery of being – what it is supposed to study – (such a Philosophy) reduces itself into a midget and thwarts its own reason.

But we need to stop at this point, because herein lies the very germ of the Encyclical, the very crux of the controversy over the validity of its message. In the aforementioned article, Flores D'Arcais claims to have found a contradiction in the *Fides et ratio*, insofar as it seems to attribute an autonomy to Philosophy, of which Philosophy itself shall be stripped later. It seems clear, at least to me, that this particular author's notion of rational autonomy is univocal, and that for the most part, it is tinged with *pathos* rather than with *logos*. In its common usage in Politics or in Business Management, for example, the meaning of the term "autonomy" is already clearly differentiated from that of "independence." We say that a geographical region is autonomous, or that a university or a company division is autonomous, without meaning to say the least that such entities cannot receive any outside influence, or that they cannot be subject to rules coming from a higher instance other than themselves. As a matter of fact, no one and nothing in this world is completely autonomous, because the whole of reality forms a web of interactions and intertwinings. Certainly, no science could claim to be completely autonomous, since all of them depend on that portion of reality under study, on the first principles of knowledge and the general laws of Logic, aside from being in constant interdisciplinary contact – now, more than ever – with other fields of knowledge. What these rationalist claims seem to evoke, with certain delay and in Kantian terms, is the Enlightened rejection of all tutelage other than the self-imposed, the emancipation of one who dares to think for herself and thus free herself from a culpable intellectual age of minority. But at this stage, we already know how to discern that which Gadamer used to call "the prejudice against all forms of prejudice." Be it for good or for evil, it is impossible to start from scratch and avoid all preconceptions. Hence, what we have to be careful about is to be conscious of our own fundamental attitudes and to try, at least, to be reasonable and open-minded.

But this brings us back to the paradox to which we have previously referred. The Christian thinker cannot nor should prescind from her faith when she philosophizes. Moreover, it is her own faith that incites the believer not to impose on herself pre-set limits to her rational inquiries. In this sense, one could claim to be more free than another who stubbornly encloses herself in her Rationalism. But why does the full use of reason have to come under the command of an instance which is not purely rational? Have we not said that the knowledge of faith necessarily has to take recourse to the help extended by Philosophy?

Everything seems to indicate that we are trapped in a vicious circle, one in which faith and reason demand each other and support one another. Robert Spaemann has dealt with this all-important problem directly and has given it a solution that is somehow pre-figured in the title of his work, "*Fides et ratio: Der hermeneutische Zirkel,*" published in the German edition of *L'Osservatore romano* on January 29, 1999. According to Spaemann, the cultural quandary with which the life of Christian Faith and its transmission in the twentieth century has to come to grips with is precisely that of the radical Nietzschean hermeneutic, which rejects the acceptance of a universally valid truth, or at least, one that blocks the path that leads to it for all those who may be intellectually prepared to do so. Nietzsche ask, "What is the truth?" And he responds: "A host of metaphors, metonymies, in short, a sum of human relations which have been highlighted, extrapolated and adorned, both poetically and rhetorically, and which, after its prolonged use, a people has considered fixed, canonical and binding; truths are illusions which people have forgotten to be so; metaphors which have been over-used and thus lacking in force, coins which have lost their mint-marks and thus are no longer considered coins, but scrap metal." Truth is an illusion; it is that kind of error without which a certain species of living things – human beings – would be incapable of survival. Once we have discovered for ourselves and uncovered or exposed to others the real state of things, we find ourselves in the terrible situation of having to announce the "death of God," which amounts to denying any divine character in the truth. The truth is dissolved in a multitude of interpretations, in the interests of the self-serving, in the power of the power hungry, in the historical vicissitudes of its apparent glimmer. According to present-day Deconstructionists, it then becomes necessary to tear down the great epic narratives, those solemn discourses which pretend to put us before reality itself. Because reality is never present in the immediacy, but rather, it is always mediated by our constructs, by our hidden values, by our modes of interpreting empirical data. We have to tear down the illusory logic of our language, in which the acceptance of God, and therefore, the acceptance of truth finds its ultimate hiding place. In *Twilight of the Idols*, Nietzsche did not at all speak in vain when he uttered: "I fear that we are not going to rid ourselves of God because we still believe in Grammar."

Before such an attempt to unmask the "all too human" mediations which simulate whatever it is they hide, the Church holds that a cultural hermeneutic, a non-vicious circle, but rather, a *"Zirkel des Verstehens"* (in Spaemann's own words) is possible. In terms of present-day Epistemology, one could say that the Catholic position is one of moderate cognitivism. The Catholic position maintains, as the Encyclical itself attests, that "no historical form of philosophy can legitimately claim to embrace the totality of truth, nor to be the complete explanation of the human being, of the world and of the human being's relationship with God" (§51). But it is equally far from defending, in the manner of radical hermeneutics, that there is no authentic understanding of the nature of reality. It is not true that all purported knowledge leads to error rather than to the truth. Knowledge by itself does not generate error; instead, through different ways and means, it brings us closer to the truth, albeit always in a limited manner, which needs ulterior contrasts and checks of all sorts. And here is where the virtuous circle of understanding comes in. Starting out from reason, we advance towards a fuller understanding of faith, while faith itself provides us with a critical discernment of our rational ambitions.

Therefore, the Encyclical meets the most burning cultural issue of our time head on, on its own terrain, which is none other than the epistemological interpretation of our discourses on reality. The only difference being, that instead of heading towards an enfeebled relativism, it raises its aim towards the Metaphysics of Knowledge. Hence, we are not simply before a mere repetition of hackneyed expressions. In consequence, the conceptual models essayed in the recent past are no longer useful in analyzing problems with a different slant. As Inciarte has reminded us, the tectonic paradigm, which statically arranged the different bodies of knowledge horizontally, in layers, is no longer useful. It may even prove to be an obstacle in finding a more appropriate interpretive paradigm. Rather, we now have to make use of a vertical and dynamic structure, which renders possible the transit from faith to reason and from reason to faith, as a progressive and mutually enriching discernment, which does not at all lead to unsolvable paradoxes or to vicious circles. On the contrary, John Paul II maintains that the actual relationship between faith and reason demands a keen effort of discernment, since both faith and reason, being isolated, have become impoverished and weakened each other. The Pope continues,

> Deprived of what Revelation offers, reason has taken sidetracks which expose it to the danger of losing sight of its final goal. Deprived of reason, faith has stressed feeling and experience, and so runs the risk of no longer being a universal proposition. It is an illusion to think that faith, tied to weak reasoning, might be more penetrating; on the contrary, faith then runs the grave risk of withering into myth or superstition. By the same token, reason which is unrelated to an adult faith is not prompted to turn its gaze to the newness and radicality of being. This is why I make this strong and insistent appeal – not, I trust, untimely – that faith and philosophy recover the profound unity which allows them to stand in harmony with their nature without compromising their mutual autonomy (§48).

To my knowledge, here lies the most profound and original teaching that this Encyclical provides to philosophers. That is to say, that the mysteries of faith do not limit reason; they offer, instead, the very possibility of breaking open the horizon, of creating an opening to what lies beyond that to which Philosophy, with its own resources, could never aspire, without loss of its own identity and without sacrificing its own methods. When it seems as if Philosophy has reached its limits, when it has stumbled upon undecipherable enigmas, when it has wallowed in its own suspicions, and when it has no choice but to melancholically fold its own sails, then comes the spark which opens new and – in a certain sense – limitless perspective. This is not a pious *desideratum*; rather, it is a strict account of what has occurred in the history of human thought. Those who insist on opposing Christianity to a "scientific world view" do not realize that positive science itself, such as it is understood in the modern sense, would not have been possible, were it not for the demystification of nature which immediately follows from a creationist world view. The same thing happens with History. As Umberto Eco repeats in his dia-

logues with Cardinal Carlo Maria Martini, "Christianity invented History."
And the same thing happens with the notions of freedom, person, spirit, truth,
immortality, love, providence, virtue, tolerance, respect and a personal God,
among many others which, would be uncomprehensible today, had it not been
for Christian tradition, which of course includes the Salvation History of the
Jews. All of these concepts and realities have been considered by Philosophy
from a rational perspective, and in a couple of cases, it has trodden an exclusively philosophical path to reach them. Man's greatness becomes manifest
when he is able to elaborate "a philosophy in which there shines even a glimmer of the truth of Christ" (§104); because – in the words of the Second
Vatican Council – "the mystery of man could only be deciphered, in truth, in
the mystery of the Incarnate Word" (*Gaudium et spes*, §22).

John Paul II understands, therefore, that the "remembrance" of the mission of Philosophy has become very necessary at present. But he does not
refer to a momentary concern but to a prophetic one: from the viewpoint of a
higher reason, which makes of Philosophy one of the keys of this historical
crossroads, enigmatically expressed at the end of the millennium. "With its
enduring appeal to the search for truth, philosophy has the great responsibility of forming thought and culture, and now it must strive resolutely to recover its original vocation. This is why – the Roman Pontiff adds – I have felt
both the need and the duty to address this theme so that, on the threshold of
the third millennium of the Christian era, humanity may come to a clearer
sense of the great resources with which it has been endowed and may commit
itself with renewed courage to implement the plan of salvation of which its
history is part" (§6).

Such a vocation has been threshed out by the Encyclical in an impressive
series of texts which reveal how the Christian Faith and Theology itself
encourage human thought to transcend itself. "Men and women are on a journey of discovery which is humanly unstoppable – a search for the truth and a
search for a person to whom they might entrust themselves. Christian faith
comes to meet them, offering the concrete possibility of reaching the goal
which they seek" (§33). Apparently, it is difficult, if not impossible, to discover the ultimate meaning of reality, in the midst of a cultural milieu which
does not seem to accept any truth other than that arrived at through consensus
and the neutralization of values, hardly admitting anything that is not either
provisional or the product of convention. "Nonetheless, in the light of faith
which finds in Jesus Christ this ultimate meaning, I cannot," thus says the
Pope,

> but encourage philosophers – be they Christian or not – to trust in the
> power of human reason and not set themselves goals that are too
> modest in their philosophizing. The lesson of history in this millen-

nium now drawing to a close shows that this is the path to follow: it is necessary not to abandon the passion for ultimate truth, the eagerness to search for it or the audacity to forge new paths in the search. It is faith which stirs reason to move beyond all isolation and willingly to run risks so that it may attain whatever is beautiful, good and true. Faith thus becomes the convinced and convincing advocate of reason" (§56).

Karol Wojtyla, the philosopher, does not conform to the superficiality of current thought. But neither does he end up in the nostalgia of a better past. He proposes, like no other, a *passion for truth* in dialogue with the most popular intellectual currents of the present moment, among which the postmodern *"pensiero devole,"* in the manner of Vattimo, which invites us to follow in the shadow of post-Metaphysical thought, and for which the death of God and the abolition of human dignity are necessary starting points, is a specially meaningful reference for this particular issue.

Where shall we draw strength in order to face this skeptic relativism as widespread as it is rooted in the *Lebensformen* of modern capitalism? In the words of John Paul II, *the deep waters* (cf. §16) in which one may quench her thirst and replenish energies lie in that open and receptive confidence in an unmerited gift as contained in that splendid phrase from St. Paul which is the *obedience of faith* (cf. *Rom* 1: 5; 16: 26). But have we not agreed that Christianity was the great obstacle for free philosophical thought and for a science that were not to find continuous barriers in an authoritarian orthodoxy? The answer is no. Many others, I among them, have never given in, not even in difficult moments, as when Althusser affirmed that Marxism was *the Science.* We never accepted that caricature, ever so alienated from historical reality, which at present could only find its way in pamphlets of popular science or some weekly magazines. What is certain, I repeat, is that the central concepts of modern thought and current world view at the very base of empirical science could only have arisen and developed in a non-anthropocentric and humanist medium provided by the vision of the human being and physical reality furnished by Christianity. As a matter of fact, Christian thought has been extraordinarily fertile so as to keep reason awake and prod it towards scientific adventures which would not have been possible departing from Greco-Latin wisdom or Oriental Mysticism, not to mention its late-modern audio-visual version in the New Age movement.

The most original and provocative trait of this Encyclical is that for the first time, it neatly draws out the consequences that an intelligent analysis of intellectual history contributes to the effective and contemporary profession of both Theology and Philosophy. These two branches of knowledge cross-fertilized each other, so to speak. Because a deep and genuine understanding of the Christian Faith is possible only from the viewpoint of a transcendent Philosophy, one that is determined "to move from *phenomenon* to *foundation*" (§83). And Philosophy, for its part, overcomes its decadent narcissistic tendency, as a completely self-absorbed Rationalism, condemned to one or another form of Nihilism, as Kierkegaard, Dostoyevsky and Nietzsche himself had foretold, when Christian Revelation opens for it doors to unknown heights. Heidegger takes cunning advantage of this event, but he falls into error, even from the perspective of his own principles, when he maintains in his *Introduction to Metaphysics* that the expression "Christian Philosophy" is an oxymoron, the squaring of the circle, because the philosopher-believer would already have an answer – that is, creation – to the question, "Why being, instead of nothing?". He did not seem to have noticed that such a response should have been considered by him to be *ontic*, rather than *ontological*.

A peek into this mystery breaks the iron cage of ideological and ethnocentric thought, the same one of totalitarian political praxis and of an acquisitive and individualistic economy. Wojtyla calls the assumption of this fair risk the *boldness of reason* (cf. §48). It is the flip-side of the *obedience of faith*. The Christian philosopher knows himself to be a child of God. And unlike the slave, he "knows what his master is doing" (Jn 15: 15). Such a situation, far from inviting one to restraint and prudence, beckons her instead to scale the heights of thought and to try out once more a grand intellectual tradition about to complete two thousand years of existence.

"Were theologians to refuse the help of philosophy, they would run the risk of doing philosophy unwittingly and locking themselves within thought structures poorly adapted to the understanding of faith. Were philosophers, for their part, to shun theology completely, they would be forced to master on their own the contents of Christian faith, as has been the case with some modern philosophers. Either way, the grounding principles of autonomy which every science rightly wants guaranteed would be seriously threatened" (§77). With a shade less of drama, one may add that to try to speak in prose without knowing how, never yields satisfactory results, as was the case of Moliere's character, just like laboriously trying to discover the Mediterranean Sea, or playing hide-and-seek with oneself. In short, "the content of revelation can never debase the discoveries and legitimate autonomy of reason. Yet, conscious that it cannot set itself up us an absolute and exclusive value, reason on its part must never lose its capacity to question and to be questioned" (§79).

This is the backdrop against which the Magisterium of the Catholic Church once more displays *the enduring originality of the thought of St. Thomas Aquinas* (cf. §43–48), as a serene expression of a manner of thought based on faith, in which Philosophy and Theology complement each other harmoniously, free from confusion or shrillness. In light of these reflections, no one should find it odd, much less be scandalized, that the Magisterium has repeatedly praised the merits of Saint Thomas's teachings, and has singled them out as a guide for theological studies, as well as an orientation for philosophical research, that many of the Christian philosophers of today would do ill to ignore. Neither is it a case of mere serendipity that many of the intellectuals who have converted in this century have felt the need to study the same Thomas Aquinas that their previous, biased formation prevented them from approaching. Such is the case of Maritain, Gilson, Chesterton, García Morente, Flannery O'Connor, Alasdair MacIntyre or Saint Edith Stein, among many others. The Encyclical likewise reminds us that the intellectual depth of the Second Vatican Council – splendidly reflected in the Catechism of the Catholic Church – was due to the work of theologians, the majority of whom were formed in the shade of the contemporary renewal of Thomism, many of whom later on followed that path to which their own research inclined them. Karol Wojtyla clarifies that what is important is not

> to take a position on properly philosophical questions nor to demand adherence to particular theses. The Magisterium's intention has always been to show how St. Thomas is an authentic model for all who seek the truth. In his thinking, the demands of reason and the power of faith found the most elevated synthesis ever attained by human thought, for he could defend the radical newness introduced by revelation without ever demeaning the venture proper to reason (§78).

John Paul II does well to celebrate that the topic of tradition has surfaced in these past few decades. Faced with a Philosophy based on a radical and systematic suspicion, Gadamer has opened a path towards a balanced hermeneutics that surpasses the exaggerations of both Historicism and radical Critique. For his part, MacIntyre shows us that the Enlightenment project of analysis and thought outside of any known tradition is illusory, and at the same time, that a genuinely philosophical tradition projects us beyond itself, to confront rival versions and to try and decide through which one could the truth be found. Meanwhile, Charles Taylor defends the modern appeal for authenticity, but – through a heavily-nuanced version of the *"Zirkel des Verstehens"* – he warns us that in order not to trivialize this desire, it is necessary to interpret one's own cultural identity through *strong evaluations* of an ethical and religious nature. The Encyclical underscores the fact that "the appeal to tradition is not a mere remembrance of the past; it involves rather the recognition of a cultural heritage which belongs to all of humanity. Indeed, it may be said that it is we who belong to the tradition and that it is not ours to dispose of at will. Precisely by being rooted in the tradition will we able today to develop for the future an original, new and constructive mode of thinking" (§85). Lest we forget, the evaluation that *Fides et ratio* makes of multiculturalism is a model of rigor and objectivity. The multiplicity of cultures simultaneously lived in the present economically and communications-wise globalized world constitutes enormous wealth, no doubt, if genuine dialogue were to be attained among them. On the other hand, this could completely degenerate into some superficial relativism if each of these diverse cultures were to be considered as water-tight compartments, thus ignoring their structural constants and the analogy of their religious references. In the end, I would daresay, fragmentary multiculturalism is a power strategy that trivializes the variety and variations of the *Lebensformen*, while imposing on the weak the non-negotiable conceptions of the strong. Evidently, that is a card that present Christian thought would not like to play. "To believe it possible to know a universally valid truth is in no way to encourage intolerance; on the contrary, it is the essential condition for sincere and authentic dialogue between persons. On this basis alone is it possible to overcome divisions and to journey together toward full truth, walking those paths known only to the Spirit of the Risen Lord" (§92).

In the *Critique of Pure Reason* Kant makes use of the comely metaphor of the dove that could not fly in a phenomenon vacuum. John Paul II is, doubtless, more bold as he sustains in the brief exordium of the Encyclical that "faith and reason are like two wings on which the human spirit rises to the contemplation of truth." Once again, it is an invitation to be free from fear, and to risk some form of thought that befits the dignity of the human person.

Such an invitation becomes explicit and solemn towards the end of this powerful document: "I appeal also to *philosophers*, and to all *teachers of philosophy*, asking them to have the courage to recover, in the flow of an enduringly valid philosophical tradition, the range of authentic wisdom and truth – metaphysical truth included – which is proper to philosophical enquiry. They should be open to the impelling questions which arise from the word of God and they should be strong enough to shape their thought and discussion in response to that challenge. Let them always strive for truth, alert to the good which truth contains. Then they will be able to formulate the genuine ethics which humanity need so urgently at this particular time. The Church follows the work of philosophers with interest and appreciation, and they should rest assured of her respect to the rightful autonomy of their discipline. I would want especially to encourage believers working in the philosophical field to illumine the range of human activity by the exercise of a reason which grows more penetrating and assured because of the support it receives from faith" (§106).

Certainly, the Christian thinker could say, together with Saint Paul, that he knows where, or better still, in Whom he has placed his trust. He knows that faith is a rational obedience that "illumines every human being that comes to this world" (John 1. 9), on the condition that such a human being – conscious of his great weakness and the dignity of his calling – were to leave its solitude and bravely open itself up to receive a gift which at the same time strengthens and surpasses human intelligence.

Fides et Ratio, Political Philosophy, and Thomas Aquinas

Mary M. Keys

In this paper I propose to weave together two strands of the argument advanced by John Paul II in his encyclical letter *Fides et Ratio*. Concretely, I would like to consider the case John Paul II makes, at least implicitly, for the renewal of political philosophy, together with his development of previous papal pronouncements on the perennial value of Thomas Aquinas's thought.

Political philosophy in Fides et Ratio

The term "political philosophy" occurs nowhere in the encyclical. Yet I would argue that it is presupposed by John Paul II's overall argument, and implicit in a wide range of his recommendations.[1] The Pope encourages scholars to turn their attention once again "to man," that is, to human nature as impelled to seek wisdom and to be open to God's revelation and grace (§107, §43). He underlines the importance of "ask[ing] radical questions about the meaning of human, personal and social existence," in the hope that philosophy might be able to provide some solid (albeit never exhaustive) answers to these crucial queries (§5; emphasis added). John Paul II argues from both philosophy and from Sacred Scripture that human beings are naturally social creatures, whose fulfillment requires a participation in a variety of communities, traditions, and interpersonal relationships; who will not be happy or wise locked in their isolated individuality; who require self-transcendence (social, metaphysical, and ultimately religious) for their self-fulfillment (cf. §21, 23, 25, 31-32, 81, 85, and 101). He is clearly concerned that social theory and practice governed by "atheistic humanism," or limited by various versions of relativism, positivism, or pragmatism, will yield a dehumanizing politics (see §46, 89, 98; cf. *Evangelium Vitae*, §69). John Paul II laments contemporary theology's tendency to disdain philosophy's cooperation in favor of a primary or exclusive reliance on the "human sciences" (given the context, we can presume he is referring primarily to the behavioral social sciences which posit a sharp fact-value distinction; see §61). Finally,

John Paul II indicates the reasons why Catholic moral theology has remained open to, and indeed dependent upon, ethical and social philosophy:

> In the New Testament, human life is much less governed by pre-scriptions than in the Old Testament. Life in the Spirit leads believers to the freedom and responsibility which surpass the Law. Yet the Gospel and the apostolic writings still set forth both general principles of Christian conduct and specific teachings and precepts. In order *to apply these to the particular circumstances of individual and communal life, Christians must be able to engage their conscience and the power of their reason. In other words, moral theology requires a sound philosophical vision of human nature and society, as well as of the general principles of ethical decision making* (§68, emphasis added).

From all this I conclude that we should see in *Fides et Ratio* a call to reinvigorate political philosophy in its classical sense, as the overarching science of man in his social and civic orientation, hence of law, justice, and forms of government, in function, *of the good life for the human person.* Political philosophy thus defined is arguably the queen of the practical sciences, which John Paul II is so eager to reorient towards the truth about the human good (cf. §25).

Fides et Ratio on Thomas Aquinas

If the place of political philosophy in the encyclical's argument is not self-evident, the importance *Fides et Ratio* accords to the thought of Thomas Aquinas certainly is. In the section of chapter 5 entitled, "The enduring originality of the thought of St. Thomas Aquinas" (§43-44; cf. also 57-58 and 78), John Paul II makes special mention of several characteristics of Aquinas's work. The first is Thomas's account of the ""non-contradictory relationship between faith and reason;" in particular, his recognition "that nature, philosophy's proper concern, could contribute to the understanding of divine revelation," while reason in turn requires the light of faith to attain its perfection. John Paul II further cites Aquinas's "impartial love for truth," whatever or whomever its source, and his eager dialogue with Greco-Roman, Jewish, and Islamic thinkers; his insight into "the primacy of the wisdom which is a gift of the Holy Spirit" and which "enables judgment according to the divine truth," while giving due weight to theological and philosophical wisdom (and, we might add, practical or prudential wisdom); and finally his conviction of and emphasis on truth's universality, objectivity, and transcendence.

In my opinion, each of the above-mentioned features of Aquinas's thought holds important implications and opens interesting investigative horizons for students of political philosophy. But constraints of time and space compel me to choose just one theme, the last one listed. For the remainder of this paper, I would like to focus on the essential openness of human nature to what is universal; or, more specifically, on the *universal* dimension of the human good. Where does the thought of John Paul II point us on this score? And, on this issue, will his recommendation to consider Aquinas's writings be helpful to students of political theory?

Universality, Particularity, and the Good Life

In *Fides et Ratio*, the Pope is most interested in highlighting what is *universal* in humanity, in human experience, in the human quest to know, and in the objects of that knowledge (cf. §14, 23, 24, 27, 38, 44, 69). Philosophy and theology, human wisdom and the wisdom of the Cross, are united in overcoming (more or less perfectly, more or less definitively) the barriers which separate people, the aspects of human lives most marked by differences which particularize and divide. Together with this emphasis on universality is a focus (so characteristic of John Paul II) on "the human person," concretely here on his or her search for meaning, for an integrated life harmonizing the demands and possibilities of faith and reason, and merging thought with action in a consistent manner. The encyclical, therefore, can leave the reader with the impression that the Pope sees human life as an endeavor of personality to participate as fully as possible in universality. Human existence appears between two poles, that of the individual person and the universality or totality of wisdom, of the Word of God. Particularity can appear by default as something to be down-played, even to be left behind in the striving for the universal.[2]

This is certainly an appropriate focus for a treatment of faith and reason, one of the main points of which is to affirm philosophy's calling to probe what is shared, what is common both *in praedicando* and *in causando* in nature and especially in human nature. John Paul II seeks to persuade citizens and scholars at the close of the millennium not to abandon that "typically philosophic and critical thinking which is concerned with the universal."

Indeed, this kind of thinking is required for a fruitful exchange between cultures. What I wish to emphasize is the duty to go beyond the particular and the concrete, lest the prime task of demonstrating the universality of faith's content be abandoned. Nor should it be forgotten that the specific contribution of philosophical enquiry enables us to discern in different cultures "not what people think but what the objective truth is."[3] It is not an array of human opinions but truth alone which can be of help to theology (§69).

The attentive reader will note that *Fides et Ratio* also acknowledges the importance of the "communal" aspect of human life: the familial and social character of human existence (§31), and the centrality of traditions in particular (§70–72, 85, 101). John Paul II is convinced of the irreplaceable role of particularity in human life, especially in its social, cultural, and political dimensions. However, for a full appreciation of this aspect of the Pope's thought, it is necessary to read *Fides et Ratio* together with John Paul's 1995 *Address to the United Nations General Assembly* (hereafter cited as *UN*).[4]

In that address, on the occasion of the UN's fiftieth anniversary, John Paul II argues that the rights and duties of *nations* – broadly, of polities, peoples, and ethnic groups – must be considered more deeply, in the context of domestic politics as well as in international relations. The pontiff cites several features of modernity which propel humanity in the direction of ever-increasing globalization and uniformity. "And yet," he notes,

> precisely against this horizon of universality we see the powerful re-emergence of certain ethnic and cultural consciousness, as it were an explosive need for identity and survival, a sort of counterweight to the tendency toward uniformity. This is a phenomenon which must not be underestimated and regarded as a simple leftover of the past. It demands serious interpretation, and a closer examination on the levels of anthropology, ethics and law.[5]

This tension between the particular and the universal can be considered immanent in human beings. By virtue of sharing in the same human nature, people automatically feel that they are members of one great family, as is in fact the case. But as a result of the concrete historical conditioning of this same nature, they are necessarily bound in a more intense way to particular human groups, beginning with the family and going on to the various groups to which they belong and up to the whole of their ethnic and cultural group, which is called, not be accident, a "nation," from the word, *nasci*: to be born. This term, enriched with another one, *patria*, evokes the reality of the family. "The human condition thus finds itself between these two poles – universality and particularity – with a vital tension between them; an inevitable tension, but singularly fruitful if they are lived in a calm and balanced way" (UN §7, emphasis added).

It is clear from the remainder of John Paul II's address, as well as from the argument of *Fides et Ratio*, that the key requirement for this "calm and balanced" way of living the tension, is an awareness of the *priority of universal moral truths* – regarding the *good* of the human person and of human society, whence flow duties and rights – *to any political, cultural, or social particularities*. John Paul II stresses the existence of a natural or "universal" moral law, "a moral logic which is built into human life and which makes possible dialogue between individuals and peoples. If we want a century of violent coercion to be succeeded by a century of persuasion, we must find a way to discuss the human future intelligibly. The universal moral law written on the human heart is precisely that kind of 'grammar' which is needed if the world is to engage this discussion of its future" (*UN* §3; cf. *UN* §8–10, and §92).

Legal Justice as a Moral Virtue

In the fifth book of the *Nihomachean Ethics*, Aristotle praises "legal justice," that virtue which disposes a person to will and to perform law-abiding acts. He notes that, in a certain sense, this justice comprises the whole of virtue, insofar as a person can employ acts of any other ethical virtue in the service of this form of justice.[6] Legal justice is, it seems, the key virtue of man as a "political animal." However, the attentive reader is left wondering how legal justice can be a universally praiseworthy quality, when humans must often, perhaps always, live under deficient and even deforming codes of civil law. It would seem that, to salvage the status of legal justice as both legal *and* ethically virtuous, some transpolitical type or rule would be needed.

I want to argue that Thomas Aquinas's treatment of this virtue in the *Summa Theologiae* reflects just that ineradicable tension between universality and particularity underscored by John Paul II. My argument, which here I can only sketch, has three basic parts:

> 1. Thomas's opening article concerning legal justice in the *Secunda secundae* is deliberately ambiguous regarding *which type of law* is the rule and measure of justice as a general virtue (see *ST* II-II 58,5; cf. 90, 2).[7]
>
> 2. This ambiguity opens up the possibility that natural law is the real or ultimate rule of legal justice; and there is evidence from the *Prima secundae* to support this conclusion (see *ST* I-II 100,12).[8]
>
> 3. However, in the bulk of the discussion in the *Secunda secundae*, Thomas employs primarily classical conceptions of legal justice as a civic or political virtue, hence governed by the human law of a particular polity (see *ST* II-II 58,7-8; cf. 59,1).[9]

Aquinas's notion of general or legal justice thus appears as an analogous one. The legal justice governed by natural law cannot simply replace that justice ruled by human law, nor vice versa. Human beings, nature's curious combination of matter and spirit, possess in reason or intellect a powerful principle of universality. Yet their limited, contingent being also requires heed paid to the claims of particularity. Human nature is *both* broadly social *and* specifically political. In one sense, for human life and human nature the fully general justice, dependent upon natural law, is *too* general; in another, it is not comprehensive enough. Put another way, natural law requires *both* "completion" *and* "specification" or "determination" by means of human law. It requires completion in order to be suited to guide and direct the common way of life of a given political community.

Aquinas's two "general" or "legal" justices, to speak somewhat loosely, and the tension which at least potentially exists between them, reflects his view of human nature as characterized by the union of universality and particularity. From this union flow the requirements of properly human "completeness." Persons possessed of general justice on the truly universal level of practical reason, of natural law,[10] will see the importance of cultivating all the human virtues. Moreover, they will recognize and desire them as tending to the betterment not of themselves alone, but also of their families, political societies, and the other associations to which they may belong. They will also be aware of the necessity of positive law, to complete the general moral principles by rendering them more determinate; to fill out their country's common way of life and create a genuine political community. It would seem that a person possessing the virtue of "natural legal justice" will recognize the necessity of cultivating "political legal justice." If the precepts directing the latter are in harmony with natural right and natural law, civic general justice will then seem the fully comprehensive social virtue.

And yet, paradoxically, civic legal justice simultaneously stands revealed as narrower, more dependent upon contingency and partiality and convention, however prudently crafted and essential these may be to human existence. As such, it is more prone to err, to deform the human person; more apt to produce and propagate confusion between the truly virtuous and the merely expedient, between the essential and the accidental, between the forest and the trees. In a case of conflict between positive law and natural law, the truly "generally just" individual will reject the former as guide under the tutelage and direction of the latter. The person guided by this universally humane rule of goodness and virtue will recognize the legitimacy and delicacy of the particular. But he cannot sacrifice the regime in his own soul to it.[11] In refusing to do so, he does not sacrifice the common good to his purely personal benefit. Rather, if he acts with prudence, this person upholds the universally human order of goodness, the prior and transcendent rule of any good community. At the least, he thereby recalls for his society and his fellows what sort of polity and persons they should strive to be.

Concluding Remarks

The argument of *Fides et Ratio* urges social scientists, and particularly political philosophers in the classical sense of the term, to dare to seek the truth about man and his good. John Paul II encourages us to weigh seriously the arguments made on these matters by thinkers such as Thomas Aquinas, who combine appreciation for the scope and power of reason with openness to mystery and revelation. Both John Paul II and Aquinas hold out the moderate yet ennobling prospect of *a political philosophy*, of a *politics*, which does justice to both universal and particular dimensions of the human good, and to the ineradicable tension that exists between them. From all this, we citizens of the second and third millennia have, I believe, much to learn.

Notes

1 I am grateful to Tom Hibbs of Boston College for calling this aspect of the encyclical to my attention, and for suggesting the connection between John Paul's argument and some recent work by French political theorist Pierre Manent, e.g., *City of Man* (Princeton University Press, 1998).

2. I am grateful to Grace Goodell of Johns Hopkins University for a lively conversation at the outset of this Summer Institute, in which she forcefully argued this interpretation of *Fides et Ratio* and helped me clarify my own response to it.

3. Thomas Aquinas, *De Caelo* 1. 22.

4. The text of this address (*Address to the United Nations General Assembly*) is currently available for your convenience at the following website: http://www.christusrex.org/www1/pope/UN-speech.htm.

5. *Address to the United Nations General Assembly.*

6. Cf. *NE* 1129a 27–30a 14.

7. "Justice, as stated above (58, 2) directs man in his relations with other men. Now this may happen in two ways: first as regards his relations with individuals, secondly as regards his relations with others in general, insofar as a man who serves a community, serves all those who are included in that community. Accordingly justice in its proper acceptation can be directed to another in both these senses. Now it is evident that all who are included in a community, stand in relation to that community as parts to a whole, while a part as such belongs to a whole, so that whatever is the good of a part can be directed to the good of the whole. It follows therefore that the good of any virtue, whether such virtue direct man in relation to himself, or in relation to certain other individual persons, is referable to the common good, to which justice directs: so that all acts of virtue can pertain to justice, insofar as it directs man to the common good. It is in this sense that justice is called a general virtue. And

since it belongs to law to direct to the common good, as stated above (I-II 90, 2), it follows that the justice which is in this way styled general, is called legal justice, because thereby man is in harmony with the law which directs [the] acts of all the virtues to the common good." *Summa Theologiae* II-II, q. 58, a. 5 (trans. Fathers of the English Dominican Province, Christian Classics, 1981).

8. "[T]he moral and judicial precepts, either in general or also in particular, contained that which is just in itself: but the moral precepts contained that which is just in itself according to that *general justice* which is *every virtue*, according to the *Ethics* 5.1; whereas the judicial precepts belonged to *special justice*, which is about contracts connected with the human mode of life between one man and another." *Summa Theologiae* I-II, q. 100, a. 12.

9. "The Philosopher says (*NE* 5.1) that *many are able to be virtuous in matters affecting themselves, but are unable to be virtuous in matters relating to others*, and (*Pol.* 3.2) that *the virtue of the good man is not strictly the same as the virtue of the good citizen*. Now the virtue of a good citizen is *general justice*, whereby a man is directed to the common good. Therefore general justice is not the same as virtue in general, and it is possible to have one without the other." *Summa Theologiae* II-II, q. 58, a. 6, s.c. This explicitly political characterization of legal justice continues throughout the *corpus articuli* and into the following articles as well.

10. Note that according to Thomas, positive laws deviating from the natural law are deemed not only *unjust*, but *illegal* as well (see *inter alia Summa Theologiae* I-II, q. 96, a. 4). The "legal justice" which has the natural law for its rule is thus the fully *general* and, again to our surprise, paradigmatically *legal* virtue.

11. Cf. Plato's *Republic* IX, 591a–92b.

Verbum Mentis:
Philosophical or Theological Doctrine?
John O'Callaghan

"In the beginning was the Word; and the Word was with God; and the Word was God." So begins the Gospel according to St. John. And according to venerable scholastic and neo-scholastic traditions of commentary, so also is planted the seed for the centerpiece of St. Thomas's philosophical account of how the faculty of intellect functions in understanding, the *verbum mentis*. At the risk of great oversimplification that ignores signficant differences between these traditions of commentary, the basic idea of the *verbum mentis* is that the mind of human beings is an image of the Trinity, to the extent that it is constituted by mind, intellect, and will. In particular, just as the Word of God (Christ) proceeds from the Father, similarly in the human mind a mental word, thus *verbum mentis*, proceeds from or is expressed by the intellectual power, which *verbum mentis* exists in the mind and is signified by a vocal word when we speak. So expressed in the mind, it constitutes the understanding of extramental things. I have just begun the research for this topic, and I do not have much time here to do anything more than make bald indefensible assertions, so I will not say much about the medieval background for this discussion, in particular its roots in St. Augustine's *De trinitate*. I simply want to claim that the *verbum mentis* is no part *at all* of St. Thomas's philosophical account of cognition. The danger occurs precisely when it is divorced from its properly theological setting, and erected into a philosophical thesis in St. Thomas, as if it is one of the *preambles of faith*, philosophically attainable and an essential element of a philosophical psychology, yet revealed since necessary for salvation, a doctrine akin to the incorruptibility of the soul. Unfortunately, I do not have time to consider the properly philosophical difficulties that I think are associated with this picture of the mind, but can only approach it from the perspective of the interpretation of St. Thomas's writing.[1] From that perspective, I think the discussion displays St. Thomas's subtle respect for the autonomy of philosophy, even as it is used within theology.

The importance of the *verbum mentis* to St. Thomas's philosophical psychology is stressed across a wide variety of 20th century authors, including perhaps most famously Jacques Maritain, Etienne Gilson, and Bernard Lonergan;[2] and of course it has much deeper roots in more ancient traditions of interpretation. More recently, in his efforts to contrast St. Thomas's Aristotelianism unfavorably with the anti-Aristotelianism of Peter John Olivi, and William Ockham, Robert Pasnau attributes this "theory of the *verbum*" to St. Thomas as part of "the most impressive and coherent statement of the dominant Aristotelian theory of cognition"[3] in the middle ages. A classic exposition of the *verbum mentis* by a figure more sympathetic to St. Thomas is provided by Joseph Peifer in his work *The Concept in Thomism.*[4] His discussion is in turn heavily influenced by the sixteenth and seventeenth century Portuguese theologian and commentator Poinsot, more widely known as John of St. Thomas; Maritain's interpretation is similarly indebted. A particularly powerful expression of the structure of the interpretation is that the human person cannot understand an object in the world unless he expresses within himself a mental *entity* that serves as a representation of that object; that representation is the *verbum mentis*. The mental word is the extra-mental object's *being present to the intellect*. By abstraction, the possible intellect has impressed upon it an intelligible species, the *species impressa*, that renders it, the possible intellect, capable of expressing or producing an intelligible species, the *species expressa*, in a representation of the object known. The expressed species (*species expressa*) or representation is identified with the *concept* which is in turn identified with the *verbum mentis*. It would be misleading to suggest that all of these figures share all the details of this underlying account of the *verbum mentis*. Lonergan, for example, would not necessarily share the view that the intellect expresses an *entity* distinct from the act.[5] Nonetheless, as a whole this underlying structure remains a powerful account of the *verbum mentis*, and is in many ways the subject of criticism in contemporary philosophy for its commitment to *mental representations* as mental entities upon which the intellect's acts bear in knowing the world.[6]

Peifer is committed to the *distinct entity* account, and states a number of theses about this *concept* identified with the *verbum mentis*, as for instance, "as we use exterior words to speak our thoughts to others, so we use interior words to speak our thoughts to ourselves."[7] This speaking of the concept to ourselves is necessary in order to know the extra-mental thing. Another way in which Peifer puts this is "understanding we speak within ourselves what we know, and we know what we speak. Speaking what we know, we express a word to ourselves in which we know what we know."

Finally, the strength of this scholastic and neo-scholastic tradition of interpretation displays itself when some commentators do not simply claim that it is essential to St. Thomas's philosophical psychology, but go on to claim that in his interpretations of Aristotle's works, St. Thomas attributes the *verbum mentis* to Aristotle in his account of the signification of words at the beginning of the *Peri hermeneias*. This is what Lonergan does in the introductory chapters of his classic *Verbum*. In the *Peri hermeneias*, Aristotle famously (or infamously depending upon your perspective) wrote:

> Now spoken sounds are symbols of affections in the soul, and written marks symbols of spoken sounds. And just as written marks are not the same for all men, neither are spoken sounds. But what these are in the first place signs of – affections of the soul – are the same for all; and what these affections are likenesses of – actual things – are also the same. These matters have been discussed in the work on the soul and do not belong to the present subject.[8]

Summarizing this central text from the *Peri hermeneias*, Lonergan writes:

> [C]ommonly [St. Thomas] asked what outer words meant and answered that, in the first instance, they meant inner words. The proof was quite simple. We discourse on "man" and on the "triangle." What are we talking about? Certainly, we are not talking about real things directly, else we should all be Platonists. Directly, we are talking about objects of thought, *inner words*, and only indirectly, only in so far as our *inner words* have an objective reference, are we talking of real things.[9]

Claude Pannacio provides a very similar account when he writes:

> The mental *verbum* or concept is the prime significate of the corresponding external word. . . . [Aquinas] thus interprets Aristotle's famous passage in the *Peri hermeneias* about the *passio animae* (i.e., affections in the soul) being the significate of the external word as referring to what Augustine and he call the *verbum mentis*.[10]

Even our own John Haldane, who wishes to deny the formation of inner entities that serve as mental representations, and who would deny Peifer's picture of an inner dialogue with ourselves as a means for understanding extramental things, nonetheless displays the power of, as well as his indebtedness to this scholastic and neo-scholastic tradition. Explaining why St. Thomas thinks words must signify concepts, he defends in Fregean terms the role of the *verbum mentis* thus, "the *verbum mentis* gives the *sense* of a term, and in that capacity is signified by it, but *referentially* the term takes us to the world and specifies an extramental nature."[11] John's intent is to provide a more benign interpretation of the *verbum mentis* acceptable in these Fregean terms to contemporary philosophers. However, those influenced by Frege would presumably balk at the apparent identification of the *sense* of a term with something *mental*, whatever its underlying ontology happens to be. In any case, John, like these other neo-scholastic commentators, identifies the concept with the *verbum mentis*. My claim, however, is that all these commentators are mistaken and the *verbum mentis* plays no philosophical role in St. Thomas.

As I have said, there are important differences between the underlying philosophical accounts that these various scholastic and neo-scholastic commentators provide of the *verbum mentis*. But I do not intend to consider those philosophical differences here. Want I want to address is the interpretive problem, since amidst their differences all these advocates share the common interpretive position, that the *verbum mentis* is a philosophical doctrine in St. Thomas, whatever the underlying philosophical account of that doctrine turns out to be. Let me turn then to this interpretive problem.

It would be absurd to claim that St. Thomas does not use the *verbum mentis*. So why do I seem to have claimed it? St. Thomas uses the theme in several of his early discussions, particularly the *Commentary on the Sentences of Peter Lombard*, the *Disputed Questions on Truth*, and the *Summa Contra Gentiles*. A classic expression of it is given in the *Summa Contra Gentiles* when he writes: the *interior word* conceived is a certain *ratio* and likeness of a thing understood.[12] Maritain provides an exhaustive bibliography of the texts in the first appendix to *The Degrees of Knowing*.[13] The fifth *Quodlibetal* question is interesting because there St. Thomas does not refer to it as a *verbum mentis*, but rather a *verbum cordis*, a *word of the heart*. I will argue later that the application of *verbum* to the intellect's concepts is a theological metaphor, and this use of *verbum cordis* for the same thing would support that view, unless, of course, it forms an integral part of St. Thomas's philosophical cardiology. In any case, the texts cited by Maritain are exhaustive, and are typically passages in which St. Thomas is making remarks about intellectual activity and knowing extra-mental things, and the advocates of the *verbum mentis* make great use of them.

Consider, for example two places in the *Summa*: I, q. 34, a. 1; and II–I, q. 93, a. 1, ad 2. In question 34, a. 1, St. Thomas asks "Whether 'Word' should be said essentially or personally in God." After giving a brief summary of the *Peri hermeneias* passage, and its background in Aristotle's *De anima*, he claims two things, first "it is spoken words which are most manifestly and commonly called words," and second "primarily and principally the interior concept of the mind is called a word; secondarily the vocal sound itself that signifies the interior concept is called a word,"[14] since as a sound it is only a word because it signifies a concept. What is interesting, however, is that he does not attribute this second claim to Aristotle, though he has just summarized Aristotle. Instead, he cites theological authority in the person of St. John Damascene in the *De fide orthodoxa*, who had "posited these mode . . . of the term word." In question 93 (Pt. II–I), he is enquiring into whether the eternal law is a supreme exemplar existing in God, and he will conclude that the eternal law is expressed in the Divine Verbum. There again he writes

> the vocal word is something uttered from the mouth of a man, but this word expresses what human words are intended to signify. The same applies to the mental word of a man, which is nothing other than some mental concept by which a man gives mental expression to those things which he cognizes.[15]

But here he simply refers the reader back to what is written in the earlier question 34, and he immediately goes on to write "so it is in the divine Verbum, . . . as appears from Augustine in the *De Trinitate*." I want to make two quick points about these discussions in the *Summa*, first the topic under consideration is clearly a theological topic, *Christ as Dei Verbum*, and second, the authorities appealed to for what is said about the human mental word are also clearly theological, namely St. John Damascence and St. Augustine.

In any case, there *is* also evidence for the claim of some of the advocates' that the *verbum mentis* is an entity distinct from the act of intellect that produces it. Peifer quotes *De potentia*, q. 8, a. 1 in which St. Thomas writes that the conception of the intellect differs (*differt*) from the thing that is understood, the intelligible species by which the intellect is in act, and the act of understanding. He also quotes the *De veritate* (q. 4, a. 2) where St. Thomas writes, "this conception is the effect of the act of understanding," and the response to the seventh objection in that article, where he writes "but the intellect has in itself something proceeding from it, not only in the manner of an operation, but also in the manner of a thing produced."[16] It is important to note in this context, however, that the language of "differs" does not of itself indicate distinction of *entities* in St. Thomas. Form and matter differ in a material thing, without being distinct entities. Similarly, essence and existence differ in a created thing, without being distinct entities. Nonetheless, the last two citations certainly suggest that the concept is a distinct entity as an effect of the act of understanding. I have no intention of disputing that in *those* texts.

What I dispute is their importance. Most of the classic texts that are cited are early texts that have a very strong Augustinian flavor to them set against the background of the *De trinitate*, along with strong Aristotelian elements. What ought to be alarming to the advocates of the *verbum mentis*, however, are those discussions in which it is lacking, namely St. Thomas's last, most detailed and developed philosophical discussions of the substance and facul-

ties of the human person, the *Commentary on the De anima* and the content
of questions 75–89 of the first part of the *Summa*. I take this to be a striking
textual fact for the reader. In the *Summa, the* discussion of the *Divine Verbum*
goes all the way up to and through question 74. Then silence. St. Thomas
begins q. 75 with the intention to "first to consider those things that pertain to
the essence of the soul; second, those which pertain to its powers, and third
those that pertain to its acts." When in question 79, he turns to the *power* of
intellect or understanding, and in questions 84–89 to the *act* of intellect or
understanding, what is striking is that he makes absolutely no mention of the
verbum mentis. Not three times, not twice, not once. Nor does the *verbum
mentis* occur even once in St. Thomas most detailed account of the signification of *words*, the *Commentary on the Peri hermeneias*, even though when he
discusses the divine names in question 13 of the first part of the *Summa*, he
relies very heavily upon the themes he will soon investigate in his commentary on the *Peri hermeneias*. But in question 13 he makes no mention of the
verbum mentis. The advocates of the *verbum mentis* typically pass over these
texts in silence, and give no sign that they are aware that it does not occur in
those discussions. Because they take it to be the essential key to St. Thomas's
philosophical account of understanding, they are forced by this silence of St.
Thomas to appeal to earlier, much more exclusively theological discussions.
But then the contrast of the *Commentary on the De anima*, the *Commentary
on the Peri hermeneias*, and particularly the discussion in the *Summa* of the
essence, powers, and acts of the soul, is striking by contrast. For the advocates, in practice it is as if Aquinas had not written the commentaries or questions 75–89.

Typically, the only citation to the *Summa* will be a passage in question 85,
article 2, near where Aquinas denies that the *intelligible species* is known
prior to extra-mental things. In response to the third objection, St. Thomas
writes:

> [Two operations are found in the intellect.] In the first place the pas-
> sion of the possible intellect may be considered insofar as it is
> informed by the intelligible species. Which having been formed it
> forms in the second place either a definition or a division or a com-
> position, which is signified through an articulated sound. Hence the
> *ratio* which the name signifies is the definition; and the enunciation
> signifies a composition or division of intellect. Therefore articulated
> sounds do not signify the intelligible species, but that which the intel-
> lect forms for itself in order to judge of exterior things.[17]

What is being distinguished here is, of course, the operation of the agent
intellect from the operation of the possible intellect. The agent intellect ren-

ders the possible intellect capable of its act with respect to an object by informing it with the *intelligible species* that has been abstracted from some extra-mental thing. Because of its similarity to the earlier texts in which St. Thomas will apply 'verbum mentis' to "what the intellect forms for itself in order to judge of exterior things," this reference provides the advocates with the foot in the door, or, as I would like to claim, the opening to Pandora's box, for attributing the entire philosophical theory of the *verbum mentis* to the *Summa* discussion.

There are however two very interesting features of this text. First, it does not claim that what the intellect forms in forming definitions, and so on, differs from the act of intellect, as some of the earlier texts appear to do. Second, it makes no mention *at all* of the *verbum mentis*. That of course may just be an oversight on St. Thomas part, though it is difficult to see how he could fail to mention it throughout the entire discussion of 75–89, and not just in this passage, when, on the other hand, he mentions it in the other contexts within the *Summa* that I have already discussed.

In any case, it seems to be upon the principle of rough similarity that the advocates use to attribute the *verbum mentis* the passage from the *Summa*, that they also attribute it to St. Thomas's interpretation of Aristotle, as in Lonergan and Pannacio. A reader of St. Thomas's commentary on Aristotle's *Peri hermeneias* should be startled by the claim that in our speech we are "directly" talking about inner mental words, and "indirectly" talking about extramental things, as well as Pannacio's textual claim that St. Thomas interprets the "famous passage from the *Peri hermeneias*" in such a way that the concept is the "prime significate of the corresponding external word." I have shown elsewhere that this latter claim is simply false.[18] St. Thomas quite clearly departs from Boethius and Ammonius, the commentators whom he is engaging in his interpretation of the *Peri hermeneias* passage. They do hold the view about the direct and indirect signification of words, roughly described by Lonergan and Pannacio. St. Thomas does not. But the really startling claim is Pannacio's that St. Thomas *identifies* Augustine's *verbum mentis* with Aristotle's *passions of the soul*.

Where is this interpretation coming from? Is it thoroughly groundless? No. In the case of Lonergan, it is simply his assumption that what is going on in the *Commentary on the Peri hermeneias* is really nothing other than what St. Thomas had to say in earlier texts like the *Sentences Commentary*, the *Disputed Questions on Truth*, and so on. In the case of Pannacio, it is not based upon the *Commentary* itself; how could it be, since the *Commentary* never refers to the *verbum mentis*? Rather, it is actually based upon St. Thomas's commentary on the opening passages of the Gospel of John. This commentary was written between 1270–72, roughly at the same time as, and even a little after the first part of the *Summa* and the Aristotelian commentaries in question, in stark contrast to most of the early texts often written ten or more years earlier that are usually cited by the advocates in defense of the *verbum mentis*, though many of the advocates cite the Gospel of John as well.

Pannacio simply cites the commentary on John for his evidence of how St. Thomas interprets Aristotle, but does not explain it. Allow me to try. St. Thomas is trying to explain the meaning of *Verbum*, that is, the Latin scriptural name of the Second Person of the Trinity found in the beginning of John's Gospel. There St. Thomas cites the *Peri hermeneias* for the familiar thesis that "vocal utterances are signs of those things which are passions in the soul." Of course we have seen this in the discussion of question 34 in the *Summa*. But the quotation from Aristotle makes no mention of a *verbum mentis*. St. Thomas continues by writing that "it is customary in Scripture ("*consuetum est . . . in Scriptura*") for things signified to be named by the names of the things that signify, as for example in ICorinthians 10. 1 [it says] 'and the rock was Christ.'" Here, the thing that signifies is a rock, and the thing that it signifies is Christ. But the *name* of the thing that signifies is "rock." Thus, as is "customary in Scripture," the name *rock* that properly applies to the rock which signifies Christ, is metaphorically applied to Christ, when Scripture says "the rock was Christ." All well and good. What has this to do with the *Peri hermeneias*? Well, the passion of the soul is signified. A vocal utterance, "passion of the soul," is what signifies it. But 'word' is the name that we apply to vocal utterances that signify. Thus, consistent with the "custom of Scripture," 'word' is applied to what is signified (the passion of the soul), as well as to what signifies (the vocal utterance). We have a sequence of analogies, 'word' to 'rock,' 'passion of the soul' to rock, and passion of the soul to Christ. It is on the basis of these analogies, that Pannacio takes St. Thomas to interpret the *Peri hermeneias* passage as committed to a *verbum mentis*. In any case, St. Thomas concludes, "it is clear then that what is intrinsic to our soul which is signified by our extrinsic word ought nevertheless itself be called a word." However, just as in question 85, article 2 of the *Summa* nothing in the subsequent discussions indicates that the *ratio* is a distinct *entity* from the species or the act that it informs. All it says is that speaking properly words signify the *ratio* (the form *absolutely considered*), not the species (the form *considered as actually informing* the act.)

But now consider whether this discussion in the *Commentary on the Gospel of John* is in fact a philosophical discussion, that is, whether it provides a substantive philosophical account of the cognitive process to call the definition that the intellect forms a *verbum mentis*. First, notice that all St. Thomas claims is that what is within our soul is appropriately "called" a *verbum* because of what is in fact a *verbum*, a verbal utterance. He does not say that the passion of the soul *is* a word. Indeed, if we look back at the *Summa* passages that do refer to the *verbum mentis*, all they claim is that the mental concept is "called" a verbum. This distinction between what is *called* X, and what *is* X, is not an unimportant distinction in St. Thomas. So for instance, he will often write that the soul can be "called" intellect or mind from its highest power which "is" intellect or mind; in so calling it, there is no suggestion that the soul "is" a power, though intellect *is* a power. The soul can properly be *called* intellect or mind, even though it *is* not intellect or mind. It is an analogous use of 'intellect' or 'mind' applied to the soul. But here, with regard to calling the passion of the soul a *verbum*, the case is different. No philosophical justification is given for applying 'word' to the passion of the soul. None is even attempted; no appeal is made to anything in Aristotle's *De intrepretatione*, or *De anima*, or elsewhere.

On the contrary, he is not explaining the *Peri hermeneias*. Rather, he presupposes it as understood, and appeals to it for part of an account of a scriptural passage about the Second Person of the Trinity. It only provides him with the thesis that words signify passions of the soul; it gives him nothing else, and he no longer appeals to it throughout the rest of the passage. Instead, the scriptural passage is explained by an appeal to Aristotle's work *in conjunction with* "the custom of Scripture." This appeal to Scripture dovetails nicely with the *Summa* discussions that appeal to the theological authority of St. Augustine and St. John Damascene. But what does the real work in calling the passion of the soul a *verbum* is not the Aristotelian passage; rather it is the "custom of Scripture." There is no suggestion that this is Aristotle's "custom," or that St. Thomas wishes to interpret him that way. Indeed, the example that justifies calling the passion of the soul a *verbum*, "the rock was Christ," is not even an instance of *analogous* predication, but an instance of what St. Thomas in other places identifies as *metaphorical* predication.

So, the case is not even analogous to the case of calling the soul intellect or mind. It is clear from the *Commentary on John* that the justification for calling a passion of the soul a *verbum* is not philosophical, but theological, which practice in turn is justified by participation in Scriptural custom. And the use does not even seem to be analogous, but rather metaphorical.[19] None of it indicates that this *verbum* is an entity distinct from the act of understanding and the form of that act. So, to call what the intellect does in defining things the expression of a mental word is not a philosophical claim, but a theological metaphor used for a theological purpose, to speak theologically of how man is an image of the divine Trinity. Indeed, if we turn back to the *Summa*, that is precisely how it is used, when St. Thomas picks up the *Verbum* theme again after question 89, in the discussion of the image of God in man in question 93 of the first part. Just a few short questions after St. Thomas has given us a philosophical discussion of the soul, its powers and acts that makes no reference to the *verbum mentis*, he now asks how it is that man is an image of God. His answer, starting from the revealed doctrine of the Trinity with Christ as *Verbum Dei*, is that "it is *possible to say* that there is in rational creatures an image of the uncreated Trinity, in which there is found a procession of a word according to intellect and a procession of love according to will."[20] Notice the emphasis on "it is *possible to say*," not "it *must* be said." One article later, he again cites the authority of Augustine in calling the mental concept a word. So, in light of his commentary on the Gospel of John, I am confident when I claim that St. Thomas knew the *verbum mentis* is a theological discussion, not a philosophical one, even if many of his scholastic and neo-scholastic commentators do not recognize it.

What is the lesson to be drawn from this? It is clear that the advocates of the *verbum mentis*, some consciously, others unconsciously, want the theological discourse to dictate the terms of the philosophical. St. Thomas's approach is quite different. Indeed, his actual practice exemplifies just what he described in one place as one of the roles of philosophy within theology, namely, "to make known through certain *likenesses* those things which are of the faith, just as Augustine in the book *De trinitate* uses many likenesses taken from the teachings of the philosophers in order to make manifest the Trinity."[21] The marvelous coincidence here is that the discussion of the *De trinitate* that St. Thomas seems to have in mind, in giving an example of how the doctrines of the philosophers can be used by the theologians, is Augustine's discussion of the *Verbum*. The Aristotelian discussion provides nothing more than a "likeness" in terms of the passions of the soul for the discussion of the *Divine Verbum*. But the image taken from the philosophical discussion is *not* the *Verbum*. The *Verbum* comes from Scripture itself,[22] not Aristotle. It is not a philosophical discussion, nor, in general, a part of St. Thomas philosophical discussion of cognition. And the theological discussion is not normative for the philosophical, but presupposes it if a "likeness" is to be drawn from it.

I may be wrong to dismiss the philosophical importance of the *verbum mentis*, but at least I have a principled reason for doing so. On the other hand, the advocates need to explain its complete absence from the philosophical discussions, as well as the legitimacy of using the theological discussion as a normative principle for determining the content of what they themselves argue is a philosophical position. Indeed, I think the difference between the philosophical and the theological makes the discussion all the more interesting, and Aquinas's use of philosophy within theology all the more subtle. As Rev. Pinckaers said so elegantly in his paper, "as his faith increased, so also did the rigor of his reason." (Though one might piously add that it it could only be due to the miracle of Faith, that the rigor of Aquinas's thought could increase beyond what is displayed in his earlier works.) But in the context of the Pope's encyclical, I don't want to emphasize so much the philosophical and theological content of the discussions, which some may argue with, or think no longer useful for contemporary philosophy and theology. That we can argue over, but it is an argument for another time. On this specific point of the *verbum mentis*, which is just an example of so many other instances, St. Thomas provides us with the model of how to use philosophy within theology, while respecting the autonomy of philosophy. Whatever philosophy may happen to be under consideration, if it is a genuine philosophy, the theologian need not, indeed should not make it say something it does not, and need not say. With St. Thomas as our guide in this at least, we are better able to appreciate the graceful dance of human reason unaided by revelation with human reason elevated by grace and informed by revelation. Let us all give thanks to our teachers, and the One Teacher by whom they teach.

Notes

1 But see my *Thomist Realism and the Linguistic Turn: Toward a More Perfect Form of Existence*. Forthcoming from the University of Notre Dame Press, Fall of 2000.

2. For Maritain see *The Degrees of Knowledge* (New York: Charles Scribner's Sons, 1959), *passim*, especially Appendix I on "The Concept." For Gilson see *The Christian Philosophy of St. Thomas Aquinas* (New York: Random House, 1956), pp. 223–35. For Lonergan see *Verbum: Word and Idea in Aquinas*, ed. David B. Burrell, C.S.C. (Notre Dame: University of Notre Dame Press, 1967), *passim*, but especially Ch.1.

3. Robert Pasnau, *Theories of Cognition in the Later Middle Ages* (Cambridge: Cambridge University Press, 1997), p. vii.

4. New York: Bookman Assoc., 1952.

5. I owe this point to David Burrell, C.S.C., in conversation.

6. See my *Thomist Realism and the Linguistic Turn* (note 1 above).

7. John Peifer, *The Concept in Thomism* (New York: Bookman Associates, 1952), p. 158.

8. Aristotle, *Aristotle's Categories and De Interpretatione*, trans. John L. Ackrill (Oxford: Clarendon Press, 1963), p. 43.

9. *Verbum*, p. 2.

10. Claude Pannacio, "From Mental Word to Mental Language," *Philosophical Topics* 20:2 (1992), p. 128.

11. "The Life of Signs," *Review of Metaphysics* 47 (March 1994), p. 468.

12. Bk. IV, cap. 11, #14.

13. In my reading, those that are most often cited are *De potentia*, q.8, a.1; *Summa Theologiae* I, q. 34, a. 1, ad 3; I–II, q. 93, a. 1 ad 2; *Summa Contra Gentiles* IV, cap. 11, #14; *Quodlibetum* V, q. 5, a. 2, ad 1; a. 9 ad 1; *In Joannem Evang.*, cap. I, lect. 1; *De veritate*, q. 4, a. 2, q. 9, a. 4, ad 1, 7, 9.

14. "Manifestius autem et communius in nobis dicitur verbum quod voce pro-fertur, quod quidem ab interiori procedit quantum ad duo quae in verbo exte-riori inveniuntur, scilicet, vox ipsa et significatio vocis. Vox enim significat intellectus conceptum, secundum Philosophum in libro *Periherm.*, et iterum vox ex imaginatione procedit, ut in libro *De anima* dicitur. Vox autem quae non est significativa verbum dici non potest; ex hoc ergo dicitur verbum vox exterior, quia significat interiorem mentis conceptum. Sic igitur primo et prin-cipaliter interior mentis conceptus verbum dicitur; secundario vero ipsa vox interioris conceptus significativa; tertio vera ipsa imaginatio vocis verbum dicitur. Et hos tres modos Verbi ponit Damascenus." Aquinas, *Summa Theologiae* I, q. 34, a. 1.

15. "Verbum enim vocale est quiddam ab ore hominis prolatum, sed hoc verbo exprimuntur quae verbis humanis significantur; et eadem ratio est de verbo hominis mentali, quod nihil est aliud quam quiddam mente conceptum quo homo exprimit mentaliter ea de quibus cogitat. Sic igitur in divinis ipsum Verbum, quod est conceptio paterni intellectus, personaliter dicitur; sed omnia quaecumque sunt in scientia Patris, sive essentialia sive personalia sive etiam Dei opera, exprimuntur hoc Verbo, ut Patet per Augustinum in *XV de Trin.*"

16. "Ipsa enim conceptio est *effectus* actus intelligendi." *QDV,* q. 4, a. 2; "Sed intellectus habet in seipso aliquid progrediens ab eo, non solum per modum operationis, sed etiam *per modum rei operatae*. Et ideo verbum significantur ut res procedens." Ibid., ad 7.

17. "[Duplex] operatio coniungitur in intellectu. Nam primo quidem consid-eratur passio intellectus possibilis secundum quod informatur specie intelligi-bili. Qua quidem formatus format secundo vel definitionem vel divisionem vel compositionem, quae per vocem significatur. Unde ratio quam significant nomen, est definitio; et enuntiatio significat compositionem et divisionem intellectus. Non ergo voces significant ipsas species intelligibiles, sed ea quae intellectus sibi format ad iudicandum de rebus exterioribus." *ST* I, q. 85, a. 2, ad 3.

18. See my *Thomist Realism and the Linguistic Turn*, Ch. 3, *passim* (note 1 above).

19. But see *ST* I, q. 34, a. 1, ad 1.

20. "In creatura rationali, in qua invenitur processio verbi secundum intellectum et processio amoris secundum voluntatem, potest dici imago Trinitatis increatae per quandam repraesentationem speciei." *ST* I, q. 93, a. 6.

21. *Expositio Super Librum Boethii De Trinitate*, q. 2, a. 3 *respondeo*: "ad notificandum per aliquas similitudines ea quae sunt fidei, sicut Augstinus in libro De trinitate utitur multis similitudinibus ex doctrinis philosophicis sumptis ad manifestandum trinitatem."

22. This is not to exclude, of course, philosophical influences in St. John's milieu that provide a context for his use of *Logos* to express the divine revelation in Scripture.

Entrusting Ourselves:
Fides et ratio and Augustine's *De utilitate credendi*
Anne Barbeau Gardiner

In *Fides et Ratio*, Pope John Paul declares that "[i]n believing, we entrust ourselves to the knowledge acquired by other people" (§32). Such entrusting comes naturally to us, for, as he explains, "there are in the life of a human being many more truths which are simply believed than truths which are acquired by way of personal verification" (§31). This is especially the case for us who have come late in history: "Who in the end could forge anew the paths of experience and thought which have yielded the treasure of human wisdom and religion? This means that the human being – the one who seeks the truth – is also the one who lives by belief" (§31). We are dependent, then, upon the past and upon those who have transmitted to us the accumulation of human wisdom and tradition. The Pope speaks also of a "trusting dialogue" between friends as another form of entrusting ourselves, noting that ancient philosophers proposed "friendship as one of the most appropriate contexts for sound philosophical enquiry" (§33).

But besides these universal forms of entrusting, there is another kind that has its roots in the Bible. The Pope points out that "biblical man" understood himself "only as 'being in relation' – with himself, with people, with the world and with God" (§21). In particular, the Chosen People were dependent for their belief upon those to whom God had spoken directly and did not approach the truth by way of theory and abstraction, as the Greeks did (§16), but by way of entrusting themselves to holy men whom God himself had entrusted with his revealed word. Theirs was the God of Abraham and Jacob, of Moses and the Prophets. With the Incarnation of Christ, this "being in relation" was brought to fullness: God immersed himself in time to speak to us "as friends" and take us personally "into communion" with him (§10–11).

Fides et Ratio is pervaded by this biblical sense of fiduciary trust as the ground of our quest for truth. The Pope sees each of us as on a journey toward "a truth recognized as final, a truth which confers a certitude no longer open to doubt" (§27). But interestingly enough, he thinks that this "ulterior truth" about the meaning of life can be attained "not only by way of reason but also through trusting acquiescence to other persons who can guarantee the authenticity and certainty of the truth itself" (§33). One may ask, though, how is it possible to ascertain who is worthy of our trusting acquiescence? How is one to distinguish between a Jacques Maritain and a Teilhard de Chardin? The Pope does not answer this question in the present encyclical. He simply asserts that God has endowed us with "inherent capacities of thought" to enable us "to encounter and recognize a truth of this kind" (§33). That is, we have the ability to discern, by the grace of the Holy Spirit, the persons we ought to trust By engaging ourselves in trust – in an age gone mad with individualism—we will avoid using our freedom only for ourselves. For the Pope remarks, in *Crossing the Threshold of Hope*: "If we cannot accept the prospect of giving ourselves as a gift, then the danger of a selfish freedom will always be present."[1]

St. Augustine makes a similar point, but in sterner language, in *De utilitate credendi*: "It is authority alone which moves fools to hasten unto wisdom."[2] That is to say, only a person speaking with authority for the Church can quickly set on the right path one who is just a beginner on the journey to truth. Such a beginner would seriously delay his progress if he went about to reinvent the wheel, that is, if he tried to rediscover by himself all that God had already revealed to the Church and which a Catholic teacher was able to transmit to him. Just as one who goes to court puts his trust in an expert in the law rather than trying to master the law by himself, so a searcher after truth entrusts himself to a guide who is a fitting conduit for the deposit of Catholic truth about God and man.

The idea of personal entrustment that informs *Fides et Ratio* is related to the principle of "personalism" which the Pope developed in some of his previous works, such as *Love and Responsibility*[3] and *Crossing the Threshold of Hope*. In the latter, he wrote, "This principle [of personalism] is an attempt to translate the commandment of love into the language of philosophical ethics. The person is a being for whom the only suitable dimension is love." And there he added: "Man affirms himself most completely by giving of himself."[4] It seems, then, that this entrusting of ourselves which he urges in the recent encyclical is an affirmation – in an age of depersonalization and lovelessness – of our personhood and our need for love. The Pope finds it beautiful and rich that our journey towards truth should have been designed by Providence to be personal and loving, to be in some sense, incarnational. Our entrusting of ourselves to others, he declares, is "often humanly richer than mere evidence, because it involves an interpersonal relationship and brings into play not only a person's capacity to know but also the deeper capacity to entrust oneself to others, to enter into a relationship with them which is intimate and enduring" (§32). Indeed, he adds, "the capacity to entrust oneself and one's life to another person and the decision to do so are among the most significant and expressive of human acts" (§33).

Here we have a glimpse into the very heart of Christianity. For the entrusting and interdependence of believers within the Mystical Body of Christ, which is the Church, is a reflection of the *communio personarum* of the Trinity. The Pope speaks of a real and abiding intimacy of persons as lying at the core of reality. Personhood is inscribed into the ground of being itself. It follows, then, that our journey towards truth will deeply involve our being persons related by trust to one another. Men and women are really on a double quest, he explains, "a search for the truth and a search for a person to whom they might entrust themselves" (§33). These two searches converge at the point where we meet Jesus Christ, who is "Truth in Person, Truth "embodied in a living and personal way" (§34), who invites us to entrust ourselves to him and fully realize what we are when he says, "Come, follow me." Through the Incarnation, the Pope explains, Christ "fully reveals man to himself" (§60). Our Savior shows us how precious our human form is which he did not disdain to take for himself. From now on, God "takes a human face" (§12), enters history, and speaks to us with a "living voice" in the Church to whom Christ said, in the person of his Apostles: "He who hears you, hears me" (Luke 10. 16).

A similar motif of self-entrusting is woven deep into the fabric of *De utilitate credendi*. Augustine wrote this treatise when he was still only a deacon. He observes here that for the one who cannot come to the truth by himself, a guide is near at hand in the Catholic Church to make him ready, to cleanse and purify him for his journey. It would be "ungrateful" of him to refuse the guidance that God has provided with so much labor.[5] Augustine urges his friend Honoratus, who had followed him earlier into Manicheeism, now to "entrust yourself to good teachers of Catholic Christianity."[6] Augustine explains that he himself had needed to entrust himself to the guidance of such a Catholic teacher – Ambrose, bishop of Milan. Whatever gifts and skills he and Honoratus may have in the sight of the world, they are still only "fools," Augustine insists, when it comes to the true "knowledge" of God and man.[7] Beginners like themselves need to trust wiser men like Ambrose, rather than follow their own judgment.

One cannot help but be struck by Augustine's humility when he explicitly includes himself, as well as Honoratus, among the "fools." In *Fides et Ratio*, the Pope remarks aptly that faith "liberates reason from presumption" and teaches it "humility" (§76). Augustine is a perfect example of this when, at mid-life, he entrusts himself like a child to the holy and learned bishop of Milan. In another section of his recent encyclical, the Pope cites the *Confessions*, where Augustine remarks, regarding his first steps in the Catholic faith, that he found it "modest and not in the least misleading to be told by the Church to believe what could not be demonstrated." In Manicheeism, on the contrary, he had begun with a proud pretense of ration-

ality and ended up embracing the most absurd beliefs. One cannot help but
compare his trajectory as a Manichean to that of some modern thinkers, who
started with an exorbitant idea of the autonomy of reason and ended up
embracing totalitarian ideologies like Maoism and Stalinism.

Like Augustine, the Pope alludes to the Wisdom books of the Bible and
speaks of the "fool" as one who may be skilled in learning, who may know
many things in the sight of the world, but who is incapable of fixing his gaze
on what really matters in life. Such a person needs to have his reason set free
by way of entrusting himself to another. This entrusting will set him speedily
on the quest for the ultimate meaning of existence (§18). What is desired
when we entrust ourselves, the Pope explains, is not philosophical truth but
"the truth of the person – what the person is and what the person reveals from
deep within." It seems that in this kind of trust, love mediates the truth directly from one heart to another, as in the Eucharist. The poet John Dryden
describes such a process well, in a poem called "Eleonora" (1692), where he
gives us a model of the Catholic saint. This saint is so much wiser than the
friends who entrust themselves to her that he compares her to "swelling Seas"
commingling with "gentle Rivers." But as these unequal waters merge in the
love of friendship, the truth of each person is fully communicated:

> For 'tis the bliss of Friendship's holy state
> To mix their Minds, and to communicate;
> Though Bodies cannot, Souls can penetrate
> ("Eleonora," lines 250–52).

This is what the Pope is speaking of in *Fides et ratio* – a friendship of
souls where the mutual self-giving is like Holy Communion. When Dryden
uses the word communicate for the way minds and souls mix and penetrate
each other, he alludes to Holy Communion. For even in the mid-eighteenth
century, two generations after him, the first meaning of the term communicate
in Samuel Johnson's Dictionary (1755) was still, to receive Holy
Communion.

Self-entrusting, then, is profound communication in the context of true
friendship. What we see in such friendship is what the Pope calls "faithful
self-giving" on both sides, that is, a commingling of tides, a sharing of gifts
that is dynamic and fruitful because of a mutual trust that produces "fullness
of certainty and security." In this loving context, truth is relayed from heart to
heart and leads the beginner gently from the knowledge of belief to that of
experience. As the Pope explains, "knowledge through belief, grounded as it
is on trust between persons, is linked to truth: in the act of believing, men and
women entrust themselves to the truth which the other declares to them"
(§32). In this day and age, when friendship is too often set aside for the sake

of private ambition, it is good to be reminded of its inexpressible value in the quest for truth.

One of the subtexts of *Fides et Ratio* is that many moderns are unable to entrust themselves to others because of their radical individualism. They have fallen into an "ever deepening introversion, without reference of any kind to the transcendent" (§81). They exalt their individual freedom of thought into an absolute, and regard their private reason as having total sovereignty when it comes to deciding what is good and evil or what is true. Indeed, they even think they can determine their "own truth, different from the truth of others" (§98). The Pope thinks this exorbitant idea of autonomy which is rampant in the modern world is a recapitulation of the Fall of Man. For Original Sin was just such a refusal of entrustment for the sake of a radical idea of personal freedom: "the blindness of pride deceived our first parents into thinking themselves sovereign and autonomous, and into thinking that they could ignore the knowledge which comes from God" (§22).

Like Pope John Paul II, the Catholic poet Alexander Pope spoke of this modern pride in the sovereignty of reason – a pride already pervasive among 18th-century intellectuals – as an echo of Original Sin:

> In Pride, in reas'ning Pride, our error lies;
> All quit their sphere, and rush into the skies.
> Pride still is aiming at the blest abodes,
> Men would be Angels, Angels would be Gods.
> Aspiring to be Gods, if Angels fell,
> Aspiring to be Angels, Men rebel . . . (*An Essay on Man*, 1:123–30).

In a chapter on the legacy of Descartes in *Three Reformers*, Jacques Maritain likewise speaks of a serious disease of the modern mind – the sin of angelism. The modern aspires to think like an angel, Maritain declares, that is, to be entirely independent of things, as if he were a disembodied spirit, and to be a unique species all to himself. But by such a "denaturing of human reason," he goes "beyond the limits" of our species. For he even claims for our intelligence "the perfect autonomy and the perfect immanence, the absolute independence . . . of the uncreated intelligence."[8] But even as modern man usurps this "superhuman condition" of mind, he marches, ironically enough, toward an ever greater brutalization and depersonalization of his species. Civilization founders because the more he tries to think like an angel, the more he acts like a beast.

From the viewpoint of a contemporary solipsist or postmodern, the idea of entrusting oneself to another might seem to be the opposite of personal freedom and dignity. But this is not the case. The Pope explains that the "grandeur of the human being" does not lie in self-sufficiency, but "in choosing to enter the truth, to make a home under the shade of Wisdom and dwell there" (§107). Our freedom is "real but limited," for we are only creatures. We have a "seed" of freedom which we are meant to cultivate by an openness to truth. But all too often we use our freedom merely to choose "finite, limited and ephemeral goods," thereby losing all passion for truth and allowing our reason to be shackled. Jesus Christ came to free our reason and to animate it in pursuit of the truth. Indeed, our "freedom itself needs to be set free."[9]

And so, just as Augustine urged Honoratus – who had long been shackled to Manicheeism because of its initial appeal to his pride in human reason – to find freedom by entrusting himself to a Catholic teacher, so the Pope urges the modern thinker, imprisoned by what Maritain calls the sin of angelism, to entrust himself to the "Good Teacher," the "living voice" of the Gospel. For the humanity of persons is "all the more affirmed the more they entrust themselves to the Gospel and open themselves to Christ" (§102). In *Veritatis splendor*, too, the Pope had noted that when we entrust ourselves to the guidance of the Magisterium, we are far from being demeaned or diminished. Indeed, we become more fully ourselves, because the Church does not bring to our conscience "truths which are extraneous to it," but rather unfolds and confirms what was already latent there from the beginning.[10] The Pope assures us that though the knowledge acquired by our entrusting ourselves to other persons seems at first "an imperfect form of knowledge," it can afterwards be "perfected gradually through personal accumulation of evidence."[11] "Faith accepts divine truth as it is," and then a new horizon opens up that "stirs reason to move beyond all isolation and willingly to run risks so that it may attain whatever is beautiful, good and true."[12] Entrusting ourselves leads, then, to a level of ardor and courage in the pursuit of truth that would otherwise have been lacking. Reason itself now "grows more penetrating and assured because of the support it receives from faith."[13]

This is not just a hypothesis, the Pope insists. It is something that has already been shown in history. For the Church Fathers "succeeded in disclosing completely all that remained implicit and preliminary in the thinking of the great philosophers of antiquity" (§40). He adds that "a good part of modern and contemporary philosophy would not exist without this stimulus of the word of God" (§76). But, of course, this great debt of theirs to Christianity is precisely what most modern philosophers will ignore or even deny. And, as Rev. Stanley Jaki has shown, the immense debt of modern science to Christianity is also their well-kept secret. And here I cannot help but recall John Dryden's apt reproach, in *Religio Laici* (1682), to the Deist philosopher of his day for ignoring his debt to Judaeo-Christianity. Dryden tells him that his idea of a Creator, of a universe designed according to the Divine Mind, and of personal rewards or punishments after death were all truths given to the Deist by the very Bible he claims he has renounced:

Vain, wretched Creature, how art thou misled
To think thy Wit these God-like Notions bred!
These Truths are not the product of thy Mind,
But dropt from Heaven, and of a Nobler kind.
Reveal'd Religion first inform'd thy Sight,
And Reason saw not, till Faith sprung the Light (lines 62–68).

Thus, the 17th-Century Deist repudiating his roots is the father of the postmodern who sees nothing important as having been conceived before the "Early Modern Period."

But the beauty of self-entrusting for the sake of truth, of holy friendship, is that it can span the centuries and millenia. Dante entrusted himself to Virgil in his journey through Hell and Purgatory more than a thousand years after Virgil's bodily death. And there have been many "sons" of St. Benedict and St. Francis down the centuries. In *Fides et Ratio*, the Pope speaks of how the writings of St. Anselm and St. Thomas Aquinas still inspire us across the ages. He mentions also the blessed martyrs who personally witness the truth to us by the sacrifice of their lives. By their "act of trusting abandonment to Christ," he says, they are for us who live after them the "most authentic witnesses to the truth about existence." They invite us to "confidence" and "emulation," persuading us to belief by a "love that has no need of lengthy arguments." Indeed, they "stir in us a profound trust because they give voice to what we already feel" (§32). Assuredly, those who inspire "emulation" and "trust" by their personal sacrifice are, in a manner of speaking, still alive to us as persons, as friends, across the ages.

It seems, then, that there is nothing degrading to our human freedom and dignity when we entrust ourselves to each other for the sake of truth. As the Pope observes in *Fides et Ratio*, truth itself is set in "the context of interpersonal communication." The Pope points to the Blessed Mother, the Seat of Wisdom, as the best example of how personal entrusting does not diminish our dignity. For "in giving her assent to Gabriel's word, Mary lost nothing of her true humanity and freedom." She is our model "in giving birth to the Truth and treasuring it in her heart" (§108). Through her, the Truth himself came into the world as a Person. Likewise, in *Veritatis splendor*, the Pope cited St. Ambrose as saying that Our Lady herself is the "model" for every Christian in her trustful self-giving. And both recent encyclicals conclude with the Pope's entrusting us – that is his word – to Mary, Seat of Wisdom.

Ultimately, self-entrusting for the sake of truth has a Trinitarian dimension. For as Jesus entrusted his Apostles with his word, saying "He who hears you, hears me" (Luke 10. 16), so he acknowledged that the Father had, in turn, entrusted him: "The word which you hear is not mine but the Father's who sent me." In *Redemptor Hominis* (1979), the Pope explains this passage as meaning that the word of Christ is the "property" of God himself, since "even He, 'the only Son,' who lives 'in the bosom of the Father,' when transmitting that truth as a prophet and teacher, feels the need to stress that He is acting in full fidelity to its divine source."[14] And so, the Church guides to whom we entrust ourselves to learn about the truth have themselves been entrusted with the word coming from the Father through the Son. Truth, then, has an ineffably Personal source within the Trinity.

In *Sign of Contradiction*, the Pope speaks of the love between the Persons of the Trinity as a parallel to our *communio personarum* within the Church. He says that we offer to each other here in the Mystical Body "gifts of truth and love" in the same way as do the three Persons in God throughout eternity. When Jesus prayed for us to be one (John 17. 21), the Pope says he implied "a certain similarity between the unity of the divine Persons and the unity of the sons of God in truth and charity."[15] Now this is a very profound insight into the revealed truth of man's having been created as *imago Dei*. Man was made personal just like God, to be in loving intimacy with others. As we read in Genesis, "It is not good for man to be alone."

The Mystical Body of Christ is the place, then, of fraternity and friendships. It is the redeemed garden of mutual self-entrustings spreading in, and taming a wild, alienated world. The Church offers to the rest of mankind a beautiful image of the Personal love in the Trinity. Indeed, in this encyclical, the Pope himself offers an image of this love. He seems to stand waiting with widespread arms, like the old father in the Parable of the Prodigal Son, waiting for his erring modern son to return and entrust himself, that the entire family of Christ may rejoice and communicate together.

Notes

1. Pope John Paul II, *Crossing the Threshold of Hope*, ed. Vittorio Messori (New York: Alfred A. Knopf, 1994), p. 202.

2. Augustine, *De utilitate credendi*, §34; trans. C. L. Cornish, Nicene & Post-Nicene Fathers, 38 vols. (Oxford, 1873–1887), vol. 3, pp. 337–43.

3. Karol Wojtyla, *Love and Responsibility*, trans. H. T. Willetta (New York: Farrar, Straus, Giroux, 1981).

4. *Crossing*, pp. 201–2.

5. *De utilitate credendi*, §35.

6. Ibid., §36.

7. Ibid., §27

8. J. Maritain, *Three Reformers* (New York: Apollo, 1970), p. 79.

9. Pope John Paul II, *Veritatis splendor* (1993), §86.

10. *Veritatis Splendor*, §64.

11. Ibid., §32.

12. Ibid., §44 and 56.

13. Ibid., §106.

14. Pope John Paul II, *Redemptor Hominis* (1979), §19.

15. Karol Wojtyla, *Sign of Contradiction* (New York: Seabury Press, 1979), p. 20.

Death, Immortality and Resurrection
Rev. Peter Hunter, O.P.

Many of the talks this week have been brilliant theoretical expositions of the relationship of reason and faith, but I'm a practical man, and I thought I would offer a practical example of a rather nice situation where an interesting relation of faith to reason appears. This example concerns two issues, one in analytical philosophy and one in the thought of Thomas Aquinas, which I shall try to argue resemble each other in such a way that a resolution of an apparent antinomy in a discussion about body and soul in Aquinas can suggest a way to go forward in the other issue, which is the evaluation of the phenomenon of death in analytical philosophy. The treatment which follows is my understanding of what Rev. David Albert Jones, O.P. has written on the issue in a draft of his doctoral thesis (Blackfriars, Oxford) on the theological assessment of whether death is a good or a bad thing. Any insights are to be attributed to Rev. Jones, any deficiencies to me.

Rev. Jones began his study of this topic because he became interested in the fact that Augustine, although disposed to think that death was a good thing by his Neo-Platonic background, because of his reading of Scripture on the topic, came to think of death as always *per se* a tragedy. Rev. Jones began to think about the proper Christian attitude to death, and in the process of this needed to address the arguments about death in the analytical tradition. He discovered that analytical philosophers wrote very little about death, but a lot of what they did write centered basically on two developments; one a reconsideration of arguments of Lucretius aiming to demonstrate that death is not to be feared; and the other pointing out the unsatisfactory nature of never-ending existence.

Lucretius argues in book III of *De Rerum Naturae* that death is not to be feared. Two arguments in particular get rehearsed by analytical philosophers. The first claims that because we will not be around once we are dead, we should not fear the state of being dead. Some philosophers say that fear of death is irrational and rests on the mistaken assumption that being dead will be an awful state to be in, when in fact it is no state at all. The other argument rests on the idea that death is undesirable because it brings about nonexistence. But we didn't exist before our births, and yet no one seems worried that they once did not exist, only that at some time they will not exist. This is irrational, says Lucretius, for pre-natal and post-mortem nonexistence are symmetrical.

Thomas Nagel is one philosopher who argues against Lucretius.[1] He sees that what people fear in death is not some state of nonexistence. That truly would be irrational, for it is surely right that nonexistence is not a state. I think Nagel is somewhat confused as to exactly why it is bad for me to lose my life. Philosophers supporting Lucretius ask how death can harm me if I am not around as the result of it to be harmed, so Nagel goes through arguments to try to show that people can be harmed even when they are dead (by defamation, for example),[2] which to my mind is besides the point, and prone to just the error Nagel detects in Lucretius. Nevertheless, I think he is right that death, seen as my extinction, is an evil. This is evident simply from the consideration of it as the loss of the good of life, which is good simpliciter and not simply in combination with the other goods it makes possible (happiness, health or what have you). What the person who hates death realizes (perhaps unconsciously) is that death is precisely the extinction of life, and that life is good *per se*, or what amounts to the same thing, that human beings, considered simply as existing, as living, are good. Notice that belief in the immortality of the soul does not substantially change this analysis, for it seems right to doubt that a soul could have any kind of really human existence when separated from the body. Some philosophers who follow Frege in his discussion of existence see this analysis of life as good *simpliciter* and consequently death as evil as involving the mistake of thinking that existence is a predicate, but I wonder if such philosophers would see the will to self-preservation as irrational, and if not, on what grounds they would base it.

Moreover, in contradistinction to the situation with other animals, human death is particularly the stuff of outrage and tragedy, for death seems to take more than it has a right to. If Aquinas and Aristotle are right to say that understanding involves the mind becoming, in a way, the thing it understands, then human death is the death of a whole world. That is to say, the mental life of a human being ought not to be within the reach of death, for death is about the corruption of the material body. Certainly, we are our bodies – I am not a Cartesian – but humans exhibit some behavior that is more than bodily, more than simply material. The human being, as linguistic, can think about his own death. Even if Freud, among others, is right that I cannot imagine my own death, and though we might agree with Wittgenstein that death is not an event in my life but its horizon,[3] still I can view this horizon with disquiet as that which robs me of my existence, my humanity, and "not go gentle into that good night. Rage, rage against the dying of the light," as Dylan Thomas pleads with his dying father to do.

On the other hand, Bernard Williams, among others, points out to us the undesirability of never-ending earthly life. In his article "The Makropulos Case," he uses a story of a man deprived of the possibility of death, an enduring theme of Western literature, making an appearance for example in an ancient piece of anti-Semitic propaganda, the story of the Wandering Jew. Williams claims that deathless life would ultimately be tedious, filled with suffering and destructive of all kinds of human values which rely on the fragility of human life. In many of the stories on this theme, the undying individual must watch loved ones pass away, and the victims of this inability to die, for that is how the stories invariably present them, come to despair of any sense to existence and frequently pray vainly for death to come upon them. In the words of one of the songs in a popular film version of such a story, "Highlander," "Who wants to live forever?" Some philosophers complain that Williams's conclusion follows from inessential aspects of the story – that Makropulos suffers the infirmity of extreme old age, for example – but I think that Williams's story captures quite well what it would be like if death escaped us here on earth.

Other authors point out that if life is to be compared to a story,[4] it must have an end in order to have a proper dramatic shape. Or if you prefer, a life without an end would be devoid of finality, and that might end up robbing existence of any kind of meaning. To make sense, a temporal existence must come to an end, to a completion. Deathless life would be like a newspaper serial that went on century after century. Ultimately, the story wouldn't be able to go anywhere, for it wouldn't ultimately have anywhere to go to. It might be interesting for a few years or decades, but in the end, it would just be tedious and repetitious. It might be objected that we can imagine a life where I could spend my time doing philosophy, becoming more and more wise and that this would give a finality to life without introducing a cessation of existence, but such a possibility ignores the fact of bodily decay which to my mind is a central fact of bodily, temporal existence.

So perhaps it is true both that death is an evil, as bringing an extinction to life, which is a *per se* good, and that life without some kind of completion or fulfillment would be tedious and ultimately meaningless. There is at least suggestive evidence that this is true. Consider the fact that when a ten-year-old dies, we are particularly shocked and angry, while with an octogenarian, especially someone who lived well, death seems perhaps sad, but also somehow acceptable and even perhaps appropriate. In the ten-year-old, we are more aware of the outrage of death as extinction while with the octogenarian, we see the closure it brings to earthly existence. (It is important to see that the death of the octogenarian is still, though, an extinction, and the death of the ten-year-old still brings a finality to his life, though an untimely one.) So perhaps we can accept that philosophy tells us that death has two apparently contradictory faces, the Grim Reaper, to be hated and feared, and a more benign character, who brings things to a proper conclusion. It is interesting to note that while we have a name for the first face, the latter lacks one: death as we know it has more of the former character than the latter.

At this point, Rev. Jones introduces a certain argument of Thomas Aquinas, which I hope you will see immediately has relevance to the arguments I have just presented. Aquinas believes on philosophical grounds that: (1) the soul is naturally immortal; (2) the body is naturally moral; (3) the soul is naturally joined to the body. I am told by Christopher Martin that sometimes Aquinas does not seem to think that (1) can be demonstrated by reason, but certainly in the *Summa Contra Gentiles*, for example, he offers several arguments for its truth.

But as you can see, if (1), (2), and (3) are all true, then the human being is a rather odd creature. His make-up seems to involve a naturally unnatural state! So just like the discussion of death in analytical philosophy, Aquinas' philosophical discussion of the human person leads him into an apparent antimony. Aquinas can then say two things.[5] Firstly, this condition used to have a resolution, when Adam, though naturally mortal, had the supernatural gift of immortality, lost due to the Fall. Secondly, this unnatural condition will be resolved, since there will be a resurrection of the body.

Clearly, the form of the two predicaments (of death, and the unnatural nature of humanity) is rather similar – an apparent antimony proposed to us by philosophy. So perhaps the first antimony has a resolution rather like the second. Perhaps some theological doctrine can make sense of the two faces of death. What makes us more confident is that the arguments are not just similar in form – there is an intrinsic connection of their matter too. The fact that the human being has a material body is what gives him a life story, inserted into time, and which suggests that a finite span of life is appropriate, while the immateriality of the human soul, the soul's intellectual life, are what make man's extinction outrageous.

And we are not disappointed. Aquinas and Augustine both say that Adam in his original state would have died in a sense, only his death would have been only in the aspect of a completion, of a glorification.[6] But after the Fall, death becomes an extinction. And thinking to our own future, through the Redemption won in Christ, death is a foe which has been defeated, which has lost its sting, (though it remains an enemy) and through the Resurrection of the Body, death is transformed in the end into a way to completion, to simple closure, once again and is not ultimately able to make us extinct.

Notes

1 He does so, for example, in "Death," *Nous* IV: 1, pp. 73–80.

2. Steve Baldner pointed out to me that this consideration is not so far-fetched as it might seem. Aristotle wonders in Book I of the *Nicomachean Ethics* whether I might be said to be harmed after my death.

3. Wittgenstein, *Tractatus Logico-Philosophicus*, §6.4311.

4. For example, J. Malpas, "Death and the Unity of Life," in *Death and Philosophy*, eds. R. C. Solomon and J. Malpas (London, 1998).

5. What follows here is only a sketch of Aquinas' position, but I hope enough has been said to show the similarity between the two positions.

6. Thomas Aquinas, *Summa Theologiae* I, q. 97, a. 4; Augustine *De Genesi ad Litteram* VI, 23.

Contributors

Benedict Ashley, O.P., St. Louis University, St. Louis, Missouri

Steven Baldner, Department of Philosophy, Saint Francis Xavier, Nova Scotia

Rémi Brague, Université de Paris, Sorbonne

Angelo Campodonico, Universitá di Genova, Italy

William E. Carroll, Department of History, Cornell College, Iowa

Louis Chammings, Institut National de l'Audiovisuel, Paris

Jude Dougherty, Dean emeritus, School of Philosophy, The Catholic University of America, Washington, D.C.

Leo Elders, S.V.D., Instituut voor Wijsbegeerte, Rolduc, Kerkrade, The Netherlands

Anne Gardiner, Brewster, New York

Grace Goodell, School of Advanced International Studies, Johns Hopkins University, Washington, D.C.

John J. Haldane, School of Philosophical and Anthropological Studies, University of St. Andrews, Scotland

John Hittinger, Department of Philosophy, USAF Academy, Colorado

Jennifer Hockenbery, Department of Philosophy, Mt. Mary College, Milwaukee, Wisconsin

Peter E. Hodgson, Corpus Christi College, Oxford, UK

William J. Hoye, Katholisch-Theologische Fakultät, Universität Münster, Germany

Peter Hunter, O.P., Blackfriars, Oxford, UK

Mary M. Keys, Department of Government, University of Notre Dame

Alejandro Llano, Instituto de Antropologia y Etica, Universidad de Navarra, Spain

Ralph McInerny, Director, Jacques Maritain Center, University of Notre Dame

Christopher Martin, Center for Thomistic Studies, University of St. Thomas, Texas

Cyrille Michon, Université de Paris, Sorbonne

John O'Callaghan, Department of Philosophy, Creighton University, Omaha, Nebraska

Servais Th. Pinckaers, O.P., Albertinum, Fribourg, Switzerland

Vittorio Possenti, University of Venice, Italy

Roger Pouivet, Université de Rennes, Institut de Philosophie, Rennes

Mario Enrique Sacchi, Member of The Pontifical Roman Academy of St. Thomas Aquinas and of the Catholic Religion, Editor, *Sapientia*, Buenos Aires

Michael Sherwin, O.P., Department of Theology, University of Notre Dame

Steve Snyder, Pontifical College Josephinum, Columbus, Ohio